Early Modern Virginia

John Smith, *A Map of Virginia* (London, 1612). (Courtesy of the Library of Virginia)

EARLY AMERICAN HISTORIES
Douglas Bradburn, John C. Coombs, and S. Max Edelson, Editors

Early Modern Virginia
Reconsidering the Old Dominion

Edited by Douglas Bradburn
and John C. Coombs

University of Virginia Press / Charlottesville and London

University of Virginia Press
© 2011 by the Rector and Visitors of the University of Virginia
All rights reserved
Printed in the United States of America on acid-free paper

First published 2011
First paperback edition published 2013
ISBN 978-0-8139-3502-7 (paper)

9 8 7 6 5 4 3 2 1

The Library of Congress has cataloged the hardcover edition as follows:
LIBRARY OF CONGRESS CATALOGING-IN-PUBLICATION DATA
Early modern Virginia : reconsidering the Old Dominion / edited by
  Douglas Bradburn and John C. Coombs.
    p. cm.
  Includes bibliographical references and index.
  ISBN 978-0-8139-3149-4 (cloth : alk. paper) —ISBN 978-0-8139-3170-8
(e-book)
    1. Virginia—History—17th century. 2. Virginia—Social conditions—17th century. 3. Virginia—Economic conditions—17th century.
I. Bradburn, Douglas, 1972– II. Coombs, John C., 1966–
F229.E19 2011
975.5'02—dc22
                                                                    2011007984

Contents

Preface   vii

Introduction
Lorena S. Walsh   1

The Eschatological Origins of the English Empire
Douglas Bradburn   15

Mutual Appraisals: The Shifting Paradigms of the English, Spanish, and Powhatans in Tsenacomoco, 1560–1622
Camilla Townsend   57

The Rise and Fall of the Virginia-Dutch Connection in the Seventeenth Century
Victor Enthoven and Wim Klooster   90

"To Seeke for Justice": Gender, Servitude, and Household Governance in the Early Modern Chesapeake
Terri L. Snyder   128

Deference, Defiance, and the Language of Office in Seventeenth-Century Virginia
Alexander B. Haskell   158

Middle Plantation's Changing Landscape: Persistence,
Continuity, and the Building of Community
Philip Levy — 185

"Scatter'd upon the English Seats": Indian Identity and
Land Occupancy in the Rappahannock River Valley
Edward DuBois Ragan — 207

Beyond the "Origins Debate": Rethinking the Rise of
Virginia Slavery
John C. Coombs — 239

Transatlantic Politics and the Africanization of
Virginia's Labor Force, 1688–1712
William A. Pettigrew — 279

Conclusion: The Future of Chesapeake Studies
Philip D. Morgan — 300

Notes on Contributors — 333

Index — 337

Preface

Early Modern Virginia: Reconsidering the Old Dominion seeks to spur fresh work, to ask new questions (and old questions again), and to help further understanding of the development, settlement, and nature of life in Virginia's first century. The idea for the volume emerged during our collaboration on a historiographic essay—"Smoke and Mirrors: Reinterpreting the Society and Economy of the Seventeenth-Century Chesapeake"—that sought to show the potential for new directions in the early history of the region. The essay argued that recent work and new perspectives revealed the weakness of prevailing interpretations of the economic character and social development of the Tobacco Coast colonies. But rather than suggest a new master narrative to take the place of the old grand orthodoxy, the article stressed the need for more research—on a variety of long-neglected topics. This essay collection, along with the symposium that preceded it, is part of that effort, not to redefine the field, but to suggest new angles of view, new approaches, and new arguments that help advance our ability to understand the nature of life in early America. With essays employing a variety of methodologies, analytical strategies, and types of evidence, this volume explores a wide range of topics that touch upon numerous aspects of the lived and imagined experience of the early American world: from religion to government, trade to imperialism, slavery to Native American society, landscape to the sexual politics of the household. Each of the essays is based on new original research by an international group of historians.

To begin, these essays are specifically about Virginia and how it fits into the early modern world, considered broadly. Because much of the last generation of work on the Chesapeake generalized from the sources and records of colonial Maryland, Virginia's unique problems have often been lost in too-easy assumptions of regional homogeneity in all things. And yet the volume is not a collection of local histories. As the essays show, analysis of the problems that confronted the peoples of early Virginia often require contexts that reach beyond county lines, colonial borders, and imperial boundaries. Far from narrowing our comprehension of the Chesapeake, focusing solely on Virginia advances our understanding of both the limits and true potential of regional approaches to the history of early British America.

We have chosen to emphasize "early modern" Virginia, rather than "colonial," as a way to break down the artificial barriers that too often separate early American historians from the great problems and literature of the early modern world. "Colonial" implies a teleology; it suggests a timeless meaning of empire; it assumes an essential parochialism about the people who inhabited these shifting societies; and it creates a sense that these places (with the exception of their commercial connections) were largely self-contained, sealed off from the bigger trends and cultural life of the contemporary world. "Early modern" is, of course, no less of a historiographic construction. But "early modern" speaks to a broadly held consensus about the problems and character of the postmedieval, premodern world, which saw the rise of the nation-states in Europe, the problems of organized war and state formation, the expansion of European societies throughout the Atlantic, and the birth of large-scale merchant and financial capitalism. It was a time marked by a transformation in the unity of Christendom; an explosion in the trading and use of enslaved men and women; an unprecedented mingling and mixing of peoples, ideas, worldviews, and cosmologies from disparate areas of the globe; and the aggressive conquest of the Americas. The story of Virginia in the seventeenth and early eighteenth century is a story of the early modern world, and we all should aspire to resist the tempting complacency of the familiar categories and constructs of American history.

The essays in this volume were all presented at an intimate symposium held in August 2007 at the Robert H. Smith International Center for Jefferson Studies at Monticello. The four-hundredth anniversary year of Virginia's founding seemed an especially appropriate time to reflect upon how the story of England's first colony in America has been told. The symposium brought together numerous experts, along with the volume's contributors, not only to critique the essays but help stimulate a more general dialogue about the past, present, and future state of the field. This workshop-style presentation of the papers greatly aided in the development of the arguments and shaped the perspectives of the essays in this volume. For their generous participation and commentary at the symposium, we especially thank James Axtell, Deanna Beecham, Peter V. Bergstrom, Warren M. Billings, Edward Bond, Holly Brewer, Lois Green Carr, Patrick Griffin, David Hancock, Richard Holway, James Horn, Julia King, Jon Kukla, John Ruston Pagan, Jean B. Russo, J. Elliot Russo, Brent Tarter, Thad W. Tate, and Camille Wells. This gathering would not have been possible without the financial and intellectual support of our generous host Andrew Jackson O'Shaunessy, Saunders Director of the Robert H. Smith International Center for Jefferson Studies. The invaluable administrative support of Joan Hairfield, also of Monticello, made the planning and arrangements of the events smooth and enjoyable. Hampden-Sydney College, SUNY-Binghamton University, the John D. Rockefeller Library at Colonial Williamsburg, and the Virginia Foundation for the Humanities provided the financial assistance without which the symposium could not have been held and for which we are extremely grateful. And Justin C. Schauer, of Richmond, Virginia, graciously allowed us to work at his beautiful Church Hill home, helping to alleviate much of the drudgery of copy-editing. This book is dedicated to Jackson Caroline Coombs and Charles and Samuel Bradburn, our children, with love.

Early Modern Virginia

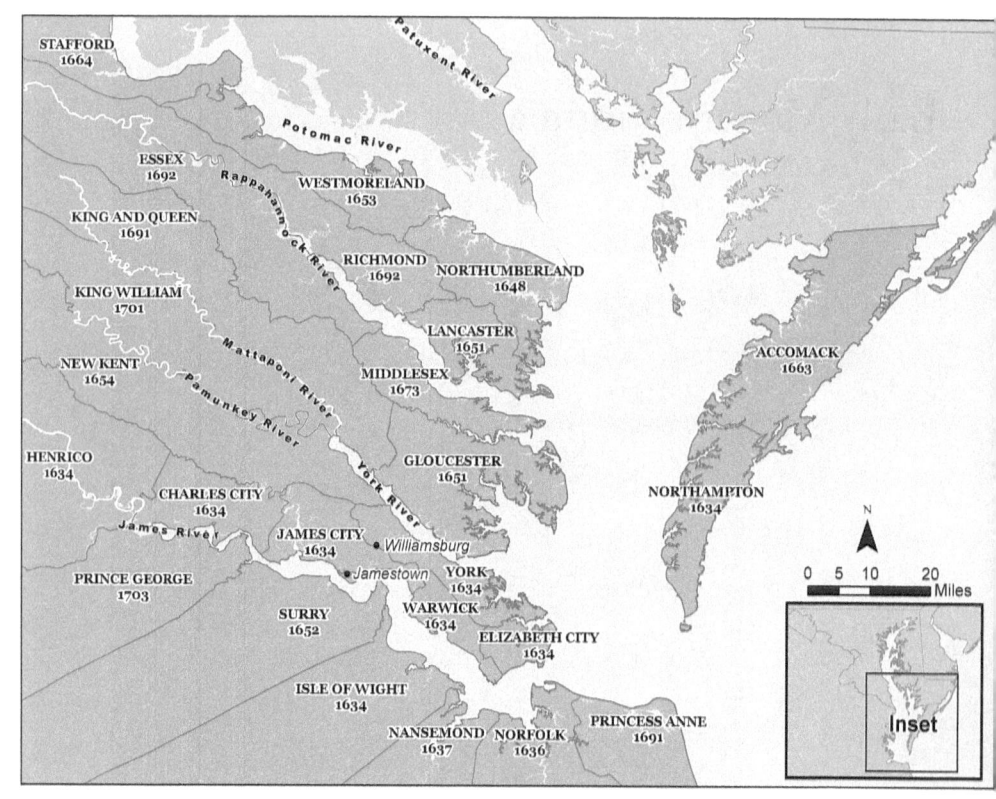

Virginia counties established through 1703. (Map by Kevin Heard, GIS Core Facility, Binghamton University)

Introduction

LORENA S. WALSH

Early Modern Virginia continues in a long tradition of edited volumes showcasing new research on the Chesapeake. The first such volume (*Law, Society, and Politics in Early Maryland*) appeared in 1977, incorporating essays stemming from a conference held at the Maryland State Archives in Annapolis in 1974. Another edited collection (*The Chesapeake in the Seventeenth Century*), dealing with both Virginia and Maryland, followed two years later containing essays resulting from a second regional history conference also held in 1974 at College Park, Maryland. This book presented the most innovative new work on Chesapeake history and continues up to the present to be an assigned reading in college history courses. Nine years later *Colonial Chesapeake Society*, another still frequently assigned reading, brought together selected papers originally presented at two conferences held in 1984 in honor of Maryland's 350th anniversary; one emphasized the seventeenth-century Chesapeake and the other, the eighteenth century. Two subsequent essay collections that present research undertaken since the mid-1980s have had a more restricted circulation. A fourth volume of unrevised essays dealing primarily with Virginia and Maryland, but other areas as well, resulted from a 1992 conference in College Park, Maryland, honoring Lois Green Carr. A fifth book had its beginning in papers presented at a roundtable discussion of new directions in Chesapeake history at an annual Omohundro Institute Conference in 2002.[1]

The essays in the present volume are similarly the product of a prior preparatory symposium, but they address a wider range of topics—both geographically and intellectually—than did the earlier works, reflecting the diverse directions in which the field of early American history has moved in the 1990s and 2000s. And, unlike the previous compilations, they are exclusively devoted to Virginia during the period between the era of initial settlement (which has received an outpouring of scholarly attention and reinterpretation elicited by the 2007 four-hundredth anniversary of the founding of Jamestown) and the golden age of the early eighteenth century. This time the editors deliberately chose to narrow the focus to the Old Dominion in order to redress the imbalance of scholarship that has long privileged later-established, smaller, and less populous Maryland over its older, larger, and more populated sister Chesapeake colony.[2]

In the 1970s and 1980s many historians of the Old Dominion were slower to embrace the issues and methods of the new social history than were those of the "Chesapeake School" centered in and primarily studying Maryland. That the more recently settled of the two "Fruitful Sisters" should garner the most attention was in part an artifact of record preservation and location. More of Maryland's early provincial and county records have survived than have those of Virginia, and they were conveniently housed, well curated, and well cataloged in the Maryland State Archives. The second reason is the greater volume of long-term, systematic research on a number of Maryland counties undertaken by museum-based historians working for Historic St. Mary's City and Historic Annapolis with support from the National Science Foundation and the National Endowment for the Humanities. Teamwork and collaboration enabled these historians to assemble larger databases than most individual scholars have the time, energy, and resources to compile, and to publish research findings, mostly in the form of journal articles or essays, relatively quickly. Third, the location of the museum-based research teams in the Maryland State Archives facilitated regular interchange among the sizable number of independent scholars who were also researching early Chesapeake subjects in the archives. Since almost all shared an enthusiasm for the topics and methods of the new social history, ensuing publications often dealt with the same sets of issues explored in a number of different Maryland locations. And shared topics and approaches frequently led, for better or for worse, to widespread sharing and widespread cross-citing of conclusions.[3]

Virginia scholars, in contrast, faced not only the obstacles of more of that colony's early records having been lost to courthouse fires and Civil War chaos and conflagrations but also the logistical hurdle of Virginia county records remaining housed in scores of individual, widely scattered county courthouses. To some extent, the heroic efforts of the Mormon Church in microfilming Virginia county court records and the housing of these copies in the Virginia State Library overcame some of the logistical obstacles. However, the poor quality of some of the microfilm, and the stipulation that access to sometimes invaluable loose papers housed in individual county courthouses required permission (not always forthcoming) of individual county clerks, discouraged historians of the Old Dominion from pursuing research in more than one Virginia county. Darrett B. and Anita H. Rutman's study of Middlesex County and James R. Perry's book on the early Virginia Eastern Shore used the county study model so extensively employed in Maryland. Many other Virginia historians, however, worked in relative isolation and continued to pursue the more traditional topics of politics and of the character and activities of elites.[4]

Others wrote dissertations on selected aspects of the history of individual counties that were not subsequently made into monographs and hence not widely disseminated outside academic circles. Colonial Williamsburg's Department of Historical Research also undertook a systematic study of the records of York, one of the best-documented early-settled Virginia counties. The biographical files assembled under NEH-sponsored grants continue to constitute an invaluable resource mined by museum personnel and independent researchers alike. One of the main focuses of this museum-directed research was to describe and explain the development of towns in the Chesapeake region, a topic with limited applicability to the rest of the region in the seventeenth and early eighteenth centuries, aside from Anne Arundel County, Maryland, where Historic Annapolis researchers shared similar interests and eventually undertook similar research. But here, too, the results of these ambitious studies remain confined to relatively inaccessible research reports and seminar papers. Consequently, Edmund Morgan's *American Slavery, American Freedom*, appearing in 1975 before the more detailed county studies were available and now in its thirty-fifth year, remains the most comprehensive account of the economic and social development of the Old Dominion in the seventeenth century.[5]

While the outpouring of local studies underscored both significant similarities and significant differences in economic and social development and in material culture between localities, as was also the case with the outpouring of New England town studies that had initially sparked parallel explorations of Chesapeake counties, teachers and publishers began calling for grand syntheses that would summarize and make sense of the increasingly unwieldy and sometimes contradictory welter of local works. Allan Kulikoff tackled this ambitious task, interpreting developments throughout the region through a combination of staple theory, developmental models rooted in explanations previously devised for Maryland, and a Marxist perspective on issues of opportunity and class formation. Other grand syntheses summarizing findings for the region and situating it in the wider context of other British American colonies appeared in the mid- to late 1980s. John J. McCusker and Russell R. Menard's *Economic History of British America, 1607–1789* interprets developments in the thirteen mainland colonies (including the Upper South), Canada, and the West Indies through the lens of staple theory. Jack P. Greene argues in *Pursuits of Happiness* that the distinctive demographic, social, and economic patterns first identified for the seventeenth-century Chesapeake characterized the experience of most colonists in British America rather than representing a peripheral and deviant pattern. Instead, Greene contended that it was New England that was atypical. And in *Albion's Seed* David Hackett Fischer argues for the direct transfer of specific English regional cultures to specific mainland colonial regions. Fischer's contentions generated considerable controversy; the other syntheses have been generally accepted among Chesapeake scholars. In any event, whatever the intention of the authors, the effect of these grand syntheses has been more to deter than to stimulate additional research on the issues addressed in them, especially for the seventeenth century.[6]

For a long time the similarities between the two colonies appeared to outweigh differences. The centrality of tobacco to the economies of both, an abundance of land and acute shortages of labor, similar systems of local government, the prevalence of high mortality regimes, immigrant societies with a preponderance of males, truncated family life, labor systems that shifted from indentured servants to slaves by the end of the century, and the prevalence of an attenuated material culture and impermanent forms of architecture appeared to justify treating the region as a relatively homogenous whole, with the exception of the lower Eastern Shore and the counties on the south bank of the lower James River, where tobacco soon became a peripheral crop. The greater volume and greater coherence of research on Maryland made it easy to substitute Maryland models where Virginia evidence was absent, sparse, or yet to be collected. Such assumptions were reinforced by reference to maps delineating county boundaries (unweighted for differing population densities), which show that in the 1660s and 1670s the geographic expanse bordering on Chesapeake Bay occupied by the two colonies was similar in size. That the area of the Old Dominion organized into counties expanded dramatically in the early eighteenth century, spilling over into Virginia's vast Piedmont region and dwarfing tightly bounded Maryland was more or less passed over.

By the mid-1980s, young scholars looking for dissertation topics began to view early Chesapeake history as overcrowded and overdone, and shifted the locus of new research to the Lower South, the middle colonies, the backcountry, and the mid-eighteenth-century Chesapeake. Moreover, as many of the scholars associated with the Chesapeake School moved on to jobs far removed from the Annapolis archives, they developed other interests at the same time as distance diminished opportunities for interchange and collaboration. In addition, members of the Maryland research teams were determined to accomplish the maximum amount of research possible with available grant funds and consequently deferred drafting and polishing of results for publication for later, on the scholars' "own time." While the research targets were usually met and sometimes exceeded, the strategy did not facilitate collaborative writing. Planned synthesizing monographs fell by the wayside as individual authors were overwhelmed with teaching duties and museum assignments, as two or more collaborating authors were unable to obtain simultaneous funding for writing, and as unresolved disagreements within individual research teams about which model of colonial development supplied the best explanation for the patterns observed stymied progress on projected joint monographs. During the same decade, some Virginia scholars did begin to question the applicability of Maryland-based conclusions regarding economic cycles and demographic trends to Virginia. Researchers of the Old Dominion, however, had little or no interest in undertaking more Virginia county studies in order either to test Maryland-based economic and social models or to generate alternative explanations. The new social history either moved on to other places or was superseded by other approaches. For the Chesapeake, team efforts tended to give way to individual research projects of smaller, sometimes microhistorical, scope.[7]

New work on the Virginia economy has continued to appear sporadically. David Scott Hardin was among the first, along with Darrett B. Rutman and Anita H. Rutman, to ask how economic trends in the Virginia sweet-scented tobacco region may have differed from those in oronoco-growing areas, and Hardin was the first to carefully delineate the distribution of soils suitable for growing it. Lorena S. Walsh subsequently analyzed diverging trends in sweet-scented, oronoco, and peripheral tobacco-growing areas. Douglas Bradburn and John C. Coombs are among the first Virginia scholars to begin employing the new evidence on regional economic diversity to re-examine larger questions such as the consolidation of gentry power, opportunity for poor whites, and the rise of slavery.[8]

In the past two decades a few other scholars of the region resisted the trend toward moving on to other locales or to later time periods. Warren Billings has continued to publish new research on Virginia's seventeenth-century legal, institutional, and labor history. James Horn wrote on the early social history of the region, employing examples from both Virginia and Maryland, and Holly Brewer published an influential essay on the impact of entail in the Old Dominion. Several decades' worth of research on regional living standards and consumer behavior by historians, architectural historians, and material culture specialists finally came into print in a volume of collected essays appearing in 1994. The emphasis in *Of Consuming Interests*, however, is on the eighteenth century, and many of the authors only briefly summarize their seventeenth-century research before turning to lengthy discussions of material culture in the subsequent century. By the 1990s early Virginia also began to be represented in the relatively new field of environmental history. But much of the research specific to the Old Dominion has so far been confined to conference papers.[9]

Some of the contributors to *Early Modern Virginia* now further develop topics that dominated the interests of earlier Chesapeake School scholars. Economics was one of the primary subjects, and in "The Rise and Fall of the Virginia-Dutch Connection in the Seventeenth Century," Victor Enthoven and Wim Klooster present new evidence on the extent of Virginia-Dutch trade in the seventeenth century—prior to 1651 when England sanctioned it, in the 1660s and 1670s when hostilities alternated with clandestine trade, and after 1680 when direct commercial contact ended but Amsterdam remained a major market for Virginia tobacco. In "Middle Plantation's Changing Landscape: Persistence, Continuity, and the Building of Community," continuing the school's strong interest in material culture, Philip Levy traces the evolving built environment—an important component of living standards and a reflection of elite pretensions—from mid-seventeenth-century frontier settlement through Middle Plantation's early transformation into Virginia's eventually fashionable capital of Williamsburg.

Two areas that figured prominently in more traditional histories of early

America but received less attention from Chesapeake School historians are politics and religion. The Maryland-based scholars were more interested in social and demographic issues and in quantitative rather than qualitative approaches. Given their main goal of uncovering more about the lives of common people, they put comparatively little time and effort into writing on the doings of elites. Here Alexander B. Haskell's essay "Deference, Defiance, and the Language of Office in Seventeenth-Century Virginia" tackles issues of identity and negotiated authority, in which scholars have taken considerable interest since the 1980s. Through a thoughtful analysis of the vocabulary of office and its relation to deference, Haskell furthers understanding of both elite assumptions and ordinary settlers' political behaviors and underscores the importance of critically reading literary evidence.

In addition to neglecting topics emphasized by traditional mainstream historians and privileging perceived regional economic and social similarities over inadequately explored regional differences, the initial research questions of the Chesapeake School were also in part data driven, with researchers mining the most widely available local records—county court records, deeds, wills, and probate inventories that held so much promise for learning systematically about the lives of relatively ordinary white men and women. Despite a commitment to present the history of all marginalized people, those best represented in the local records took precedence. The sources were by nature much fuller for men, but, again prodded in part by museum programming needs, Chesapeake scholars were soon discovering innovative ways for using records generated by men to learn more about the lives of women. Research and writing on early Virginia women (as well as on women in early Maryland and in both colonies in the eighteenth century) has continued, as witnessed by the publications of Suzanne D. Lebsock, Joan Gunderson, Virginia Bernhard, Kathleen M. Brown, Linda L. Sturtz, and Terri L. Snyder. Here, in "'To Seeke for Justice': Gender, Servitude, and Household Governance in the Early Modern Chesapeake," Snyder combines three themes that have long interested Chesapeake School historians—strategies women used to challenge patriarchal privilege, neighborhood sanctioning of residents who violated standards of accepted behavior, and the limited intervention of the legal system in household governance.[10]

Blacks are even more sparsely documented in local records, except when they appear as property in wills, probate inventories, and in Virginia land claims. Russell Menard made innovative use of the probate listings to delineate the demography of blacks on Maryland's lower western shore, a method that scholars continue to employ for other parts of the region. The exceptionally full parish registers for Middlesex County enabled Darrett and Anita Rutman and Charles Wetherell to explore mortality trends and seasonal patterns of births and deaths for blacks as well as whites. But when it came to other aspects of the lives of blacks on the Tobacco Coast, quantitative-minded scholars were slow to move beyond demographic issues. At first Allan Kulikoff was among the few Chesapeake historians willing to plunge into the new and initially contentious arena of African American history. Distaste for the heated and often acrimonious debates over the legitimacy, viability, and direction of the field, as well as the sometimes dubious (and decidedly unquantifiable) assertions made in some early studies concentrating on African American "culture," deterred many in the Chesapeake school from moving beyond the kinds of quantifiable documentary evidence with which they were most comfortable.[11]

Much has changed since the mid-1980s. First, African American studies has become a well-established branch in both history and historical archaeology. Given the dearth of documentary evidence, archaeology has proved especially critical to understanding the material and cultural lives of Africans and their creole descendants in the early Chesapeake. Scholars have also developed new research methods, such as group biography, that use property records generated by slaveholding whites to recover more elements of the history of the enslaved.[12]

And, as with research on white women, area museums' need to present reputable public programs on African Americans elicited (and continues to elicit) much of the scholarship on early Chesapeake blacks. Moreover, museum-sponsored collaborations between historians, archaeologists, and curators have enhanced understanding of physical realities beyond what archival research alone affords. And historians and archaeologists who collaborate with museum interpreters have gained more comfort and confidence in writing about controversial topics and have learned from interpreters' hard-won skills in presenting controversial material in compelling but nonconfrontational ways. Finally, the compilation of the Trans-Atlantic Slave Trade Database, which makes possible the tracing of geographic origins of forced African migrants, has recently opened new possibilities for exploring cultural continuities as well as discontinuities and the process of creolization.[13]

One of the topics that has continued to generate new interest and to elicit reinterpretation is the status of early Africans in Virginia. Robert

McColley and Alden T. Vaughan aptly survey evidence and interpretations up to the mid-1980s. William Thorndale and Martha McCartney have analyzed a previously unknown census documenting the presence of thirty-two blacks in Virginia in 1620. Michael J. Guasco and April Lee Hatfield began exploring the Iberian roots of racial slavery in the English colonies. Jonathan A. Bush introduces fresh arguments about the application of commercial law designating enslaved Africans as property in the absence of parliamentary acts defining and regulating slavery in the early English colonies. Linda M. Heywood and John K. Thornton innovatively explore the African background of the first blacks in Virginia and conclude that most Africans brought to the English colonies in the early seventeenth century were held in indefinite service, if not outright slavery. Tim Hashaw makes a strong argument for most of the early Africans being held in lifelong slavery. And John C. Coombs has introduced a cogent critique of the transition to racial slavery in Virginia that argues that colonial elites deliberately embraced slavery much earlier than previously thought. In this volume Coombs further develops these arguments in "Beyond the 'Origins Debate': Rethinking the Rise of Virginia Slavery."[14]

While Africans and Afro-Virginians are being more fully incorporated in historical narratives despite the limitations of available sources, this has often not been the case with Native Americans, the group most poorly represented in European-generated documents. In many conventional accounts, Indians begin dropping out the story after 1622 and rarely appear in Chesapeake narratives after 1644 except for episodic accounts of diplomatic missions or incursions by nonresident groups. And until recently, few postcontact archaeological site reports were available to compensate for exceedingly sparse documentary records. The main exception has been Helen Rountree's works on the Powhatans and James D. Rice's examination of Algonquian groups in the Potomac River basin. In this volume Camilla Townsend's essay "Mutual Appraisals: The Shifting Paradigms of the English, Spanish, and Powhatans in Tsenacomoco, 1560–1622" furthers understanding of Native motivations. Edward D. Ragan's essay "'Scatter'd upon the English Seats': Indian Identity and Land Occupancy in the Rappahannock River Valley" helps, like Rice's book, to fill a long-standing historiographical gap, dealing as it does with the adaptive survival strategies of Native American groups other than the Powhatans and with interactions between Algonquian residents and Europeans throughout the century.[15]

Finally, histories of the Old Dominion are just beginning to incorporate a wider Atlantic dimension that might serve to counter the Chesapeake School's more narrow focus on domestic contexts and explanations. April Lee Hatfield's *Atlantic Virginia* is the first book-length treatment of the subject. Many of the books and essays published for the four-hundredth anniversary of the Jamestown settlement include an Atlantic perspective, as do many of the most recent works on early Africans in the region. Since the early Chesapeake remained predominantly a land of immigrants until the end of the seventeenth century, more widespread adoption of pan-Atlantic approaches holds promise for fresh interpretations of issues new and old. In this volume Douglas Bradburn demonstrates that Protestant apocalyptic rhetoric informed early-seventeenth-century English imperial plans, and Camilla Townsend's essay, mentioned above, traces interactions between English, Spanish, and Powhatans and the reasons Spanish and Native American rulers chose not to act against the English intruders, thus allowing the first English outpost to survive.[16]

Thus some of the essays in *Early Modern Virginia* revisit older issues, exploring the extent to which Virginia examples prove or disprove prior explanations. Some offer critiques and major reinterpretations of earlier paradigms. And some break new ground by addressing previously neglected topics. Although there remains widespread agreement that there were indeed elements of regional culture that Virginia and Maryland shared, there is also an overdue recognition of significant regional (and subregional) differences that must be taken into account in crafting more satisfactory and nuanced explanations of historical change.

Notes

1. The essay collections are Aubrey C. Land, Lois Green Carr, and Edward C. Papenfuse, eds., *Law, Society, and Politics in Early Maryland* (Baltimore, 1977); Thad W. Tate and David L. Ammerman, eds., *The Chesapeake in the Seventeenth Century: Essays on Anglo-American Society* (Chapel Hill, NC, 1979); Lois Green Carr, Philip D. Morgan, and Jean B. Russo, eds., *Colonial Chesapeake Society* (Chapel Hill, NC, 1988); *Lois Green Carr: The Chesapeake and Beyond—A Celebration* (Crownsville, MD, 1992); and Debra Meyers and Melanie Perreault, eds., *Colonial Chesapeake: New Perspectives* (Lanham, MD, 2006). Sponsors of the various conferences represented in these essay collections include the Omohundro Institute of Early American History and Culture; Historic St. Mary's City; the Maryland State Archives; the Department of History at the University of Maryland, College Park; Johns Hopkins University; St. Mary's College of Maryland; and the Maryland Humanities Council.

2. The Robert H. Smith International Center for Jefferson Studies, Hampden-

Sydney College, SUNY-Binghamton University, the John D. Rockefeller Library at Colonial Williamsburg, and the Virginia Foundation for the Humanities provided financial assistance for the 2007 symposium.

3. "Fruitful Sisters" alludes to John Hammond, *Leah and Rachael; or, The Two Fruitful Sisters Virginia and Mary-Land* [1656], in Clayton Colman Hall, ed., *Narratives of Early Maryland, 1633–1684: Original Narratives of Early American History* (New York, 1910), 277–308. For discussions of Chesapeake School historians' cross citations that have tended to transform working hypotheses into uncritically accepted explanations, see Anita H. Rutman, "Still Planting the Seeds of Hope: The Recent Literature of the Early Chesapeake Region," *Virginia Magazine of History and Biography* 95 (1987): 3–24; and Douglas Bradburn and John C. Coombs, "Smoke and Mirrors: Reinterpreting the Society and Economy of the Seventeenth-Century Chesapeake," *Atlantic Studies* 3 (2006): 131–57.

4. Darrett B. Rutman and Anita H. Rutman, *A Place in Time: Middlesex County, Virginia, 1650–1750* (New York, 1984); James R. Perry, *The Formation of a Society on Virginia's Eastern Shore, 1615–1655* (Chapel Hill, NC, 1990).

5. Edmund S. Morgan, *American Slavery, American Freedom: The Ordeal of Colonial Virginia* (New York, 1975).

6. Allan Kulikoff, *Tobacco and Slaves: The Development of Southern Cultures in the Chesapeake, 1680–1800* (Chapel Hill, NC, 1986); John J. McCusker and Russell R. Menard, *The Economy of British America, 1607–1789* (Chapel Hill, NC, 1985); Jack P. Greene, *Pursuits of Happiness: The Social Development of Early Modern British Colonies and the Formation of American Culture* (Chapel Hill, NC, 1988); David Hackett Fischer, *Albion's Seed: Four British Folkways in America* (New York, 1989). For scholars' reactions, see "Forum: *Albion's Seed: Four British Folkways:* A Symposium," *William and Mary Quarterly,* 3rd ser., 48 (1991), 224–308. *The Economy of British America* was envisioned as a preliminary work identifying needs and opportunities for future research. However, as a conference assessing the impact of the book over the past fifteen years revealed, its conclusions are still widely and largely uncritically accepted as the final word on economic issues, and few scholars have pursued the research needs McCusker and Menard delineated. See Cathy Matson, ed., *The Economy of Early America: Historical Perspectives and New Directions* (University Park, PA, 2006).

7. For a summary of research published in the 1980s and a questioning of the applicability of Maryland models, see Anita Rutman, "Still Planting the Seeds of Hope."

8. David Scott Hardin, "'Alterations They Have Made at This Day': Environment, Agriculture, and Landscape Change in Essex County, Virginia, 1600–1782" (Ph.D. diss., University of Maryland, 1995); Lorena S. Walsh, "Summing the Parts: Implications for Estimating Chesapeake Output and Income Subregionally," *William and Mary Quarterly,* 3rd ser., 56 (1999): 53–94; Walsh, *Motives of Honor, Pleasure, and Profit: Plantation Management in the Colonial Chesapeake, 1607–1763* (Chapel Hill, NC, 2010); Bradburn and Coombs, "Smoke and Mirrors."

9. Warren M. Billings, "The Law of Servants and Slaves in Seventeenth-Century Virginia," *Virginia Magazine of History and Biography* 99 (1991): 45–62; Billings, "Sir William Berkeley and the Diversification of the Virginia Economy," *Virginia Magazine of History and Biography* 104 (1996): 433–54; Billings, *Sir William Berkeley and the Forging of Colonial Virginia* (Baton Rouge, 2004); Billings, *A Little Parliament: The Virginia General Assembly in the Seventeenth Century* (Richmond, 2004); James P. Horn, *Adapting to a New World: English Society in the Seventeenth-Century Chesapeake* (Chapel Hill, NC, 1994); Holly Brewer,

"Entailing Aristocracy in Colonial Virginia: 'Ancient Feudal Restraints' and Revolutionary Reform," *William and Mary Quarterly*, 3rd ser., 54 (1997): 307–46. For living standards and consumer behavior, see Cary Carson, Ronald Hoffman, and Peter J. Albert, eds., *Of Consuming Interests: The Style of Life in the Eighteenth Century* (Charlottesville, VA, 1994); and Lois Green Carr, "Emigration and the Standard of Living: The Seventeenth Century Chesapeake," *Journal of Economic History* 52 (1992): 271–91. Examples of environmental history include Timothy Silver, *A New Face on the Countryside: Indians, Colonists, and Slaves in South Atlantic Forests, 1500–1800* (Cambridge, 1990); Philip D. Curtin, Grace S. Brush, and George W. Fisher, eds., *Discovering the Chesapeake: The History of an Ecosystem* (Baltimore, 2001); Virginia DeJohn Anderson, "Animals into the Wilderness: The Development of Livestock Husbandry in the Seventeenth Century Chesapeake," *William and Mary Quarterly*, 3rd ser., 59 (2002), 377–408; and Jack Temple Kirby, *Poquosin: A Study of Rural Landscape and Society* (Chapel Hill, NC, 1995).

10. Suzanne D. Lebsock, *"A Share of Honour": Virginia Women, 1600–1945* (Richmond, 1984); Joan Gunderson, "The Double Bonds of Race and Sex: Black and White Women in the Colonial Virginia Parish," *Journal of Southern History* 52 (1986): 351–72; Virginia Bernhard, "'Men, Women and Children' at Jamestown: Population and Gender in Early Virginia, 1607–1610," *Journal of Southern History* 58 (1992): 599–618; Kathleen M. Brown, *Good Wives, Nasty Wenches, and Anxious Patriarchs: Gender, Race, and Power in Colonial Virginia* (Chapel Hill, NC, 1996); Linda L. Sturtz, *Within Her Power: Propertied Women in Colonial America* (New York, 2002); Terri L. Snyder, *Brabbling Women: Disorderly Speech and the Law in Early Virginia* (Ithaca, NY, 2003).

11. Russell R. Menard, "The Maryland Slave Population, 1658–1730: A Demographic Profile of Blacks in Four Counties," *William and Mary Quarterly*, 3rd ser., 32 (1975): 29–54; Darrett B. Rutman, Charles Wetherell, and Anita H. Rutman, "Rhythms of Life: Black and White Seasonality in the Early Chesapeake," *Journal of Interdisciplinary History* 11 (1980): 29–53.

12. For example, Lorena S. Walsh, *From Calabar to Carter's Grove: The History of a Virginia Slave Community* (Charlottesville, VA, 1997).

13. For example, Garrett Randall Fesler, "From Houses to Homes: An Archaeological Case Study of Household Formation at the Utopia Slave Quarter, ca. 1675 to 1775" (Ph.D. diss., University of Virginia, 2004); Patricia M. Samford, *Subfloor Pits and the Archaeology of Slavery in Colonial Virginia* (Tuscaloosa, AL, 2007); and Willie Graham et al., "Adaptation and Innovation: Archeological and Architectural Perspectives on the Seventeenth-Century Chesapeake," *William and Mary Quarterly* 3rd ser., 64 (2007): 451–522. The Trans-Atlantic Slave Trade Database is available at http://www.slavevoyages.org.

14. Robert McColley, "Slavery in Virginia, 1619–1660: A Reexamination," in Robert H. Abzug and Stephen E. Maizlish, eds., *New Perspectives on Race and Slavery in America: Essays in Honor of Kenneth M. Stampp* (Lexington, KY, 1986), 11–24; Alden T. Vaughan, "Blacks in Virginia: Evidence from the First Decade," in Vaughan, *Roots of American Racism: Essays on the Colonial Experience* (New York, 1995), 128–35. For the census see William Thorndale, "The Virginia Census of 1619," *Magazine of Virginia Genealogy* 33 (1995): 155–70; and Martha W. McCartney, "An Early Virginia Census Reprised," *Archaeological Society of Virginia Quarterly Bulletin* 54 (1999): 182–87. McCartney demonstrated that the document originated in 1620. For Iberian roots, see Michael J. Guasco, "'Encounters, Identities, and Human Bondage': The Foundations of Racial Slavery in the English

Atlantic World" (Ph.D. diss., College of William and Mary, 2000); and April Lee Hatfield, "A 'Very Wary People in Their Bargaining' or 'Very Good Marchandise': English Traders' Views of Free and Enslaved Africans, 1550–1650," *Slavery and Abolition* 25 (2004): 1–17. For slave laws or their absence, see Jonathan A. Bush, "Free to Enslave: The Foundations of Colonial American Slave Law," *Yale Journal of Law and the Humanities* 5 (1993): 417–70; and Bush, "The British Constitution and the Creation of American Slavery," in Paul Finkelman, ed., *Slavery and the Law* (Madison, WI, 1997), 379–418. For the status of early Virginia blacks, see Linda M. Heywood and John K. Thornton, *Central Africans, Atlantic Creoles, and the Foundation of the Americas, 1585–1660* (New York, 2007); Tim Hashaw, *The Birth of Black America: The First African Americans and the Pursuit of Freedom at Jamestown* (New York, 2007); and John C. Coombs, "Building 'The Machine': The Development of Slavery and Slave Society in Early Colonial Virginia" (Ph.D. diss., College of William and Mary, 2004).

15. Helen Rountree, *The Powhatan Indians of Virginia: Their Traditional Culture* (Norman, OK, 1989); Rountree, *Pocahontas's People : The Powhatan Indians of Virginia through Four Centuries* (Norman, OK, 1990); *Powhatan Foreign Relations, 1500–1722* (Charlottesville, VA, 1993); Rountree and Thomas E. Davidson, *Eastern Shore Indians of Virginia and Maryland* (Charlottesville, VA, 1997); James D. Rice, *Nature and History in the Potomac Country: From Hunter-Gatherers to the Age of Jefferson* (Baltimore, 2009).

16. April Lee Hatfield, *Atlantic Virginia: Intercolonial Relations in the Seventeenth Century* (Philadelphia, 2004). Essay collections derived from conferences related to the 2007 Jamestown anniversary include Robert Appelbaum and John Wood Sweet, eds., *Envisioning an English Empire: Jamestown and the Making of the North Atlantic World* (Philadelphia, 2005); and Peter C. Mancall, ed., *The Atlantic World and Virginia, 1550–1624* (Chapel Hill, NC, 2007).

 The Eschatological Origins
of the English Empire

Douglas Bradburn

In 1612 an important front in the long struggle between Satan and the saints, in the mind of many Englishmen, was a little military camp in a country the English called Virginia. Twice a day, officers of the guard would lead the motley collection of settlers in a prayer of exhortation, begging God to help them "build up the walls of Jerusalem." They were engaged, as Sir Thomas Dale, "high marshall" of the colony, enthusiastically acknowledged, "in Religious Warfare."[1] They had left their homes because of God's "motion & work in our hearts," with the intention "principally to honor thy name, & advance the kingdom of thy son." They implored Him to crush their enemies, open the minds of the Indians to the True Religion, end Native taunts and blasphemies, and "let wickedness, superstition, ignorance & idolatry perish at the presence of thee our God."[2] Not content to merely convert or kill the Indians, the prayer called upon God to "call in the Jews together with the fullness of the gentiles" that "thy name may be glorious in all the world." Only then would they "with all thine elect people" come to see the face of God "and be filled with the light thereof for evermore."[3]

The prayer, and Dale's vision of religious warfare, were loaded with Protestant apocalyptic rhetoric, an eschatological perspective that framed, for many Englishmen and Englishwomen, the meaning of the transformations their world was experiencing in the late sixteenth and early seventeenth century.[4] As part of their Reformation, English Protestants were encouraged to look into recent and ancient history to discover the secrets of God's providential design, or as John Foxe's *Book of Martyrs* noted, of seeking out examples "from the primitive age to these latter tymes of ours" of God's plan for the true Church. Foxe depicted historical time as a long struggle between Christ and Antichrist, a contest for the fate of humanity in which contemporary events exhibited clear signs of a climactic fight, and in which the saints would triumph over the forces of the devil. For those who embraced such logic, England was not only the equivalent of Israel, the chosen nation, but was the natural epitome, protector, and hope of the Reformation.[5] Foxe's vision and Dale's mission are the crucial pillars that supported, sustained, and encouraged the expansion of England's empire. Both as a refinement of English national pride and an expectation of international Protestantism, such eschatological thinking provided the fundamental framework for the expansion of the English from the exploits of Drake in the 1580s to Oliver Cromwell's "Western Design" in the 1650s.

Historians of early English expansion and colonial America have tended to downplay the place of religious fervor in the colonization and settlement of Virginia. David Armitage, for instance, in his recent study of the ideas surrounding early English dominion overseas, emphasizes the rationalism—indeed "Oxonian Aristotelianism"—of the two great compilers and promoters of English expansion, Richard Hakluyt the younger and Samuel Purchas. He dismisses any connection to the overt piety of these apparently practical men. Andrew Fitzmaurice, for his part, attempts to fold all promotional material into a rather secular "humanist" ideology, which he argues "dominated colonizing projects."[6]

For early Americanists, Virginia still exists as an easy foil for New England, useful for pedagogy and general analysis as an economic enterprise, which contrasts so nicely with the various religious designs of Massachusetts, Plymouth, Connecticut, New Haven, and Rhode Island. Englishmen in Virginia are most clearly seen as adventurers: desperate, greedy, and violent, while the English in the New England colonies, although they could run into radicalism and bigotry and could kill Indians with equal ferocity, are generally seen as hardworking, pious, and well intentioned. Although numerous historians have repeatedly stressed the religious tenor of certain aspects of the Virginia story, from promotion to actual practice in the colony, there still remains a deep disjunction between Virginia's primary status as a place striving more for profit than for God and New England's place in the long argument over faith and religious authority in early American society. Even those historians who catch the similarity between the militant fervor of Elizabethan England and the movements of the Puritans of the 1630s downplay the common links that necessarily extended through the Virginian project.[7]

This essay explores those continuities—of personalities, of ideas, and of worldviews—that shaped the general context and impulse of English expansion from the 1580s through the 1650s. First, we find the expansion of England dominated by a militant internationalist Protestant ideology that drove the timing, meaning, and success of colonizing and trading enterprises throughout the Atlantic world and greatly influenced English interest in the East Indies. Second, as an intellectual concern eschatological thinking affected nearly every substantial inquiry into the causes and nature of things that affected colonization: the drive to perfect technological achievements; to explore, chart, and map the world; to study and catalog its mysteries; to expand the study of languages; and to advance knowledge of the hidden truth of God. These two tendencies—the one militant and aggressive, the other probing, experimental, and intellectual—were part of an eschatological worldview that often reinforced, sustained, and justified the other and are both crucial to understanding the nature and dynamic of English expansion in the seventeenth century.

Virginia exists as a central part of this story and connects the people and dreams of the Elizabethan adventurers to the assumptions of the latter-day roundheads. Properly understood, eschatological visions for the place and meaning of England in God's mysterious but increasingly evident design shaped the origins of the English empire. The changes in the mission between the initial settlements in Virginia and the later exodus to New England do not reflect different priorities, but the shifting politics of the English state church. Virginia and New England share a common eschatological origin. To reveal this broad context we will follow two tracks: one an analysis of the people who systematically encouraged and engaged in the creation of English colonies from the 1580s through the 1650s, and the other an examination of the intellectual milieu that nourished and explained that movement.

"At the Helm of the Imperial Ship, of the Most Parte of Christendom"

The most militant Protestants of the sixteenth and seventeenth centuries believed that England needed to play a leading role among the Protestant states in Europe. Specifically, such zealots argued that England needed an aggressively anti-Spanish, anti-Hapsburg policy that would stop the Spanish drive to reverse the progress of the Reformation and establish a universal monarchy in alliance with Rome. Such a perspective became increasingly important in the face of nearly continuous religious civil wars in France from the 1550s to the 1590s, the creation and expansion of the Jesuit order, the rise of Philip II to power in the Spanish empire with his grand strategy of "messianic imperialism," the ever more confessional character of the Dutch revolt, and the religious alliances of numerous German states.[8]

Within England, the leaders of the movement to assert English power in the cause of international Protestantism were drawn from the ranks of Marian exiles and their sympathetic supporters. In the church this included people eager to ensure continuing reformation in the English Church so that practices matched theology—that is, the "Puritan" movement. At court, this aggressive perspective was shared by a constellation of courtiers and ministers closely tied to the interest of Robert Dudley, Earl of Leicester (after 1584), whose brother had married the presumptive queen, Jane Grey, and whose family had fought against the accession of Queen Mary. This included Elizabeth's "spymaster" and principle secretary after 1576, Sir Francis Walsingham. A Marian exile, Walsingham maintained strong links to the Huguenots in France. Famous names associated with the group include Sir Philip Sidney, who married Walsingham's daughter Frances; Robert Devereux, 2nd Earl of Essex, who married Frances after Sidney's death at the battle of Zutphen; and Robert Rich, 3rd Baron Rich, who married Devereux's sister, Penelope, and who championed Puritanism in East Anglia. Rich owned the largest personal fleet in England by the end of the sixteenth century. This group played a driving role in all the English expansionist projects of the 1570s and 1580s, including the efforts of Martin Frobisher to discover the Northwest Passage, the Elizabethan attempts to settle parts of Munster and Ulster in Ireland, the Roanoke voyages of Sir Walter Raleigh, and the privateering of Sir Francis Drake. Walsingham was one of the largest shareholders of Drake's circumnavigation voyage, and he early supported the attempted mission of his stepson Christopher Carteill to map and make contacts in the Far East.[9]

The desire for active English participation in the cause of international Protestantism was intimately bound into eschatological thought, which could be either apocalyptic or more gradual, but which fundamentally understood the progress in Christendom in the late sixteenth and early seventeenth centuries as component elements of the prophetic events promised in scripture concerning the ultimate fate of humanity. In addition to the constant preaching of some of England's leading churchmen, including bishops Thomas Cranmer, Nicholas Ridley, John Ponet, John Aylmer, John Jewel, and Edwin Sandys (archbishop of York, Marian exile, and father of

Edwin Sandys of the Virginia Company), a direct correspondence between the fate of the Reformation in England and God's plan was given popularity by the joint efforts of John Bale and John Foxe. Both Marian exiles, Bale and Foxe associated the suffering of English reformers with the experience of the earliest Christian churches and connected these "latter day" events with the coming of the millennium. The prophecies of the book of Daniel and of the New Jerusalem, Babylon, and Whore of Babylon in the book of Revelation were given vivid meaning to justify the struggles of the Reformation generally and England's split with Rome specifically. John Bale's *The Image of Both Churches* and John Foxe's *Acts and Monuments, of These Latter and Perilous Days* linked the problems of the Reformation with earlier medieval apocalypticism by distinguishing between the "true church" of Christ and the false church of "antichrist." The pope was the Antichrist, and the institutional power of the papacy represented Babylon. The Roman Catholic Church was a false church, as described in the book of Revelation. The Hapsburgs of Spain and the Holy Roman Empire, with their lust for universal dominion, figured as the famous Whore of Babylon, but other international Catholics loomed large, including the Leaguers of France, the Jesuit order, Mary Queen of Scots, and any number of intestine papists. Much of this interpretation of "latter day" events was directly infused in the marginalia of the Geneva Bible itself, the most widely published English vernacular Bible into the second decade of the seventeenth century.[10]

John Foxe continued to update his *Acts and Monuments* to take into account the most recent evidence of God's unfolding plan for England and Christendom. His 1570 version was ordered into all the orphanages and city companies of London, all the cathedrals, the bishops' halls and chambers, numerous colleges of Oxford and Cambridge, and countless parish churches. By 1577 the book was ubiquitous. Francis Drake sailed with a copy in 1577 on his eventual circumnavigation of the world, forced his Spanish prisoners to listen to him read from it, and colored in the engravings and plates on the slow days at sea. He wrote from his successful raid on Cadiz in 1587 thanking the recently deceased John Foxe for his prayers.[11]

The existence of the Spanish empire in the Americas (and after 1580 in the East) played a preeminent role in spurring English desire for an aggressive Protestant expansion beyond the British Isles. The English privateers John Hawkins and Francis Drake sailed with, and often were commissioned by, the Huguenot pirates and the Dutch Sea Beggars. The exploits of Drake and the behavior of the Spanish in the New World played a prominent role in the official and unofficial justifications for aggressive English involvement overseas. Richard Hakluyt devoted numerous chapters of his "Discourse on Western Planting" to excoriating the behavior and effect of the Spanish dominion overseas. Had not the wealth of the Indies allowed Philip II to harass the Protestants of the Low Countries, corrupt the court of Portugal, foment intestine wars in Europe, fund rebels in Scotland and Ireland, torture and murder English sailors the world over, and enslave the natives of the Americas, all in the service of "the great Anti-Christ of Rome"? As for the pope, who supported the pretenses of Spain to govern the world, Hakluyt referred his readers to the work of John Bale, wherein the true nature of the pontiff's cruelty and authority were revealed.[12]

Before Hakluyt, however, the first great theorist of English empire was the polymath John Dee. Our modern mind, which draws strict lines between science, religion, and magic, can barely grasp the inner life of "Dr." John Dee, who even by the end of his own lifetime had become little more than a misunderstood, if charismatic, necromancer.[13] Born in England, trained at the university of Louvain—one of the premier centers of "new Learning" in Europe—by the age of twenty-five he was lecturing at Paris on Euclidian geometry. An intimate friend of Girardus Mercator, Dee is thought to have brought the first globes based upon Mercator's projections to England. At the court of Edward VI, Dee received the close patronage of the Duchess of Northumberland, whose son Henry Percy would later patronize Thomas Hariot. And Dee was obsessed with eschatological thinking. Dee thought numerology and the Bible could help discern the final days. Impatient to discover the mysteries of God's hand in the world, Dee turned increasingly to "secret knowledge," conjuring spirits and angels, pestering them with questions about the nature of things, and believing himself to be a seer and perhaps a prophet.[14] After 1583, when he traveled to the court of Rufus II of Bohemia, Dee constantly harangued crowds about the coming end of times. The pope worried that he was trying to start another heresy. But unlike numerous continental occultists, cosmographers, and mystics, Dee explicitly tied the future fate of mankind to the fortunes of England.

In the heady beginning of England's overseas empire, properly inaugurated by Francis Drake's bold circumnavigation of the world in 1577–82, Dee's prophecy of a "British Empire"—he is the first to use the term in print—placed England at the center of a New World, revealed by the new Truth of the latter days. Dee's *General and Rare Memorials Pertayning to the*

Perfect Arte of Navigation presented a vigorous argument for the importance of naval superiority to the prosperity and strength of Britain, called upon an aggressive reorganization of the state to support such a navy, and expounded on the economic benefits such support would provide in the fisheries, in the mechanical arts, and in the development of trade. And Dee believed that God had wished, and promised, that it would be so.

The frontispiece of Dee's essay, which he personally designed, is a mélange of rich symbolism. Elizabeth is depicted as the fulfillment of a prophecy made before the beginning of time. Mingling Greek, Latin, Hebrew, and English, as well as symbols of the occult, dynastic emblems of the Tudors, marks of astrology, and the secrets of Cabala, Dee attempted to present a definitive interpretation of the eschatological importance of English expansion and navigation. There sits Elizabeth "at the HELM of the IMPERIAL SHIP, of the most parte of Christendom," guiding the voyages of discovery, protected by an angel bearing the cross of St. George, and governed herself by the God of Israel, enveloped in the providential sun.[15] This sun, with its omnipotent rays, has a prominent place on the frontispiece of Foxe's *Book of Martyrs*, connecting the trials of ancient Israel, the struggles of the early Christians before Constantine, and the English martyrs before Elizabeth. Dee tied Elizabeth and England into an unfolding of biblical time, revealed by the secrets of the new mathematics, new geographical knowledge, new perfections in the mechanical arts, new study of the stars, and new close reading of the Bible. As Dee noted, the "HEAVENLY KING" had recently made "the Way and Means, most evident, easie, and Compendious." Time, history, and prophecy were all collapsed to show the importance of this present moment. Dee was a man in search of God's Truth, and he used all the practices available in the sixteenth century to discover it.[16]

While Dee was wrong about the date the world would end, he was right about the "British Empire," which would come to rule the waves through the development of a commanding navy. Until he left England in 1583, Dee played an important role in the community of men engaged in voyages of discovery. He was influential in the circle around Leicester and was particularly close to Sir Philip Sidney (Leicester's nephew) and Sir Edward Dyer (Leicester's secretary), who had been tutored by Dee in chemistry and whose own interest in cartography and cosmography mirrored Dee's. He was a friend of Christopher Hatton, privy councilor, one of the leaders of the Protestant internationalist interest in Elizabeth's court. He met often with Richard Hakluyt the elder, providing him with numerous maps and

Frontispiece to John Dee's *General and Rare Memorials Pertayning to the Perfect Arte of Navigation* (London, 1578). (Reproduced courtesy of the Huntington Library, San Marino, California)

globes. Richard Hakluyt the younger was a "protégé" of the Sidney group, and he relied on Dee's writings, knowledge of the voyages of exploration, legal and economic justifications, and new geographical information in his construction of the "Discourse on Western Planting."[17] Dee advised Humphrey Gilbert the day before Humphrey completed his anti-Spanish tract in support of the search for the Northwest Passage entitled "How her Majesty may Annoy the King of Spain."[18] He advised Sebastian Cabot on his 1553 mission to the Northeast and prepared maps and instructions for the voyages of John Davis,[19] Adrian Gilbert, Francis Drake, Martin Frobisher, and Walter Raleigh. He drafted manuscripts justifying English dominion overseas for the consideration of Elizabeth I, Francis Walsingham, and William Cecil, Lord Burghley in 1577–78.[20] In 1580 Dee presented Queen Elizabeth with a parchment manuscript providing her with proof of her "Titles to Foreign Lands," and declaring her an empress. The next year he wrote a treatise on the propagation of Christianity to the Native Americans, whom he called the "Infidels of Atlantis."[21] Dee was well known to Thomas Hariot and Henry Percy, later 9th Earl of Northumberland (called the "wizard Earl" because of his interest in astronomy and chemistry), and the backers of Drake.[22]

While Dee's later career saw him obsessed with occultist practices, divining from crystals, and necromancy, he was neither insane nor confused. He knew exactly what he was after, and he represents a powerful tendency shared by all the "scientists" engaged with the colonization projects: an attempt to shape and understand the world through the perfection of new knowledge.[23] Dee shared this fascination with Richard Hakluyt and Thomas Hariot, himself a mathematical genius, who wrote on navigation, tutored the Sidneys and Raleigh on mathematics, navigation, and astronomy. He was patronized by Raleigh and paid a pension by Northumberland. Hariot was sent by Raleigh to Roanoke, where he engaged in an extensive study of the flora and fauna of North Carolina; the language, habits, and manners of the native people; and the economic potential of the colony. Although these tendencies have been described as fundamentally "scientific," or humanistic, the effort to reveal the secrets of the world in the late sixteenth and early seventeenth centuries was ultimately bound into an eschatological view of historical time. As Hariot himself noted, all of his visits to the Native towns of "Virginia" included an aggressive assertion of the Truth of the Bible and a confirmation that "all things have beene and were to be done according" to God's original and unchanging design.[24] The exciting new world that was being increasingly revealed by the new science of geography, the improvements of cartography, the perfection of mathematics, and the rise of real astronomy was itself a growing light in the world prophesied in the Bible, a source considered by all of these men to be God's revealed Truth.

All of these men were influenced by humanist techniques and traditions (which are too often anachronistically separated from the earnest piety of the times),[25] but they were transcending the obsessions of late humanism. The classics and ancient learning were not, generally, read in opposition to scripture but in light of it. The creation of the Geneva Bible was possible only because of humanist interests in ancient languages, while humanist techniques in the study of history informed Bale, Foxe, and Hakluyt. John Dee was a devotee not only of the study of ancient languages and the discovery of ancient knowledge (he had a manuscript library of over four thousand works) but of the experimentation advocated by Roger Bacon. But the discovery of Truth through study, learning, and experimentation was not secular or purely "scientific" in any useful sense of the word; it was performed in the service of God's unfolding providential design and for the use of mankind, so that humanity could again achieve dominion over nature.[26] John Napier, known as the inventor of logarithms—who was a friend of Edward Briggs, mathematician, auditor of the Virginia Company, friend of Nicholas Ferrar, and client of Robert Rich, 2nd Earl of Warwick—was more famous for his intense study of the machinations of the Antichrist. In 1593 Napier published his *Plaine Discovery of the Whole Revelation of St. John*, a massive and obscure exegesis on the book of Revelation that predicted the world would end in 1700.[27] And Aristotle, with his cyclical model of history, was never enough. As Walter Raleigh emphatically noted, "I shall never bee perswaded, that GOD hath shut up all light and Learning within the Lanthorne of Aristotle's braines." Aristotle, like all great materialists, was good at explaining how things work but never the cosmic Why.[28]

The great advantage these men possessed over the ancients was knowledge of Why: the holy scripture—God's word—and increasingly, a better understanding of the world. Bale, Foxe, Hakluyt, and Raleigh each broke out of the cyclical models of constant chance and change that characterized the work of the humanist historians of England, such as Polydore Vergil. Instead, they wrote history with an eschatological time line, which had a beginning and (ultimately) an end. With such a model, the improvements of the sixteenth century—from printing to mapmaking—portended important things, as the prophets had predicted. The younger Hakluyt recognized this instantly when he was shown by his cousin a comparison of the

Ptolemaic World (the limit of ancient geographic knowledge) with the new world of Ortelius. Explaining that the moderns knew much more than the ancients about the shape and character of the world, and arguing that the diversity of things drove a natural propensity toward mutual dependence, the elder Hakluyt asked his protégé to reflect on the prophecy of the 107th Psalm, which notes that "they that go down to the sea in ships, that do business in great waters" would, in Hakluyt's terms, "see the works of the Lord, and his wonders in the deepe." As David Sacks has argued, Hakluyt interpreted this moment as a calling from God to aid in the rediscovery of the world, closed to man since the fall from Paradise. Hakluyt's *Principle Navigations*, which he claimed was patterned on the compilations of John Bale and John Foxe, can be seen as a type of ecclesiastical history, structured to show the progressive unification of the world through the various voyages of discovery. Hakluyt, through his literary endeavors and his sponsorship of discovery and colonization, would help rebuild Solomon's Temple.[29]

So utilitarian perfection—in mechanical arts, mathematics, natural history, navigation, astronomy, and the study of languages—served eschatological ends. Francis Bacon made this explicit in his treatise *The Advancement of Learning*, which condemned an obsessive fascination of the late humanists for ancient authors and the mere niceties of rhetoric and logic. Bacon favored work on the practical arts, such as the study of astronomy, navigation, mathematics, and the natural world, which could provide "a rich storehouse for the glory of the Creator and the relief of man's estate."[30]

And Bacon linked the advancement of knowledge directly to the prophecy of the book of Daniel. As he wrote in his *Valerious Termininus*, the prelude to his attempts to create a new grand system of modern knowledge, "all knowledge appeareth to be a plant of God's own planting," and the extent to which that plant could be seen to flourish was ultimately "the providence of God; not only by a general providence but by a special prophecy," which "was appointed to this autumn of the world." Thus, "in the prophecy of Daniel" when discussing the "latter times," it is written, "*Many shall pass to and fro, and science shall be increased*," which Bacon took to be a reference to "the opening of the world by navigation and commerce and the further discovery of knowledge."[31] Bacon's works would be considered by Puritans "as the philosophical complement to Foxe's *Book of Martyrs*."[32] Eventually God, through mankind's efforts, would reveal the mysteries of the world, and man would regain dominion over nature. To help reveal the changes in the world, Bacon recommended new types of history and natural philosophy, including "histories of Cosmography" (such as Hakluyt's *Principal Voyages*) and "Providential history," to seek out God's judgments in postbiblical times.[33]

An example of such an attempt at providential history is Walter Raleigh's massive *History of the World*, which first appeared in 1614. In this tome written for Prince Henry, Raleigh represented the story of mankind as a progress from first fall to the last judgment, with the purpose of investigating the seminal judgments of God upon mankind. For "the judgments of God are ever unchangeable," wrote Raleigh, and He would never approve in one age "that which he hath cursed in another." In explaining his method and defending the notion of providential history, Raleigh used examples from the recent past to show that man could glimpse the providence of God and his mysteries and to explain the rise and fall of kings and kingdoms by an awareness of God's powerful guiding hand. He rejected "*Aristotles* rotten ground" for "this doctrine of Faith." The world had a certain creator and must certainly have an end, as explained in holy scripture. As a work of history it appealed to opponents of the divine right of kings, and its enthusiasm for seeking after the mysteries of providential design recommended it to Puritans. Raleigh noted his own concern for the end of days clearly, arguing that "the long day of mankind" was "drawing fast towards an evening and the world's tragedy and time near at an end."[34] Published eleven times before 1687, the book was "heartily endorsed by Cromwell."[35]

So the sophisticated eschatological thinking of the learned nicely framed the more popular apocalyptic militant Protestantism that fueled the drive for war with Spain. Raleigh stood astride both tendencies nicely, as did Northumberland, Leicester, Essex, and the Sidneys. Raleigh's public image as the enemy of Spain and the hero of the cause of Protestantism, martyred for mysteries of state most likely tied to the plots of the Spanish Ambassador, only served to strengthen the tie between English expansion across the Atlantic, the providence of God, and the future of Protestantism. As Thomas Scott noted in one of his twenty-five essays against the Spanish Match and in favor a close union between England and the Dutch Republic, if Raleigh had escaped the plots of Gondomar, he would have "made a new conquest of the West Indies."[36] In his *Vox Populi*, Scott understood the "West Indian voyages" and all the investments in "Virginea or the Bermudas" as a crucial part of the Protestant cause, which could "perhaps raise another England" to withstand "new Spaine in America."[37] Scott placed the conflict in purely eschatological terms, "we [the English] being for Christ and he [Spain] for Anti-Christ."[38]

"The Lost Flocke Triumphant"

Before the early 1580s, foreign policy in Elizabeth's court fluctuated between plans for open war with Spain, funding for the Dutch rebels, support for the Huguenots in France and attempts to keep such efforts informal or to stop them entirely.[39] Events on the continent and within the British Isles, however, helped shift English strategy into open alliance with the states in the Netherlands (and war with Spain) by the mid-1580s, at precisely the time the Roanoke voyages received the sanction and support of Elizabeth.[40] From 1585 to the end of the war in 1604, numerous tracts, sermons, and pamphlets placed the fight with Spain directly into an eschatological worldview.[41] The war with Spain, which provided military experience for a generation of leaders who would later figure prominently in the English schemes in the Americas, was cast and justified as a religious war. In nearly two decades of employment in strategic confessional wars: in the West Indies, in the Netherlands under the command of Leicester, during the Armada fight, in France in support of the Huguenot Henry of Navarre, in the taking of Cadiz in 1596 under Essex and Raleigh, and against the rebels in Ireland under Essex, English military forces were dominated by a militant internationalist Protestantism and filled with advocates of ongoing Reformation. By the middle of the 1590s, English Jesuit Robert Parsons noted that of the three religions in England—"protestants, puritans, and papists"—the Puritans had "a great part of the best captains and soldiers on their side" as well as the bulk of commanders and sailors in the "navy."[42] These military men in the navy, on privateers, and in the various forces deployed in the Netherlands and Ireland played a crucial role in the settlement and promotion of the Virginia project.[43]

Peace with Spain at the accession of King James VI of Scotland to the throne of England was not the end of anti-Spanish sentiment or of firm belief in the Protestant cause, but it did break up the dominance of the anti-Spanish block at the center of English court politics. Nevertheless, the garrisons in the Netherlands remained, the governor of Flushing being Robert Sidney, the younger brother of Sir Philip and nephew of Leicester, who continued to promote an aggressive Protestant foreign policy. As Viscount Lisle, Sidney was a member of the king's Council for Virginia (1609) and a member of the East India and Northwest Passage companies. As a child in Leicester's household, he had been tutored in mathematics, chemistry, and navigation by John Dee and Thomas Hariot.[44]

After formal peace, many of the navy men simply obtained commissions from the States General and continued attacking the Spanish until the twelve-year truce of 1608. Their ships were often based out of Flushing, where Sidney was governor. The most important owner of these vessels was Robert Rich, 3rd Baron Rich, who had ships at both Flushing and Middleburg and whose family kept a representative in Amsterdam after 1604.[45] His grandfather was Richard Rich, notorious for betraying and perjuring himself to convict Thomas More, at the behest of Henry VIII, for which he was rewarded with the plunder of numerous monasteries—the foundation of the Rich family fortune. The 3rd Baron Rich was a strong patron of the Elizabethan Puritan movement, holding reformed meetings at his estate in Essex, protecting radical preachers throughout East Anglia, and building a stable and formidable influence in Parliament. In 1604 Rich controlled at least fifty and possibly as many as seventy-five manors in Essex County and at least twenty livings.[46] He served under his brother-in-law Essex in the mission to Cadiz and represented Elizabeth at the French court in the late 1590s, during which he worked to support the passage of the Edict of Nantes. At the end of the war with Spain, Rich owned the largest private fleet of ships in England, which he continued to employ, now with letters of marque from the Dutch Republic or the Duke of Savoy against the common enemy Spain.[47] His son, Robert, 2nd Earl of Warwick after 1618, continued the mission of Raleigh, mixing the privateering tradition with colonization, and, as we will see, became a dominant force in the establishment of the English Atlantic empire.

In addition to the continuous links between the English soldiers and sailors in the Netherlands, the close relationship of the Virginia voyages to the eschatological Protestantism of the 1580s and 1590s can be best glimpsed within England in the court interest of Henry Stuart, Prince of Wales. Henry's court, officially formed at his being made Prince of Wales in 1610 but informally organized as early as 1606, presented itself (much like the eighteenth-century courts of the Prince of Wales) as the center of opposition to official government policy.[48] Henry exhibited none of the inclinations for *politique* compromise that so informed James I's attitude toward foreign policy. As Henry's biographer wrote, "at no point does he emerge as anything other than violently anti-Catholic."[49]

As early as 1604 Henry associated himself closely with the old war party and the cause of Protestantism throughout Europe. He was an ardent defender of Walter Raleigh, tried to get him released from the Tower, and attempted to have his estate restored. He was violently anti-Spanish, a tendency encouraged by his personal chaplains, some of whom had served with Essex.[50] He had a massive portrait of Prince Maurice of Nassau hung in St. James's palace and pressed to get Maurice inducted into the Order of the Garter. He enthusiastically pushed for his sister Elizabeth's marriage to the leader of Protestant princes in Germany, Frederick of the Palatinate. He supported strengthening the maritime power of England and patronized and protected the master shipbuilder Phineus Pett, who designed the first English three-deck man-of-war, the *Prince Royall*. If war broke out with Spain—and he hoped it would, the sooner the better—he knew exactly the strategy he would pursue: attack the West Indies. During the Julich-Cleves succession crisis in 1609, he relished the outbreak of a major confessional conflict in Europe. At his death numerous projects large and small were discovered among his papers, most of them tending toward "active intervention in the affairs of Protestant Germany and Huguenot France."[51]

And Henry was enthusiastic for colonization. He was an active supporter of the Virginia voyages of 1606 and a substantial adventurer in 1609.[52] He provided a patent for Robert Harcourt to revive Raleigh's Guiana project and open a trading colony at the Wiapoco.[53] With Sir Dudley Digges and Sir Thomas Smith he helped fund Henry Hudson's voyage of 1610. As "Supreme Protector" of the "Merchant Discoverers of the North-West Passage" the prince sent Henry Button on a mission to seek out a northwest passage, going so far as to give him instructions on shipboard behavior: "Let there be a religious care throughout your shippes." Button, a member of the Virginia Company, was the first Englishman to winter on the west side of Hudson Bay, and he named North and South Wales after the prince. Henry employed Sir Thomas Roe, a member of the Virginia Council, on an exploration of Guiana and the West Indies, another precedent for Raleigh's fateful descent on the Amazon in 1616–17.[54] Like the circles of Leicester, Sidney, Northumberland, and Raleigh, Prince Henry also promoted the new learning, the useful arts, mathematics, navigation, astronomy, and architecture.[55]

Numerous people encouraged the prince's important role in the renewed mission of discovery and colonization and celebrated his efforts as part of the cause of international Protestantism, which he relished. Huguenot Pierre Erondelle, at the behest of Richard Hakluyt, translated the expeditions of Samuel Champlain and dedicated the translation to Henry as the "Bright Starre of the North." "God hath necessitated in his Prophecie," he wrote, that great princes needed to be "nurturing Mothers of the Church" and "manage magnanimous actions, such as the peopling of lands, placing of Colonies, erecting of civill Governementes, and propagating of the Gospel of Christ." Such actions would bring in "the Lords harvest, to spread the name which must gather the elect from the utmost endes of the world." And finally, he observed, "Your poore Virginians doe seem to implore your Princely aide" to help them "shake off the yoke of the devil," who had "hitherto made them live worse than beasts" but now would be "brought into the fold of Christ."[56] Henry's librarian, the mathematician and cosmographer Edward Wright—who was himself connected to the Sidney circle around Dee and Hariot—dedicated the second edition of his *Certaine Errors in Navigation* to Henry. Wright interpreted the voyages of discovery and colonization as a way to reunite the world, restore man's dominion over nature, and "in the end come to the saving knowledge of the true God."[57] William Crashaw, who would preach to the Virginia Company on the sailing of Lord De la Warr, called upon Henry's leadership in clearly apocalyptic terms:

> Go forward, Princely Salomon, and walke still in the waeis of David, your Kingly Father: so shall our Israel be happy and blessed by you: and all the world shall praise God for you; for on whom are the eies of Christendom set, but upon you & your father's house? Surely, the hope of the Christian world is, that God hath appointed and annointed our gracious Sovereigne, and his royall issue, to hold up his religion in these declining daies, and to give the Whore of Babylon that foil & fall, from which she may never rise.

He further exhorted the prince to "hate the whore and make her desolate & eate her flesh, and burn her with fire."[58]

The Virginia voyages of 1606 and the reorganization of the Virginia charter, which created the king's Council for Virginia of 1609, was dominated by people with connections to the international Protestant cause and the emerging court of the Prince of Wales. With two exceptions, all the peers of the realm on the governing Council for Virginia had served in the wars in the Netherlands, France, Ireland, or at sea between 1585 and 1604 and were closely connected to the old Leicester/Essex group, Sir Walter Raleigh, Prince Henry, or all three. Many of them were heroes of the struggle. George, Lord Carew was the second cousin of Walter Raleigh, had fought with Essex at Cadiz and against the Azores, helped crush the Irish rebellion, and repelled the Spanish landings at Kinsale in 1601. Thomas Cecil, Earl of Exeter, served in the Netherlands in the 1580s and became governor of Brill, one of the "cautionary" towns; he and his brother Sir Edward Cecil, who served Price Maurice until 1609 and was also a member of the Council for Virginia, were closely associated with Prince Henry. Exeter would later receive a special commission to find and expel Jesuits from England. William, Earl of Pembroke, was a nephew of Sir Philip Sidney and Robert Sidney, the governor of Flushing. He served with Essex at Cadiz, attempted to free Raleigh from the Tower, was involved with the East India Company until 1614, and was brought into the Somers Islands Company, which named a tribe for him in those islands. He was an original member of the Council for New England, an incorporator of the Guiana Company in 1627, and a patentee of thirty thousand acres in Virginia in 1620. He was violently anti-Spanish. The eschatological pamphleteer Sir Thomas Scott was his personal chaplain.[59] And of course there was Thomas West, 3rd Baron De la Warr, governor of Virginia, who served in Ireland with Essex, to whom his wife was related.[60]

To these luminaries we could add numerous commoners on the council, the most important being Sir Thomas Smith, treasurer of the company. Smith's brother had fought at Cadiz with Essex and Raleigh and was knighted posthumously by Essex for gallantry. Smith himself was implicated in the Essex plot: Essex dined with him on the day of his arrest, and Smith was expected to raise the armed bands of London, of which he was the head, in support of Essex. For his efforts Smith spent two years in the Tower. As is well known, Smith championed English merchant capital, serving as governor of the East India, Muscovy, French, and Bermuda companies; he was a longtime treasurer of the Virginia Company and a major investor in the Northwest Passage Company, the English mission to the Senegal River in Africa, and an assault on the Corsairs in the Mediterranean. At his death his widow married Robert Sidney, now the new 1st Earl of Leicester.[61] Another commoner, Sir Dudley Digges, a member of the prince's household, was the son of Thomas Digges, the astronomer, mathematician, and pioneer in the invention of the microscope, who was himself a close associate of John Dee and another client protected by Leicester's patronage. Digges would become one of the important parliamentary leaders of the anti-Spanish faction in English politics, along with a number of other members of the Virginia Council. He was interested in the voyages of Henry Hudson and was a major investor, with the Prince of Wales, in the Northwest Passage expeditions. He was a member of the Bermuda Company and of the council of the New England Company.[62]

That these leaders shared an eschatological vision of history and England's place as the elect nation is evident in the ministers they patronized and the way they advertised their mission. It was never considered an economic venture in the vulgar sense of the term. The whole project was directly connected with the wars of Elizabeth and the ongoing fight against Antichrist, and many of the same people were directly involved. William Crashaw, educated at the Puritan-dominated St. John's College, Cambridge, invoked all the old messianic imperialism by calling King James and Prince Henry *"new Constantines or Charles the Great"*[63] (honors that John Foxe had given to Elizabeth), both of whom figured large in Protestant apocalyptic schemes of providential design. The mission to Virginia was not an economic one and could promise no "present profit" and therefore was only patronized by converted and sanctified men who sought to build up "the walls of Jerusalem."[64] "Remember," Crashaw noted, calling for the prayers of the people for support, "the end of this voyage is the destruction of the devils kingdom, and propagation of the Gospel."[65] The weakness of Virginia, the smallness of numbers, the trials and tribulations, the starvation and privations, and the discontents in the government were no different than the experiences of the Israelites in the time of Saul and only proved that God had taken the project in hand. "Thus hath God used to set on foote, and lay the beginnings of greatest matters," Crashaw observed, "that his power might be seene in weaknesse and that it might appear to be the work of God and not mens."[66]

Nearly all the clergy employed by the company to defend its reputation, promote the mission, and serve in Virginia in these years came from the most aggressive militant training grounds of English reforming Protestantism: Emmanuel College, Cambridge; St. John's College, Cambridge; Queen's College and Magdalen Hall, Oxford.[67] And they all placed the settlement of Virginia into grand eschatological visions. Typical is the ministry of Alexander Whitaker, the son of William Whitaker, regius professor of divinity at St. John's, Cambridge, who served in Virginia at the church built at Henricus. By 1612 he had seen the "many adversities of this Plantation." But such problems were not surprising, "for wheresoever any goodnesse shall begin to bud forth, the Divell will labour by all meanes to nip it in the head." The vigor of the devil in Virginia was similar to his "practice to discourage the Israelites from the conquest of Canaan." It was the fundamental battle, "for the Devill knowing that where Christ wins, he losethe."[68] Attempting to rally support in England, Whitaker finished vigorously: "You ... whose hearts God hath stirred up to build Him a Temple, and conquer a Kingdome for Him here" go "forth boldly and remember that you fight under the banner of Jesus Christ."[69]

While we might expect such rhetoric from the clergy associated with and employed by the company, and much more can be cited,[70] the merchants and soldier leadership spoke with eschatological fervor as well. During a speech to the company, Alderman Robert Johnson, later son-in-law of Sir Thomas Smith, not only thought the Virginia colony would provide employment for "many thousands" but would stop the flow of disaffected young men to "Rome and Rheims," where "after a little hammering" by the Jesuit "[Robert] Parson and his *Imps*," they become fit instruments for the villainous designs of international Catholicism.[71] After detailing all the popish plots, lies, and treasons committed by "the combination of Jesuits" and "that Arch Atheist in chief," the pope, Johnson insisted that papists were not wanted in Virginia, and he called upon the company "not to harbor this viperous broode in your bosome, which will eat out and consume the wombe of their mother."[72]

In numerous parts of his speech, Johnson connected the Virginia mission with a broader eschatological scope, drawing on ancient, biblical, and historical predictions. He referred to a "Blinde Prophecy" of "one of the Sibyalls," which asserted that "before the ende of the world there shall be a discoverie of all Nations: which shall come to bee knowne and acquainted together, as one neighbor with another, which since the confusion of tounges have been obscure and hid."[73] He expressed true wonder "that for an hundred years and more, the wealth and riches of the East and West should runne no other current but into one coffer," the treasury of Spain, which spent the wealth on the Jesuits: "a factious crew of newly created Friers, and that for no more speciall end, than with instigating bloddy plottes to pierce the heart of a Christian State and true religion." Johnson thought the current voyages were re-enacting the triumphs of "those Undaughted *English* and *Scottish* Captaines, that so often ventured their lives and spilt their blood, to reconquer Palestine from the Turkes and Sarezens." At the end of his speech he referred to the great English martyr John Frith, burned as a heretic for denying transubstantiation and purgatory in 1533. Frith predicted great wonders that would "be wrought by *Scots* and *English*, before the coming of Christ."[74] In exile in the 1520s Frith had translated Patrick Hamilton's "Revelation of the Antichrist," which condemned the pope and the hierarchical apparatus of the Church. His life and writings were particularly encouraged for the consideration of the "young."[75] Johnson would continue these musings in his 1612 offering, "The new life of Virginia," which compared Queen Elizabeth's early failed attempts in the New World to King David's failures to build the temple that Solomon eventually achieved, just as King James succeeded in building Virginia: "this Temple for the Lord."[76]

It was precisely because of these eschatological visions and the international Protestant credentials of the people involved in shepherding the Virginia project that the company would aggressively defend its activities with recourse to eschatological themes and reinterpret the history of the colony with a close eye to God's providential design. The suffering of the early colonists, the shipwreck and survival of the *Sea Venture* on Bermuda, and the subsequent persistence and stabilization of the colony under Lord De La Warr, Sir Thomas Gates, and Sir Thomas Dale, was a perfect emerging narrative for men who looked to the Bible to understand the mysteries of providence. One of the earliest publications concerning the wreck of the *Sea Venture* set the tone. *The Lost Flocke Triumphant* was a description in verse by Richard Rich, younger brother of Sir Nathaniel Rich (cousin and close ally of Sir Robert Rich, later Earl of Warwick), who described himself as a "soldier." In this piece he celebrated the character of the commanders of the cause, who were all connected to the heroic Protestantism of the 1580s and 1590s, the providence of God, and the religious nature of the mission. The actors were "men of worthy fame," the "noble Delaware," the "worthy Sr. Thomas Gates," the "valiant Captain Mr. Christopher Newport," and George Percy, "brother unto *Northumberland*," who "hope[d] to plant a Nation, which none before that stood." The work was done "to glorifie the Lord" and "to no other end."[77]

All the subsequent histories of this episode and the histories of the founding of Bermuda written in the company period supported this interpretation. For Ralph Hamor the company was "by the providence of God, miraculously wracked and saved upon the hopeful *Sumer* Islands."[78] Robert Johnson asked, "Who can withstand the Counsel of God that sits in the stearne of all actions" as he described the storm that sent the *Sea Venture* at "least an hundred leagues to the southward," where "by the miraculous hand of God and industrie of the Captaines, all the people escaped safe to land and not a man perished."[79] Edmund Howe's *Chronicle* made clear that the "discovery of these islands," was evidence "of the speciall Mercy, and divine providence of Almighty God."[80] William Crashaw used the "marvelous and indeed miraculous deliverance" of the *Sea Venture* on Bermuda as the centerpiece of no less than two of the four reasons that had "convinced [him] to beeleeve that God himselfe is the Founder and favourer of this Plantation."[81]

William Strachey, secretary of Virginia, educated at Emmanuel College, Cambridge, who was shipwrecked on the island and wrote a famous letter describing the wreck and subsequent survival of the party on Bermuda, used the occasion to reveal his own enthusiasm for eschatological thinking. Not only did God's mercy and miraculous deliverance save the party at sea, but by revealing the Bermuda Islands to be habitable and not, as most men thought, filled with devils and evil spirits, God had shown that "Truth was the daughter of Time"—a startling discovery that revealed the faith of God's promise in the prophecies to reopen light in the world.[82] Francis Bacon used exactly this phrase—"that Truth is the daughter of Time"—in *Cogitata et Visa*, an aggressive defense of the fundamentally providential and eschatological course of history.[83] William Crashaw made these arguments evident in his introduction to Silvestre Jourdain's "Plaine Description of the Barmudas."[84] The end of times mirrored God's creation, where every day God revealed more and more truth. And that is why "the great secrets in nature, and as admirable perfections in art, and as rare inventions, and profitable experiments" are "daily discovered in these latter ages." It had not been two hundred years "since the admirable art of Printing was found out," which subsequently led to the propagation of the Gospel and the "destruction of Poperie." Neither Aristotle nor the apostles understood the relationship of the compass to the poles, by which the navigation of the great seas and the discovery of "the new world of America" became possible. In the same way, God made known the "poor Virginia plantation" and "the hidden and long concealed truth, about the Islands of Bermuda."[85]

After the arrival of Gates and Thomas Dale in Virginia, no one who visited the colony could have missed the character of the mission. It was, as Dale himself noted, "Religious Warfare." If a visitor was not persuaded by the twice-daily prayer calling for God's help in vanquishing "Satan and his ministers," the pious rigor of Dale's laws, "Divine, Morall and Martial," would have convinced them. Or they might have run into Ralph Hamor, secretary of the colony, raving about "Anamonites and Horonites," the villains of the book of the prophet Nehemiah, who attempted to stop the Jews from rebuilding the Second Temple.[86] Nehemiah described the Jews, harried by the expected attacks of their enemies, as toiling with tools in one hand and weapons in the other to repair the walls of Jerusalem—an image of particular significance to the experience of the English in Virginia.[87] It is fitting that this period of religious warfare—"five yeeres of intestine warre"—would end with the conversion and marriage of Pocahontas.[88] "Were it but for the gaining of this one soule," Dale noted, "I will think my time, toile, and present stay well spent."[89] Her husband, John Rolfe, was one of the "Lost Flocke" miraculously saved at Bermuda, and his own piety has been well attested, as he wrote of the Virginia project: "What a crown of glory, shall be set upon their heads who shall faithfully labour herein."[90]

The peace that came with the marriage would see the first serious efforts to promote the conversion of the Indians in Virginia.[91] Henry, Earl of Southampton; Edwin Sandys; George Sandys; Dudley Digges; Robert Rich, Earl of Warwick; and Nicholas Ferrar were particularly interested in this endeavor, which was intended to culminate with a college at Henrico. The archbishop of Canterbury announced and raised money for the college, and the East India Company raised donations on its ships.[92] Patrick Copland, a preacher from the East India Company—and eventual minister in Bermuda—raised funds at the Cape of Good Hope for the school in Virginia. Copland directly connected these efforts to the prophecy of the book of Daniel 12:3 that "they that turn many to righteousness, shall shine as stars for ever and ever."[93] Although the effort was never particularly well organized, and much depended upon the personal activities of George Thorpe, the uprising and massacre designed by Opechancanough—foiled, the Virginia Company asserted, by the aid of God through the converted Indians—ended any immediate hopes for such a transformation. Once again, the settlers were reduced like the Jews in the book of Nehemiah, as one survivor plaintively noted, "working with our Hoe in one hand & our Peece or Sword in the other."[94]

Hearing of the attack of the Indians, the Council for Virginia supported the minister's call for "holy war" against the natives, and the apocalyptic preacher Joseph Mede compared the assaults of the Indians to "the massacres now in France & other parts of Christendome."[95] Within a year he would begin work on his *Clavis Apocalyptica* (later published in English as *The Key to the Millennium*), an "enormously popular" study that sketched out the relationship of the book of Revelation to the events of the sixteenth and seventeenth centuries.[96] And he associated the natives, in light of the failures to convert massive numbers, with the denizens of "Gog and Magog" of Revelation, who resisted the efforts of the godly in the prophecies of the end of times.[97]

As the company fell apart as a result of internal divisions, caused in part by dislocations created by the uprising, in part by intrigue related to the attempts of James I to promote the Spanish Match, and in part by gross mismanagement,[98] Samuel Purchas reiterated the holy cause of the Virginia mission and hoped for its continuation. Purchas began with the beginning: "In the beginning God created heaven and earth." "God is the beginning and the end, the Alpha and Omega, the first and the last," so "the first and last thing therefore in this Virginian argument considerable, is God." From here Purchas placed the Virginia story into a clearly eschatological context, from Adam to the glorious Queen Elizabeth.[99] The legal authority of the English to hold Virginia mirrored the authority God gave Moses to hold the land of Canaan, which the Jews purchased with their blood.[100] The many products and economic benefits provided by exploitation of the resources of Virginia mimicked the commerce and products that aided Solomon in the construction of the temple. The increase in seamen, which accompanied the rise in trade caused by the Virginia voyages, would create hardened soldiers to protect the English state, who would learn, "like the Jewes of Nehemiahs time, to use the Sword with one hand, and instruments of labour with the other."[101] The spread of the Gospel, both by settlement and conversion, would prove the destiny of God's plan for Virginia: "And Saviours shall thus come on Mount Zion to judge the Mount of Esau, and the Kingdome (of Virginia) shall be Lord." So the Virginia adventures would "overcome both Men and Devills, and espouse Virginia to one husband, presenting her as a chast Virgin to Christ."[102] The project of Virginia was but a part of a larger piece, the establishment of empire, as the "Kingdome thus multiplyed into Kingdomes," with Scotland and England true sisters, while "Virginia, New England, Newfoundland" together with "Bermuda, and the other islands" could be the "adopted and legall daughters of England."[103]

Warwick's Empire

Sir Thomas Dale, writing to the unidentified minister "M.D.M.," noted that "you have ever given me encouragements to persevere in this Religious Warfare." Worried that M.D.M. perceived a flagging enthusiasm among the people who had "undertooke the business," Dale assured his friend that he still served God, "in whose Vinyard I labor, whose Church with greedy appetite I desire to erect." Henry Stuart, Prince of Wales, was Dale's great patron, "his glorious master," who would have "ennamelled with his favours the labours I undertake, for God's cause."[104] As Dale put it, "Hee was the Great Captaine of our Israel, the hope to have builded up this heavenly New Jerusalem." Dale named the settlement he established at Henrico in his honor, and he perceived (rightly) that Henry's death had "quenched" the enthusiasm for the project. Virginia stood at the edge of failure, "in desperate hazard."[105]

With the death of Prince Henry, a new "Great Captain" of "our Israel" began to emerge as a guiding force of the struggling project, and he shared not only an eschatological vision of England's place in history and the world but the means and ambition to carry on the cause: Sir Robert Rich, after 1618 the 2nd Earl of Warwick. Beginning in 1612, with the creation of another charter for the Virginia Company and the subsidiary establishment of Somers Isles Company, Sir Robert Rich began to appear as a major investor, promoter, and entrepreneur in the English Atlantic world, engaged in all aspects of the emergent English expansion: "trade, plunder and settlement." Caught up in privateering controversies, both in the West and East in the second decade of the seventeenth century, by the end of the decade he had become a dominant force in the future progress and meaning of English colonization, a prominence that would continue until his death in 1658.[106]

Well known to be one of the "Puritan grandees" allied in opposition to Laudian reforms in the 1630s, Warwick came from a long line of infamous English Protestants and was connected by kin and experience to the international Protestant cause. His uncle was Robert Devereux, 2nd Earl of Essex, with whom his father had served at Cadiz. His brother, Henry Rich, later Earl of Holland, the first governor of the Massachusetts Bay Company, was knighted at the investiture of Henry, Prince of Wales. The prince himself approved the final list of candidates. Warwick and Holland were cousins of Robert Devereux, 3rd Earl of Essex, a childhood friend and confidant of Prince Henry. Warwick's other younger brother, Sir Charles Rich, served closely with the 3rd Earl of Essex in the attempts to regain the Palatinate in the 1620s. Throughout the 1620s Warwick and his cousin Sir Nathaniel Rich, along with Sir Dudley Digges and numerous other Virginia Company stalwarts, were leaders of the attempt to crush the Spanish Match, establish private funding for the efforts to recover the Palatinate, and create a West Indian company to wrest the West Indies from Spanish control. The anti-Spanish pamphleteer Thomas Scott, who wrote most of his essays on service in the Netherlands, was certainly connected with the Rich circle. A minister at Norwich and Ipswich, both Puritan towns in Essex County, which the Rich family dominated, Scott later became the personal chaplain of William Herbert, Earl of Pembroke; a member of the Virginia, Northwest Passage, Bermuda, and East India companies; and a personal ally of Warwick in the House of Lords.

Knighted in 1604 at the accession of King James, Sir Robert Rich, 2nd Earl of Warwick, died in 1658, at the end of an era. The extent to which Sir Robert engaged with his father in the early period of privateering is not altogether clear. By 1609 Rich was clearly interested in English expansion and colonization and appeared as a member of the Virginia Company. He was part of the *leadership* of every major and almost every minor colonization effort of the first half of the seventeenth century. He was a strong Puritan, educated at Emmanuel College, Cambridge (at the same time as William Strachey), where he became a lifelong friend of Oliver Cromwell, whose daughter married his grandson and heir. His connections to the birth of the English empire are extensive and represent only a small portion of his wide-ranging influence. He was a leader of the Virginia project both before and after the dissolution of the company, a founding member and longtime governor of the Bermuda company, an organizer of a failed expedition to settle Guiana (which eventually led to the settlement of St. Kitts and Nevis), a founder of the Guinea Company, a leader in the movement to revive the second Virginia company in 1620 (the Plymouth company), a founder of the New England Company, a friend and supporter of the Dorchester Company, a leader of a fleet to the West Indies to seize the Spanish treasure fleet in 1626, a founder and leader of the Providence Island Company, and one of the original proprietors of the Bahamas. As president of the Council for New England, he and his allies succeeded in getting the Massachusetts Bay Company charter through a hostile court, transferring the government to New England, and getting a separate charter for Plymouth in 1630. He was actively engaged and invested with the rising "New Merchants" in London and associated with Maurice Thompson, who would dominate the trading relations of all the Atlantic colonies into the 1650s. He sold the patent for the eventual settlement of Saybrook under John Winthrop Jr. and Henry Vane to his colleagues on the Providence Island venture, Lord Say and Sele and Lord Brooke. In 1638, he purchased the proprietary rights of the Earl of Pembroke to Trinidad, Tobago, St. Bernard, and Barbados. He commanded the navy for Parliament until 1645 and again from 1648 to 1649. In 1643, Parliament, at war with King Charles I, made Warwick "governor in chief and lord high admiral" of all the plantations and islands "within the bounds and coasts of America," the first and only position of its kind in English history. In this office Warwick granted the founding charter to Rhode Island and Providence Plantations, which served as the fundamental constitution of the province and later the state into the nineteenth century.

Attempting to fully incorporate Warwick's extensive influence into the making of the English empire between 1607 and 1651 is beyond the scope of this essay, as it would entail a flood of names and dates, of cross connections and fatal influences encompassing nearly every Atlantic colony. But a sketch should reveal the significance of the continuity of the godly cause in the English Atlantic from the collapse of the Virginia Company to the Navigation Act of 1651.

As one of the founders of Bermuda, Rich coordinated the development of the colony and his own estates on the island, including the "Warwick Tribe," in close contact with his cousin Sir Nathaniel Rich and their factor on the island, Nathaniel's brother, Robert Rich. As early as 1617 one of Warwick's privateers, Captain John Powell, brought a "good store of neggars" to the Rich and company holdings on the island. This shipment gives Rich the distinction of being the first English plantation owner to use enslaved Africans in quantity. Bermuda quickly gained the reputation of a privateering hub, heavily populated by "Men of Warr and Pirates," who earned the support of the local population for their frequent trade and for "robbinge the Spanyards (as being lyms of Antechrist)."[107] Aware of the usefulness and demand for African labor, Rich quickly put together the Guinea Company in 1618 and continued encouraging his privateers to sell slaves in the Americas.

One of these privateering captains was Samuel Argall. Connected with the Rich privateering interest as early as 1606, and employed by the Virginia Company in 1607 to find a quicker route to Virginia, Argall shared ownership with Sir Robert Rich in the *Treasurer,* a ship with which he achieved both fame and infamy. In 1613, Argall used the ship to aid in his kidnapping of Pocahontas and in the same year destroyed the French settlement at Saint-Sauveur (on the Penobscot River), which he accomplished by killing numerous men in a raid, abandoning those he did not kill on a tiny skiff without provisions, torturing "with great cruelty" the two Jesuits at the settlement, and taking numerous prisoners back to Jamestown, where they were put to hard labor.[108] Dale enthusiastically supported "this worthy Gentleman captain Argall."[109] When Dale returned to England in 1616, Argall governed Virginia in the spirit of Dale's strict religious and martial law until he was displaced by Sir George Yeardley. Argall, with Rich (now Warwick), sponsored the privateering voyage of Captain Daniel Elfrith on the *Treasurer*, which arrived in Virginia with a shipload of slaves within days of its consort, *The White Lion*, a Dutch privateer, which sold the "20. and odd" Africans it carried in August 1619.[110] Being turned away from Virginia because of concern over the legitimacy of his cargo, Elfrith sold his slaves to the Rich holdings in Bermuda, where he stayed until the late 1620s. Elfrith's daughter married Rich family man Philip Bell, who would become the first governor of the Puritan colony of Providence Island and, later, governor of Barbados. Elfrith was appointed the first admiral of Providence Island, which engaged in a war against Spain that Warwick had been waging privately his whole life.[111] Argall himself became an active member of the Council for New England and admiral of New England in 1622. He commanded the failed attack on Cadiz in 1625.

Rich, now 2nd Earl of Warwick, following the example of Sir Walter Raleigh, organized the Amazon Company in 1619 in partnership with Captain Robert North, Raleigh's second (and Warwick's cousin) on his late failed Guiana voyage. The effort succeeded in landing numerous colonists, only to abandon them as King James forced Warwick to renounce his patent in the face of the revived possibility of a Spanish match for Prince Charles. At this moment, also under pressure from James's Spanish designs, Edwin Sandys disclaimed any company involvement in the unlawful privateering of Warwick and Argall's *Treasurer*—a move that created a fatal breach between Sandys and Warwick, which led directly to the collapse of the Virginia Company. Unable to control the Virginia Company, Warwick, with the help of Sir Ferdinando Gorges, another veteran of the Netherlands wars and a cousin of Raleigh, reanimated the second Virginia Company, now revamped as the Plymouth Company. He encouraged the pilgrims to migrate from Leyden and played a major role protecting their settlement within the limits of his patent.[112]

As a major patent holder in the New England Company in the 1620s, Warwick had always associated New England with the religious cause. But times were changing in England, and the rise of Anti-Calvinism in the English church would reshape the parameters of the godly fight and the place of the Americas in the unfolding of English dominion overseas. The English state church until the late 1620s was Calvinist in doctrine, clarified by the Lambeth articles of 1595 and by the official representatives of the English church at the Synod of Dort in 1619, which condemned any theology of grace through works or sacraments, such as Arminianism, as heresy. But the findings of the Synod of Dort were never completely incorporated by King James I, and during his period of flirtation with the Spanish from 1620 to 1624, he not only allowed a Catholic bishop within England but stopped prosecuting recusants and began supporting some English churchmen whose attitudes were clearly anti-Calvinist, like William Laud. The easy association of Puritanism with a doctrinal and theological stance only emerged in the late 1620s, employed by people who supported the Laudian reforms of the 1630s. Before this period, Puritans certainly existed—they were people who wished to reform many of the liturgical practices and governing structures of the English Church—but they were largely indistinguishable from the mainstream of English theological reasoning. The Church of England, then, at least until the mid-1620s, when Archbishop Abbot lost his privileges, was a Calvinist church.[113]

The Rich interest within England aggressively attempted to stop the spread of anti-Calvinism in the English church in the 1620s. Warwick was the main mover of the York House Conference, at which he sponsored a debate over the character of the English church that pitted Calvinists like his friend the Puritan John Preston—who taught Rich's son at Emmanuel College—and the rising anti-Calvinist group. Highlights of the debate included a long argument related to whether or not the pope was the Antichrist, with Warwick—and a number of other grandees associated with English expansion—arguing in the affirmative.[114] But the York Conference ended in stalemate, and shortly thereafter, Archbishop Abbot—an old friend of the court of Prince Henry—lost his powers of appointment. In the Parliament of 1628 Sir Nathaniel Rich led the drive to condemn the anti-Calvinist views of Richard Montagu. As Rich declared in the House of Commons, he was "sorry any man here" could speak "in defense of . . . Arminianism."[115] But like the York House Conference, the Parliament of 1628 failed to stop the transformation of the English church.

As the naval war with Spain ended—during which Warwick's privateers charted the location of Providence Island—and with the war in Europe broadening in scope, the failure of England to lead the Protestant cause, combined with the rise of anti-Calvinism in the church, promised a grim future for the godly. Warwick would prove pivotal in the effort of numerous dissatisfied Englishmen and women to escape the trend by emigrating to the Americas. He was the friend of John Winthrop, the patron of Hugh Peter, and a protector of John Stoughton and numerous other ministers closely associated with the New England settlements. In 1628 Warwick, with fellow travelers Lord Say and Sele, Lord Brooke, John Pym, and Richard Knightly (all of whom would later be involved in the Providence Island Company, shortly to be formed), sitting as part of the "New England Company for the Settlement of Massachusetts Bay," sent Netherlands veteran John Endicott to Massachusetts to prepare the way for an expected exodus.[116]

The plantations in New England were justified in precisely the same terms used in the Virginia colonization literature of 1609. John White—friend of Warwick's client Richard Hooker—acknowledged that the settlement of colonies would expand shipping, produce necessary commodities, and expand the wealth of the realm, but the great purpose of settling colonies must be "the opening of the eyes of those poor ignorant soules, and discovering unto them the glorious mystery of Jesus Christ." This action would fulfill the prophecy of the end of days. As White argued, numerous men of note "both for place and learning in the Church" had shown that the "course held by God from the beginning in the propagation of Religion, falls in this last age, upon the Westerne parts of the world." In fact, he asserted, our "Savior's prophecy, Mathew 24.27 points out such a progress of the Gospell." Recent events showed that God was unfolding his design by revealing the secrets of the loadstone and the existence of so many unknown nations. God had revealed the New World and left "this great and glorious worke to this age of the world." Look, White exhorted his readers, for "the nearness of the Jewes conversion, before which, it is conceived by the most that the fullness of the *Gentiles* must come in according to the Apostles prophecy." That this day cannot be "farre off appears by the fulfilling of the prophecies."[117]

When Warwick is placed at the center of the story, the New England settlements of the late 1620s and the 1630s were not a shift from but a continuation of the eschatologically informed mission of the Virginia companies of 1606 and 1609. What had changed was the political context of the English church. The English plantations had always claimed to represent the leading edge of the battle against the Antichrist, as Thomas Scott and Samuel Purchas had reminded English readers in the mid-1620s. They had always claimed that the end of times was near and that the colonization of the Americas—by the godly of England—would play a crucial role, already designed, in the fulfillment of the scriptural prophesies. But as England itself fell under the power of papist tendencies, the exodus to the Americas became a defensive refuge in the latter times. Thus numerous pamphleteers needed to defend their actions against the critique of separatism, a problem the early movements, seen as the extension of a militant reforming mission of the English church, did not have.

So the great migrations of the 1630s, in which tens of thousands of English men and women fled the rising tide of Antichrist within England represent a continuation of trends, attitudes, and personalities that had always called for the discovery and settlement of America in eschatological terms.[118] There were differences in the processes of internal development that would shape different polities throughout the English Atlantic, but the impulse for the initial settlements have a common eschatological root, which has been too often ignored.[119] In fact, by 1641, when John Pym—a close ally with Warwick against Arminianism since the early 1620s and a fellow leader of the Providence Island Company—could so blithely suggest that the "Sixty thousand able persons of this Nation" in "New England, Virginia, and the Caribe Islands, and in the Bermudas" could easily conquer New Spain and thereby destroy the "great support of Popery in all parts of Christendome," he reflected the fact that the English Atlantic had always been associated with the great Protestant cause.[120]

Like the other leaders of that cause, Warwick patronized the leading advances of the new learning. In 1619 he gave the mathematician Henry Briggs, an active member of the Virginia Company, a share in one of the tribes of Bermuda. Briggs was a teacher of mathematics at anti-Catholic Gresham College, collaborated with Edward Wright in numerous projects to improve the teaching and techniques of English navigation and astronomy, and was an admirer of Thomas Hariot. One of the leading promoters of the use of logarithms, Briggs wrote a tract in support of William Baffin's expedition to find the Northwest Passage, which was published by the Virginia Company in one of its promotional tracts and called for the conversion of the natives of America.[121]

Through Briggs we can connect Warwick to the "spiritual Brotherhood" associated with Samuel Hartlib, Jan Comenius, and John Dury, which played such an important role in the English scientific transformation of the mid-seventeenth century, and which Charles Webster has shown was deeply obsessed with Baconian eschatological thinking and often directly involved in explicit apocalyptic predictions.[122] Numerous other Warwick connections also place him in a position of patronage, protection, and influence with this group. With Sir Nathaniel Rich, Warwick helped financially support Samuel

Hartlib in the 1630s.[123] Warwick's personal chaplain, John Gauden, encouraged Parliament in 1641 to invite Jan Comenius and John Dury to England, in the first month of the Long Parliament's meeting.[124] Warwick controlled the Felsted School in Essex, which served as a major incubator for Puritan scientists and preachers in the 1630s and 1640s. His colleagues in colonial projects, including Lord Brooke, Lord Say and Sele, John Pym, Henry Mildmay, Richard Knightly, Maurice Thompson, and numerous others, were patrons of or, like Brooke, direct collaborators with the "Brotherhood." Warwick himself supported numerous leading figures of Hartlib's "Invisible College," which sought out the utopian potential of the new learning in an effort to regain "Dominion over Nature," including the management of plantations, the creation of universal education, and the potential for universal language. The "College" provides the clearest example of the supposed "practical" ends of mercantilism being applied for godly, eschatological purposes. Heaven resembled a godly utopia, with all things serving their proper purpose, all resources at the command of perfect centralized design. "Science" could serve to make a paradise of Earth, restore man's dominion over nature, and bring on the end of times. So the college stimulated and provided a forum for the new political economists like Benjamin Worsley who would come to design and justify the regulations of England's empire.[125]

Benjamin Worsley's manuscript "Proffits humbly presented to this kingdome" took these interests in the perfectibility of commonwealths and social utopianism to practical ends. He wished to see saltpeter factories encouraged, husbandry and all methods of tillage improved, fisheries perfected, and sheep preserved from "sickness" so that their wool could flourish. Plantations should be extended and more fully settled, and the navy should be encouraged and shipping increased. The benefits of these and other improvements would be manifest: specie would be increased, commodities would be cheaper, more money would be available for productive use, and the "Poore in the Kingdome may be this way maintained." To what end? Why should the commonwealth play such an active role in the regulation of its own economy, imperial and local? Here Worsley revealed his Baconian eschatological pedigree: the improvement in the condition of man would assure that England could "sitt as judge and Umpire of all Christian differences"; thus, as "Peace makers" they could show themselves the true children of God and inherit the kingdom of heaven. The Gospel would be propagated "into other unknowne partes"; "the Jews could be converted," which he thought "shortly to be expected and without doubt at hand"; and there could be a Union and "reconciliation throughout all the Christian at least all the Protestant Churches."[126]

Worsley developed these ideas into a systematic program for controlling the trading relationships of England's colonies, and in particular he developed a model plan he wished to see applied in Virginia. The main thrust of his ideas can be found directly in much of the work of the Parliament's council on trade, including the act of 1650, which was intended to stop trade with those colonies still supporting the king, but which also restrained all trade with "any of the English Plantations in America" without a proper license. While the relationship of Worsley to the more famous Navigation Act of 1651 is unclear, he had a major impact on the design of Restoration policy toward the colonies, including the creation of the councils of trade and plantations, under the patronage of Shaftesbury.[127] And Worsley defended the 1651 act in *The Advocate* of 1652, comparing Dutch encroachments with the "Design of *Spain*" to "get the Universal Monarchie of Christendom." Worsley introduced his arguments by confidently asserting "the Belief of the Coming of [God's] appearance, and the breaking forth, very shortly, of his Glorie."[128]

The Navigation Act of 1651 was the product of a directly apocalyptic tendency, fomented by the righteous anger of Oliver St. John (a member of the Providence Island Company with Warwick), along with many of the Rumpers, at the behavior of the Dutch during a failed attempt to rejuvenate the Anglo-Dutch union. St. John returned from his disappointing mission in 1650 roused by the belief that the Dutch would "repent of having rejected our offers." In a rich examination of the ideological context of the passage of the Navigation Act and the coming of the first Anglo-Dutch war, Steven Pincus has shown that both the act and the war reflected, not simple economic motives, but the belief of the Rump, and the popular crowds in London, that the "rod of the Lord" needed to give justice to the Dutch, fallen Protestants who had joined "the great Antichristian interest." In the summer of 1651 when the Navigation Act was passed through Parliament, the war drums sounded, and the editor of the London *Weekly Intelligencer* noted that "All things conspire to shew that the end of the world is at hand."[129]

But fighting with Protestants remained a highly dubious proposition for much of the political nation, and as Cromwell dismissed the Rump, he moved the country toward a foreign policy upon which everyone could agree—the Western Design—a glorious plan to finally wrest New Spain from the whore of Babylon.[130]

And yet by 1655 Cromwell had abandoned an overtly apocalyptic foreign policy,[131] as England began to follow the evident trends of confessional politics in Europe and the Americas in the 1640s and 1650s. The Rump had failed to create a godly society. Wars of religion were endless and ultimately unwinnable. Thirty years of war in Europe had changed very little, and the 1648 Treaty of Westphalia dismissed religion as a legitimate future motive for conflict and diplomatic intrigue. In America during the English Civil War, the conflicts over loyalty to the Crown or Parliament rarely replicated the alignments within England itself, as a dynamic based upon the local interests of the colonies informed the politics of loyalty.[132] Only in Maryland, which had its share of Catholics and Jesuits, was anything approaching a "religious war" fought.[133] Religion would no longer be a legitimate reason of state in England after the Restoration, and new contexts for the purpose and meaning of the empire based upon conflicting visions of commerce and dominion would struggle for ascendancy. The age of religious wars had ended.[134]

The men and women who built, imagined, and supported English expansion in the early seventeenth century did not live on bread alone. If they had, Virginia would have been abandoned, slavery would not have come to North America when it did, the English would not have colonized the West Indies, and New England would not have become a New England. From the "wizard" John Dee to the economist Benjamin Worsley, the pace and meaning of English expansion was dependent upon an eschatological worldview that justified, motivated, and created the first English empire. Without the strong pressure of militant reforming Protestantism and the grand millennialism of English Christianity, the English would not have created settlement colonies in the seventeenth century, or at least they would not have created the colonies they did, when they did. The motif of the initial expansion of England, from the voyages of Francis Drake to the final Western Design of Oliver Cromwell, was above all else religious. Yet it was a strain of eschatological religiosity that incorporated concerns we would later come to consider merely scientific, political, and economic, but which possessed, for its advocates, a real power to transform the world according to God's plan and promise.

It is perhaps counterintuitive to assert that the origins of something can come from people obsessed with the end of time, but as Samuel Purchas noted, "the end of a thing is the beginning," and Creation mirrored Redemption: "a Glorious Circle."[135]

In this last age, Time doth new worlds display,
That Christ a church, o'er all the Earth may have,
His righteousness shall barbarous realms away,
If there first love, more civil lands will leave
America to Europe may succeed
God may of Stones raise up Abra[ham's] seed.[136]
—William Alexander, Earl Sterling, Proprietor of Nova Scotia, 1616

Notes

1. Samuel Purchas, *Hakluytus Posthumus; or, Purchas his Pilgrimes, Contayning a History of the World in Sea Voyages and Lande Travells by Englishmen and Others*, 26 vols. (New York, 1906), 19:102–3 (hereafter *Purchas his Pilgrimes*).

2. "A Prayer duly said Morning and Evening upon the Court of Guard, either by the Captain of the watch himself, or by some one of his principal officers," in *Lawes Divine, Morall and Martiall, &c* (London, 1612), n.p.

3. Ibid.

4. "Eschatology," considered broadly, is nothing more than a concern with the end of the world, the last days of humanity, and the final judgment. Such thinking has had a place in all of the world's religions and numerous secular societies and was a crucial concern of Europeans, both Protestant and Catholic, engaged with problems stemming from the breakdown of Roman Catholic hegemony in the sixteenth century.

5. John Foxe, *Actes and monuments of matters most speciall and memorable, happenyng in the Church with an uniuersall history of the same, wherein is set forth at large the whole race and course of the Church, from the primitive age to these latter tymes of ours, with the bloudy times, horrible troubles, and great persecutions agaynst the true martyrs of Christ, sought and wrought as well by heathen emperours, as nowe lately practised by Romish prelates, especially in this realme of England and Scotland* . . . , 3 vols. (London, 1684). See also, William Haller, *Foxe's Book of Martyrs and the Elect Nation* (London, 1963); Patrick Collinson, *The Elizabethan Puritan Movement* (London, 1967), 21, 24–25; Paul Christianson, *Reformers and Babylon: English Apocalyptic Visions from the Reformation to the Civil War* (Toronto, 1978).

6. David Armitage, *Ideological Origins of the British Empire* (Cambridge, 2000); Andrew Fitzmaurice, *Humanism and America: An Intellectual History of English Colonisation, 1500–1625*, (Cambridge, 2004), 1. There is little doubt that the early context of colonial expansion is part of the Renaissance worldview, which drew upon numerous classical tropes, including a conception of commerce and virtue, even manhood, that might be called "civic humanism." We might also find numerous analogies with late medieval chivalric culture in the posturing of the adventurers. But the English, at least, rejected classical conceptions of historical time—and that makes all the difference. For more directly economic motives, see G. L. Beer, *Origins of the British Colonial System* (New York, 1908); Charles Andrews, *The Colonial Period of American History*, 4 vols. (New Haven, CT, 1936); and David Beers Quinn, *England and the Discovery of America* (New York, 1974). Alison Games, in her recent broad analysis of the global reach of English expansion in the century after 1560, suggests that religion is simply one of the many attributes that shaped the way En-

glish "cosmopolitans" interacted with the peoples and the places they met. While that is true enough, her study, which she describes as a "vantage" on English expansion, tends to create a slightly skewed portrait of mainsprings of English colonization projects, by an overemphasis on some of the marginal players. This is not to suggest that the English did not interact with the globe in many diverse ways in this period, but that without an understanding of the driving significance of eschatological thinking, it all looks like a chaos of "adaptability" and "flexibility," two concepts that are obviously but not really distinctively "English" in this century of expansion. See Alison Games, *The Web of Empire: English Cosmopolitans in an Age of Expansion, 1550–1650* (New York, 2009), 1–15, quote from 7.

7. Some exceptions include Louis B. Wright, *Religion and Empire: The Alliance between Piety and Commerce in English Expansion, 1558–1626* (Chapel Hill, NC, 1942); Perry Miller, "The Religious Impulse in the Founding of Virginia: Religion and Society in the Early Literature," *William and Mary Quarterly*, 3rd ser., 5 (October 1948): 492–522, and 6 (January 1949): 24–41. John Parker, "Religion and the Virginia Colony, 1609–10," in K. R. Andrews, N. P. Canny, and P. E. H. Hair, eds., *The Westward Enterprise: English Activities in Ireland, the Atlantic, and America, 1480–1650* (Liverpool, 1978), downplays the continuities between the 1580s and the 1610s. Karen Ordahl Kupperman, *Providence Island, 1630–1641: The Other Puritan Colony* (Cambridge, 1995); Kupperman, *The Jamestown Project* (Cambridge, MA, 2007). Edward L. Bond, *Damned Souls in a Tobacco Colony* (Macon, GA, 2000) gives a strikingly original interpretation of religious experience to the making of the polity in seventeenth-century Virginia, with which this essay is generally compatible.

8. I am well aware of the current debate over the real nature of the "wars of religion" in early modern historiography, but I tend to follow the persuasive arguments of Paul Douglas Lockhart, *Frederik II and the Protestant Cause: Denmark's Role in the Wars of Religion, 1559–1596* (Leiden, Netherlands, 2004), 4–7, that "any effort to divorce the study of international politics and the making of foreign policy from their confessional backgrounds, at least in pre-Westphalian Europe, is inherently a futile one." On the "messianic imperialism" of Philip II, see Geoffrey Parker, *The Grand Strategy of Philip II* (New Haven, CT, 1998); Bodo Nischan, *Prince, People, and Confession: The Second Reformation in Brandenburg* (Philadelphia, 1994); and John M. Headley, Hans J. Hillerbrand, and Anthony J. Papias, eds., *Confessionalization in Europe, 1555–1700* (Aldershot, UK, 2004). On the increasing religious polarization of the Dutch revolt, see Jonathan Israel, *The Dutch Republic: Its Rise, Greatness and Fall, 1477–1806* (Oxford, 1995), 179–230.

9. Collinson, *Puritan Movement;* Christopher Durston and Jacqueline Eales, *The Culture of English Puritanism, 1560–1700* (London, 1996); Wallace T. MacCaffrey, *Queen Elizabeth and the Making of Policy, 1572–1588* (Princeton, NJ, 1981); Simon Adams, "Faction, Clientage and Party: English Politics, 1550–1603," *History Today* 32 (1982): 33–39.

10. Christianson, *Reformers and Babylon;* Richard Bauckman, *Tudor Apocalypse: Sixteenth Century Apocalypticism, Millennarianism, and the English Reformation: From John Bale to John Foxe and Thomas Brightman* (Appleford, UK 1978).

11. William Haller, *The Elect Nation: The Meaning and Relevance of Foxe's Book of Martyrs* (New York, 1963), 221; John Cummins, *Francis Drake* (New York, 1995), 112.

12. E. G. R. Taylor, ed., *The Original Writings & Correspondence of the Two Richard Hakluyts, with Introduction and Notes* (London, 1935), 2:302.

13. Peter French, *John Dee: The World of an Elizabethan Magus* (London, 1972).

14. See Méric Casaubon, ed., *A True and Faithful Relation of What Passed for many Years*

Between Dr. John Dee (A Mathematician of Great Fame in Q. Eliz. And King James their Reignes) and Some Spirits: Tending (had it Succeeded) to a General Alteration of most States and Kingdoms in the World . . . (London, 1659).

15. John Dee, *General and Rare Memorials Pertayning to the Perfect Arte of Navigation* (London, 1578, 1588), 53.

16. Ibid. See also Walter Trattner, "God and Expansion in Elizabethan England: John Dee, 1527–1583," *Journal of the History of Ideas* 25 (January–March 1964): 17–34.

17. Ken MacMillan, "Discourse on History, Geography, and Law: John Dee and the Limits of the British Empire, 1576–1580," *Canadian Journal of History* (April 2001): n.p.

18. John Dee, *The Private Diary of Doctor John Dee*, ed. James Orchard Halliwell (London, 1842), 4–3, 5, 8.

19. Davis, an author of a few navigational tracts, would later serve as a retainer of Essex, and at his behest he would serve the Dutch as the chief navigator in a voyage to the East Indies in the 1580s and lead the first voyage of the East India Company to the East. Alexander Brown, *The Genesis of the United States*, 2 vols. (New York, NY, 1890) 2:875.

20. MacMillan, "Discourse on History."

21. Parks, *Richard Hakluyt*, 48–49; E. G. R. Taylor, *Tudor Geography, 1485–1583* (New York, NY, 1968), 135.

22. Henry Percy's younger brother George would emigrate to Virginia and serve as deputy governor until 1612. His daughter, Lady Anne Percy, married John West, brother of Thomas West, 3rd Baron De La Warr.

23. A sensitive treatment of Dee and his context is Deborah E. Harkness, *John Dee's Conversations with Angels: Cabala, Alchemy, and the End of Nature* (Cambridge, 1999).

24. Thomas Hariot, *A brief and true Report of the new found land of Virginia* (London, 1588), F2.

25. Erasmus himself had a powerful philosophy of Christ and distinguished between "true Christianity" and the false church. See Israel, *Dutch Republic*, 45–47. For a conflation of humanism with antireligious science, see Armitage, *Ideological Origins*; and Fitzmaurice, *Humanism and America*.

26. Christianson, *Reformers and Babylon*, 37.

27. Christopher Hill, *Intellectual Origins of the English Revolution Revisited* (Oxford, 1997), 9, 38–39,

28. John Kenyon, *The History Men: The Historical Profession in England Since the Renaissance* (Pittsburgh, 1983); [Walter Raleigh], *The History of the World* (London: Walter Burre, 1614), preface, A3, D2 quote on 19. Raleigh also commented, "The wisest of the Naturalists (if Aristotle bee hee) could never so much as define, but by the Action and effect, telling us what it workes (which all men know as well as he) but not what it is," D3.

29. David Sacks, "Richard Hakluyt's Navigations in Time, History, Epic, and Empire," *Modern Language Quarterly* 67 (March 2006): 31–62. I have relied heavily on Sacks for my interpretation of Hakluyt and thank him for his generous help. See also Hill, *Intellectual Origins*, 11–12, 39–40, 120–22, 138–47.

30. Francis Bacon, *Advancement of Learning* (1605), book 1, iv, vii.

31. Francis Bacon, "Valerious Termininus," in James Spedding et al., eds., *The Works of Francis Bacon*, 14 vols. (London, 1861–1872), 3:220–21.

32. Charles Webster, *The Great Instauration: Science, Medicine and Reform* (New York, 1975), 25.

33. Sacks, "Navigations," 31–62; Hill, *Intellectual Origins*, 120–22; Webster, *Instauration*, 20–23.

34. Raleigh, *History of the World*, 213.

35. Ibid., preface, A3, D2; Kenyon, *The History Men*, 19.

36. Hill, *Intellectual Origins*, 184.

37. For the importance of Scott, see Steven Pincus, "From Holy Cause to Economic Interest: The Study of Population and the Invention of the State," in Alan Houston and Steven Pincus, eds., *A Nation Transformed: England after the Restoration* (Cambridge, UK, 2001), 272–90; and Thomas Scott, *Vox Populi; or, Newes from Spayne* (London, 1620), n.p. [9, 10].

38. Thomas Scott, *The Belgick Pismire* (London, 1623), n.p. [5].

39. For a recent encapsulation of the extensive literature on Elizabethan foreign policy and the ongoing historiographical debate, see Susan Doran, *Elizabeth I and Foreign Policy, 1558–1603* (London, 2000).

40. The successful Spanish conquest of Portugal in 1580; the successes of Alexander Farnese, Prince of Parma, in recapturing much of the Spanish Netherlands; the discovery of the Throckmorton Plot in 1583 by which the Spanish ambassador and the Duke of Guise conspired with Mary Queen of Scots to overturn Elizabeth; the death of the Duke of Anjou in 1584, which opened up the French throne to the Huguenot leader Henry of Navarre; and the subsequent Treaty of Joinville of 1585, in which the Spanish united with the Duke of Guise and his new league to assure a Catholic succession in France, all pressed Elizabeth into the Treaty of Nonsuch in 1585, in which she allied with the States General; took over the cautionary towns of Flushing, Brill, and Rammekens; and began cobbling together an alliance of Protestant princes in Europe, which eventually included James VI of Scotland and the erratic John Casamir of the Palatinate.

41. James Aske, *Elizabeth Triumphans* (London, 1588), 11; Oliver Pigge, *Meditations* (London, 1589), 33; Robert Greene, *The Spanish masquerade* (London, 1598), B2–B3; Thomas Tynne, *A Preparation against the Prognosticall Dangers of this Year, 1588* (London, 1588), B6; Robert Pricket, *A Soldier's Wish unto his Sovereign Lord King James* (London, 1603) C2v.

42. R. Dolman [Robert Parsons], *A Conference About the Next Succession to the Crowne of Ingland* (Antwerp, 1596), 33.

43. Of the many soldiers and sailors engaged in the Virginia project from 1606 to 1620, numerous names of the leadership of the colony, both in England and America stand out: Henry Percy, Earl of Northumberland; George Percy; Sir Thomas Gates; Sir George Sommers; Sir Thomas Dale; Christopher Newport; Robert Sidney; Captain John Martin, who sailed with Drake and died in Virginia in 1629; and Sir Henry Mannering.

44. *Oxford Dictionary of National Biography*.

45. Arthur Percival Newton, *Colonizing Activities of English Puritans* (New Haven, CT, 1914), 16–17. Flushing and Middleburg would be the leading early ports for the Virginia/Dutch tobacco trade.

46. Mary Elizabeth Bohannnon, "The Essex Election of 1604," *English Historical Review* 48 (July 1933): 396–98.

47. Newton, *Colonizing Activities*, 16–17.

48. Hill, *Intellectual Origins*, 22–23.

49. Roy Strong, *Henry, Prince of Wales, and England's Lost Renaissance* (London, 1986), 85, particularly 52–55.

50. Strong, *Henry, Prince of Wales*, 53.

51. Ibid., 76–77, 84–85; John Chamberlain to Dudley Carleton, November 12, 1612, in John Chamberlain, *Letters*, ed. N. E. McClure, 3 vols. (Philadelphia, 1939), 1:390; *Calendar of State Papers, Venetian*, ed. R. Brown et al., 38 vols. (London, 1864–1947), 12:450, 453–54, 470.

52. Robert Tindall, whom Henry sent on the first voyage, sent a journal of the trip and a draft of the river back with Christopher Newport's return voyage. Strong, *Henry, Prince of Wales*, 61. On Henry's funding for Virginia in 1609, see *Calendar of State Papers, Venetian*, 11:237.

53. *Purchas his Pilgrimes*, 16:358; Newton, *Colonizing Activities*, 26.

54. Strong, *Henry, Prince of Wales*, 60–63, quote on 62.

55. Strong, *Henry, Prince of Wales*; Hill, *Intellectual Origins*, 190–95.

56. Marc Lescarbot, *Nova Francia; or, The Description of that part of New France*, trans. P. Erondell (London, 1609), n.p. [1–3].

57. Edward Wright, *Certaine Errors in Navigation* . . . (London, 1610), n.p.

58. William Crashaw, "Crashaw's Epistle Dedicatory," in Brown, *Genesis of the United States*, 2:616.

59. *Oxford Dictionary of National Biography*; Hill, *Intellectual Origins*, 184; Brown, *Genesis of the United States*, 2:921.

60. *Oxford Dictionary of National Biography*.

61. Brown, *Genesis of the United States*, 2:1017.

62. Ibid., 2:879.

63. William Crashaw, *A Sermon Preached in London Before the right honourable the Lord Lawarre, "A New-Year's Gift to Virginiae"* (London, 1610), I, 2; Strong, *Henry*, 62.

64. Crashaw, *A Sermon Preached*, E3.

65. Ibid., n.p. [11].

66. Ibid., E4.

67. Robert Gray, St. Johns, Richard Crakenthrope, Queens, etc. See the excellent piece by Thomas P. Chadwick, "Canvassing for the Colonies: Comparative Representations of the Recruitment and Mobilization of Trans-Atlantic Emigrants in Britain, 1580–1620 and 1660–1710," Atlantic History Seminar Working Paper 04CR002, March 2004, 9.

68. Whitaker to Thomas Smythe, July 28, 1612, in Brown, *Genesis of the United States*, 2:578–79.

69. Alexander Whitaker, "Good News from Virginia," in Brown, *Genesis of the United States*, 2:588.

70. See Miller, "The Religious Impulse"; and Parker, "Religion and the Virginia Colony."

71. Robert Johnson, *Nova Britannia* (London, 1609), D3.

72. Ibid.

73. Ibid., n.p. [15].

74. Ibid., n.p. [18].

75. See John Day, comp., *The Whole Workes of W. Tyndall, John Firth, and Doct. Barnes, three worthy martyrs, and Principal leaders of this Church of England* (London, 1573), p. Aii.

76. Robert Johnson, *The New Life of Virginea* (London, 1612), B3.

77. R[obert] Rich, *The Lost Flocke Triumphant* (London, 1610), B2.

78. Ralph Hamor, *A true Discourse on the Present State of Virginia* (London, 1614), 16.

79. Johnson, *The New Life of Virginea*, C.
80. Howe, *The Annals or General Chronicle of England* (London, 1615), in Brown, *Genesis of the United States*, 2:754.
81. William Crashaw, "Crashaw's Epistle Dedicatory," in Brown, *Genesis of the United States*, 2:616.
82. *Purchas his Pilgrimes*, 19:14.
83. Bacon, *Cogitata et Visa*, in *Works*, 3:612–13. See also, Webster, *Instauration*, 23.
84. [Silvestre Jourdain], *A Plaine Description of the Barmudas, now called the Summer Islands* (London, 1613), in Peter Force, ed., *Tracts and other Papers relating principally to the Origin, Settlement, and Progress of the Colonies in North America*, 4 vols. (Washington, D.C. 1836–46.) 3:1–15.
85. Jourdain, *A Plaine Description*, 1–3.
86. Ralph Hamor, "To the Reader," in *Discourse*, n.p. [5].
87. "Each took his weapon even to the water." Nehemiah 4:23. For a telling sequence of letters describing the situation in this period, see Don Diego de Molina to Don Diego Sarmineto de Acuña, April 30, 1614, in which the unfortunate Molina, writing in a field "with a root" notes that "I am convinced that the Lord brought me hither . . . to become the Moses of these unfortunate people." Brown, *Genesis of the United States*, 2:743–45.
88. Hamor, *Discourse*, 2.
89. Ibid., 55.
90. On Rolfe, see Miller, "The Religious Impulse," 500–501.
91. Bond, *Damned Souls*, 114–18.
92. "America and West Indies: Addenda 1623," no. 124, December 14, 1623,*Calendar of State Papers Colonial*, Addendum 1574–1677, 9:63.
93. Patrick Copland, *A Declaration how the monies* . . . (London, n.d.); quote in Copland, *Virginia's God Be Thanked* (London, 1622), 2.
94. *Purchas his Pilgrimes*, 19:210–11.
95. *Records of the Virginia Company*, 3:671–72; Robert C. Johnson, ed., "The Indian Massacre of 1622: Some Correspondence of the Reverend Joseph Mead [sic]," *Virginia Magazine of History and Biography* 71 (1963): 408.
96. On Joseph Mede and his relationship to Baconian eschatological thought, see Webster, *Instauration*, 9–11.
97. J. Bowman, "Is America the New Jerusalem or Gog and Magog?" *Proceedings of the Leeds Philosophical and Literary Society* 6 (1950): 445–52.
98. Wesley Craven, *The Dissolution of the Virginia Company: The Failure of a Colonial Experiment* (New York, 1932), is still the definitive account, but I believe it is ripe for revisions. Craven successfully refuted much mythology about the collapse of the company but made the economic motives too deterministic of people's behavior. The split between Rich and Sandys cannot be properly considered an economic grievance, although there was money involved. The shifting alliances of the Spanish Match, interwoven with problems related to particular personalities, shaped many of the internal conflicts of the moment.
99. Samuel Purchas, "Virginias Verger; or, A Discourse shewing the benefits which may grow to this Kingdome from American English Plantations, and specially those of Virginia and Summer Islands," in *Purchas his Pilgrimes*, 19:218–67, quotations on 218.
100. Purchas actually provided numerous "legal" justifications for the Virginia project, including the law of nature and nations, as it relates both to states and individuals, that is,

cohabitation and commerce, war and conquest, but also "first discovery, first actual possession, prescription, gift, session, and livery of siesin, sale for price, and I mention not the natural inheritance of the English their naturally borne and the unnatural outcries of so many unnaturally murdered, of just vengeance of rooting out the authors and actors of so prodigious injustice." *Purchas his Pilgrimes*, 19:224–25.

101. Ibid., 19:259.

102. Ibid., 19:231.

103. Ibid., 19:238.

104. Also described as "sometime servant to the Prince Henry." See "King James to Dudley Carleton, November 11, 1617, and Sir Dudley Carleton to Secretary, February 4, 1618, *Calendar of State Papers Colonial*, 9:55. Carleton noted that Dale was fortunate in this matter "especially at this time of division and distraction, when they can agree in nothing but in being close handed." Ibid., 9:55–56. Dale left the service of the Dutch the very day they paid his past expenses, which enflamed opinion about Dale, as Dale left to do service in the East Indies. Ibid., 9:56.

105. *Purchas his Pilgrimes*, 19:102–3.

106. The two most important works about Warwick's activities overseas remain Newton, *Colonizing Activities*; and W. Frank Craven, "The Earl of Warwick, A Speculator in Piracy," *Hispanic American Historical Review* 10 (November 1930): 457–79. Other works build on these, including Kupperman, *Providence Island*; Robert Brenner, *Merchants and Revolution: Commercial Change, Political Conflict, and London's Overseas Traders, 1550–1653* (Princeton, NJ, 1993); and Andrews, *Colonial Period*. A definitive biography of Warwick remains to be written; the biographical sketch that follows is based largely on the aforementioned sources and the *Calendar of State Papers Colonial*, the *Oxford Dictionary of National Biography*, and *The Records of the Virginia Company*.

107. Virginia Court Session, May 31, 1620, *Records of the Virginia Company*, 1:367.

108. *Calendar of State Papers Colonial*, 9:51. Of this episode, Sir Thomas Edmondes reported rumors in Paris that Argall employed "greatest cruelty" against the Jesuits. Ibid. In *Purchas his Pilgrimes*, 19:101–2, Ralph Hamor describes a very different version of events. On the *Treasurer*, see *Records of the Virginia Company*, 1:323, 367, 3:219, 241–42, 418–23.

109. *Purchas his Pilgrimes*, 19:102.

110. Engel Sluiter, "New Light on the '20. and Odd Negroes' Arriving in Virginia, August 1619," *William and Mary Quarterly*, 3rd ser., 54 (April 1997): 395–98.

111. Michael Jarvis and Jeroen van Driel, "The Vingboons Chart of the James River, Virginia, circa 1617," *William and Mary Quarterly*, 3rd ser., 54 (April 1997): 392–94.

112. Warwick's later close colleague in the New England and Providence Island Company, Robert Greville, Lord Brooke, was a student at Leyden and supportive of John Robinson's ministry there. Brooke's adoptive father, the poet Sir Fulke Greville, was a companion of Raleigh and, as his gravestone proclaimed, was "friend to Sir Philip Sidney." Robert E. L. Strider II, *Robert Greville, Lord Brooke* (Cambridge, MA, 1958), 4. Fulke Greville ruminated about the impending end of time in Fulke Greville (Baron Brooke), *Poems and Dramas of Fulke Greville: First Lord Brooke*, ed. Geoffrey Bullough, 2 vols. (Oxford, 1945), 1:224–25.

113. This point has been debated widely, but see Nicholas Tyacke, *Anti-Calvinists: The Rise of English Arminianism, 1590–1640* (Oxford, 1987); Patrick Collinson, *The Religion of the Protestants: The Church in English Society, 1559–1625* (Oxford, 1982); Peter Lake, "Calvin-

ism and the English Church, 1570–1635," *Past and Present* 114 (1987): 32–76; Peter White, *Predestination, Policy and Polemic: Conflict and Consensus in the English Church from the Reformation to the Civil War* (Cambridge, 1992); White, "The Rise of Arminianism Reconsidered," *Past and Present* 101 (1983), 34–54; and White, "The Rise of Arminianism Reconsidered: A Rejoinder," *Past and Present* 115 (1987), 217–19.

114. Tyacke, *Anti-Calvinists*, 164–80.

115. Mary Frear Keeler, Maija Jansson Cole, and William B. Bidwell, eds. *Commons Debates, 1628*, 6 vols. (Rochester, NY, 1978), 4:321.

116. Andrews, *Colonial Period*, 1:430–61.

117. John White, *The Planters Plea; or, The grounds of plantations examined* (London, 1630), 16, 12, 14. For more extensive discussion of the mission of the New England settlements, see Perry Miller, *The New England Mind: The Seventeenth Century* (1939; reprint, Cambridge, MA, 1954); and Miller, *Errand into the Wilderness* (Cambridge, MA, 1956).

118. Alison Games could have gone much further in her suggestions about the pietistic nature of the British Atlantic in the 1630s and misses the continuity from the early missions. See Alison Games, *Migrations and the Origins of the English Atlantic* (Cambridge, MA, 1999), 132–62.

119. T. K. Rabb, *Merchant and Gentry Investment in the Expansion of England, 1575–1630* (Cambridge, MA, 1967), 88.

120. John Pym, *A Speech Delivered in Parliament, By a Worthy Member Thereof, And a Most Faithful Well-Wisher to the Church and Common-weale; concerning the Grievances of the Kingdom* (London, 1641), 38. George Calvert, Lord Baltimore's Maryland was the exception that proves the rule. Unable to work with the likes of Warwick (his distant cousin), Pembroke, Digges, Argall, and others, Baltimore gained his first sole proprietary patent—for a settlement of "Avalon" (Newfoundland)—in the spring of 1623 when James was eager for his Spanish Match and making numerous concessions to Catholic toleration in England. This was around the time when Calvert converted to Catholicism. Unable to make an effective settlement in the bitter cold of Newfoundland, Calvert (now Baltimore) set his hopes on a part of the Chesapeake basin and gained his charter for Maryland in 1632, the same moment that Laud was being raised to archbishop of Canterbury. The colony was immediately embroiled in religious conflict and ultimately religious war.

121. Edward Waterhouse, *Declaration of the State of the Colony and Affaires in Virginia* (London, 1622). Waterhouse was a Virginia colonist, giving one of the first published reports of the massacre and listing the dead. Briggs's tract is in ibid., 45–50.

122. Webster, *Instauration*.

123. Ibid., 42–43.

124. Hill, *Intellectual Origins*, 90–95.

125. Webster, *Instauration*, 370–81.

126. Benjamin Worsley, "Proffits humble presented to this Kingdome," in Webster, *Instauration*, 540–46.

127. Charles Webster, "Engineering for Universal Reform from the Invisible College to the Navigation Act," in Mark Greenglass, Michael Leslie, and Timothy Raylor, eds., *Samuel Hartlib and Universal Reformation: Studies in Intellectual Communication* (Cambridge 1994), 213–35.

128. Benjamin Worsley, *The Advocate* (London, 1652), 1, B.

129. Steven C. A. Pincus, *Protestantism and Patriotism: Ideologies and the Making of En-*

glish Foreign Policy, 1650–1668 (Cambridge, 1996), 40–79, quotes on 40; *Weekly Intelligencer* quoted at 76.

130. Karen Ordahl Kupperman, "Errand to the Indies: Puritan Colonization from Providence Island through the Western Design," *William and Mary Quarterly*, 3rd ser., 45 (January 1988): 70–99.

131. Pincus, *Protestantism and Patriotism*, 149–98.

132. Excellent on the problems of the war in Virginia is Bond, *Damned Souls*, 145–75. For the rest, see Carla Pestana, *The English Atlantic in an Age of Revolution, 1641–1660* (Cambridge, MA, 2004).

133. See, for instance, Roger Heaman, *An Additional Brief Narrative of a late Bloody Design against the Protestants of Ann Arundel County in Maryland in the Country of Virginia* (London, 1655).

134. It took the New Englanders a little longer to realize this fact. See Pincus, "From Holy Cause to Economic Interest," 272–90.

135. *Purchas his Pilgrimes*, 19:230.

136. William Alexander, "Doomsday," in Brown, *Genesis of the United States*, 2:758. Alexander was granted a patent for "New Scotland," or Nova Scotia, comprising much of British Canada.

Mutual Appraisals

The Shifting Paradigms of the English, Spanish, and Powhatans in Tsenacomoco, 1560–1622

CAMILLA TOWNSEND

In the early years of the Virginia colony, as the settlement teetered on the edge of extinction, two sets of people watched every move the English made and drew their own conclusions. Messengers flew back and forth to Powhatan, paramount chief of the tribes of Tsenacomoco, reporting every detail. Across the sea in Madrid, Philip III received a deluge of reports from his ambassador in England, who had found that sailors returning from Jamestown could often be induced to speak for a fair price. Some who had Powhatan's ear urged him to step up the attacks against the strangers; the Spanish ambassador in London urged his king to annihilate the struggling colony while it was still young. The two monarchs, however, remained relatively unperturbed and thought it best to let things go on as they were. The Spaniard knew too much and the Indian too little to be able to see the long term clearly. They would each learn their error in the next fifteen years, but by then it would be too late. In the interstices of their shifting paradigms, Jamestown was forged.[1]

Paquiquineo Travels the World

A long history of relevant events, known to both the Spanish and the Indians but not the English, affected the thinking of several key players.[2] In 1563, more than forty years before the founding of Jamestown, a kinsman of Powhatan's named Paquiquineo had stood in a stone chamber in the Dominican convent in Mexico City and desperately tried to outmaneuver the provincial head of the order, attempting to negotiate a return to his homeland, whence he had been taken against his will. It was a long story, without a clear beginning or, as far as Paquiquineo could see, a clear end.

From the time of their taking of the Caribbean, the Spanish had used the islands as a base to send out exploratory expeditions in all viable directions. Even after some had made their way toward the mainland that would soon be called "Mexico" and discovered the rich Aztec kingdom, others had continued to investigate different regions, including the coast of Florida and points north, hoping against hope that they would be equally lucky. It soon became clear, however, that Mexico was the destination of choice. There, people who had relied on farming for many centuries lived in settled villages and were accustomed to paying tribute to conquering overlords. When the militarily powerful Spanish told the indigenous that henceforth they were to labor part of each year on their conquerors' behalf, most of them chose to comply rather than protest. Individual ethnic states—or parts thereof—were given out in *encomienda*. A Spaniard received the right to demand labor and tribute and, in exchange, accepted responsibility for the people's spiritual well-being. When the Spanish discovered silver mines in Mexico in addition to the valuable Indians, they felt that their good fortune was complete.

Still, early hopes that the lands to the north might prove a "New Andalusia"—a country as lovely and productive as southern Spain—died hard among some individuals, especially those who stood no chance of receiving an encomienda in Mexico or in the more recently discovered Inca territories. In the 1550s, after the French began to exhibit designs on the region, there was another burst of interest on the part of the Spanish. Philip II soon became convinced that efforts to colonize the region were a costly waste of time.[3] The seminomadic Indians seemed absolutely unwilling to farm for the colonizers, pay them tribute, or even permanently respect their authority. They would simply melt away into the woods, reappearing later at inopportune moments. Philip did not, however, learn the lesson quickly enough to save Paquiquineo and his companion from years of agony.

In 1561, Antonio Velázquez was hired to transport supplies to a new settlement that Spanish authorities in Mexico were attempting to plant at Santa Elena (now South Carolina's Parris Island). A storm drove them further north than they had intended, and they made landfall in July in the Chesapeake Bay, which the Spanish called Bahía de Santa María. Two Indians who had apparently had contact with other passing Europeans—or knew others who had—demonstrated through signs that they were willing to come aboard Velázquez's vessel to trade. The natives were young men, just the right age to be taken away and trained as translators. Some Spaniards claimed that the two had volunteered to go, but the usual modus operandi in such cases was not to ask permission. Nor does it seem possible that without any common language the Indians could have given their consent to such a scheme; moreover, another Spaniard gave the game away, indicating that the young men had said their families would have no way of knowing what had happened to them.[4]

Paquiquineo was from a noble family based in the peninsula between the rivers now known as the James and the York. He was probably Chiskiak, but could also have been Paspahegh or Kecoughtan. Like most noblemen, he had kin in more than one group.[5] He and his companion had undoubtedly been sent to establish relations with the newcomers, who were known to carry valuable goods. Indeed, tribes to the south, who had regular contact with either the Spaniards or some of their Muskogean-speaking allies, were rapidly gaining the upper hand in long-distance trade relations.[6] Even when the ship set sail, Paquiquineo may have remained calm, knowing the local coast well and feeling certain that he would be able to make his way back. But then the ship turned its back to the coast and headed out to open sea. He would have had no reason to believe at that point that he would ever see his people again.

They docked in Portugal in August and then made their way to Seville to do the necessary paperwork. While Velázquez wrote his report and answered questions, he also requested money from the House of Trade to buy clothing for Paquiquineo so that he could be presented to the king in Madrid. Since he was a prince, the young Indian might well prove valuable. The request was approved. In all formal correspondence, Paquiquineo was simply referred to as the "princely person" brought over by Velázquez, but the accountant doling out the money laboriously spelled out his name: the word was strange to him and he wanted to be sure to get it right.[7]

Paquiquineo must have been a quick study. By the time he was presented to the king, he had learned enough Spanish to convey to the monarch that he wanted to go home. Clearly, efforts would have been made to convert him to Christianity, but up till then, he remained an unrepentant pagan. Still, the king prided himself on his sympathy for the Indians and saw a promising opportunity to make an ally of an indigenous prince from a previously hostile land. He gave orders that Paquiquineo and his companion were to be sent out in the next convoy to New Spain, captained by Pedro

Menéndez de Avilés. The ships would go first to New Spain and then on their return trip drop the two off at their homeland, along with certain Dominican friars who hoped to do some good on those wild shores.[8]

They arrived in Mexico in August 1562 at San Juan de Ulúa, near Veracruz. Paquiquineo learned that he would have to travel up into the heart of this country, to Mexico City, to meet with members of the Dominican order and plan the small mission that was to accompany him home. After a long trek up into the pine forests, they crossed the ring of mountains that surrounded a great central valley. Everywhere this world teemed with people who looked like him but who toiled in the fields like the peasants in Spain. The travelers walked along hard-packed dirt roads that had been made long ago by Indians who owed at least nominal allegiance to Moctezuma, now dead for forty years. The old people remembered the days of their youth, before the Spanish came. They still spoke of it among themselves.[9] Paquiquineo could not have learned much Nahuatl, but he could communicate in Spanish with the Indians who surrounded him.

Mexico City was an extraordinary metropolis. In 1519, before the arrival of Hernando Cortés, its population, at about a quarter of a million, had been larger than that of any city in Spain. In the forty years that followed, it had known devastation and drastic reorganization, but its teeming markets and busy byways had endured. The first Dominicans had arrived in 1526 and had built their massive convent on the foundations of a demolished temple of the old order. Thither went Paquiquineo.

In the close quarters of the city, among people who had no acquired immunities, disease had run rampant since the first outbreak of smallpox in 1520. The sickness still attacked newcomers with frightening rapidity. Almost immediately, Paquiquineo and his compatriot succumbed. "They got so ill," wrote the provincial of the order, "and arrived at such a point, that it was not thought that they would escape." The friars in their long robes approached Paquiquineo in his fevered state to ask yet again if he would like to be baptized and save himself. Now he said yes. When nothing seemed to be happening, he asked again, with urgency, for salvation. The friars decided he had demonstrated his will sufficiently; a priest baptized him, giving him the Christian name of their viceroy, Don Luis de Velasco.[10]

The man now named Don Luis was young and strong; he and his companion were given good food and good care. They recovered. Even as they convalesced, the exuberant friars began to teach them their faith. Don Luis impressed them all. "He has a fine presence and mental capacity," wrote the provincial. Indeed, Fray Pedro de Feria had come to rest certain hopes for his order squarely on the young man's shoulders. It seemed to him that the illness had been ordained. "Our Lord has ordered all of this business... and chosen this Indian as a means to aid all that land [of the Chesapeake]." The Dominicans would organize a great mission, and Don Luis would be the intermediary who would make it work. The order could use such a success, for the Franciscans had arrived in Mexico first and had acquired far more power in this new land than the Dominicans. If the Dominicans could be the ones to tame the supposedly untamable wilderness of the North, their prestige would grow enormously. Don Luis encouraged the Provincial's enthusiasm and told him what he wished to hear: that his people were peace loving and would welcome the friars to their land. The sooner they were off, the better.

Paquiquineo's strategy, however, proved disastrous, in that it worked too well. Feria approached Captain Menéndez about sending out some Dominican volunteers, extensive supplies, and maybe forty or fifty soldiers, and Menéndez flatly refused. He could not devote so much space to their needs without having received orders to do so from Spain. He could still, of course, take the Indians and one or two Dominican volunteers as originally planned. Feria thought quickly. He was entirely unwilling to let Paquiquineo leave them and see his order lose such an opportunity. However, he could hardly keep the two Indian guests prisoner against their will. A solution offered itself. As he wrote to the king, "Seeing that these [two] are now Christians and members of the faith, and that if they were returned to their lands alone and without ministers to keep them in the faith, ... and were to go back to their rites and idolatries and thus be lost [to perdition], *their baptism would have caused them a greater condemnation.* Permitting it seems a great inhumanity." He continued boldly that it would be "an offense to Our Lord and even to Your Majesty to return them to their lands. It is believed that it was so ordered only supposing them to be infidels, as they were when they left your kingdom."

Feria spoke to Don Luis and his companion about the situation. Don Luis wanted to go, and the convoy had orders to take him; if they did not let him go, he said, he could appeal to the king, who had commanded that he be taken home. But Feria explained that he had spoken to the archbishop—a Dominican to whom he was closely connected and who was one of the ultimate powers in the land, along with the viceroy—and the archbishop had interceded with Menéndez and informed him that they could not take the men north because of the danger to their souls.[11] Of course they were at full liberty to leave the convent if they chose or even to return with Menéndez to Spain and seek another audience with the king. Paquiquineo may have thought about renouncing his newfound faith—he may even have brought it up—but he would quickly have come to see that now that he was a Christian, he was subject to the Inquisition, and apostasy was a sin punishable by death. "They said," wrote Feria with quiet pleasure, "that if they were not going to their own land, they preferred to stay here than to go to Spain."[12]

Paquiquineo, however, was far from giving up. He probably spoke directly to Menéndez, who would later remember his eagerness. He definitely cultivated his connection to his patron, the viceroy for whom he was named, Don Luis de Velasco. The viceroy knew the value of a good Indian intermediary. The Spanish had long depended on them. His own younger brother was married to a woman whose stepdaughter was a child born to Doña Marina, who had proved invaluable at the time of the conquest of Moctezuma. Don Luis actually offered to pay out of his own pocket some of the expenses to be incurred by the Dominicans once the king gave his permission.[13]

Three years would go by before anything happened. At first the Dominicans undoubtedly continued to dream of future glories and wait for authorization. But the next year, in 1564, the viceroy died suddenly. Indians lined the streets to watch the great funeral procession. For the next few years, in the ensuing power vacuum, chaos reigned; there would have been little reason to believe that a major Dominican undertaking could be expected to launch itself, especially without its primary financial backer. While Don Luis lived out his days in Mexico City, he would have been witness to a great crisis among the indigenous nobility who worked as scribes and artisans for the Dominicans and other religious. They were suddenly told that they, too, would for the first time have to pay tribute to the Spanish government, which in this time of trouble needed more funds. Those who protested were carted ignominiously off to prison in irons. "We are a conquered people," wailed the sons of men who had once ruled the Aztec empire.[14]

Then suddenly in early 1566, the governing council of Mexico City received a direct order from the king to send Don Luis and a few Dominican friars to Menéndez de Avilés, who awaited them in Havana.[15] The year before, Menéndez had been named *adelantado* of Florida and the regions to the north—which the king still had not quite given up on—and Menéndez needed Don Luis. He had used his influence to have the young man removed from the custody of the zealous Dominicans.

By August Paquiquineo was on a ship leaving the port at Havana with thirty-seven soldiers and two Dominican friars who had come from Mexico with him. The rest of the story is well known to scholars of early Virginia. The briefest of summaries will suffice. Don Luis—living cheek-by-jowl aboard ship with thirty-seven armed Spanish men who had only hostile things to say about the Indians of his homeland—did not recognize (or claimed not to recognize) any familiar landmarks. A storm blew them off course, and because of the direction of the winds, the captain decided to make for Spain, where Don Luis stayed for several long years. He lived with the Jesuits in Seville, whom Menéndez had begun to court in the hope that they might join him in taming the coast of North America. Don Luis promised that if they went he would serve them as Timothy had served the apostle Paul. Finally, in 1570, he sailed from Spain with a delegation of Jesuit volunteers. They landed in Havana, made final preparations, and set off northward. No soldiers could be spared to accompany them, but Don Luis assured them that it would not matter. Within weeks, they landed in Tsenacomoco, and Paquiquineo was greeted joyfully by his kin, just as he had promised he would be. He did his best to make the friars comfortable while they wrote their last letters home and sent the missives off on the returning ship. Then, after ten years, Don Luis went home to his village.[16]

When a Spanish supply ship returned the next year and found no one to greet them, they kidnapped an Indian and learned from him that the Jesuits were dead. Only one young boy was left alive. It was that boy who would later tell the Spanish that Don Luis himself had led the war party that came to kill the foreigners. The next year, Menéndez himself, whose rage knew no bounds in this case, led the expedition that came to seek revenge. They seized hostages in order to secure the return of the young boy they had learned was still alive, and once they had him in their custody, they demanded the return of Don Luis as well. Unbeknownst to them, however, their hostages were not from Don Luis's tribe, and thus the Spanish stood no chance of having him turned over to them. After a few days, they killed most of their prisoners and sailed away, determined never to return.

The Spanish had had enough. Mexico and Peru sent silver every year. The farmlands in those countries spread mile after mile, willing Indian hands working in the fields. Recently, French settlements along the Florida coast that had seemed threatening had been found and destroyed. That the wild lands might be hiding a northwest passage to the Pacific seemed less and less likely with each passing decade, and in any case, it no longer mattered much to the Spanish: in 1565, one of their galleons had found the winds that made it possible to sail from Manila to Acapulco. The connection to Asia was secure.

In addition, it seemed the conquest of the north country, besides being of relatively little value, was virtually impossible. In the past, the most effective conquests had always been made with the help of intermediaries, and there could have been no more promising figure than Don Luis—young, keenly intelligent, and royal. If Spanish efforts with him had been in vain—he who had been the cultivated pet of a king and viceroy—there seemed no reason to believe they would succeed with others of his land. Without any useful Indians, conquest was not worth attempting.

The Spanish Appraise Jamestown

For the next thirty years, from the point of view of the Spanish, there were no major developments in the region of the Chesapeake. They kept a watchful eye on the English attempts to settle at Roanoke, as rumors circulated that valuable mines had been found there, but their political focus was closer to home.[17] In 1585 the Anglo-Spanish War began, leading to the sending of the Armada to invade England, which ended in humiliating defeat and debt. After the old king died in 1598, his son, Philip III, faced extraordinary pressure to forge a reign of peace. In 1604, the Treaty of London brought an end to hostilities with England, and by 1606, the Spanish were busily engaged in attempting to negotiate a truce with the rebels in the Netherlands. Many hoped that the Spanish and English royal lines would someday even be united by marriage.[18] It was at that moment, in March of 1606, that the Spanish ambassador in London sent a hasty message that the English were planning yet another attempt to colonize areas to the north, despite earlier failed efforts not only at Roanoke but also in Canada.[19]

The ambassador, Don Pedro de Zúñiga, did not report any more developments for over a year, and when more news was forthcoming, it was not of an alarming nature. In January 1607, he mentioned a plan to send two vessels per month from London and two from Plymouth till they had succeeded in transporting upward of two thousand men to the new settlement, but then he added that investment capital was in short supply. The king answered briefly that he wanted regular reports on Virginia, as "its contiguity increases the vigilance which it is necessary to bestow upon all the Indies and their commerce." The most important issue was, of course, not what plans the English made for Jamestown, but "whether they make any progress there." He knew how easy it was to make plans for the region; carrying them out was another matter. In August the ambassador reported that Captain Christopher Newport had come back from Jamestown disappointed. The country, as the Spanish well knew, was not populous. As the ambassador wrote, "They fell in with a King who had in all 150 men."[20]

In September, Don Pedro fell ill, and as he lay in his sickbed, the news he received from his spies seemed more dismal to him than it had before. The English, he decided, were not responding to reports of the inhospitable land as he had thought they would. They must, he surmised, simply be determined to create for themselves a secure base for their piratical activities. As he concluded, "There have combined merchants and other persons who desire to establish themselves there; because it appears to them the most suitable place that they have discovered for privateering and making attacks upon the merchant fleets of Your Majesty." Two weeks later he added, "It appears clearly to me now that it is not their intention to plant colonies, but to send out pirates from there, since they do not take women, but only men."[21]

A few days later, the agitated ambassador received an audience with King James. The monarch's two-year-old daughter had died only days before, but he did his best. James first tried to make the case that he had not thought land so far north really belonged to Spain, but meeting only with steely rage, he retreated to the position that his subjects were not going to Virginia with his blessing. If Spain really controlled the area well enough to find and attack the settlement and punish the people there, he certainly would have no reason to complain or (implicitly) to declare war. He wondered why his people persisted in going to so "sterile" a place with no "great riches"—thereby reminding the ambassador that it probably was not worth fighting about—and feigned surprise at the idea that his own people might be planning to create a pirates' cove. He would speak to them, but could not possibly order them to return. To do that would be to acquiesce to the idea that all of America belonged to Spain, even beyond the territory that Spain actually controlled.[22]

The ambassador's report infuriated certain men in the court of Philip III. His council concluded that the settlement should be attacked immediately while it was still small and would be easy to uproot. They suggested that the small Windward Fleet stationed in the Indies be deployed. The king responded vaguely, "Let such measures be taken in this business as may now and hereafter appear proper." He then arranged to have military authorities turn the proposal down, noting that "The driving out of the English from Virginia by the Fleet stationed to the windward will be postponed for a long time."[23]

The Spanish king has sometimes been accused of being a fool in this matter, but such an interpretation is far from the truth. To begin with, the Iberians did not yet know exactly where Jamestown Island was. Philip was being asked to deplete his treasury by sending an entire fleet out looking for a needle in a haystack. If they ever found the settlement and attacked it, they risked reopening hostilities with England, the last thing that he—or indeed, even the most belligerent councilors—really wanted. They would do all this in order to destroy a colony that had almost no chance of flourishing and certainly would never make anyone rich. True, English privateering vessels might use it as a safe harbor, but it was naïve to think that if the English lost Jamestown, they would lose their inclination toward piracy.

Don Pedro de Zúñiga, surrounded by constant talk of Jamestown at the British court, and less well informed of the general situation in the northern territories of the Indies than was his king, saw the situation differently. He continued to send dire warnings, for which the monarch thanked him in a rather breezy tone before moving on to more pressing business, such as the situation in the Netherlands. In June of 1608 Zúñiga managed to buy a colonist's letter from a sailor (who had been engaged to deliver it to someone else), and over the summer obtained a copy of an actual map of the colony. It included the names of over sixty Indian villages—and Indian villages, all Spaniards knew, were the centerpiece of potential wealth. Both items were forwarded to the king.[24]

The ambassador's concerns proved somewhat contagious. In Madrid, another group, the Council for War in the Indies (one of whose members served on the well-informed king's council) now joined Zúñiga in advising an attack against the fledgling colony. The war council suggested that ten galleons under construction at Dunkirk—which had been intended for use in the Netherlands, but which probably would not be needed there, since peace seemed imminent—should immediately be sent to do the job. In this period, the king had the majority of his council persuaded that they should remain perfectly calm. The members of the king's council were nothing if not diplomatic, however. They wrote back that the council for war made a good point and that the ships should be brought to Spain while they considered what was best to be done. Meanwhile, they requested that the council of war communicate with the governor of Florida and order him to organize a small reconnaissance mission.[25]

In the spring of 1609, as Jamestown was being reorganized under a second and potentially more effective charter, Zúñiga's tone became increasingly strident. The Baron of Arundel, who had been passed over as a leader in favor of Lord De La Warr, had come to report to him all that he knew of the venture. He said that the English were growing increasingly bold, since Philip III had not yet taken steps to wipe out the colony, and he pointed out that several of the colony's new leaders came straight from fighting in the Netherlands. They even planned to offer a general pardon to all pirates who would take refuge there. "The thing is so perfect," Zúñiga wrote, "for making use of these pirates, that Your Majesty will not be able to get the silver from the Indies, unless a very large force should be kept there." One of his sources had promised him further important news. "All he can say," the ambassador reported, "is that there has been found a moderate mine of silver and that the best part of England cannot be compared with that country." Such a statement would certainly have made Philip suspicious, as he thought he knew it to be false. "I understand," continued Zúñiga, "that as soon as they are well fortified they will kill that King and the savages, so as to obtain possession of everything."[26] Reading those words, Philip may well have been tempted to stop reading. The idea of killing all the indigenous inhabitants was truly ludicrous. It was from Indians that early colonists obtained food, and once a region was pacified, it was Indians who formed the backbone of the labor force. If there really was a silver mine, for example, who would work it if the Indians were dead?[27] Having failed to comment on the Jamestown situation for months, the king now wrote to the ambassador thanking him for keeping him informed but suggesting that he not put too much stock in whatever the embittered Baron of Arundel might say.[28]

As further proof of the seriousness of the situation, Zúñiga had enclosed with one of his letters a promotional pamphlet distributed by the Virginia Company. The king was given a translation into Spanish; however, the text would only have deepened his conviction that there was nothing in Virginia worth fighting for. In trying to prove that the Indians would be no threat and did not deserve what they had, the author of the pamphlet wrote, "The natives are savages who live in troops like cattle—some dressed in furs and others naked—without any discipline or law of life than the law of Nature."

The situation, then, was just as well-informed Spaniards had thought: the Indians in that region were nomads, or at least partly nomadic, and could never be distributed in encomiendas. They were without value. The propagandist continued, "They are well-disposed and eager to learn a better mode of life." But those Spaniards who knew the shocking story of Don Luis knew differently. Those Indians would never be persuaded to give up their wild ways and embrace a Christian life.[29]

In 1610, after issuing several more warnings, Zúñiga was replaced by another ambassador, Don Alonso de Velasco, who was decidedly less excitable. He recognized immediately how very dire the situation in Jamestown really was, beginning his first letter to Spain as follows:

> Sire: From Virginia there has come ... a ship of those that remained there lately, and those who arrived in it, report that the Indians hold the English surrounded in the strong place which they had erected there, having killed the larger part of them, and the others left so entirely without provisions that they thought it impossible to escape, because the survivors eat the dead.... The swine which they carried there ... the Indians killed, and almost all who came in this vessel died from having eaten dogs, cat skins and other vile stuff.[30]

Particularly because the colony was so weak, Velasco recommended sending a force to finish it off—as Zúñiga in his parting words of advice had undoubtedly urged him to say—but perusing his letter, most readers could not help but conclude that such a step would be entirely unnecessary, in that the colony was dying on its own.

That same summer of 1610, Philip III and his advisers received an opposing sworn statement about Jamestown given by an Irish sailor who had been encouraged by the Church to give testimony. "Francis Maguel" claimed he had been in Jamestown for eight months. For reasons of his own—perhaps to please a priest, or earn some extra cash—he chose to spin a magnificent yarn. He said the settlers had found a mine that yielded gold, silver, and copper. Amid the ducks and pheasants that filled the land, there were "an infinite supply of peacocks." The Indians, having been taught how evil the Spanish were, had agreed to come over to the English side, give up their gods, and become Christians. They knew of a water route to the western sea and had promised to show it to the colonists.[31] The king forwarded the statement to Velasco in London for comment. Velasco responded that it was not to be believed. He had made a friend of the merchant Sir William Monson, several of whose employees had gone to Jamestown as sailors hoping to discover a land of opportunity and had returned with horror in their faces.[32]

In the meantime, the governor of Florida had indeed sent out the requested exploratory expedition, and by early 1611, its report, was also in the hands of the king. Captain Francisco Fernández de Ecija was an experienced hand in the Indies. Reading his report side by side with the materials being produced by the Virginia Company is a disorienting experience for the modern reader. They seem at first to have been written in different centuries—as indeed they were, in effect. The Spanish were not the neophytes the English were but had decades of experience in the region by then.[33] Recognizing that the Indians were at the center of the drama, real people with complex languages, without whom nothing of significance could be learned, Ecija opened with a careful explanation of his party's translation capabilities. They were dependent on an indigenous woman named María de Miranda from Santa Elena, whom they had known for some time, as she was married to a Spaniard living in Saint Augustine. She spoke several Muskogean languages. At each point in his narrative, Ecija paused to explain how the translation chain in a particular spot worked, if in fact they were out of a region where María could find someone with whom she could communicate effectively. Ecija also brought with him one Juan de Santiago, a Spaniard who had sailed with the ships that traveled to Don Luis's land in 1570, 1571, and 1572.[34]

After questioning Indians up and down the coast about the English—what they knew about them and what their own relations with the Anglos were—they at length sailed into the Chesapeake Bay. There they met with an English ship larger than their own (it was Samuel Argall's ship, destined at a later day to kidnap Pocahontas) and decided to retreat. They thus could not say with certainty where the actual settlement was.

This document was read by a number of parties in Spain, not just by the king and his closest advisers. Among them were people who had no more experience in the Americas than did the English and were rather vague about realities there: a single report was not enough to educate them. The ever-bellicose council for war in the Indies wrote a response to the document that beautifully illustrates the ways in which a text can be misread by those who choose to do so. These readers smoothed out the communication difficulties, saying only that the interpreter was "an Indian woman, a native of those provinces and having their language." A reference in the original document to the Indians' belief that the English had some women with them was radically transformed: "There were many women and children who went about through the fields and houses of the neighboring Indians." The presence of occasional ships at Jamestown indicated that "every day many [ships] came and went." They were sure the English were planning to travel overland "until they shall come to New Mexico, New Galicia, Vizcaya and [the mines of] Zacatecas." The enemy could then easily "fortify themselves in the ports of the [Pacific] sea and there make ships and overrun the whole coast of New Spain ... Peru and China." Last but not least, these readers asserted that Ecija's report indicated that "there are many Indians [in Virginia] very well provided with the fruits of the earth and other supplies." They themselves had no way of understanding how little the picture conveyed by Ecija resembled that conveyed by early observers of the sedentary Indians like the Aztecs elsewhere in the Americas. In the end, they recommended sending some four or five thousand men immediately. The council for war in the Indies would naturally be glad to take upon itself the task of organizing such a force.[35]

It is perhaps not surprising that the king—who had read Ecija's actual report, as well as hundreds of other communications from the colonies over the years—settled for sending out another exploratory mission with the goal of obtaining the exact location of Jamestown and getting a good view of it.[36] Thus it was that Don Diego Molina of the royal navy was sent from Spain to Havana with orders to travel along the North American coast pretending to be a civilian seeking a certain wrecked ship. He had with him as his pilot one Francis Lymbry, probably an Irishman, who was married to a Spanish woman and had served as a mercenary for the Spanish fighting the Barbary pirates. He spoke Castilian so well that he often passed for a native. He was not as clever as he thought, however: he did not realize that as a British subject and a noted navigator, he was under surveillance by English spies serving in Spain. His lack of awareness was to cost him dearly.[37]

Molina and his crew made for the Chesapeake Bay, and there, rather than running from the English they met, they hailed them and asked their help, offering the story of the wrecked ship and pretending to be lost. At first the English offered to bring them as guests to Jamestown, but soon became suspicious of their presence and decided to imprison the three men who had come to parlay with them—Don Diego Molina himself, the ensign Marcos Antonio Perez, and Francis Lymbry, or "Maestro Antonio."

An English navigator named John Clark had already been sent aboard the Spanish ship to guide it upriver; now he was taken prisoner by the infuriated Spanish and found himself sailing toward Cuba in shackles. Later he would win renown for himself as the mate of the *Mayflower*, but on that dismal evening in 1611, he probably believed his career was over.[38]

Clark was questioned in Havana and then later in Madrid. Both times he told the truth about Jamestown as he knew it. The truth, of course, was comforting to his interlocutors. He reported that there definitely was no gold or silver, only iron, pitch, and very good timber. He admitted that the Indians varied in their attitude and certainly could not be counted on as loyal servants. When asked what they wore, he said they clothed themselves in deerskins, thus confirming, in Spanish minds, the impression that these people were very different from the textile-producing farmers of the southern lands.[39] Even the cause-seeking council for war in the Indies was divided as to how to respond, and the king's council of state simply concluded that Clark's testimony proved the colony to be worthless.[40]

At about the same time, Velasco, the ambassador in London, still consulting with sailors who were intimates in the household of the merchant William Monson, sent the king a report that time would prove to be stunningly apt. He agreed that there were no precious metals, only iron, pitch, and timber. It was true that the land was as fertile as some people said, but that fact did the colonists little good. "The Indians are warlike and pursue them continually," Velasco reported, "so that they cannot come out into the country without great danger." Any notion of setting up a seigniorial society based on the distribution of encomiendas was out of the question: "It does not appear that they will be able to maintain themselves, unless they bring over so large a number of people that they can make themselves Lords of the Country, as the Indians now are."[41] For the colony to be a viable enterprise, in short, the English would literally have to replace the indigenous population with a settler population. To the Spanish, the notion would have seemed almost amusing.

The king and his council essentially lost all interest in Jamestown from that point on. Ironically, by early 1613, the English had become convinced that the Armada was on the verge of seeking to demolish the colony. It is not clear who circulated that rumor so industriously, though one can guess it may have been the council members themselves. There was absolutely no truth to it. In the spring of 1613, Philip wrote to Velasco about other matters. He thanked him for keeping him up to date about Jamestown, "although it is understood," he said, "that for the present the colonization and fortification of Virginia by the English cannot cause any apprehension."[42]

If the king worried about Virginia at all, it was only in that he feared the dreadful conditions there would kill poor Diego Molina, who had gone at his express bidding. The young ensign with him had in fact died, as they would later learn. The Spanish had been offering for two years to exchange John Clark for the beleaguered prisoners, but nothing had come of it. Toward the end of 1613, a letter from Molina was delivered to Velasco in London. An Italian sailor had agreed to hide it in the sole of his shoe and deliver it to the Spanish ambassador. The text of that letter is famous to historians of Jamestown for its description of the dismal state of affairs in the colony. Molina hoped that his asserting that the fortifications were so weak "that a kick could destroy them" would bring the Armada, looking for an easy victory, but his statement had the opposite effect. The letter only became more evidence that Jamestown could never amount to a threat. Though the Spanish government asked for him regularly, Molina languished for another three years, becoming increasingly penitent for his past sins and more and more convinced he would never see his children again. At length, in 1616, he and Lymbry were put aboard ship with Jamestown's acting governor, Sir Thomas Dale. Perhaps now the English finally felt safe in sending such a tale bearer home, for Pocahontas's peacemaking marriage to John Rolfe had strengthened the colony considerably. Officials in London were well aware of Lymbry's real identity and had informed Dale of it. They had probably given Dale his instructions: he hanged Lymbry at sea, thus eliminating the need for an ugly trial at home. Don Diego, though shaken, made it alive to London, and the exchange for John Clark was soon effected. The Spanish king rewarded Molina with a thousand ducats, and then, at his request, sent him to Mexico with a letter instructing the government to give him his back pay from the time he sailed in 1611 through to the present all in one lump sum. Molina apparently still felt that the Americas were a land of promise. It was only Virginia he hoped never to see again.[43]

Back in London, a new Spanish ambassador, a jocular man, dearly loved to tell the apocryphal story of two thieves who, when faced with hanging or being sent to Virginia, opted for hanging. He said that though the situation there was apparently somewhat better since peace had been made with the Indians, it still was not a land that others would want. Having no alternatives, however, it seemed to satisfy the English. "They preserve those places very carefully," he wrote. "I feel sure," he closed his letter, "that they will never give them up."[44] And Philip III was content that it should be so.

The English Adjust Their Sights

It is perhaps not surprising that the Spanish king needed some time to confirm to his satisfaction that the Indians in Virginia were seminomadic and absolutely "untamable," for the English themselves—from whom he was ultimately getting most of his information—did not understand the situation at first. Their leaders had read about Spanish experiences and at first had no way of understanding that much of what they had learned was irrelevant to them. Pietro Martire d'Anghiera's *De rebus oceanicis et orbe novo decades tres* had been translated into English by Richard Eden in 1555 as *The Decades of the New World,* and Francisco López de Gómara's Spanish narrative about Hernando Cortés's exploits in Mexico had appeared in 1578. Other accounts were in circulation as well, and many would later be included by Richard Hakluyt and Samuel Purchas in their noteworthy compendia.[45]

Information about Virginia itself, however, was hard to come by. After a stay at Roanoke, the scholar Thomas Hariot had published in 1590 his *Brief and True Report of the New Found Land of Virginia.* Now, of course, it is evident that he was describing a culture entirely dissimilar to that of the people of Mexico. His readers, however, did not recognize that. An Indian was an Indian, they assumed. Spanish experience showed that Indians could be taught to respect the authority of Christians. Hariot himself, in fact, though he probably would have acknowledged (if asked) that what he was observing did not resemble what was reported about Mexico, insisted that the Virginia natives were intelligent and desirous of being taught. The misapprehensions about what would be possible in this different context were undoubtedly exacerbated by the fact that the cultures of the Caribbean, featured in *The Decades,* were in fact very similar to those of the Virginia Tidewater. There, too, the indigenous farmed part of the year and hunted, fished, and gathered in other seasons. The only reason the Caribbean people had eventually been brought into tribute-paying submission was that they were trapped on islands and could not retreat into endless woods.[46] The English, however, thought they had a useful model. The instructions issued to the Virginia Company were that they should look for silver and gold mines as well as a passage to the South Sea. If these could not be found, they were directed to make a fortune through trade and by sending home goods worth cash—pitch, tar, dried fish, pearls, etc. They did not need to plant food, as the Indians would provide it in tribute payments.[47]

The extent to which the English had imbibed the notion that they would be able to make the Indians work for them is exemplified in the writings of

William Strachey, a highly rational man educated in the classical tradition and a careful observer by nature. He had visited Jamestown in 1609, when things can hardly be said to have been going well with the natives. Yet even he, writing in 1610, still assumed that the Indians of Virginia could be reduced to virtual serfdom. Reality had not been able to do away with his preconceived notions and expectations. He thought his perception that Powhatan had used force in constructing his chieftainship fit well with what he had learned of Mexico and Peru, where enemies of the Aztecs and Incas had been particularly eager to aid the Spanish. He did not understand that the peoples in those places, both enemies and friends, were already sedentary, full-time agriculturalists who would no more think of running away to the woods than he would himself. He was sure of the Virginia Indians' goodwill, writing that "when they shall understand how the tribute which they shall pay unto his Majestie [King James] shal be far lesse then that which Powhatan exacteth from them, who robbes them as you have heard of all they have."[48] Powhatan's enemies, however, would not prove as useful to the English as the Tlaxcalans, for example, once were to Hernando Cortés.

The Indians themselves, Strachey believed, would soon learn the benefits of tilling the soil on behalf of English overlords:

> English Garrisons shall not only be provided of Corne, and their storehowses of marchandizes, but the Naturallas being thus constrained to paye duly this Their Tribute will Clense double as much grownd as they doe [now].... Although (peradventure) this may seeme a burthen at the first, until they have acquainted themselves with another kind of life, and perceive themselves indeed to become thereby more civill, as likewise to enjoy the rest of their owne more freely then under Powhatan, they will fynd themselves in far better estate, then now they are.

Strachey had given some thought as to how exactly the difficult transition might be made. Besides reading about Spanish experiences, Strachey had at his disposal the evidence given by a sea captain named Ellis who had spent some time in Peru. He said that the key to Spanish success apparently lay in favoring the chiefs, who were thereby motivated to press their people to accept the new arrangements: "The Cassiques or Comaunders of Indian Townes in Peru, whom the Virginians call Weroances, although they paie unto the king of Spayne great Tribute, yet because they make exchaunge with the Spaniards for what remaynes, they ... keepe great Hospitality and are rich in their furniture horses and Cattell." It was certainly worth making sure the chiefs were left well-off, for without them, the Spanish would apparently "not be able to make the Twent[i]eth part of the profit" that they currently did. This was because it was the chiefs who guaranteed that their people would work on behalf of the Spanish, paying tribute in time and goods:

> They furnish out of their severall Territoryes, not so few as 50,000 people to worke in the [silver] mines of Potosi, who after so many monethes travaile are returned into their Countryes, and 50,000 others by another Company of Cassiques provided to supplie them: in New Spain they doe the like, for the naturall people gather all the Schuchinella [Cochineal] which the Spaniards have and receave no more for a weekes labour then so much money as will buy them a pott of wyne to drinck drunck the Satterday night.

Strachey waxed on enthusiastically: "Surely all this being delivered in fitt termes, by some perfect Interpreter, and to men that are Capable ynough of understanding, yt may beget a faire concept in them, of us and our proceedings, and leave them well satisffyed."[49]

Strachey, despite all his reading—and his relatively accurate portrayal of the system then in place in Mexico and Peru—did not know the story of Paquiquineo. He was comfortably polishing his prose in England while other men learned how naïve English expectations had been. Many of them paid for the mistake with their lives. John Smith, on the front lines, rapidly learned to see the situation clearly. He grew tired of those critics back home who persisted in clinging to wrongheaded ideas and assuming that the colony's failures were the fault of the colonists. "To cleare us from the worlds blind ignorant censure, these few words may suffise to any reasonable understanding," he said. He explained: "It was the Spaniards good hap to happen in those parts, where were infinite numbers of people, whoe had manured the ground with that providence, that it afforded victual at all times: and time had brought them to that perfection, they had the use of gold and silver, and the most of such commoditie, as their countrie afforded, so that what the Spaniards got, was only the spoile and pillage of those countrie people, and not the labours of their owne hands."[50] Up to this point, Smith demonstrated his skills as a proto-ethnographer of sorts and confined himself to analytical language. Then, remembering his own frustrations, he suddenly fell into a fit of pique: "But had those fruitfull Countries, beene as Salvage, as barbarous, as ill peopled, as little planted, laboured and manured as Virginia, the [Spaniards'] proper labours (it is likely) would have produced as small profit as ours." The task of the English was large indeed:

> We chanced in a lande, even as God made it. Where we found only an idle, improvident, scattered people ... [w]hich ere we could bring to recompence our paines, defray our charges and satisfie our adventurers, we were to discover the country, subdue the people, bring them to be tractable, civil, and industrious, and teach them trades, that the fruits of their labours might make us recompence, or plant such colonies of our owne that must first make provision how to live of themselves ere they can bring to perfection the commodities of the country.[51]

At the time he wrote, in 1612, Smith by no means believed the thing was impossible. He hinted that the notion he had embedded in this paragraph—that the English must seek to replace the Indians themselves—was key. He himself was no longer in Virginia, but others must carry on, he asserted, now that they had found "the right course how to proceed." Most Englishmen were not yet ready to hear such words, but within a decade, they would be.

The Powhatans Shift Their Strategy

If the English had less experience and thus a more limited understanding of the region than did the Spanish, the Indians were at an even greater disadvantage. They were not, of course, confused about the realities of Tsenacomoco, but they were at first ill-equipped to read all the signals they were given by the Europeans. They had to learn what it was that the English expected of them before they could determine how best to attempt to save themselves from such a fate. It was a tall order.

Paquiquineo, like all noblemen from the land between the James and the York Rivers, was almost certainly in some way related to Powhatan; in later years the Chickahominy apparently envisioned him as Powhatan's elder kinsman.[52] Since he was a young man in 1561, he was clearly somewhat older than Powhatan, but he was not many years removed. It is highly likely that the two would have met after Paquiquineo's return in 1570. In the 1580s and 1590s, Powhatan's gradual transformation from a chief of six tribes to the high chief of at least twenty was in full swing, so he must have been of some stature even in the 1570s.

We can never know exactly how much the story of Paquiquineo's travels influenced Powhatan. It clearly would have done so to some degree, however, whether he got it firsthand from "Don Luis" himself or secondhand from others. At an absolute minimum, Powhatan's people learned two valuable lessons from those events: (1) though from a far-distant land, the strangers had ways of repeatedly finding exactly the same spot, even after the passage of many years; and (2) the strangers' bodies, covered in metal clothing, were relatively invulnerable, and their weapons highly dangerous. Most likely, Powhatan learned far more than this: he was probably told about the dense population of other parts of the world, the frightening extent of the Spanish empire and the efforts of the people called "English" to compete on the high seas. Specifics about the nature of European society would have been very difficult for one man to convey to a world of people who had no frame of reference whatsoever, though Paquiquineo may well have tried.[53]

Powhatan, of course, left us no diplomatic correspondence. We cannot eavesdrop on his conversations with his advisers as effectively as we can on Philip III's. However, the record of his actions and of the statements he made as written down by the English—especially the ever-astute John Smith—allows us to interpret at least some part of what he was thinking. In addition, we can cross-check Smith's assertions about Powhatan's policies by reading what the Spaniard Ecija claimed Powhatan's close neighbors understood about the situation as of mid-1609.

Interestingly, when Powhatan first learned in the spring of 1607 that the strangers were setting up camp within his dominions, he did what numerous other politically powerfully groups did at first contact as well: he organized a military strike, hoping to establish dominance, but he kept his own hands clean, in case it was not successful.[54] While about half the English were wandering up- and downriver looking for friendly natives and hoping to trade for food, all the tribes of the lower James (the Appomattock, the Weyanock, the Paspahegh, the Quioccohannock, and the Chiskiak) banded together and attacked the settlers encamped on Jamestown Island. With the element of surprise in their favor, no fortifications yet built, and half the English absent, the Indians might have been victorious. But they had yet to learn about shipboard guns. The English on board opened fire, spreading grapeshot among the camp's assailants, killing several instantaneously and leaving numerous others wounded. The warriors retreated.[55]

Powhatan sent representatives shortly thereafter to explain that certain tribes were implacably set against the strangers, but that he himself would attempt to work out the affair. His observers saw that the strangers were building a fort; as soon as it was finished, the captain of the lead ship turned about and went home, obviously carrying news of the settlement's location to the land across the sea. Powhatan certainly would have understood that this was not a good development. It is undoubtedly no accident that for the next several months nothing happened. The settlers sickened and died in extraordinary numbers, rendering them far more vulnerable than they had been before, but Powhatan made no move to destroy them. Rather, he seemed interested in tying them to him by succoring them, for numerous Indians brought food to trade. His previous knowledge of Europeans, combined with the more immediate data he had gathered from the failed military assault, taught him that there was not much he could do either to drive these people away permanently or to render them subservient in a definitive sense. But he could perhaps use strategy to make them into useful trading partners even as he gathered more information. It was important that he bind them to himself rather than risk allowing them to form some sort of alliance with one of his many enemies or perhaps even one of the tribes only recently conquered by him, a number of whom resented his dominance.[56]

In recent years, we have been so eager to restore Powhatan and his people their dignity that we have focused entirely on the settlers' early dependence on the Indians to obtain enough corn to live. Powhatan, however, knew that their inability to gather enough nourishment for themselves did not change certain facts. Europeans could come and go from his lands; he could not find theirs. They could bring over more men at any time even if he killed the ones who were here. And killing them would cause enormous loss of life. The victory would be so costly that he might never regain his current standing among his people; his paramountcy could disintegrate. The strangers could fire from their boats and retreat; he had no such horrendously destructive weapons. They wore metal helmets and breastplates; his own warriors had none.

Powhatan could not know why these bumbling strangers, who seemed unable to read the most obvious cues of nature, had such extraordinary accoutrements. He could not know that they were the cultural heirs of people who had been sedentary farmers for many thousands of years, while his own people had only begun to settle down for part of each year to plant corn, beans, and squash about three hundred years earlier. Far to the south, at the center of the long-distance trade network that touched his shores, the Mexicans who had developed corn had been farming longer, but even they were neophytes in comparison to Old World peoples. None of them had been dedicated to such a lifestyle long enough to move out of the stone age and into the iron age. The Europeans, however, had.[57] So it was that in 1607, Powhatan, despite his manifest intelligence, had a problem. And he knew it.

The best he could do would be to use strategy to try to retain the upper hand, to make the strangers into useful trading partners who provided him with metal goods that other Indians wanted. The danger, of course, was that rather than simply being useful to him, they might ultimately reduce him and his people to submission. Paquiquineo's story had certainly taught him that the latter was always a possibility. He seized what opportunities he could to improve his position. When John Smith traveled up the Chickahominy River and into Pamunkey territory, Powhatan's kinsman Opechancanough seized him, and Powhatan interrogated him. As Smith remembered the incident only a matter of weeks later, the question of the "cause of their coming" was the one that seemed to be of paramount importance to the chief. And several years later, when Smith copied out some sentences that he had taken down in his earliest efforts to learn the language, he found in his papers: "Casa cunnakack, peya quagh acquintin uttasantasough?" (In how many daies will there come hither any more English ships?)[58] For this issue, certainly, was the key. The hundreds of warriors under Powhatan's command could keep control of a few dozen hungry English men—despite their marvelous weaponry and metal clothing—if no more were coming. To the south, populous tribes had held the Spanish at bay for years, as only relatively few Europeans had chosen to come. If more came, however, it would be a different matter.

Powhatan's strategy involved more than seeking information. He tried to bind John Smith to him with some sort of promise of friendship or even fictive kinship; Smith's reporting of the incident is contradictory enough that we will never be certain of what happened. And the chief attempted to make a friend of the Englishmen's leader, Captain Newport, inviting him to visit as soon as soon as he returned from London. Of course he insisted that the visit be in his territory, where he was the stronger man and the English uncertain of the lay of the land. When Newport came, he turned over to his care a young boy named Namontack, who would live with the English and learn their ways, and he accepted into his own household an English boy named Thomas Savage. Perhaps most importantly, Powhatan arranged for his people to sell food to the colonists; the Indians would receive some metal goods in exchange.

We know that Powhatan was feeling somewhat uncertain of how best to proceed because in the spring of 1608, he changed his policy. Perhaps some of his advisers who advocated another course won the day after a series of discussions. English building activities indicated that the strangers had no intention of leaving but only of welcoming more of their number; in addition, the settlers began to perform military exercises outside the fort, a gesture that could only have appeared threatening. There may also have been incidents of abuse directed at the women, who were often the ones who visited the fort and sold the English food. Our English sources do not comment on the matter, but it is hardly a stretch of the imagination. For any or all of these reasons, Powhatan apparently decided that he was in danger of appearing weak, and he began to allow his people to harass the strangers when they were found alone or in small groups outside the fort. A frontal attack, he had decided, would never do, but he thought he could make his point another way.

The violence of the Englishmen's reprisal was certainly illuminating. They took several Indians hostage. When the Indians responded by taking two straggling colonists prisoner, the English donned their armor, boarded their small boat, and approached the nearby Paspahegh village. They shot fire bolts into several longhouses, thus setting them alight, and then sprayed shot into the Indian settlement. Fragments of lead flew everywhere, wounding many, possibly dozens. The Paspahegh immediately sued for peace and released their prisoners. The English released only one of theirs.

Understandably, Powhatan reverted to diplomacy and strategy. He had twice seen what the English could do if he engaged in warfare. It was enough; he wanted no more of it. He sent his daughter Pocahontas along with one of his advisers to negotiate for the other prisoners and then continued to allow her to visit the fort and learn some English. When Namontack returned from England with Newport in the fall, he clearly spent some time conversing with him.

What he learned from Namontack—or through Namontack, using him as a translator—may have been more decisive in his mind than we have previously realized, or perhaps the colonists' insatiable demands for food simply grew too unbearable. For whichever reason, within a matter of weeks, by the end of the year 1608, Powhatan made a major decision. He had clearly attained certainty in his mind as to what the settlers wanted: they desired his people to pay a regular tribute of corn. It was in fact to be tribute, not trade: the Indians were to receive only the most minimal recompense in metal goods. Furthermore, the English intended to use violence to obtain the tribute if it was not freely given. They already had done so in a number of villages. The Powhatans would, in effect, be a conquered people. He could not accept that, nor would his followers.

By Christmas, because the colonists were meeting with so much resistance in their efforts to gather corn from the Indians, they concluded that "it was Powhatans policy to starve us." In January they went upriver to his village to pressure him directly. He would not give them corn but would only sell it at a high price. Smith claimed the indigenous prince then made his current thinking clear by asking some pointed questions: "What will it availe you, to take that perforce, you may quietly have with love, or to destroy them that provide you food? What can you get by war, when we can hide our provision and flie to the woodes, whereby you must famish by wronging us your friends?" Over the next few days, the colonists tried to extract corn from neighboring territories. They were tense, as they could see the Indians were angry, and they thought they saw ambushes everywhere they went. The Indians delayed them in several places. It turned out to be a screen. By the time Smith and his men returned to the king's village, they found it entirely abandoned: the people had packed up their provisions and disappeared, just as Powhatan had threatened. Smith explained in frustration, "There was nothing now to be had." He had earlier warned his men, some of whom were inclined to shoot first and ask questions later, "If we should each kill our man and so proceede with al in this [king's] house, the rest will all fly, then we shall get no more."[59]

Back at Jamestown, the colonists were soon to learn that other chiefs agreed with Powhatan. If they paid tribute, there would be no end to it. They would become drones, and their own children would go half-hungry. Instead, they should offer the newcomers friendship, meaning voluntary trade, and threaten to remove themselves from the scene entirely if their offer were rejected. The Paspahegh sent a messenger, who warned: "You will have the worst by our absence, for we can plant anywhere, though with more labour, and we know you cannot live if you want our harvest, and that reliefe we bring you; if you promise us peace we will believe you; if you proceed in reveng, we will abandon the Countrie."[60]

Such speeches convinced Smith that the English had entirely misread the situation; they needed to take a different approach than had the Spaniards. We can believe that Smith recorded relatively accurate summaries of what the chiefs said, partly because events unfolded in keeping with just such an Indian policy, but also because what he claimed the Indians understood seems to have been known far and wide. Six months later, in the middle of 1609, the Spanish captain Ecija spoke to Indians who regularly traveled four days north to a village called "Daxe," whose people traded regularly with those of the James River. From them they had learned that "the English had them [the Indians] sow [corn], for they did not bother with sowing, but with fortifying." The said fort and the military capabilities of the English were daunting, despite their limited numbers, for "a ship came from England every year laden with supplies and munition."[61]

Indeed, it seems to have been generally understood along the coast that despite the attractive qualities of European hatchets and hoes, it was nevertheless dangerous to traffic with them. If Europeans developed a grudge against a certain tribe, it could spell disaster, and they understood perfectly well that the Spanish and English hated each other. An Indian who was known to have participated in trade with the English at first refused to discuss it with María, the Spaniards' interpreter, "for fear of both of them [the English and Spanish]." Later, some Indians actually got into a violent quarrel when one group learned that the other had already given away to the Spanish the fact that they traded with the English.[62]

In late 1609, Powhatan's new policy was tested. John Smith had sailed home, and the new president unwisely challenged the interdiction and took some men to find Powhatan's new settlement and demand corn. The Indians risked all and killed as many as they could, even though they knew the survivors, fleeing on their boat, would tell the tale and demand retribution. It did not matter: they would melt into the woods again before the colonists could return. They simply had to make their point clear—that the settlers must stay in Jamestown and not venture out making demands.

If nothing else had changed, the new indigenous policy would have been effective. But more English came. In May of 1610, the new governor, Lord De la Warr, arrived with his flotilla. Within three months, the increased English population, now well armed and well supplied, launched a violent campaign of a kind that they had not risked before. They began with the now infamous attack against the Paspahegh, in which dozens of warriors were run through with swords and the chief's children tossed into the water and shot while they still struggled. A veritable war ensued for several years.

The Indians fought in the only way they could: killing colonists whom they found alone or in small groups. In 1613, Powhatan's daughter was kidnapped; a year later, she was still in captivity, and he acceded to her proposition—brought to him by messengers—that she marry one of the colonists in order to effect a truce. Two years later, in 1616, he sent at least one high-level adviser with his daughter on a trip to England, where they assiduously gathered information.[63]

What Powhatan may not have known was that almost as soon as he realized his people faced the prospect of serfdom and began to strategize to save them from that fate, the English began to change their plans. For it was in this period that the English were hesitantly formulating the idea that they should simply eliminate the Indians and repopulate Virginia with settlers. The Spanish ambassador heard it from a returning sailor in 1611, and John Smith alluded to the notion in print in 1612. Military men with experience in Ireland were an influential voice in the colonial project: the possibility of killing the locals, perhaps always near the surface, was now being voiced. If Powhatan saw such devastation on the horizon, the new knowledge destroyed his few remaining years. Certainly those who lived to return from London had begun to understand what the future held. One of them, Uttamatomakin, agitated among his peers for several years. In March of 1622, as the pace of colonial encroachments on Indian land had only increased, Opechancanough, the new paramount chief, launched a major attack on the settlements along the James River, killing perhaps a quarter of the colonists.

But it was too late. The only permanent result of the affair was that the English openly concluded that the Indians would have to be removed. The colonists could not be stopped at this point. Early on, the Spanish might have attacked by sea, had their king known less; the Powhatans might have attacked unceasingly by land, had their king known more. Jamestown would not then have been the first successful English colony.

Even so, such a turn of events would only have delayed matters. The territory was never going to be worth a major war to the Spanish, and the Indians were never going to be able to close the gap that millennia of Old World agriculture had wrought. Philip III and Powhatan might have lived out their days in greater peace of mind, but they could not have spared their grandchildren in a permanent sense. We can derive no important lessons about contingency from this tale. What we *can* learn from paying close attention to the thought processes of the people involved is a greater respect for the mental leaps they had to make in a world that was in fact new to all of them.

Notes

1. This essay speaks of the decisions of the king of Spain and the paramount chief of the Powhatans as though each were an independent actor whose words and deeds came from him alone, but such usage is purely a writing convention. In fact, each monarch operated in conjunction with a council. It is even possible to imagine that the kings as individuals had little real control. Some have argued that the true power behind Philip III was the Duke of Lerma; others that Opechancanough, as military chief, dominated Powhatan. I believe the record indicates in both cases that the rulers were key players in their governing councils but certainly not the only players. Rather than mentioning the ruler "and his council" at every turn, however, I refer simply to "the king" or "the chief" *except* when differences of opinion among the advisers need to be spelled out.

2. There has been a great deal of recent interest in the indigenous figure once known only as "Don Luis de Velasco." In a recent landmark volume, no fewer than three essays treat the subject: Daniel K. Richter, "Tsenacommacah and the Atlantic World"; James Horn, "Imperfect Understandings: Rumor, Knowledge, and Uncertainty in Early Virginia"; and J. H. Elliott, "The Iberian Atlantic and Virginia," all in Peter C. Mancall, ed., *The Atlantic World and Virginia, 1550–1624* (Chapel Hill: University of North Carolina Press, 2007). All three offer paradigms within which we may understand the events that occurred. Here I attempt to offer a different perspective by bringing to bear new data found in the Archivo General de Indias in Seville and certain sixteenth-century indigenous annals from Mexico City.

3. Paul Hoffman has documented this period in great depth in *A New Andalucia and a Way to the Orient: The American Southeast during the Sixteenth Century* (Baton Rouge: Louisiana State University Press, 1990).

4. Archivo General de Indias (AGI), Contratación 5167, book 2, Cartas a Su Majestad, September 1561, ff. 110 and 112. For later contradictory statements about the young man's having come by choice, see Clifford M. Lewis and Albert J. Loomie, *The Spanish Jesuits Mission in Virginia, 1570–1572* (Chapel Hill: University of North Carolina Press, 1953). Some of the statements made much later claim that Don Luis was a middle-aged man at the time of his abduction, but those observers who were involved in the events all agree that he was very young.

5. All Spanish accounts agree that he was from a princely family, and events in the Chesapeake after his return do in fact indicate that he had social and political power in the area inhabited by the Paspahegh, Kecoughtan, and Chiskiak. On intermarriage among Powhatan nobility, see my *Pocahontas and the Powhatan Dilemma* (New York: Hill and Wang, 2004), 15–17.

6. On archaeological evidence of Powhatan trade ties to the Indians of the Carolinas, see E. Randolph Turner, "Native American Protohistoric Interactions in the Powhatan Core Area," in Helen Rountree, ed., *Powhatan Foreign Relations, 1500–1722* (Charlottesville: University Press of Virginia, 1993).

7. AGI, Contaduría 286, no. 1, Datas, September 1561, f. 171. The House of Trade also promised to pay the keep for Paquiquineo's companion and for two other Indians who had been brought from Mexico to try to learn the language of the Indians at Santa Elena, though in fact as events turned out they had never even gotten there.

8. The party stopped in Seville to make final arrangements. One of the Indians from

Mexico (see preceding note), who was called Alonso de Aguirre, had been working as a bearer in the port. After he learned of the projected route, he announced that he had become too attached to Paquiquineo to be separated from him and that he, too, wished to return to New Spain so that he might then travel on to his friend's homeland. He might be useful as an interpreter, after all, as in the meantime, he had learned some of the language, apparently from Paquiquineo's companion. The Spaniards were touched and agreed to let him renounce his work in the port and return to the New World. It did not seem to occur to them that he was simply seizing an excellent opportunity to return home to Mexico. They all sailed from Sanlúcar in the spring of 1562. AGI, Contratación 5185, book 1, Cartas escritas por el Tribunal de la Contratación a particulares, March 1562, f. 130.

9. There is a rich literature written by Nahuas in Nahuatl. Much of it was produced at the request of Spaniards, but the historic annals were intended for a Nahuatl-speaking audience. The best work on the subject to date is by Susan Schroeder on the indigenous historian Chimalpahin, who would have been a contemporary of Don Luis, though he had not yet come to Mexico City.

10. AGI, México 280, Fray Pedro de Feria a Su Majestad, February 13, 1563. This long letter provides a particularly rich source, as the following paragraphs will indicate. It was discovered by Hoffman but only briefly mentioned by him in *A New Andalucia*.

11. The letter only alludes to the *arzobispo*, but in that period, the position was filled by the Dominican fray Alonso de Montúfar. For more on the man and his strategies, see Lesley Byrd Simpson, *Many Mexicos* (1941; reprint, Berkeley: University of California Press, 1966). For the most recent work on the competition between the spiritual and temporal authorities in Mexico, see Alejandro Cañeque, *The King's Living Image: The Culture and Politics of Viceregal Power in Colonial Mexico* (New York: Routledge, 2004).

12. AGI, México 280, Fray Pedro de Feria a Su Majestad, February 13, 1563 (emphasis added).

13. The famous Doña Marina had a daughter by the conquistador Juan Jaramillo. After Marina's death, Jaramillo married a Spanish woman, Beatriz de Andrada, and they raised Marina's young daughter. After Jaramillo's death, Beatriz married Francisco de Velasco, the viceroy's younger brother. For more on Doña Marina and her daughter, see my *Malintzin's Choices: An Indian Woman in the Conquest of Mexico* (Albuquerque: University of New Mexico Press, 2006). It was Fray Pedro de Feria who mentioned (see n. 10) that the viceroy was willing to fund the venture.

14. For indigenous perceptions of the crisis, see Luis Reyes García, ed., *Como te confundes? Acaso no somos conquistados? Los anales de Juan Bautista* (Mexico City: Biblioteca Lorenzo Boturini, 2001), as well as other contemporary indigenous annals written in Nahuatl.

15. AGI, México 68, Audiecia a Su Majestad, March 28, 1566, ff. 225–26. For indigenous perceptions of the crisis in Spanish authority in 1566, see García, *Los anales de Juan Bautista*, as well as other contemporary indigenous annals.

16. See Townsend, *Pocahontas*, 7–10. The Jesuit documents and contextual materials are collected in Lewis and Loomie, *The Spanish Jesuit Mission*. Charlotte Gradie did additional research on the Jesuit element of the story. See her "Spanish Jesuits in Virginia: The Mission That Failed," *Virginia Magazine of History and Biography* 96 (1988): 131–56, and "The Powhatans in the Context of the Spanish Empire," in Rountree, *Powhatan Foreign Relations*. It was Gradie who first pointed out that Don Luis may not have wanted to

bring a boat bearing soldiers only to his native land. She also reminds us that the Jesuits were sharply divided over whether or not it was worth attempting to establish a mission in the wild north country.

17. On Spanish observations of events at Roanoke, see Horn, "Imperfect Understandings."

18. Some have argued that hopes for a "Spanish match" dictated diplomatic relations between the two countries in this period. It is true that the Prince of Wales proposed to Philip III's daughter in 1623, but no marriage came of it. I myself am of the school of thought that sees such political marriages as resulting from certain political and economic realities rather than creating them. I do not see any real evidence that such hopes affected either King James's ability to curb the popular enthusiasm for colonization or King Philip's analysis of how he should respond to English expeditions.

19. Don Pedro de Zúñiga to Philip III, March 16, 1606, in Alexander Brown, ed., *The Genesis of the United States: A Series of Historical Documents Now First Printed*, vol. 1 (Boston: Houghton, Mifflin, 1892), 45–46. Zúñiga's missives were sent in cipher, then unscrambled by employees at the king's court and written out in intelligible Spanish. In that form, they were collected by Brown from the Archivo de Simancas, the repository for the State Department. He had them translated by M. Schele De Vere of the University of Virginia. De Vere's translations have been criticized (notably by Philip Barbour), but spot-checking has convinced me that De Vere made only minor errors, usually concerning unfamiliar names and places. In general his work was excellent. Barbour's real quarrel with Brown, it seems to me, was that the latter attempted to use the correspondence to prove that the Spanish really did come close to annihilating Jamestown. Barbour, on the other hand, seemed to want to prove that no one in Spain ever had any interest in doing so. See his *Jamestown Voyages under the First Charter, 1606–1609* (Cambridge: Cambridge University Press, 1969). Neither man's view is accurate, in my opinion.

20. Zúñiga to Philip III, January 24, July 30, and August 22, 1607, and Juan de Ciriza a Andres de Pedrastra, May 7, 1607, in Brown, *Genesis of the United States*, 88, 100, 104, 110.

21. Zúñiga to Philip III, September 22 and October 5, 1607, in Brown, *Genesis of the United States*, 116, 118.

22. Zúñiga to Philip III, October 8, 1607, in Brown, *Genesis of the United States*, 120–22.

23. Report of the Spanish Council of State, November 10, 1607, in Brown, *Genesis of the United States*, 126–27.

24. Zúñiga to Philip III, March 28, June 16, September 10, 1608, in Brown, *Genesis of the United States*, 147–48, 172–73, 184–85.

25. Irene Wright, "Spanish Policy toward Virginia, 1606–1612," *American Historical Review* 25, no. 3 (1920): 450–51. Wright obtained all the documents she published from the AGI.

26. Zúñiga to Philip III, March 5, 1609, in Brown, *Genesis of the United States*, 243–47.

27. African slavery already flourished in certain regions of Spanish America, but at this point it was still very much conceived of as a supplementary labor source. The richest kingdoms in Mexico and Peru existed because of the sweat of the indigenous, as was common knowledge. Indeed, the Aztec and Inca empires were still nearly synonymous with the "wealth of the Indies" in the minds of the Spaniards. Trouble spots, in their experience, were those areas where the indigenous population was thin and "savage" and in need of replacement. To the Portuguese in Brazil, of course, the situation already looked

quite different: they had found only nomadic indigenous peoples, rather than the tribute-paying sedentary populations of Mexico and Peru, and thus had grown accustomed from very early on to the idea of bringing in an alternative labor supply. Their travels along the coast of Africa made the shift particularly easy for them to make.

28. Philip III to Zúñiga, May 14, 1609, in Brown, *Genesis of the United States*, 311.

29. The translation was presented to the king April 10, 1609, and is found in Brown, *Genesis of the United States*, 260–77.

30. Don Alonso de Velasco to Philip III, June 14, 1610, in Brown, *Genesis of the Unites States*, 392.

31. "Report to the Council of what Francisco Maguel, an Irishman, learned about the state of Virginia, during the eight months he was there," July 1, 1610, in Brown, *Genesis of the United States*, 393–99.

32. Velasco to Philip III, September 30, 1610, in Brown, *Genesis of the United States*, 418–19. Monson was later imprisoned in the Tower as a suspected traitor but was released.

33. See Hoffman, *A New Andalucia*; and Joseph Hall, "Between Old World and New: Oconee Valley Residents and the Spanish Southeast, 1540–1621," in Mancall, *Atlantic World and Virginia*.

34. AGI, Patronato 261, R.11, "Report of Francisco Fernández de Ecija, as recorded by Francisco de Salazar y Zúñiga," September 1609, printed in Barbour, *Jamestown Voyages*, 2:293–319.

35. Consulta of the Council for War in the Indies, March 5, 1611, printed in Wright, "Spanish Policy," 460–62.

36. On the king's response, see his comment in the margins, transcribed in Wright, "Spanish Policy," 460, as well as the response of the Council for War in the Indies, ibid., 453.

37. The Spanish plan is outlined in Duke of Lerma to Antonio de Arostegui, November 13, 1611, in Brown, *Genesis of the United States*, 509–10. On English knowledge of Lymbry's past, see Hugh Lee to Lord Salisbury, November 2, 1611, in Brown, *Genesis of the United States*, 509, copied from the English State Paper Office; and the testimony of John Clark in Wright, "Spanish Policy," 472.

38. Wright identified John Clark as the mate of the *Mayflower*. For a narrative of the exciting drama, see the testimony of the Spanish ship pilot, Havana, 1611, in Wright, "Spanish Policy," 472–73, and its interpretation by the Duke of Lerma, together with additional detail provided him by the Cuban governor Gaspar Ruiz de Pereda, in Brown, *Genesis of the United States*, 511–22.

39. Testimony of John Clark in Havana, July 1611, and in Madrid, February 1613, in Wright, "Spanish Policy," 467–79.

40. Wright, "Spanish Policy," 457–58.

41. Velasco to Philip III, March 22, 1611, in Brown, *Genesis of the United States*, 455–56.

42. Philip III to Velasco, May 23, 1613, in Brown, *Genesis of the United States*, 631–32. For a report of the gossip reaching England about the armada, see Velasco to Philip III, January 25, 1613, ibid., 602.

43. As soon as he heard of the capture of Molina, the king ordered the governor of Cuba to send John Clark to Seville at the first opportunity. AGI, Santo Domingo 869, L. 6, f. 135, January 17, 1612. Once he had the man in Spain, he sent frequent orders to Velasco in London to arrange for the exchange; those letters are printed in Brown, *Genesis*

of the United States, 603, 621, etc. After Molina eventually was returned to Spain, he agreed to his request that he return to Mexico. AGI, Indiferente 450, L. A5, f. 195, December 14, 1618. Molina's letters of 1613 and 1614 are printed in Brown, *Genesis of the United States,* 646–54, 743–45. That Molina's original letter did not have its intended effect is revealed in a letter home from the English ambassador in Madrid, Sir John Digby to James I, September 3, 1613, ibid., 657. On the fate of Francis Lymbry, see Townsend, *Pocahontas,* 135–36.

44. Don Diego Sarmiento de Acuña, Count of Gondomar, to Philip III, December 7, 1616. In that letter he told the story of the thieves, apparently forgetting that he had already told another version of it in a letter of October 17, 1614. Both in Brown, *Genesis of the United States,* 740, 900.

45. There was of course a strain within English literature on colonization that did not advocate imitation of the Spaniards but avoidance of their brutal tactics so as to retain the moral high ground and win the loyalty of the Indians. For classic commentary on this, see Edmund Morgan, *American Slavery, American Freedom: The Ordeal of Colonial Virginia* (New York: Norton, 1975); and more recently, John Hart, *Representing the New World: The English and French Uses of the Example of Spain* (New York: Palgrave, 2001). Both Morgan and Hart agree, however, that once on the ground, English colonists were eager to follow in Spanish footsteps and even consciously modeled themselves after them. For a recent detailed discussion of the ways in which readings of Spanish texts shaped English expectations in Virginia, see April Lee Hatfield, "Spanish Colonization Literature, Powhatan Geographies, and English Perceptions of Tsenacommacah/Virginia," *Journal of Southern History* 69, no. 2 (2003), 245–82. Hatfield is especially interested in the ways in which Spanish concepts of geography—which were themselves inherited from the indigenous—shaped English ideas of the space that constituted Virginia. Here I focus more on English absorption of notions concerning indigenous people as laborers.

46. Within a century, indigenous communities there had been eliminated. The genetic stock survived through intermarriages.

47. For specific discussion of the instructions provided to the colonists, see Townsend, *Pocahontas,* 39–40, 91–92.

48. William Strachey, *The History of Travell into Virginia Britania* (London: Hakluyt Society, 1953), 92. He repeated his point, saying, "After such tyme as they shall submit themselves to the kings Majestie and consent to paie him a Trybutte to be agreed upon, Powhatan shall lay no more his exactions upon them, but they shall freely enjoy all they can geather and have a peaceable and franck trade with the English." That Strachey was fully conscious of the influence Peter Martyr's work had on his own is made evident by his calling his sections "The First Book of the First Decade" and "The Second Book of the First Decade." That the English imagined they would create a seigniorial society, as had the Spanish, is demonstrated in numerous earlier texts. See, for example, Sir George Peckham, "A True Report of the Late Discoveries . . . by Sir Humphrey Gilbert" (1583), in Peter C. Mancall, ed., *Envisioning America: English Plans for the Colonization of North America, 1580–1640* (New York: Bedford Books, 1995).

49. Mancall, *Envisioning America,* 93–94.

50. John Smith et al., "The Proceedings of the English Colonie in Virginia," 1612, in Philip Barbour, *The Complete Works of Captain John Smith* (Chapel Hill: University of North Carolina Press, 1986), 1:257. This section is actually given as being authored by Richard Wiffin, William Phettiplace, and Anas Todkill; however, scholars concur that Smith's was the real guiding hand behind "The Proceedings."

51. Ibid., 1:258.

52. The Chickahominy said they hated the Spanish for having brought Powhatan's father—indicating any elder kinsman—to their shores. They lived adjacent to the Paspahegh, and the Spanish thought they were landing in the same spot as the first expedition had when they wreaked their vengeance on them. See Ralph Hamor, *A True Discourse of the Present State of Virginia* (1615; reprint, Richmond: Virginia State Library, 1957), 13.

53. Years ago, the scholarly world floated the notion that Don Luis may actually have been Powhatan's brother (or cousin) Opechancanough, who went on to lead a rebellion against the English in later years. The idea has had a certain appeal, probably because it leaves us with one pure renegade. But it cannot possibly be true. First, Opechancanough was almost certainly Pamunkey, and definitely from the upper James and York, not the lower; he could not have been Chiskiak, Paspahegh, or Kekoughtan, and Paquiquineo had to be one of those. Second, Opechancanough and Powhatan operated in tandem, the former as the chieftaincy's military head and the latter as its political head. If Powhatan had actually had at his side a man who had ten years' experience living among Europeans, he would have behaved differently from the beginning, having access to all the information he could need. Instead, events prove that Powhatan demonstrated a clear learning curve.

54. The conquest of Mexico is full of such stories. The Tlaxcalans, for example, blamed the Otomí who lived within their borders, and the Aztecs arranged to have Cortés's expedition attacked while it was still distant from the capital, Moctezuma later dissociating himself from the event.

55. The most detailed account of the earliest days of contact is a letter from George Percy. After the first few weeks, the most detailed account is John Smith's "True Relation," sent back to England in 1608. There were numerous letters sent home, however. Literally all surviving ones have been collected by Edward Wright Haile in *Jamestown Narratives: Eyewitness Accounts of the Virginia Colony, 1607–1617* (Champlain, VA: Roundhouse, 1998). I draw my sequence of events from all of them, being careful to accept them uncritically only where they agree. I would not trust, for example, any statement made only by Francis Maguel.

56. There have been a number of excellent studies of the nature of Powhatan's paramount chieftaincy and the political tensions that were part and parcel of its very formation. For the most recent contribution, see James Rice, "Escape from Tsenacommacah: Chesapeake Algonquians and the Powhatan Menace," in Mancall, *Atlantic World and Virginia*.

57. See Jared Diamond, *Guns, Germs, and Steel: The Fates of Human Societies* (New York: Norton, 1997). Diamond is a biologist, and his writings have been hotly debated by historians. Some of what he has to say is unhelpful, but there is no doubt in my mind that his presentation of recent scientific findings concerning the locations of ancient protein-rich plants will prove to be one of the greatest scholarly contributions of the twentieth century on the subject.

58. John Smith, "A Map of Virginia," (1612) in Barbour, *Complete Works of John Smith*, 1:137.

59. John Smith, "Proceedings," in Barbour, *Complete Works of John Smith*, 1:239, 247, 256.

60. Ibid., 1:261–62.

61. Report of Captain Ecija, in Barbour, *Jamestown Voyages*, 2:301, 312.

62. Ibid., 2:315, 318.

63. For more on all these topics, including my assertion that the Indians who went to London sought information, see Townsend, *Pocahontas*.

The Rise and Fall of the Virginia-Dutch Connection in the Seventeenth Century

VICTOR ENTHOVEN AND WIM KLOOSTER

In March 1651, Virginia governor William Berkeley denounced the 1650 Act of Navigation in the strongest possible language: "The Indians, god be blessed round about us are subdued; we can onely feare the Londoners, who would faine bring us to the same poverty, wherein the *Dutch* found and relieved us; would take away the liberty of our consciences and tongues, and our right of giving and selling our goods to whom we please."[1] As this observation reveals, Dutch maritime and commercial connections had been vital for the survival of the fledgling colony. The Dutch had "relieved" the Virginians in two ways. First, they supplied the planters and colonists with all kinds of necessities in order to survive in the New World. Archeological evidence substantiates the impact of Dutch commercial links on the material culture of the early Chesapeake.[2] Second, they had shipped the fruits of Virginia—tobacco, corn, and meat—to the Old World and had marketed these products. In 1653, the London-based merchant John Bland tried to convince the authorities in England, on "behalf of the inhabitants and planters in Virginia and Maryland," of the paramount importance of the Dutch trade network and the Holland tobacco market. As Bland wrote, "If the Hollanders must not trade to *Virginia* how shall the Planters dispose of their Tobacco? The English *will* not buy it, for what the Hollanders carried thence was a sort [of] Tobacco, not desired by any other people, nor used by us in *England* but merely transport for *Holland*."[3] The port cities of Middelburg in Zeeland and later Amsterdam in Holland, where Chesapeake tobacco was cut and mixed with Dutch-grown varieties, became the dominant continental markets for Virginia tobacco. Around 1700, Holland imported almost one-third of Virginia and Maryland tobacco: 8–9 million pounds out of a total of 30 million.[4] The importance of the Dutch for the international tobacco trade and manufacturing lasted well into the eighteenth century.[5]

We may wonder what "Dutch," "English," and "Virginian" meant in the seventeenth century. Were London-born merchants active in the Virginia trade who conducted their business from Amsterdam, for instance, Dutch or English? And were Dutch-speaking settlers in Virginia Dutch Virginians? An example may illustrate the prevalence of multiple identities and allegiances. In August 1651, the *Golden Lion*, master John Jasperson of Middelburg, set sail from Amsterdam bound for Virginia, carrying spirits, clothing, and shoes. Peter de Leeuw, Govert Lachard, and a few others, all dwelling in the Spanish Netherlands, owned the ship. Its arrival in the James River the following October coincided with the passage of England's Navigation Act, which led to the seizure of over one hundred Dutch ships by English privateers in a nine-month span.[6] The *Golden Lion* was among these vessels, seized by three English ships on February 7, 1652, shortly before Virginia was brought under obedience to the Commonwealth. Several Virginia planters, including Nicolas Smith, John Bishop, Samuel Hart, and Giles Webb, had already loaded their tobacco on board the *Golden Lion*, which was bound for London.[7] Was this a Dutch, English, or Virginia enterprise? It is likely that the ship originated from the Dutch Republic but was naturalized because of the rising tension between the Commonwealth and the States General, meaning that ships' papers were obtained in a neutral port, in this case one in the Spanish Netherlands. In this essay we will call a person or his trade "Dutch" when the center of gravity of the commercial venture was the Dutch Republic. For instance, James and Jacques Thierry, both coming from London but living in and trading from Amsterdam in the 1660s and the 1670s, will be classified as "Dutch."[8] Likewise, Virginians of Dutch descent and active in Virginia-Dutch commerce will also be referred to as "Dutch."

The emphasis of this essay is on the organization of the bilateral maritime and commercial connections between Virginia and the Dutch Republic in the seventeenth century. Contacts with the Dutch colony of New Netherland will be largely left out.[9] Over time the character of Dutch-Virginia commercial relations changed profoundly. Sometimes Dutch merchants are rather notable in the archives, but at other times they are more submerged in the sources. Russell Menard's observation that the rare appearance of

Dutch traders in Maryland and Virginia records of the 1660s is an indication of their absence from the trade is questionable. We argue, drawing on different Dutch archives, that his claim that the Dutch were forced out by war and legislation after the 1650s is untenable. While Dutch trade with Virginia certainly did change dramatically during the 1660s, direct commercial contact with the Netherlands started to erode only during the 1680s.[10]

The Dutch Tobacco Market

During the seventeenth century, the international tobacco trade in the Netherlands took place at Middelburg, Rotterdam, and Amsterdam, each of which dominated the import of Virginia leaf at one point or another. The processing of the leaves into consumable stimulants took place only in Amsterdam. Amsterdam relied on overseas producers for much of its food and raw material supplies, while its principal exports consisted of commercial and shipping services, colonial products, and manufactured goods with a high import content. It was in Amsterdam where the processing and manufacturing industries of sugar, textile, and tobacco were located. During the second half of the seventeenth century, Amsterdam tobacco spinners and cutters came to specialize in the mixing of imported English colonial tobacco with the much cheaper domestic leaves. In rolling or spinning, inferior grades of tobacco were used for the insides, while the better Virginia leaf was used as exterior "wrapper," and the product was sometimes sold as "Spanish" or real "Virginia."[11]

A close relation existed between tobacco manufacturing and trade. During the second half of the seventeenth century and the first quarter of the eighteenth, Amsterdam, by then the major staple market for tobacco, became Europe's leading market for Virginia and Maryland leaf. Apart from the Chesapeake, the Caribbean and the Dutch interior were the main production areas supplying the Amsterdam manufacturers.[12] But since Caribbean tobacco, like that from Spanish South America, was imported in rolls (thus already processed), it represented a different segment of the tobacco market than the imported Chesapeake leaf. Domestic tobacco cultivation was an innovation in Dutch agriculture. Initially cultivation was stimulated by Amsterdam merchants and manufacturers who saw domestic production as a source for the stockpiles they needed in order to influence the price of tobacco on the Amsterdam market. Others—such as the ruling urban upper class, wealthy citizens, and gentry involved in trade and commercial agriculture—pioneered tobacco growing around several small towns in the central and eastern parts of the Netherlands. Prominent farmers with some education and a commercial bent were quick to adopt tobacco as a crop, and small farmers followed their lead.[13]

Prelude

Early Virginians had close contacts with the Netherlands. Several of its early leaders were "excellent old soldiers" who had served with distinction in the Low Countries, "that university of warre."[14] In 1585, following the Habsburg capture of Antwerp in the war with the rebel Dutch, Queen Elizabeth I and the States General signed the Treaty of Nonsuch. This agreement stipulated that the English crown would help the Dutch war effort against Habsburg Spain with money and troops, in compensation for which the queen received as pawns the town of Flushing and the fortress of Rammekens, both in Zeeland, and the town of Brill in the province of Holland—the so-called cautionary towns.[15] For the next three decades a substantial English community lived in Flushing, where an English civil administration and sizable garrison had been installed, until the Dutch finally paid off their debts in 1616. From 1589 until the end, Robert Sidney (1563–1626) served as governor of Flushing.[16]

During the second decade of the seventeenth century, information about Virginia arrived in the Dutch Republic, especially by way of Zeeland. Contemporary maps show that the Dutch had detailed knowledge of the plantations along the James River and about the river's navigation. Two English residents in the Netherlands would play important roles in Virginia's formative period. Sir Thomas Gates and Sir Thomas Dale were "to establish a firm market there for the benefit and increase of trade," the English ambassador in The Hague related, something that presumably would be good for the Dutch as well as the English.[17] Gates (ca. 1559–1621) was a professional soldier who fought in the Dutch war in the service of the States General. In 1603 and 1607 he paid his respects to the English governor in Flushing, Robert Sidney, before becoming one of the incorporators in the second Virginia charter (1609) and a member of the Council for the Virginia Company.[18] Gates was also among the first petitioners to King James for a charter to colonize America. He was granted leave from Dutch service, along with three other noblemen, in April 1608. A month later the new Virginia Company invited all Englishmen resident in the Netherlands to join the undertaking. Gates was named the first governor of the colony under the charter of 1609. He stayed in Virginia for only a few months in 1610, leaving in December of that year for The Hague to present his case for retaining his company and for other discussions with the States General. During this visit, he may also have planned to discuss Anglo-Dutch cooperation in Virginia, for Sir Noel Caron, the Dutch ambassador in London, had made a proposal for "joining with us in that Collonie." This would not have been an unlikely course at that time, for in Guinea and the Amazon region the Dutch and English already cooperated against the Spaniards.[19] Gates returned to the James River in May 1611. He remained in the colony for nearly three years, until April 1614, returning to Flushing via England, although he was delayed and did not rejoin his company, which had remained in the Netherlands under his lieutenant, until June 1615. Four years later, we find him serving on one of the committees of the Virginia Company.[20]

Sir Thomas Dale, too, was an English mercenary in Dutch service. In 1603 he was commissioned a captain of infantry. His wife, Elizabeth Throckmorton, was the sister of John Throckmorton, lieutenant governor of Flushing and second in command of the Sidney Regiment serving under Robert Sidney. They had only been married for a month when Throckmorton sailed to Virginia. Like Gates, Dale was granted a leave of absence by the States General in 1611 to enter the service of the Virginia Company, and he remained in Virginia until May 1616. His administration in Virginia as marshal, deputy governor, and governor was both condemned for harshness and praised for order and progress. It is unclear if he ever visited the Netherlands again. In November 1617, Dale was chosen as fleet commander for the English East India Company. One year later the States General granted him his payment for the time he had served in Virginia, and another year later he fell sick in Java, dying in early 1619.[21]

Early Commercial Contacts

Not every early Virginian with a Dutch background hailed from Zeeland. Other pioneers came from Amsterdam prior to the start of their American adventure, such as Edward Bennett, who established a plantation in Virginia and was responsible for the shipment of hundreds of settlers.[22] Several English mercenaries came with Dutch artisans in tow, eight of whom were sent by the Virginia Company in 1608 to work as glassblowers in Jamestown. The so-called Dutchmen who dwelled in Virginia in these years were not all natives of the United Provinces. The "Dutch" carpenters hired to build sawmills in 1620 arrived from Hamburg, in northern Germany. On the other hand, the Dutch identity of more than a few early settlers is obscured by the quick anglicization of their names. As Edmund Morgan remarks, "Often we learn only by chance that someone named William Westerhouse or Jenkin Price is Dutch." Another example is Meindert Doedes (known as "Mindert Doode"), a Dutch ship captain who became the founder of the Minor family.[23]

No proof has surfaced yet of direct commercial contacts between Dutchmen and English Virginia in these early years, but with the large English presence in Flushing and Middelburg and people like Sir Thomas Gates ferrying back and forth between Virginia and Flushing, English merchants, probably fellows of the Merchant Adventurers in Middelburg, started to ship Virginia tobacco to Zeeland during the second decade of the seventeenth century.[24] The Virginia Company tried to tap the resources of the Merchant Adventurers in Middelburg in 1612–13.[25] One English merchant, for example, hired the ship *Vliegende Vis* to ship tobacco to Flushing, and in 1615–16, the *Flying Hart* from Flushing exported tobacco from Virginia to Portsmouth, England. In late August 1619, a Dutch armed merchantman, in conjunction with the English privateer *Treasurer*, landed "20. and odd Negroes" at Jamestown. The ship, probably the *Witte Leeuw* (master Andries Veron), also came from Flushing.[26]

Trade without Friends

In the second quarter of the seventeenth century, a shift took place in the Dutch import trade of tobacco. As late as 1627, the province of Zeeland still dominated the tobacco trade, importing 29,199 pounds of Virginia leaf from London (or 78 percent of a total of 37,384 pounds received in the Dutch Republic), easily eclipsing Amsterdam (6,390 pounds) and Rotterdam (1,795 pounds).[27] But by 1640, because of its significant English community, Rotterdam had become a much more important tobacco market.[28] Despite these changes and notwithstanding their own growing number, Dutchmen trading with Virginia were still operating in a kind of vacuum in the years 1620 through 1640. Commercial infrastructure and trading networks were still lacking on both sides of the ocean. A small ad hoc group of traders or "adventurers" chartered vessels to carry European goods to the Chesapeake and bring back tobacco. When a vessel came home with tobacco obtained by bartering the outward cargo, the tobacco so "returned" was divided among the individual adventurers, who were under no compulsion to continue in the trade.[29]

Between 1609 and 1621 there was a cease-fire—known as the Twelve Years' Truce—in the war between the Dutch rebels and the Habsburg empire. Shortly after hostilities resumed in 1621, the Dutch West India Company was created as a chartered joint stock company. The preamble of the charter stated the most important objectives of the company as "shipping, trade, and commerce with the West Indies, Africa, and the Americas."[30] The profits made in shipping Virginia tobacco alerted the directors of the West India Company to the viability of trade with the Chesapeake. At its first meeting in November 1623, the company's directors decided both to dispatch a ship to Virginia and to forbid private ships from sailing to Virginia.[31]

Dutch private enterprise had benefited from the official ceiling of tobacco imports from Virginia and Bermuda established by King James I in 1621. The two English companies involved in tobacco imports, the Somers Isles Company and the London Company, agreed that the former ship to England the fifty-five thousand pounds to which the two colonies were limited, while the latter was to consign the remainder to Flushing and Middelburg.[32] In 1621, a large consignment of tobacco arrived in Middelburg in an English vessel.[33] Dutch merchants soon did the shipping themselves. Within a year Ambassador Carleton asked the States General to stop Dutch ships bound for Virginia. In 1623, the governor and council of Virginia reported that the Dutch "take away much [of] our Tobacco ... [b]ecause many of their commodities [such] as Sacke, sweete meates and strong Liquors are soe acceptable to the people."[34] While there are hardly any archival traces of Dutch navigating to the Chesapeake during the 1620s, the Dutch role in the export of Virginia tobacco was significant enough for the authorities in England to require as early as 1627 that all vessels leaving the colony make London their first stop, a harbinger of the Navigation Acts.[35]

As it became clear by 1629 that the West India Company could not uphold its monopoly rights, its directors began to allow private merchants in its sphere, many of whom had never left since 1621. On June 7, 1629, free colonists of New Netherland were allowed to trade in peltries in those areas where the company did not have an agent and ship them to the Netherlands. The next year, the company ceded most of its monopoly rights in

Dutch Brazil, thus making the regime in the "Dutch" Atlantic world, including Virginia, economically less restrictive.[36]

The cargoes of the ships venturing from Dutch ports to the New World included a wide array of merchandise, from liquor to cheese, pitch, and barber's chests. These shipments were high-risk undertakings because in most cases, because of a lack of contacts and the absence of a network, no prearranged deals were made about the purchase of tobacco. Ships sailed to the New World on "adventure." In Amsterdam, Rotterdam, or Middelburg, an entrepreneur—referred to as the "husband"—would take the initiative for such a venture to the other side of the ocean. First he would purchase a cargo and then hire a ship from a ship-owning company. In many cases his cargo was not sufficient to fill the whole ship, so he tried to interest his business friends in sending goods to the New World as well.

During the 1630s and early 1640s, the instructions to shipmasters and supercargoes tended to be rather vague, often listing multiple destinations in order to obtain a lucrative return cargo, although in many cases sponsoring merchants explicitly ordered the purchase of tobacco. In 1634, for instance, Marten Backer (or Martten Becker), a merchant hailing from Plymouth but residing in Amsterdam, acted as the husband of the *Engel Gabriel*. He ordered master Franck Cornelisz Kindt from Rotterdam to steer the ship on the following route: Plymouth in England, Cork in Ireland, the West Indies (in particular Barbados), Virginia, England, and back to Amsterdam. Destined for the West Indies or Virginia was a cargo of pitch. Specifically for Virginia, Becker shipped three carpenters in his service, who were to serve him there for two years.[37]

The average voyage only became risky upon arrival in Virginia. Although by the 1630s good charts were available, Dutch masters needed local pilots to navigate the Chesapeake Bay. In 1640, the vessel *'t Wapen van Leeuwarden* from Hoorn (master Dirck Cornelisz Stam), for instance, arrived in Virginia, picking up pilot "Jan Const" at Smiths Island, who piloted the ship to Jamestown.[38] Secondly, like their English rivals, Dutch merchants, masters, and supercargoes did not yet possess a well-developed local network of agents and factors who could assemble cargoes and transact business on their behalf. Hence only by spending inordinate amounts of time plying Virginia's vast system of waterways, sometimes going from plantation to plantation, were they able to sell their wares, collect their debts, and fill their ships' holds with hogsheads of tobacco.[39]

Usually the ship would stay at a safe anchorage somewhere downstream.

Master Paul Poppen (a native of Aalborg in Denmark) was ordered to sail from the port of Medemblik in Holland with his cargo to Jamestown. There he was to spend at most three months to obtain a return cargo of tobacco and then sail back to Amsterdam.[40] The plan for *'t Wapen van Leeuwarden* was that while it was anchored, the ship's carpenter would assemble a sloop or barge, for which purpose the ship's crew brought along shipbuilding materials.[41] Master Jan Jansz Visscher of the *Princess Royall* sent out two sloops, each with a crew of five, who twice had to row thirty miles to Accomack. The first time they returned with twenty-six hogsheads and the second time thirty-seven hogsheads of tobacco, which was all they could get. In the end, the ship left Virginia half empty.[42]

On many occasions a Dutch ship would arrive at the wrong time. Master David Pietersz de Vries arrived in Virginia from Tortuga on May 17, 1636. He related, "As it was out of season to obtain tobacco, I let all of my cargo lie here, and gave directions to trade when the crop of tobacco should be ripe, and I would return again when the unhealthy season should be over." A few years later Dirck Cornelisz Stam had the same experience. He was also too early, since the tobacco was not yet ready and had to be *gestreecken* (ironed). Stam left with no tobacco,[43] as did De Vries:

> The 1st of October, I began to sail up and down the river, according to my license, in order to collect my debts, but found that little tobacco had been made, and that there had been this year great mortality among the people, and large quantities of goods brought into this country by English; and that there were great frauds among the English, who had not paid each other the tobacco, and that half the ships of their own nation were not laden; so that I consider, in regard to this trade, that those who wish to trade here, must keep a house here, and continue all the year, that he may be prepared, when the tobacco comes from the field, to seize it, if he would obtain his debts. It is thus the English do among themselves; so that there is no trade for us, unless there be an overplus of tobacco, or few English ships. After I had spent the winter here, I was compelled to return, as did most all the ships, without tobacco, and to let my debts stand.[44]

De Vries made two significant suggestions to improve Dutch trade in Virginia. First, he suggested that the purchaser had to be on hand to buy it when the tobacco was ready. Second, in order to do so, it was essential to have local agents.

Realizing that as outsiders without, as yet, a local network, they needed friendship and protection, the Dutch made special efforts to associate themselves with local leaders. For this purpose, they sailed to Jamestown, not only to get refreshments but also to pay their respects to the governor or his deputy. In 1634 master Franck Cornelisz Kindt paid the governor fifty pounds of gunpowder and sixteen cannonballs. Four years later, Sir John Harvey, governor during much of the 1630s, and Richard Kemp, secretary and later acting governor, trafficked with Dutchmen, one of whom—Dirck Cornelisz Stam—brought some presents for the governor's spouse, including ribbons, lace, and silk.[45]

Dramatic Changes: "They Enjoyed the Favour of Some Friends There"

After 1640 the role of the Dutch in Virginia's trade and commerce changed dramatically, both in volume and in character. These changes can only be understood in the context of the time. The 1640s, 1650s, and 1660s were rife with war: the English Civil War, the Virginians' war against the Amerindians, and the Anglo-Dutch wars all influenced Anglo-Dutch trade. Furthermore, in 1650 the Commonwealth issued the Navigation Act, forbidding the colonials to trade with foreigners, including the Dutch. As a result of these developments, but also because of the trade's own dynamics, new networks were forged on either side of the ocean that fundamentally altered the scale and organization of the Dutch-Virginia trade.

John Pagan has already observed that the Dutch became a major force in Virginia during the English Civil War. When master De Vries returned to the Chesapeake in 1643, he counted thirty-four ships, of which four were Dutch. Eight years earlier he had counted thirty-six vessels—all of them English. In April 1644, at least four Dutch ships were loading tobacco in Virginia. There are indications that between 1643 and 1649 at least thirty-five Dutch ships sailed to Virginia. At Christmas 1648, De Vries observed that out of thirty-one ships in the colony, twelve were English, twelve were Dutch, and seven came from New England. In the same year, it was reported that a fleet of twenty-five Dutch ships was about to sail to the colony. Even the Navigation Act and the First Anglo-Dutch War did not oust the Dutch, who, as one colonist later told the High Court of Admiralty, "enjoyed the favour of some friends here."[46]

De Vries also introduced others to the Virginia trade. In 1643, master Jacob Gerritsen Blenck (ca. 1589–1652), a Rotterdam native, sailed to the Chesapeake for the first time. Upon his arrival, he met De Vries, and together they visited numerous tobacco plantations, gaining firsthand experience of the trade's ins and outs.[47] At some point in the 1640s, Blenck bought a plantation at Kecoughtan along with four other men from Rotterdam or with Rotterdam connections: Jan Jacobsen Pal, Ysbrant Vethuysen, François Vermande (who was also active in the Barbados trade) and Jan de Colonia (a dyer who occasionally invested in international shipping).[48] In 1649, this group sold the plantation through the help of Simon Overzee, a Rotterdam trader with numerous contacts in Virginia and Maryland who had settled in Virginia in 1647 and died in Maryland twelve years later.[49] The village of Kecoughtan, incidentally, was frequented by Dutchmen in the 1640s. In 1644, four Dutch ships were conducting business there simultaneously.[50]

War and Trade

In October 1642, Parliament issued a statement forbidding all trade with "any Port or place within any of His Majesties Dominions, being in Hostility," without any specification. The neutral Dutch masters and merchants had to find out for themselves if a port was off limits for them or not, at least in the eyes of Parliament. In the four years between 1643 and 1646, Parliament ships confiscated almost sixty Dutch ships.[51]

At the same time, new opportunities presented themselves to the Dutch, when King Charles I commissioned Governor William Berkeley to apprehend all ships from London and to seize all assets from Londoners living in the colony. Berkeley was more than willing to keep the London merchants at arm's length and to reach out to the Dutch.[52] Berkeley found the planters, who were involved in a bitter struggle with London-based merchants, on his side. A decade earlier, these merchants had made it clear that they aspired to full control of the Virginia trade by (1) establishing a monopoly company in London for trade with Virginia and (2) excluding of all foreign merchants from the Virginia trade, especially the Dutch.

At the time, the tobacco trade was dominated by a few powerful merchants such as Maurice, Edward, and George Thompson; Thomas Stone; and William Tucker. In 1633, their syndicate brought in 63 percent of all tobacco. In that same year, merchant-planter Tucker petitioned the Privy Council for the resurrection of the Virginia Company and demanded that the government take action to exclude the Dutch from Virginia's commerce. Tucker argued that the superior competitiveness of the Dutch would soon drive the English merchants from the trade and thus leave the planters in an even worse position—a theme frequently echoed by the merchants in the next decades, to the planters' exasperation. Opponents of the syndicate's monopoly won this battle. Following a strong plea from ten of them, including several members of the Virginia assembly, the Privy Council revoked the Thompson-Stone-Tucker monopoly contract. At the same time, the Privy Council ordered the exclusion of the Dutch from the tobacco trade, which was a victory for a rival faction of planters made up of members and allies of the syndicate.[53]

Other merchant-planters as well as many lesser planters had, however, a different opinion about the appropriate commercial role of the Dutch in the colony. In 1640, Virginia authorities issued a trading license to a Dutch (or possibly Flemish) vessel after its captain posted a bond to ensure payment of customs duties in London. The masters of several English ships filed a petition in the General Court, asking the governor and councilors to confiscate the alien's cargo. The court rejected the petition and affirmed the Dutch license on the ground that without foreigners' supplies colonists would have been left in a state of "intolerable exigency."[54]

As English politics broke down into civil war, Virginia's need for the Dutch became policy. In 1643, Virginia's colonial government, headed by William Berkeley, the trusted ally of the Dutch, passed an act encouraging Dutch-Virginia trade. Four years later,[55] in 1647, the governor, councilors, and burgesses declared that they considered the continuation of commercial relations with the Dutch essential to the colony's "being & subsistence." They also took note of rumors that English merchants had recently sponsored an act of Parliament prohibiting aliens from trading with any of England's colonies. They condemned these attempts by "some English Merchants on purpose to affright & expell the Dutch, and make way for themselves to Monopolize not onely our labours and fortunes, but even our P[er]sons." To underscore its commitment to the preservation of unrestricted commerce, the assembly again extended the invitation to the Dutch and proclaimed that anyone who caused them disturbance would suffer punishment and loss of his estates.[56] In Virginia royalist resistance was a revolt in favor of free trade.

The tobacco interest in London had to bide its time until the late summer and early autumn of 1650, when its royalist enemies were destroyed at sea and their Scottish allies defeated at Dunbar. Only then could the Commonwealth begin to consider a move against the commercial policy of the disloyal Virginians and the Dutch. From the metropolitan point of view, a more stringent commercial control of the American plantations had to be imposed, first by increasing custom revenues and then by promoting English trade. Foreigners would be excluded from trade to any of the colonies, and colonial products exported to England only. The purpose of these policies was to cut off direct trade between England's empire and continental Europe in order to integrate the practice of re-exporting colonial produce into the English customs system. Its effect was greatly to increase the price of colonial tobacco that was re-exported to European markets. These restrictive policies seriously exacerbated the situation for the planters and tended to limit their opportunities to trade, bringing down the selling price of tobacco in the colonies even further.[57]

The new London merchants, with considerable colonial interests, played a major role in seeing to the execution of the antiroyalist, antiproprietor, and anti-Dutch act of October 3, 1650, which prohibited all trade in all goods with the colonies except under license. In March 1651, Governor Berkeley responded to the news with a defiant address to the Virginia Assembly in which he linked the colonial demands for a royalist settlement in England, political autonomy, and free trade, as the quote at the beginning of this essay states. In late 1651, however, Parliament dispatched a fleet from England to subdue Virginia, around the same time that it passed the 1651 Navigation Act banning colonial trade with the Netherlands. From this time on, no European goods could be imported into England or her colonies except in English vessels or in ships belonging to the country that produced the goods or to the port from which they were usually first shipped. Furthermore, English ships were required to transport goods to England or her possessions directly from their point of origin rather than via an entrepôt such as Amsterdam. Taken together, the 1650 and 1651 acts obstructed continuation of economic cooperation between Virginians and Dutchmen and increased planters' dependence upon London merchants. By the end of 1652, the new merchants could hardly have been more satisfied with the evolution of colonial policy under the Commonwealth. The royalist revolt in the colonies had been put down, and a policy of total exclusion of the Dutch from colonial trade had been adopted. The outbreak of the First Anglo-Dutch War (1652–54) facilitated implementation of the latter measure.[58]

On the pretext of illicit trade, England had seized many Dutch ships in European waters between the adoption of the act of October 3, 1650, and the start of the war: 61 in 1650, 140 in 1651, and 106 in 1652. In these years, perhaps as many as 1,000–1,700 Dutch vessels were brought into English ports.[59] Despite these turbulent times, Dutch merchants still traded with

Virginia, but several of their tobacco-laden ships fell victim to the restrictive measures of Parliament. In 1651 the *Fortuin* with master Cornelisz Marcus was seized and brought to Yarmouth but later released.⁶⁰ A year later the *Gouden Leeuw, Liefde, Faam,* and *Fortuin* were seized by English privateers in the James River.⁶¹ But it was not that simple to oust the Dutch from Virginia. After all, "they enjoyed the favour of some friends there."⁶²

Friends in High Places

After the royalist planters and the republican Dutch had first joined hands as mutual foes of the Roundheads, Dutch merchants steadily developed their network with Virginia's ruling elite. As we've seen, Governor Berkeley had especially close ties to the Dutch. In search of Marie de Medici, to whom he was to convey a message from the king, Berkeley had visited the Netherlands in 1638. A few years later, he was trading in Virginia with an Amsterdam merchant house. Until he was ousted from office in 1652, Berkeley would stand up and protect Dutch interests while holding the London merchants at bay. His defiant stance against the act of October 3, 1650, has already been mentioned. The speech he made to the General Assembly on March 17, 1651, was sent to some friends in The Hague, who published it for distribution throughout the Netherlands and England. After the Commonwealth had taken control of Virginia, everyone was given one year to decide whether to swear loyalty to the new regime or to leave the Old Dominion. If Berkeley were to go to the Netherlands or England, he was allowed to haul his possessions "without any lett in any of the [Dutch] ports, or any molestation" whatsoever.⁶³

An important political and business ally of Berkeley's was Argoll Yeardley. The eldest son of a former governor-general, Yeardley became an active merchant-planter, who traded frequently with the Dutch. In 1649, he sailed to Rotterdam in his own vessel with a cargo of tobacco. During his stay in the city, he married Ann Custis and took her back to Virginia.⁶⁴ Family ties and common business interests reinforced Yeardley's loose alliance with like-minded merchant-planters who joined the Eastern Shore and the lower James River basin to the Holland trade. Besides Yeardley, the group included Nathaniel Littleton, Thomas Willoughby, Secretary Richard Kemp, Richard Lee, Edmund Scarborough, Yeardley's brother Francis, and Adam Thoroughgood, a Lower Norfolk County justice, whose daughter Sara had married Simon Overzee.

The network connected to Amsterdam via Berkeley through Richard

Glover, another Anglo-Dutch merchant resident of Virginia.[65] The Berkeley-Glover link drew into the mix councilors George Ludlow, Bridges Freeman, and Ralph Wormeley along with burgesses Robert Holt and Stephen Gill and numerous well-heeled independent merchant-planters: Richard Bennett, who served as a county commissioner, a burgess, and a councilor before attaining the governorship in 1652, dealt with a Rotterdam firm during the same period; Obedience Robins, a burgess and county commissioner for Accomack and Northampton, acted as Dutch trader Aries Topp's attorney in 1643 and was still doing so when he was appointed to the council in 1655; Stephen Charlton was an Eastern Shore burgess and commissioner; Edward Major, a burgess from Northampton county who eventually became speaker of the assembly, benefited from Dutch merchants' willingness to grant long-term credit to planters. These friends in high places formed only one side of a multifaceted, extended trade network along the Atlantic rim.[66]

The Dutch in Virginia

Dutch traders seem to have had a preference for the Eastern Shore, a peninsula that had been permanently settled from about 1619.[67] Jan Michielsz and Amsterdam merchant John Cornelius settled on the peninsula after having traded there for a number of years. John Johnson, Hugh Cornelius Corneliuson, Hendrick Wageman, Daniel Derrickson, Peter Jacobson, Abram van Slot, and Abraham Jansen, all residents of the Eastern Shore in 1660, may have arrived in the same way.[68] The same is true of residents of New Amsterdam who came to stay in Virginia, once again primarily on the Eastern Shore.[69]

The brothers Dirck Cornelisz Stam (b. 1608) and Arent Cornelisz Stam (1615–1646) became the leading Dutch merchants present in the Chesapeake. They were originally in the service of Killiaen van Rensselaer, the patroon of Rensselaerswijck in New Netherland (Dirck as commissary at Fort Orange); both sailed to Virginia on behalf of the patroon to conduct trade. By the late 1630s, they settled in Virginia with their families and bought 860 acres of land in Elizabeth City County as well as a parcel of land on James Island.[70] These investments and their year-round trading operations in Virginia laid the foundation for a very advantageous trade between Virginia and Amsterdam in the years to come, when the Stam brothers shipped more tobacco to Europe than any firm in England. In 1640 alone they shipped at least 60,000 pounds of tobacco from Virginia to Holland;

an additional 20,000 had to be left behind, while 16,000 was sent to London. The next year they transferred more than 100,000 pounds. The volume of their trade in Virginia tobacco during those two years greatly exceeded that of any single London merchant. In Virginia, Dirck Cornelisz Stam acted as an agent for Amsterdam merchants, bartering, for instance, linen, sugar, and other commodities for at least 10,000 pounds of tobacco in 1640, although this cargo never arrived in Amsterdam, as the ship was seized by a privateer from Dunkirk. The Stams' access to Dutch capital and credit probably contributed to their success. For example, in 1641 Arent Cornelisz Stam was able to finance certain purchases from Captain William Douglas and Company by issuing three bills of exchange for forty pounds sterling drawn upon "John Verbrugge dwelling in Amsterdam."[71] Stam granted Douglas and Company a security interest in his lands and chattels in Virginia so that the forty pounds could be recovered "in case the sayd Moneyes be not paid in Holland."[72]

Apart from the Stam brothers, there were other Dutchmen who first settled in New Netherland before moving on to Virginia.[73] Andrew Herbert arrived, for example, from New Amsterdam and William Martin from Dutch Delaware.[74] Both acquired plantations. And since New Netherland was a multinational colony, there were also non-Dutch immigrants from the Hudson to Virginia, including the German physician Georg Hack and the Bohemian Augustine Herrman. After the two colonies had established commercial links at an early stage, they drew even closer in the late 1640s and early 1650s as a result of a triangular trade operated by Amsterdam merchants.[75]

New Atlantic Networks

The English Civil War had a profound effect on Virginia-Dutch commercial relations, both in the short and long run, and both in scope and in character. During the war, navigation between the mother country and the colony was severely hampered. While Parliament got the upper hand in England, Virginia remained firmly royalist, at least until 1652. Dutch merchants like the Stam brothers dominated tobacco exportation during the war years. In the long run, many different commercial ties were established between the Dutch Republic and Virginia. They involved elite Virginians, London merchants, English and Dutch merchants operating from Amsterdam and Rotterdam, and Dutchmen settling in Virginia. During the

1640s royalist Virginia planters and republican Dutch entrepreneurs worked closely together. These contacts were so well developed by 1652 that in spite of the Commonwealth's assumption of control over the colony, the removal of Dutch ally Governor William Berkeley from office, and the onset of the First Anglo-Dutch War, Dutch ships still sailed to Virginia. Some of these vessels were seized as prizes.[76]

By the end of the 1650s, closely integrated networks relied on Dutch, English, and Virginian contacts. In July 1656 John Lugir, an English merchant living in Amsterdam, arrived in London. He had dispatched goods from Amsterdam to London, which were to be shipped from there to Virginia in an English vessel. In the colony his son took care of his business.[77] In 1659, David de Mercado (a.k.a. Jorge Nunes) hired the *Golden Flower of Plymouth* from Diego Rodrigues Arias, a merchant in London, for a trip from Plymouth to Virginia, Amsterdam, and London.[78]

The character of the trade also changed dramatically. By using their overseas contacts, Dutch merchants who had previously gambled in the hope to arrive at the right moment could now conduct year-round trading operations. If necessary, their agents used warehouses to store the tobacco when no Dutch ships were available. Deals could be made in advance, and the planters could order any kind of commodity in the Netherlands. By the time a ship left a Dutch port, it was already clear where the goods were to be taken and what kind of tobacco could be fetched where and in what amount. Thus, when the *Gouden Leeuw* left the Netherlands for the James River in August 1651, its crew knew that it would collect fifty hogsheads of tobacco upon arrival, from the agents of Cornelis Bonon and Cornelis Ackersloot, for some Amsterdam and Middelburg merchants.[79] Conversely, Virginia planters sent their tobacco in consignment to the Netherlands. In 1651, for instance, John Brown sent thirty-one hogsheads of tobacco (weighing 9,759 pounds) to Laurence Coughen in Amsterdam. For freight, offloading, and storing the tobacco, Brown owed Coughen 924:11:08 guilders. The account had to be settled through a Captain Mitchell, who would sail from Rotterdam to Virginia.[80] Similar arrangements tied Dutch ports to Maryland. In 1660, the *Golden Lyon* of London sailed to the Patuxent and Severn Rivers in Maryland to load thirty hogsheads of tobacco, which were to be delivered either at London or in Holland and Zeeland.[81]

It was also much easier now to settle one's accounts. No longer, as it had been for De Vries, was it necessary to return to the colony to collect debts. Bills of exchange could be collected by a third party, or a third party could be given power of attorney over one's business in Virginia. These extensive financial services increased the debts of Virginia and Maryland planters to merchants from Amsterdam and Rotterdam.[82] In one instance in 1664, it was revealed that prominent Maryland planters owed some forty-six bills of sale either to Edmund Custis and Company, merchants of London, or to Robert Custis, merchant of Rotterdam, and Captain Lancelot Anderson of Hull.[83]

Such arrangements fostered a lively trade, although its exact volume cannot be established. There are indications that it was, at least at times, substantial. The estimate made in an anonymous English pamphlet that Dutch vessels made up half of all European ships at anchor in Virginia to buy tobacco was, however, an exaggeration.[84]

The 1660s–1680s: More Than Meets the Eye

With the restoration of royal power over the English empire in 1660, not only did Dutch-Virginian relations change forever, but the organization of the tobacco trade underwent a profound transformation as well. After the resignation of Richard Cromwell as Lord Protector of England, Scotland, and Ireland in May 1659 and the death of Samuel Mathews as governor of Virginia the following January, Sir William Berkeley was elected governor by the General Assembly in mid-March 1660. The day Berkeley effectively took over as governor, negotiations were started for a commercial treaty with New Netherland. In mid-May, the "Articles of Amite & Commerce" between New Netherland and Virginia took effect. Merchants in the two colonies could trade freely with one another, though the Dutch would pay export duties on Virginia tobacco at the same rate as "other neighbouring English & strangers."[85]

Aside from its commercial merits, the treaty represented a most emphatic rejection of current English trade legislation, which had been designed to exclude the Dutch from the Chesapeake. It was clear that Berkeley had other plans for the colony. In upholding the economic interests of Virginia during his second stint in office, Berkeley pursued five main policies: (1) an emphasis on Virginia's importance to England and to the other colonies, (2) maintenance of Virginia's territorial integrity, (3) abolition of the restrictions that the Acts of Trade had imposed on Virginia, (4) a limit on tobacco production, and (5) encouragement of the growth of crops other than tobacco. In *A Discourse and View of Virginia*, published in England in 1663, he wrote: "Had the *Dutch Virginia*, they would make it the Fortresse, Mart and Magazin of all the *West Indies*, for ... the Rivers will securely harbour twenty thousand Ships at once; the Country produceth all things necessary for those Ships and the men that sayle in them, nothing wanting for the supplies of war or peace, but it was ever our misery not to take our aims the distance of an Age."[86] However, the new English sovereign had plans of his own, aspiring to new trade restrictions and war with the Dutch Republic.[87]

Dutch Raids on the Chesapeake

The 1660 regime change did not reduce English envy of the Dutch. To English observers Dutch superiority in international commerce seemed as great as ever, and in the newly ascendant mercantilist philosophy, Dutch gains in trade inevitably meant English losses. Virginia, however, played no significant role in the outbreak of either the Second or the Third Anglo-Dutch War. Since Dutch ships sailing to Virginia had adapted themselves to the new circumstances, disruption of their commercial activities during these two conflicts was not as severe as during the first war.[88]

The Dutch did, however, launch attacks against Virginia. On June 1, 1667, Captain Abraham Crijnssen, with a commission from the States of Zeeland, arrived with his squadron of four men-of-war and one transport at the entrance of the Chesapeake Bay. After he had taken the English colony of Suriname, he was instructed to raid Virginia. That first day he took a merchantman and a small coasting vessel outside the capes of the Chesapeake. Four days later Crijnssen defeated the lone English warship in Virginia, the frigate *Elizabeth*. Governor Berkeley organized the weak defenses of the colony, assembling the militia and arming several vessels in defense of Jamestown. When Crijnssen left after five days, he had burned the *Elizabeth* and four merchantmen, three of which were laden with tobacco. The Dutch had seized nine fully laden ships, a small vessel with sugar, and one empty ship. The colony itself, including Jamestown and the plantations, was left undamaged. The Dutch victory was humiliating but hardly disastrous; most of the tobacco fleet had survived.[89]

The Third Anglo-Dutch War (1672–74) saw more Dutch depredations. On July 11, 1673, a squadron of nine Dutch warships, commanded by Jacob Binckes and Cornelis Evertsen, entered the Chesapeake. This time the Virginians were prepared. Already in April the governor and council had ordered all militia officers to muster their troops. The coastal defenses, less than five years old, were largely empty and poorly built, and the earthworks eroded faster than they could be repaired. Fortunately for Berkeley and his militia, in June two English frigates had arrived. The two war ships and six heavily armed merchantmen sailed from Newport News to engage the Dutch at Hampton Roads. In the confusing battle that followed, one ship from Maryland—a group of Maryland tobacco ships had arrived to join the midsummer convoy to England—and four of the armed merchantmen went aground and were lost. The remaining English ships put up a gallant fight against the Dutch warships before withdrawing safely into the Elizabeth River. Meanwhile, nearly two dozen other vessels retreated to the security of Jamestown, and another dozen or so gathered under the weak fort at Nansemond. In total some eleven cargo ships were destroyed and captured with over a thousand hogsheads of tobacco. Binckes and Evertsen left the Chesapeake for New York, which they recaptured briefly in the name of the Dutch West India Company. But once again, Virginia had survived an attack.[90]

More Trade Restrictions

The 1651 Navigation Act, like other legislation of the Commonwealth period, was declared void on the Restoration of Charles II, having been passed by "usurping powers." But soon a new act replaced the old one. By the 1660s Britain's merchant marine was a shabby collection of vessels. The shipbuilding industry experienced hard times from the combined effects of the Civil War, owner backwardness, and constant, fierce competition from the Dutch. English merchants desperately wanted to weight the odds in their favor, and they pressed the new king for help. Charles was sympathetic to their plight, and in 1660, Parliament passed new legislation to protect London's maritime interests. The new laws are generally referred to as the "Navigation Acts," which (with some amendments) remained in force for nearly two centuries. The Navigation Act of 1660 required all European goods bound for America (or other colonies) to be shipped through England or Wales first. In England, the goods would be unloaded, inspected, taxed, and reloaded. The trade had to be carried in English bottoms, which included those of the colonies. The master and three-quarters of the crew had to be English. The ships had to carry certificates that they were "free" to conduct trade. Furthermore, imports of "enumerated commodities" (such as sugar, rice, and tobacco) could not be shipped to any other country without first being unloaded in England, and their duty paid, before exportation overseas. This raised the cost to the colonies and increased shipping time. Conversely, colonial imports, such as French wine or German textiles, had to be transshipped in England. Bonds were required in order to ensure compliance with all of these trading restrictions. For the Virginian planters the enforcement of the act seemed to herald a bleak future. The scheme called for a closed economic order that gathered the nation and its colonies into a transatlantic empire. For Berkeley and the assembly it was clear that a major purpose of the 1660 act was to eliminate the Dutch from the American colony. It imperiled Virginia's autonomy and institutions and jeopardized the colony's relationship with the Crown.[91]

The London-based Virginia merchant John Bland responded on "behalf of the inhabitants and planters in Virginia and Maryland" to the act of 1660's prohibiting direct import of foreign goods, writing: "I hope it will clearly appear, that the debarring the Hollanders from going to those Plantations doth not at all advance our commerce, or your majesties customes, but on the contrary, will utterly ruinate the colonies commerce and customes together in a short time; for if the Inhabitants be destroyed, of necessity the Trade there must cease."[92] In June 1661, Berkeley left for London to save whatever was possible. He did what he could to protect the interests of Virginia, distributing his *Discourse and View of Virginia* in January 1662. Haunting the lobbies of Whitehall and the Inner Court of Wards, Berkeley tirelessly pressed the Privy Council and the Council for Foreign Plantations for repeal of the offensive law. In September 1662 Berkeley was issued his instructions as governor of Virginia, which must have been disappointing. The Crown flatly refused to allow Virginians freedom of trade. As Warren Billings has argued, this outcome was inescapable given the odds against Berkeley. The persistent advocacy of the many supporters he mustered could not override the great opposition to free trade. Hence, there was no way that Charles would exempt Virginia from the commercial restrictions in the evolving navigation system. The instruction made the governor personally responsible for ensuring that the laws were faithfully executed, and he was expressly commanded to furnish a complete account of all exports, including a list showing the name, destination, and master of each ship departing the colony with a cargo of tobacco.[93]

A year later, the trade regulations were tightened further. The Staple Act of 1663 (also called the Act for the Encouragement of Trade) was an offshoot of the Navigation Acts, stating that all European goods bound for the American colonies must first land at an English port and then be reshipped to America in English vessels. England would benefit from this act by imposing custom duties on goods, and the cost would be passed to the American consumer. The English merchants would profit from handling, insurance, and shipping fees. This act also provided for a naval officer in all colonial ports to ensure that the new mercantile laws were upheld.[94]

Parliament's creation of a plantation duty system in 1673 also contributed to the effectiveness of the Navigation Laws. The Plantation Duty Act of 1673 was to meet certain difficulties that arose in the administration of the Navigation Act of 1660. The earlier act permitted colonial vessels to carry enumerated commodities from the place of production to another plantation without paying duties. Under cover of this provision, it was assumed that enumerated commodities, after being taken to a plantation, could then be sent directly to continental ports free of duty. The new act provided that, before vessels left a colonial port, bonds should be given that the enumerated commodities would be carried only to England. If bonds were not given and the commodities were taken to another colonial port, plantation duties were collected according to a prescribed schedule. The act authorized the appointment of a staff of colonial customs officials. By requiring tobacco exporters to pay customs duties in Virginia unless they posted bond to take their cargoes directly to England, these royal officials reduced the probability of illicit trade.[95]

Some historians have maintained that the 1660 and 1663 acts caused the end of direct Dutch participation in Virginia's commerce. John Pagan has pointed to the English government's decision to make colonial governors personally responsible for ensuring that the trade laws were faithfully executed as the main reason for the decline, and Russell R. Menard has observed that Dutch traders seldom appear in Maryland and Virginia records of the 1660s, which he believed might reflect the illegality of their enterprises but more likely their absence.[96] How active Dutch smugglers were remains to be seen, but it is certain that the Dutch involvement in Virginia's maritime and commercial activities did not cease during the 1660s and 1670s. There was more than meets the eye.

Masters of Disguise

During the 1660s and 1670s Dutch shipmasters, in conjunction with their friends in Holland, London, Scotland, and Virginia, made optimal use of the available range of possibilities and legal loopholes. In many cases ships equipped from Holland, both legal and illicit, used an English identity. No wonder that Menard found few traces of so-called Dutch ships in the Maryland and Virginia archives. By the time they arrived in the colonies, the Dutch ships had become English, or at least appeared to be English. While the sources do not permit measurement of the volume of this disguised trade, there are indications that it was still significant in the 1670s.[97]

The Amsterdam archives offer several cases illustrating how the Dutch became masters of disguise without violating the Navigation Acts. For example, Amsterdam merchant Daniel de Vogel represented William Brown of Plymouth, England. De Vogel had supplied a cargo of a variety of merchandise for the *Unity of Yarmouth*. According to their arrangement, the vessel was to leave Amsterdam on August 23, 1664, for Plymouth, England, where it would be reloaded. The *Unity* was then to sail to Potomac River or Appomattox Creek in Virginia, where its cargo would be offloaded, and then proceed to Maryland for tobacco. On the homeward-bound leg, the ship had to call at an English port "to pay the Kings duties" before finally going to Amsterdam.[98]

During the Second Anglo-Dutch War, in 1666, Abraham Jansz, a merchant residing in the Holland village of Graft, had purchased on behalf of Colonel Edmond Scarborough, John Michael, and Lieutenant Colonel William Kendall—all three residents and officeholders in Virginia's Accomack County—the flyboat (*fluit*) *Koning van Spanje* and had the vessel loaded with a cargo of merchandise according to their instructions. The ship sailed to Virginia, but en route to Carsten Island, master Thomas Sprieteman (a Scottish native) had to pay for his license, and the ship was confiscated. It appears that the ship was released, because in November 1667, when the war was over, the same vessel was sighted in Leith, Scotland, and Sprieteman was still master. In Leith he had changed the name of the ship from *Koning van Spanje* to *Golden Star of Peterhead*. By now, the ship's owner was one Lockwarm. Sprieteman had beaten the drum in the village in search of sailors to sail the ship to Virginia.[99]

The merchants operating from the Netherlands in the Virginia trade must have adjusted quite well to the new circumstances after 1660. On a regular basis, ships continued to be fit out in Dutch ports for voyages to Virginia. Very few vessels from the Netherlands were condemned by the Courts of Admiralty for violation of the Navigation Acts, although in 1664, three cases were brought to the Vice-Court of Admiralty in Maryland, involving alleged Dutch vessels. One of these cases involved Jacob Backer, who had chartered the sloop *Red Sterne*. He was sued by Governor Charles Calvert because the owner was allegedly a Dutch citizen of New York and therefore could not trade with the colony. The owner presented a letter from the governor of New York arguing that he, the owner, was free to trade because under a treaty between England and Holland, Dutch citizens of New York were allowed the privileges of Englishmen. The jury reached a "not guilty" verdict, and the sloop was returned to Backer.[100] A later case is that of the *Batchelor*, an English vessel seized by the Dutch in 1673 after they had retaken New York. On its way to Amsterdam under the new master Adriaan van Dort, the *Batchelor* was retaken by an English privateer and brought before the High Court of Admiralty. It was believed that the cargo of tobacco was owned by several Dutch merchants but that the former master, Englishman Philip Carteret, traveled as a passenger on board so that he could claim the tobacco if the ship was taken by an English man-of-war.[101]

Trade contacts between the Netherlands and the Chesapeake continued during the 1680s. By this time, interlopers were using merchants settled in British North America to circumvent the Acts of Navigation. Sir Josiah Child (1630–1699) noted how Amsterdam merchants obtained tobacco directly from Virginia through New York City: "The Dutch under pretence of trading to and from New-York, carry great quantities of Virginia Tobacco directly for Holland."[102]

Another example is merchant Jacob Milbourne and Captain Anthony Brockholls, deputy governor of New York from 1681 to 1688, who owned the *Susan*, a vessel that in 1687 sailed from New York to Virginia and then to Rotterdam. In addition to the *Susan*, Brockholls held an interest in at least one other vessel, the *Happy Return*, seized for trading in violation of the Navigation Acts.[103] And in August 1683 a Dutch ship heading for Virginia carrying African slaves, wine from the Canary Islands, and textiles was sighted by William Cowley.[104]

Daniel Petit, English consul in Amsterdam, constantly complained about Dutch masters not fulfilling their obligations to His Majesty by paying the required duties. One striking example was the *Vriendschap*, master Niclas Madder, which arrived in Amsterdam in August 1688: "I [Petit] have this morning arrested the ship *Friendschap*, Nicolas Madder master, lately arrived here from Virginia, without having payed . . . duties in England." The ship was "ab[ou]t 90 tunns, and was, as Madder told me, entered by him in Virginia upon his owne name and called the *Society*, he sayd also that one [John] Michael, who came in the ship from Virginia, is her true owner, and that he was but mate when he made entry of her there. One John Bornall [John Borland] a Scotsman living att Boston in New England is also come in her, as supercargo or merchant of the tobacco."[105]

On the other side of the ocean, Francis Howard, 5th Baron of Effingham and governor of Virginia (1683–88), tried to stop Dutch interloping activities as well. He commissioned several vessels to patrol the Chesapeake. One of the commanders, Thomas Allen, noted, "The Virginians are very angry that I stay here because I won't lett them cheat the King, they say I spoile their trade, and the best words I can get from them is old rogue and old dog, and when they see the ketch they say here comes the divells' ketch, and this is the best language I can get from them behind my back ... [T]hey have hired some small vessels to come when I am gone to one end of the country to fetch their Tobacco and carry it to New York or Newfoundland and from thence bring French brandy and the Tobacco they ship away for Holland, and soe cheat the King of his due."[106]

The 1690s–1720: Total War and the Demise of Direct Trade

Direct commercial contact between Virginia and the Netherlands finally came to an end in the 1690s. During the protracted wars against Louis XIV's France, both Dutch and English Atlantic commerce was profoundly disrupted by the French war on trade, the *guerre de course*. Hundreds of French, English, and Dutch merchantmen were taken as good prize.[107] The Chesapeake tobacco trade had to be protected.

The key element of this new system of imperial governance was the extension of naval power to the Chesapeake—actually a system of naval protection with two parts, which Douglas Bradburn has called the embargo and convoy regime. This system placed a limit on the total shipping allowed to England's overseas possessions, thereby limiting the size of the Atlantic trade and limiting the growth of the tobacco market with a fixed fleet of tobacco traders. This quota fleet was escorted across the Atlantic by several ships of the line, and as a result, Dutch merchants and masters withdrew almost completely from direct Chesapeake trade and navigation. Only a few "Dutch" ships are known to have sailed back and forth during the war years. Consequently, the tobacco markets in the Chesapeake, England, and the Netherlands changed profoundly.[108]

There were two major kinds of tobacco grown in the Chesapeake colonies: oronoco and sweet-scented. Oronoco, which was grown predominantly in Maryland, was stronger in flavor, while sweet-scented, which was grown on the banks of the great rivers of Virginia, had a milder taste. Sweet-scented was considered the best tobacco in the world, and as a result it brought a better price than oronoco. However, oronoco, which was not valued on the English market, was in great demand in the rest of Europe.[109]

So when the Dutch withdrew from the direct tobacco trade in the 1690s, the market for oronoco collapsed, leaving Maryland tobacco growers in great difficulty, while sweet-scented growers could take advantage of historically high prices in England.[110]

The new convoy system also transformed the London tobacco market. Larger merchants, using their contacts with the Board of Trade to manage the convoy system, squeezed out the smaller traders. As a result, by 1718 the trade in tobacco to London was dominated by only a few houses that specialized in the Chesapeake trade and nothing else.[111]

Despite these changes in Virginia and London, Amsterdam remained a dominant tobacco market. Dutch traders availed themselves of the rise in domestic tobacco production and continued to import from England instead of undertaking the high-risk voyage to Virginia themselves. By the 1690s, almost all Chesapeake tobacco arriving in the Netherlands was imported from England. English tobacco merchants became the new friends of the Amsterdam tobacco manufacturers, increasingly providing them with oronoco leaf, as shown in table 1.[112]

Small English tobacco merchants and Maryland oronoco growers suffered more than Dutch manufacturers. They found themselves unable to gain ready access to freight during the war. While within England the convoy system functioned to provide a crop of Virginia sweet-scented tobacco for English consumers, continental importation of oronoco could be seriously disrupted and costly. The Navigation Acts, the import duties, and the convoy system all led to high prices in Europe for oronoco tobacco (see table 2). In the Dutch Republic, this resulted in a boom in tobacco growing. As shown in table 3, domestic production of tobacco tripled from 6 million pounds to 18 million pounds between 1675 and 1710. As Dutch tobacco production accelerated, the Amsterdam manufacturers used a higher proportion of cheap domestic than expensive imported oronoco tobacco to produce their consumables.[113] Virginia leaf, however, would not vanish from the marketplace; the quantities of its exports to the Netherlands were increasing again by 1730. But the direct trade between Virginia and the Netherlands would only return with American independence.

Ties between Virginia and the Dutch date to the colony's earliest days. Significant numbers of Dutch ships started coming to the Chesapeake in the 1620s, usually operating without established networks and sailing in the

TABLE 1
English tobacco imports and exports and their Dutch share,
1697–1710 (millions of pounds)

			EXPORT TO HOLLAND		
	Import total	Export total	Total	% of total export	% of total import
1697	35.6	17.5	8.2	47	23
1698	31.5	22.8	7.5	33	24
1699	31.3	22.4	8.9	40	28
1700	37.8	24.9	8.1	33	21
1701	32.2	21.2	8.0	38	25
1702	37.2	14.4	6.3	44	17
1703	20.1	16.6	7.4	45	37
1704	34.9	19.7	9.3	47	27
1705	15.7	10.6	4.4	42	28
1706	19.8	11.0	5.5	50	28
1707	28.1	21.3	10.0	47	36
1708	29.0	16.6	8.4	51	29
1709	34.5	20.7	11.2	54	32
1710	23.5	15.4	8.1	53	34
Average	29.4	18.2	8.0	44	27

Sources: Data from John J. McCusker, *Historical Statistics of the United States, Earliest Times to the Present: Millennial Edition,* 5 vols., ed. Susan B. Carter et al. (New York: Cambridge University Press, 2006), table Eg1038–1045, "Tobacco Imported into England, by Origin, 1697–1775"; Jacob Price, *France and the Chesapeake: A History of the French Tobacco Monopoly, 1674–1791, and of Its Relationship to the British and American Tobacco Trades,* 2 vols. (Ann Arbor: University of Michigan Press, 1973), 2:845 (statistics 2a); and H. K. Roessingh, *Inlandse tabak: Expansie en contractie van een handelsgewas in de 17e en 18e eeuw in Nederland* (Zutphen: De Walburg Pers, 1976), 246.

Note: The actual figures are most likely higher, as Menard has already shown for the Chesapeake export to England, but because there are no new figures for the re-export to Holland, these somewhat dated figures are used.

hope of arriving at the right moment. That changed after 1640, when regular overseas contacts—including those linking merchants with high colonial officials in Virginia—allowed the Dutch to make prior deals and trade year-round. They used these networks to their advantage during the English Civil War, when they could claim a large share of the Chesapeake tobacco

TABLE 2

Prices of domestic and Virginia tobacco at the Amsterdam exchange, 1674–1737 (guilders per 100 pounds)

Year	PRICE Domestic	Virginia	Year	PRICE Domestic	Virginia
1674	25	28	1706	16	43
1675	16	26	1707	—	—
1676	25	26	1708	15	29
1677	19	30	1709	16	33
1678	—	—	1710	17	29
1679	12	18	1711	19	32
1680	—	—	1712	14	33
1681	—	—	1713	14	33
1682	16	18	1714	16	31
1683	16	24	1715	17	37
1684	—	—	1716	18	34
1685	—	—	1717	25	33
1686	19	29	1718	21	31
1687	—	—	1719	13	28
1688	13	19	1720	12	29
1689	—	—	1721	10	29
1690	—	—	1722	11	25
1691	17	25	1723	13	24
1692	17	21	1724	15	25
1693	—	—	1725	15	33
1694	14	24	1726	18	21
1695	—	—	1727	13	21
1696	15	34	1728	12	19
1697	18	35	1729	10	18
1698	—	—	1730	9	18
1699	—	—	1731	14	18
1700	—	—	1732	13	19
1701	19	18	1733	13	21
1702	—	—	1734	15	23
1703	20	37	1735	13	24
1704	—	—	1736	12	22
1705	14	30	1737	12	21

Sources: Data from Price, *France and the Chesapeake,* 852 (statistics 4); Nicolaas Posthumus, *Nederlandsche Prijsgeschiedenis,* 2 vols. (Leiden, 1943–64), 1:202–8; and Roessingh, *Inlandse tabak,* 532.

TABLE 3
Production of domestic Dutch tobacco and British imports (in millions of Amsterdam pounds)

	Domestic production	British imports
ca. 1675	6	4
ca. 1700	10	8
ca. 1710	18	7
ca. 1730	10	10
ca. 1750	12	17

Source: Data from Roessingh, *Inlandse tabak,* 340.

trade. The Navigation Acts changed the Dutch role without forcing them out. The acts, to be sure, made it more difficult for the Dutch to continue their commerce, but it nonetheless thrived during the 1660s and 1670s, as they used legal loopholes, making it even harder for modern historians to detect their presence. It was not until the 1690s that the direct connection between Virginia and the Dutch Republic ended, not primarily because of the Navigation Acts, but because of the war on trade waged by the French and the introduction of the convoy system. Henceforth, Virginia tobacco kept arriving in the Dutch Republic but solely by way of British ports.

Notes

1. H. R. McIlwaine, ed., *Journals of the House of Burgesses, 1619–1658/9* (Richmond: Colonial Press, E. Waddey, 1915), 76.

2. Robert A. Leath, "Dutch Trade and Its Influence on Seventeenth-Century Chesapeake Furniture," in Luke Beckerdite, ed., *American Furniture 1997* (Hanover, NH: University Press of New England for the Chipstone Foundation, 1997), http://www.chipstone.org/publications/1997AF/Intro/1997Contents.html. See also C. Jane Cox and Al Luckenbach, "The Dutch Connection: 'Providence' within the 17th Century Chesapeake," and Karen B. Wehner, "Transitions and Tradespeople: Artisans on the Road from Town to Colony," papers presented at the January 2007 Society for Historical Archeology Conference in Williamsburg, Virginia.

3. Quoted from "The humble Remonstrance of John Bland of London, merchants, on the behalf of the Inhabitants and Planters in Virginia and Mariland," in "Virginia and the Act of Navigation," *Virginia Magazine of History and Biography* 1 (1893–94): 147–48.

4. Hendrik Karel Roessingh, *Inlandse tabak: Expansie en contractie van een handelsgewas in de 17e en 18e eeuw in Nederland* (Zutphen: De Walburg Pers, 1976), 245–46; R. R. Menard, "The Tobacco Industry in the Chesapeake Colonies, 1617–1730: An Interpretation," *Research in Economic History* 5 (1980): 109–77, appendix.

5. Jacob M. Price, "The Economic Growth of the Chesapeake and the European Market, 1697–1775," *Journal of Economic History* 24 (1964): 500–501; Frank J. A. Broeze, "The New Economic History, the Navigation Acts, and the Continental Tobacco Market, 1770–90," *New History Review* 26, no. 4 (1973): 668–78; David Ormrod, *The Rise of Commercial Empires: England and the Netherlands in the Age of Mercantilism, 1650–1770* (Cambridge: Cambridge University Press, 2003), 183, 199.

6. Simon Groenveld, "The English Civil Wars as a Cause of the First Anglo-Dutch War, 1640–1652," *Historical Journal* 30, no. 3 (1987): 541–66.

7. Peter Wilson Coldham, ed., *English Adventurers and Emigrants, 1609–1660: Abstracts of Examinations in the High Court of Admiralty with Reference to Colonial America* (Baltimore: Genealogical Publishing, 1984), 133–40.

8. Stadsarchief Amsterdam (StA), Notarieel Archief (NA) no. 2217, November 3, 1664.

9. We have concentrated on the notarial archives, in particular of Amsterdam, and have extended the research through 1700. Furthermore, we have made extensive use of the material collected for the Virginia Colonial Records Project. See the website of the Library of Virginia, http://www.lva.lib.va.us. For contacts between Virginia and New Netherlands, see April Lee Hatfield, *Atlantic Virginia: Intercolonial Relations in the Seventeenth Century* (Philadelphia: University of Pennsylvania Press, 2004).

10. Menard, "Tobacco Industry," 152.

11. Roessingh, *Inlandse tabak*; StA, Archief Burgemeesters, portefeuille Handel (tabak).

12. Willem Frijhoff and Maarten Prak, eds., *Geschiedenis van Amsterdam: Zelfbewuste stadstaat, 1650–1813* (Amsterdam: Sun, 2005), 84.

13. Roessingh, *Inlandse tabak*.

14. William L. Shea, *The Virginia Militia in the Seventeenth Century* (Baton Rouge: Louisiana State University Press, 1983), 14.

15. Victor Enthoven, "Een stad te ver: De materiële verzorging van het garnizoen van Oostende," in Werner Thomas, ed., *De val van het nieuwe Troje: Het beleg van Oostende, 1601–1604* (Leuven: Davidsfonds, 2004), 59–71.

16. On Sidney, see Ph. Sidney, Baron De l'Isle and Dudley, *Report on the Manuscripts of Lord De L'Isle & Dudley Preserved at Penshurst Place*, 6 vols., ed. C. L. Kingsford (London: His Majesty's Stationery Office, 1925–66), 2:359 (December 29, 1598), 437 (February 9, 1599 [1600]).

17. Karen Ordahl Kupperman, *The Jamestown Project* (Cambridge, MA: Belknap, 2007), 273–74; Alexander Brown, *The First Republic in America* (Boston: Houghton Mifflin, 1898).

18. Brown, *The First Republic*, 115, 444; Conway W. Sams, *The Conquest of Virginia, the Third Attempt, 1610–1624: Virginia Founded under the Charters of 1609 and 1612: An Account Based on Original Documents of the Establishment of the Colony, by the Virginia Company of London* (New York: G. P. Putnam's, 1939), 34; Millicent V. Hay, *The Life of Robert Sidney, Earl of Leicester, 1563–1626* (Washington, DC: Folger Books, 1984); Andrew Fitzmaurice, *Humanism and America: An Intellectual History of English Colonialism, 1500–1625* (Cambridge: Cambridge University Press, 2003), 62.

19. Stephen Innes, *Creating the Commonwealth: The Economic Culture of Puritan New England* (New York: Norton, 1995), 94–96; Joyce Lorimer, *English and Irish Settlement on the River Amazon, 1550–1646* (London: Hakluyt Society, 1989); Victor Enthoven, *Zeeland en de opkomst van de Republiek: Handel en strijd in de Scheldedelta, c. 1550–1621* (Leiden: Luctor et Victor, 1996).

20. Sidney, *Report on the Manuscripts*, 3:74, 80, 4:21, 130–31, 5:233, 239, 252, 259, 260; John

Parker, *Van Meteren's Virginia, 1607–1612* (Minneapolis: University of Minnesota Press, 1961), 56, 71, 77; Edward Wright Haile, *Jamestown Narratives: Eyewitness Accounts of the Virginia Colony, the First Decade, 1607–1617* (Champlain, VA: RoundHouse, 2001), 46–47; *Resoluties der Staten-Generaal 1607–1609*, Rijks Geschiedkundige Publicatien, grote serie no. 131,(The Hague: Nijhoff, 1970), 523 (April 24, 1608), 793 (March 19, 1609); *Resoluties der Staten-Generaal 1610–1612*, Rijks Geschiedkundige Publicatien, grote serie no. 135 (The Hague: Nijhoff, 1971), 321 (February 12, 1611).

21. Shea, *The Virginia Militia*, 22–23; Haile, *Jamestown Narratives*, 45; Parker, *Van Meteren's Virginia*, 75–80; *Resoluties der Staten-Generaal 1610–1612*, Rijks Geschiedkundige Publicatien, grote serie no. 135, (The Hague: Nijhoff, 1971), 302 (January 20, 1611); *Resoluties der Staten-Generaal 1613–1616*, Rijks Geschiedkundige Publicatien, grote serie no. 151 (The Hague: Nijhoff, 1984), 333 (September 30, 1614); *Resoluties der Staten-Generaal 1617–1618*, Rijks Geschiedkundige Publicatien, grote serie no. 153 (The Hague: Nijhoff, 1975), 331, (February 6, 1618).

22. John Bennett Boddie, "Edward Bennett of London and Virginia," *William and Mary Quarterly*, 2nd ser., 13 (1933): 117–30.

23. Susan Myra Kingsbury, ed., *The Records of the Virginia Company of London: The Court Book, from the Manuscript in the Library of Congress*, 4 vols. (Washington, DC: Government Printing Office, 1906–35), 1:368, 372, 428, 2:115; Edmund S. Morgan, *American Slavery, American Freedom: The Ordeal of Colonial Virginia* (New York: Norton, 1975), 154; Philip A. Bruce, *Social Life of Virginia in the Seventeenth Century: An Inquiry into the Origin of the Higher Planting Class, Together with an Account of the Habits, Customs, and Diversions of the People* (Williamstown, MA: Corner House, 1907), 97. Westerhouse was an Amsterdam merchant whose original name was Willem Westerhuizen. Claudia Schnurmann, *Atlantische Welten: Engländer und Niederländer im amerikanisch-atlantischen Raum 1648–1713* (Cologne: Böhlau Verlag, 1998), 129n414. Other men with a Dutch background were Goslin van Netsen, Hendrick van Doveracke, and the following residents who were naturalized in the 1660s: Lawrence van Slott, Henry Wageman, Herman Keldermans, and Michael Wallandighan. Ibid., 247, 261. Yet other names are hard to retrieve because they were written phonetically in English. Pieter Claessen from Middelburg, for instance, who lived in "Warenscreek" (Warrosquyoake or Warehouse Creek?) in Virginia in 1650, may have been the same as the settler whose name was spelled Peter Clauce and Peter Clause. W. G. D. Murray, "De Rotterdamsche toeback-coopers," *Rotterdamsch jaarboekje*, 5th ser., 1 (1943): 31; Nell Marion Nugent, *Cavaliers and Pioneers: Abstracts of Virginia Land Patents and Grants, 1623–1666* (Baltimore: Genealogical Publishing, 1963), 307, 455.

24. Zeeuws Archief (ZA), Archief Baljuw van de wateren.

25. Roessingh, *Inlandse tabak*, 188–89; Enthoven, *Zeeland en de opkomst van de Republiek*, 259, 263, 305; Jan Kupp, "Dutch Notarial Acts Relating to the Tobacco Trade of Virginia, 1608–1653," *William and Mary Quarterly*, 3rd ser., 30 (1973): 653–55; George Louis Beer, *The Origins of the British Colonial System, 1578–1660* (New York: Peter Smith, 1933), 239n2; Peter Walne, "The 'Running Lottery' of the Virginia Company in Reading, 1619, and in Chester, 1619," *Virginia Magazine of History and Biography* 70 (1962): 34.

26. Rolfe to Sandys, January 1619/20, in Kingsbury, *Records of the Virginia Company*, 3:243–44; Nationaal Archief, Archieven Admiraliteitscollege 2425, Register van de Commissien ende instructien van de Admiraliteijt in Zeelland, 1606–1625, f. 163r. The pilot, Marmaduke Rayner, had close connections with the Netherlands. He actually sent an account of the first General Assembly of Virginia (August 9–14, 1619) to the English am-

bassador in The Hague. Alexander Brown, *English Politics in Early Virginia History* (Boston: Houghton Mifflin, 1901), 167; Brown, *The First Republic*, 362, 373, 379, 418, 454; Peter Wilson Coldham, "The Voyage of the *Neptune* to Virginia, 1618–1619, and the Disposition of Its Cargo," *Virginia Magazine of History and Biography* 87 (1979): 30–67; Tim Hashaw, *The Birth of Black America: The First African Americans and the Pursuit of Freedom at Jamestown* (New York: Carroll and Graf, 2007), 70–75; Linda A. Heywood and John K. Thornton, *Central Africans, Atlantic Creoles, and the Foundation of the Americas, 1585–1660* (Cambridge: Cambridge University Press), 6–7, 28.

27. London Port Book, Christmas 1626–Christmas 1627, Virginia Colonial Records Project, Survey Report no. 3,668.

28. See the website of the Rotterdam Archive under notarial deeds, http://appl.gemeentearchief.rotterdam.nl.

29. Jacob M. Price and Paul G. E. Clemens, "A Revolution of Scale in Overseas Trade: British Firms in the Chesapeake Trade, 1675–1775," *Journal of Economic History* 47, no. 1 (1987):1–43.

30. Johannes de Laet, *Jaerlyck Verhael van de Verrichtinghen der Gheoctroyeerde West-Indische Compagnie in derthien Boecken*, ed. S. P. L'Honoré Naber and J. C. M. Warnsinck, 4 vols. (The Hague: Nijhoff, 1931–1937), 1:7.

31. Enthoven, *Zeeland en de opkomst van de Republiek*, 263. In 1624, master and shipowner David Pietersz de Vries offered his ship for sale to the directors of the West India Company. He had intended to sail to Virginia, but they had not allowed him to do so. StA, NA no. 388, f. 171, April 3, 1624; see also f. 194, April 13, 1624. It is likely that Virginia actually refers to New Netherland in his deposition.

32. Philip A. Bruce, *Economic History of Virginia in the Seventeenth Century: An Inquiry into the Material Condition of the People, Based upon Original and Contemporaneous Records* 2 vols. (New York: Macmillan, 1907), 1:264–66.

33. StA, NA no. 286, ff. 237–38, May 4, 1621.

34. Sir Dudley Carleton to the Privy Council, February 5, 1622, Miscellaneous papers concerning the history of the colony of Virginia, National Archives, Kew (NAK), Colonial Office (CO) 1/2, f. 1; Virginia Colonial Records Project, Survey Report no. 623; Leath, "Dutch Trade and Its Influence."

35. Murray, "Toeback-coopers," 34. For a Dutch vessel trading in Virginia in 1625, see Beer, *Origins of the British Colonial System*, 232n2.

36. Oliver A. Rink, *Holland on the Hudson: An Economic and Social History of Dutch New York* (Ithaca, NY: Cornell University Press; Cooperstown, NY: New York State Historical Association, 1986), 106; Jaap Jacobs, *New Netherland: A Dutch Colony in Seventeenth-Century America* (Leiden: Brill, 2005), 66–67; Charles R. Boxer, *De Nederlanders in Brazilië, 1624–1654* (Amsterdam: Atlas, 1993), 99–100.

37. StA, NA no. 832, f. 474, August 3, 1634, no. 701, f. 693, August 7, 1634, no. 1224, f. 79, August 7, 1634. Probably the same ship made a trip in the summer of 1640 from Amsterdam to Dutch Brazil, the West Indies, Virginia, and New Netherland before returning to Amsterdam. StA, NA no. 1059, f. 176, December 18, 1641.

38. StA, NA no. 1626B, f. 1215, July 4, 1641.

39. John R. Pagan, "Dutch Maritime and Commercial Activity in Mid-Seventeenth-Century Virginia," *Virginia Magazine of History and Biography* 90 (1982): 486.

40. StA, NA no. 688, no folio, August 12, 1643.

41. StA, NA no. 1555, f. 1059, May 28, 1640.

42. StA, NA no. 1300, f. 102, June 14, 1651.

43. StA, NA no. 1626B, f. 1215, June 4, 1641.

44. David Peterson de Vries, *Voyages from Holland to America*, A.D. 1632–1644 (New York: Kraus Reprint, 1971), 108, 112–13.

45. Pagan, "Dutch Maritime and Commercial Activity," 489; StA, NA no. 832, f. 474, August 3, 1634, no. 1555, f. 1059, May 28, 1640.

46. De Vries, *Voyages*, 112, 183; Pagan, "Dutch Maritime and Commercial Activity," 491–93; Susie M. Ames, *Studies of the Virginia Eastern Shore in the Seventeenth Century* (Richmond: Dietz, 1940), 45; Enthoven, "An Assessment of Dutch Transatlantic Commerce," in Johannes Postma and Victor Enthoven, eds., *Dutch Transatlantic Trade and Shipping, 1585–1817* (Leiden: Brill, 2003), 403.

47. On Vermande: Gemeentearchief Rotterdam (GAR), Oud Notarieel Archief (ONA) no. 154, f. 168/259, January 23, 1649; Roelof Bijlsma, "Rotterdam's Amerika-vaart in de eerste helft der 17de eeuw," *Bijdragen voor Vaderlandsche Geschiedenis en Oudheidkunde*, 5th ser., 3 (1916): 133. Jan Jansz de Colonia (ca. 1600–ca. 1660) was the only one born outside of Rotterdam, in the town of Oudenbosch, but he soon moved to the port city: GAR, ONA no. 131, f. 36/97, March 7, 1630, no. 137, f. 307/443, October 2, 1631, no. 166, f. 28/53, March 30, 1634, no. 209, f. 10/24, September 19, 1647, no. 146, f. 243/716, August 19, 1660. On Vethuysen: GAR, ONA no. 153, f. 456/663, August 25, 1646. On Blenck: GAR, ONA no. 60 f. 177/574, February 27, 1624; Blenk's birth: GAR, ONA no. 141, f. 308/473, November 9, 1632; Blenk's burial on August 18, 1652: GAR, Doop-, Trouw- en begrafenisboeken Rotterdam no. 44.

48. GAR, ONA no. 135, f. 265/361, June 9, 1640, no. 115, f. 30/37, September 10, 1643, no. 153, f. 323/459, November 18, 1645; Pagan, "Dutch Maritime and Commercial Activity," 490; Murray, "Toeback-coopers," 30–31.

49. J. Hall Pleasants, ed., *Archives of Maryland*, vol. 51, *Proceedings of the Court of Chancery of Maryland, 1669–1679*, Court Series (5) (Baltimore: Maryland Historical Society, 1934), 66. At least one other Rotterdam merchant, the Englishman William Moseley, took up residence in Virginia. Pagan, "Dutch Maritime and Commercial Activity," 488n9. Moseley, who was still in Rotterdam in 1639, was justice of Lower Norfolk County from 1649 until his death in 1655. GAR, ONA no. 94, f. 252/429, act of January 20, 1639; "Families of Lower Norfolk and Princess Anne Counties," *Virginia Magazine of History and Biography* 5 (1898): 328.

50. StA, NA no. 1289, f. 101v–102v, July 20, 1644.

51. Lyon G. Tyler, "Virginia under the Commonwealth," *William and Mary Quarterly*, 1st ser., 1 (1893): 189–96; Carla G. Pestana, *The English Atlantic in an Age of Revolution, 1640–1661* (Cambridge, MA: Harvard University Press, 2004), 101; Simon Groenveld, *Verlopend getij: De Nederlandse Republiek en de Engelse burgeroorlog, 1640–1646* (Amsterdam: De Bataafsche Leeuw, 1984), 173–98, especially 176 and 193; StA, NA no. 1573, f. 605, October 10, 1646.

52. Richard Kemp to Charles I, September 27/October 7, 1644, *Calendar of State Papers Colonial*, 2:175–76; Groenveld, *Verlopend getij*, 206; Warren M. Billings, *Sir William Berkeley and the Forging of Colonial Virginia* (Baton Rouge: Louisiana State University Press, 2004), 99.

53. Robert Brenner, *Merchants and Revolution: Commercial Change, Political Conflict, and London's Overseas Traders, 1550–1653* (Cambridge: Cambridge University Press, 1993), 129–34; Jon Kukla, *Political Institutions in Virginia, 1619–1660* (New York: Garland, 1989), 82–86.

54. Pagan, "Dutch Maritime and Commercial Activity," 492–93; Bruce, *Economic History*, 2:306.

55. Beer, *British Colonial System*, 356.

56. Pagan, "Dutch Maritime and Commercial Activity," 493; McIlwaine, *Journals of the House of Burgesses*, 74.

57. Brenner, *Merchants and Revolution*, 585.

58. Ibid., 593, 597; Pagan, "Dutch Maritime and Commercial Activity," 494; J. E. Farnell, "The Navigation Act of 1651, the First Dutch War, and the London Merchant Company," *Economic History Review* 16 (1964): 443, 454.

59. Groenveld, "The English Civil Wars," 561; Jaap R. Bruijn, "Dutch Privateering during the Second and Third Anglo-Dutch Wars," *Low Countries History Yearbook: Acta Historiae Neerlandicae* 11 (1978): 79–93.

60. StA, NA no. 1097, f. 512, September 1, 1651, no. 1100, f. 68, May 17, 1652.

61. Coldham, *English Adventurers*, 133–39; StA NA no. 1511, f. 20, October 18, 1652, no. 1753, f. 426, August 14, 1652, no. 1753, f. 408, August 5, 1652, no. 1698, f. 1638, December 3, 1652; Pagan, "Dutch Maritime and Commercial Activity," 495; Tyler, "Virginia under the Commonwealth," 192; James R. Perry, *The Formation of a Society on Virginia's Eastern Shore, 1615–1655* (Chapel Hill: University of North Carolina Press, 1990), 218–19; Northampton County Deeds, Wills, Etc., no. 4, 1651–54, ff. 126–29, f. 144, f. 162.

62. NAK, High Court of Admiralty 13/68, ff. 122–23, quoted in Pagan, "Dutch Maritime and Commercial Activity," 497.

63. Billings, *Sir William Berkeley*, 23–24, 108, 111; Sir William Berkeley, *The Speech of the Honourable . . . 17. March 1650/1* (The Hague: Samuel Broun, 1651); William Berkeley, *De reden van de eerwaerdige sr. VVilhelm Berkley gouverneur ende capiteyn generael van Virginea, aen de gedeputeerden des volcks in de generaele vergaderinghe tot James stadt op den 27. maert, 1651. gedaen* (The Hague: Samuel Broun, 1651).

64. GAR, ONA no. 204, f. 288/435, July 26, 1643, no. 152, f. 647/957, August 29, 1643; Ralph T. Whitelaw, *Virginia's Eastern Shore: A History of Northampton and Accomack Counties*, 2 vols. (1951; reprint, Gloucester, MA: Peter Smith, 1968), 1:148–49, 108, 289. See also Kukla, *Political Institutions*, 112A–113.

65. In the 1640s, Glover, whose attorney in Virginia was Richard Lee, had a business connections with numerous Virginia planters. A list of bills and debts due to Glover in 1646 included Berkeley, George Ludlowe, Samuel Abbott, Francis Ceeley, Capt. Bridges Freeman, Augustine Warner, Robert Holte, Capt. Ralph Wormeley, Stephen Gill, Francis Coole, Robert Kinsey, George Saughier, John Chew, William Light, Richard Lee, Rowland Vauhan, Nicholas Brooke Jr., Wm. Brooke Sr. and Jr., Henry Brooke, Mrs. Mary Minifee, and Wm. Hinde. The total debt was 57,094 pounds of tobacco. Beverley Fleet, ed., *Virginia Colonial Abstracts*, vol. 24, *York County* (Baltimore: Genealogical Publishing, 1961), 66. Richard Glover may have moved from Zeeland to London in the late 1630s. In 1639, he was described as a "merchant of London." StA, NA no. 1609, ff. 43–46, June 29, 1639.

66. Billings, *Sir William Berkeley*, 95–96; Pagan, "Dutch Maritime and Commercial Activity," 489; Ames, *Studies of the Virginia Eastern Shore*, 45–49.

67. Jon Kukla, "Order and Chaos in Early America: Political and Social Stability in Pre-Restoration Virginia," *American Historical Review* 90, no. 2 (April 1985): 290n47; Charles E. Hatch, *The First Seventeen Years: Virginia, 1607–1624* (Williamsburg: Virginia 350th Anniversary Celebration Corporation, 1957), 92. The Eastern Shore was originally called Accomack County and renamed Northampton County in 1643. James R. Perry,

The Formation of a Society on Virginia's Eastern Shore, 1615–1655 (Chapel Hill: University of North Carolina Press, 1990), 9.

68. Perry, *Formation of a Society*, 150–52; Whitelaw, *Virginia's Eastern Shore;* Bruce, *Social Life of Virginia*, 260–261. Michielsz remained a merchant and became a large landowner. In his will, he left all of his "Dutch Bookes" to his younger brother. John Johnson may also have been a merchant from Graft. Nugent, *Cavaliers and Pioneers* 316, 324–25, 382. Aries Topp's real name may have been Arien Willemsz Top: GAR, ONA no. 215, f. 12/30, May 18, 1654.

69. Schnurmann, *Atlantische Welten*, 128–43; Hatfield, *Atlantic Virginia*, 97–101.

70. Nugent, *Cavaliers and Pioneers*, 98, 104–5.

71. Between 1641 and 1656 the Verbrugge Company sent fourteen ships directly from Amsterdam to Virginia. Rink, *Holland on the Hudson*, 178–80.

72. Jaap Jacobs, *Een zegenrijk gewest: Nieuw-Nederland in de zeventiende eeuw* (Amsterdam: Prometheus-Bert Bakker, 1999), 203; Jacobs, *New Netherland*, 228, 253, 484; Pagan, "Dutch Maritime and Commercial Activity," 487–88; StA, NA no. 1621A, f. 88, December 16, 1639, no. 1624, f. 394, December 19, 1639, no. 1499, f. 179, December 28, 1639, no. 1281, f. 6, January 9, 1640, no. 1281, f. 50, May 2, 1640, no. 1500, f. 13, May 9, 1640, no. 1555, f. 1059, May 28, 1640, no. 1500, f. 35, June 2, 1640, no. 1281, f. 71, June 29, 1640, no. 1333, f. 81, June 29, 1640, no. 1333, f. 82, June 29, 1640, no. 1555, f. 1113, July 30, 1640, no. 731, f. 750, August 21, 1640, no. 696, reg. 93, July 8, 1641, no. 1501, f. 165, November 26, 1641, no. 1571, f. 753, September 13, 1643.

73. Claudia Schnurmann, "Atlantic Trade and American Identities: The Correlation of Supranational Commerce, Political Opportunities, and Colonial Regionalism," in Peter A. Coclanis, ed., *The Atlantic Economy during the Seventeenth and Eighteenth Centuries: Organization, Operation, Practice, and Personnel* (Columbia: University of South Carolina Press, 2005), 186–20; April Lee Hatfield, "Dutch and New Netherland Merchants in the Seventeenth-Century English Chesapeake," in Coclanis, *The Atlantic Economy*, 205–28; John C. Appleby, "Between the Bays: Anglo-Dutch Competition in the Chesapeake and Delaware Bay Regions from the 1620s to the 1660s," *Tijdschrift voor Zeegeschiedenis* 24, no. 1 (2005): 21–42.

74. "The Randolph Manuscript," *Virginia Magazine of History and Biography* 17 (1909): 243–44.

75. On Herrman see Christian J. Koot, "The Merchant, the Map, and Empire: Augustin Herrman's Chesapeake and Interimperial Trade, 1644–73," *William and Mary Quarterly*, 3rd ser., 67 (October 2010): 603–44. StA, NA no. 1835, f. 529, October 28, 1647, no. 899, f. 448, August 1, 1648, no. 214, f. 33, May 8, 1653.

76. They included the *Fortuin, Gouden leeuw, Vaarwel, Liefde, Hoop, Jonge Honingvat, Gelderse Blom, Faam, Sint Machiel, Hartoch Leopoldus, Anna van Newcastle,* and *Maecht van Gendt.* To avoid seizure in Virginia several of these ships, such as the *Hartoch Leopoldus* and the *Maecht van Gendt,* were neutralized in ports in the Spanish Netherlands, using neutral ships' papers. The *Anna van Newcastle* would probably have used English papers. StA, NA no. 110, f. 68, May 17, 1652, no. 2280/1, f. 44, April 5, 1652, no. 1511, f. 20, October 18, 1652, no. 1837, f. 803, November 2, 1652, no. 1698, f. 1638, December 3, 1652, no. 1349, f. 19, February 27, 1653, no. 1103, f. 286, February 23, 1653, no. 2114, f. 33, May 8, 1653, no. 1891, f. 318, May 15, 1653, no. 1512, f. 3, December 2, 1653, no. 1577, f. 792, August 5, 1654, no. 2031, f. 380, October 23, 1654, no. 2197, f. 698, November 29, 1654.

77. Lothrop Withingon, "Arrivals from Virginia in 1656. Add. M. SS. 34015, Vol. II., British Museum," *William and Mary Quarterly*, 1st ser., 21 (1913): 262.

78. The *Golden Flower of Plymouth* was arrested in Amsterdam on the pretext of illicit trade. On behalf of the owner, Diego Rodrigues Arias, Rodrigues Carion and Abraham Valveerde had to settle the case. StA, NA no. 2207, f. 209, July 31, 1659.

79. StA, NA no. 1484, f. 447, December 6, 1651.

80. Northampton County Deeds and Wills, 1654–55, Laurence Coughen to John Brown, July 9, 1651, published in Warren M. Billings, ed., *The Old Dominion in the Seventeenth Century: A Documentary History of Virginia, 1606–1689* (Chapel Hill: University of North Carolina Press, 1975),184–85.

81. Bernard Christian Steiner, ed., *Archives of Maryland*, vol. 41, *Proceedings of the Provincial Court of Maryland, 1658–1662*, Court Series (3) (Baltimore: Maryland Historical Society, 1922), 406–7.

82. Fleet, *Virginia Colonial Abstracts*, 82; J. Hall Pleasants, ed., *Archives of Maryland*, vol. 52, *Proceedings of the County Court of Charles County, 1658–1666, and Manor Court of St. Clement's Manor, 1659–1672*, Court Series (6) (Baltimore: Maryland Historical Society, 1936), 622–23. In 1645, the captain of the Dutch ship *Medea* ceded debts contracted in the preceding year to Virginians Jan Gibbs, Willem Laurear, Richard Kemp, Willem Russen, Jan Gerby, and Thomas Bourbage. Act of August 14, 1645. In 1646, Dominicus Cryger commissioned boatswain Egbert Theunissen to reclaim from Francoys Farley 110 pounds of tobacco, from Robert Mason and Patrick Jackson jointly 110 pounds, and from William Carter 20 pounds. Kupp, "Calendar."

83. Pleasants, *Archives of Maryland* 52:466–76, 516–18.

84. Bruce, *Economic History*, 1:290–91; Pagan, "Dutch Maritime and Commercial Activity," 491.

85. Minnie G. Cook, "Governor Samuel Mathews, Junior," *William and Mary Quarterly*, 2nd ser., 14 (1934): 105–13; Billings, *Sir William Berkeley*, 126–27.

86. Sir William Berkeley, *A Discourse and View of Virginia* (1663; reprint, Norwalk, CT: W. H. Smith Jr., 1914), 4; Harold Lee Hitchens, "Sir William Berkeley, Virginian Economist," *William and Mary Quarterly*, 2nd ser., 18 (1938): 158–73; Joan de Lourdes Leonard, "Operation Checkmate: The Birth and Death of a Virginia Blueprint for Progress, 1660–1676," *William and Mary Quarterly*, 3rd ser., 24 (1967): 44–74.

87. For a discussion on free trade to the English colonies, see Christian J. Koot, "A 'Dangerous Principle': Free Trade Discourses in Barbados and the English Leeward Islands, 1650–1689," *Early American Studies* 5, no. 1 (Spring 2007): 132–63.

88. Not all Dutch ships evaded confiscation. One famous victim of the Second Anglo-Dutch War was the Dutch West India Company ship *Wapen van Amsterdam* (*Arms of Amsterdam*). In June 1663, English privateers captured the ship, carrying dyewood and 101 African slaves, off the Cayman Islands and brought it to Virginia. Kenneth Scott, "The *Arms of Amsterdam*: An Extract from the Records of the General Court of Virginia, 1664," *Virginia Magazine of History and Biography* 77 (1969): 406–40; E. B. O'Callaghan, *Voyages of the Slavers St. John and Arms of Amsterdam, 1659, 1663; Together with Additional Papers Illustrative of the Slave Trade under the Dutch* (Albany, NY: J. Munsell, 1867); StA, NA no. 1370, f. 79, July 4, 1664, f. 101, July 7, 1664.

89. J. C. M. Warnsinck, *Abraham Crijnssen: De verovering van Suriname en zijn aanslag op Virginië* (Amsterdam: Noord-Hollandsche Uitgeversmaatschappij, 1936), 66; Shea, *The Virginia Militia*, 89–91. For the auction of Crijnssen's prizes, see ZA, Archief Rekenkamer C 44430, f. 79, 195, 260, 263.

90. Shea, *The Virginia Militia*, 94–95; Cornelis de Waard, *De Zeeuwsche expeditie naar*

de West onder Cornelis Evertsen den Jonge, 1672–1674 (The Hague: Nijhoff, 1928), 36; Donald G. Shomette and Robert D. Haslach, *Raids on America: The Dutch Naval Campaign of 1672–1674* (Columbia: University of South Carolina Press, 1988), 139–51; Doeke Roos, *Twee eeuwen varen en vechten, 1550–1750: het admiraalsgeslacht Evertsen* (Vlissingen: ADZ, 2003), 324; StA, NA no. 4300, f. 361, September 3, 1674. The proceeds of this expedition, including the auction of three vessels and over 3,000 hogsheads of tobacco, were 115,000 guilders. ZA, Familie Verheye van Citters 30.2, De princen verovert door de Commandeurs Binckes en Everts, 1674.

91. De Lourdes Leonard, "Operation Checkmate"; Billings, *Sir William Berkeley*, 133, 140–41; David R. Owen and Michael C. Tolley, *Courts of Admiralty in Colonial America: The Maryland Experience, 1634–1776* (Durham, NC: Carolina Academic Press, 1995), 102–3; Kukla, "Order and Chaos," 294. On the several Navigation Laws, see Lawrence Averell Harper, *The English Navigation Laws: A Seventeenth-Century Experiment in Social Engineering* (New York: Columbia University Press, 1939). On the laws and Virginia, especially their effect on the coastal trade, see David C. Klingaman, *Colonial Virginia's Coastwise and Grain Trade* (New York: Arno, 1975), 21–25; and Malcolm C. Clark, "The Coastwise and Caribbean Trade of the Chesapeake Bay, 1696–1776" (Ph.D. diss., Georgetown University, 1970), 159.

92. "The humble Remonstrance of John Bland of London, merchants, on the behalf of the Inhabitants and Planters in Virginia and Mariland," in "Virginia and the Act of Navigation," *Virginia Magazine of History and Biography* 1 (1893–94): 149–51. For more on Virginia's free trade pleas, see E. A. J. Johnson, *American Economic Thought in the Seventeenth Century* (London: P. S. King and Son, 1932), especially chap. 8; and Christian J. Koot, "In Pursuit of Profit: Persistent Dutch Influence on the Inter-Imperial Trade of New York and the English Leeward Islands, 1621–1689" (Ph.D. diss., University of Delaware, 2005), 378–79.

93. Billings, *Sir William Berkeley*, 160–61; Hitchens, "Sir William Berkeley"; de Lourdes Leonard, "Operation Checkmate"; Pagan, "Dutch Maritime and Commercial Activity," 499; John. J. McCusker, "British Mercantilist Policies and the American Colonies," in Stanley L. Engerman and Robert E. Gallman, eds., *The Cambridge Economic History of the United States*, vol. 1, *The Colonial Era* (New York: Cambridge University Press, 1996), 338, 348–52.

94. Harper, *The English Navigation Laws*, 59–60; Klingaman, *Colonial Virginia's Coastwise and Grain Trade*, 13–17, 21; Clark, "The Coastwise and Caribbean Trade," 159.

95. Pagan, "Dutch Maritime and Commercial Activity," 499–500; Harper, *The English Navigation Laws*, 60–61; Klingaman, *Colonial Virginia's Coastwise and Grain Trade*, 22–23; Clark, "The Coastwise and Caribbean Trade," 161–62.

96. Pagan, "Dutch Maritime and Commercial Activity," 499; Menard, "Tobacco Industry," 152.

97. StA, NA no. 1983, f. 386, August 22, 1670; S. van Berkel, "Eene memorie over den handel der West-Indische Compagnie omstreeks 1670," *Bijdragen en Mededelingen van het Historisch Genootschap* 35 (1914): 88–104, especially 104.

98. StA, NA no. 1152 II, f. 77, August 14, 1664.

99. After laying in Leith for three weeks, Sprieteman got in a dispute with Lockwarm and was dismissed. Eventually, with a different master, the ship set sail to Virginia. StA, NA no. 3511, f. 68, November 22, 1666, no. 3416, no folio, October 11, 1668. On the illicit to-

bacco trade and Scotland, see Robert C. Nash, "The English and Scottish Tobacco Trades in the Seventeenth and Eighteenth Centuries: Legal and Illegal Trade," *Economic History Review* 35 (1982): 354–72.

100. Owen and Tolley, *Courts of Admiralty*, 255, 259.

101. Coldham, *English Adventurers*, 17–20. This is corroborated by the Survey Reports of the papers of the High Court of Admiralty in the Virginia Colonial Records Project, http://ajax.lva.lib.va.us. John F. Jameson, *Privateering and Piracy in the Colonial Period: Illustrative Documents* (New York: Macmillan, 1923); George Reese, ed., *Proceedings in the Court of Vice-Admiralty of Virginia, 1698–1775* (Richmond: Virginia State Library, 1983).

102. Josiah Child, *A New Discourse of Trade . . .* , 4th ed. (1693; reprint, London, 1740), xxiv.

103. Koot, "In Pursuit of Profit," 338; Cathy Matson, *Merchants and Empire: Trading in Colonial New York* (Baltimore: Johns Hopkins University Press, 1998), 79.

104. British Library, London, Sloane 54, Cowleys Voyage round the world, 1683–1686, f. 2, August 4/14, 1683; Schnurmann, *Atlantische Welten*, 330.

105. Schnurmann, *Atlantische Welten*, 332–35.

106. The National Archives, Kew (TNA), CO 1/63, ff. 278–81, cited in Schnurmann, *Atlantische Welten*, 330.

107. Jean S. Bromley, *Corsairs and Navies, 1660–1760* (London: Hambledon, 1987), 43–72; Johan Francke, *"Utiliteyt voor de Gemeen Saake": De Zeeuwse commissievaart en haar achterban tijdens de Negenjarige Orlog, 1688–97*, Werken uitgegeven door het Koninklijk Zeeuwsch Genootschap der Wetenschappen no. 12 (Middelburg: Koninklijk Zeeuwsch Genootschap der Wetenschappen, 2001), 308.

108. Douglas Bradburn, "The Visible Fist: The Chesapeake Tobacco Trade in War and the Purpose of Empire, 1690–1715," *William and Mary Quarterly*, 3rd ser. (forthcoming).

109. Lorena Wals, "Summing the Parts: Implications for Estimating Chesapeake Output and Income Subregionally," *William and Mary Quarterly*, 3rd ser., 56 (1999): 53–94.

110. Bradburn, "The Visible Fist"; John M. Hemphill, "Virginia and the English Commercial System, 1689–1733: Studies in the Development and Fluctuations of a Colonial Economy under Imperial Control" (Ph.D. diss., Princeton University, 1964), 5.

111. Bradburn, "The Visible Fist." On the changed scale of the trade in London, see Jacob Price and Paul G. E. Clemens, "A Revolution in Scale in Overseas Trade: British Firms in the Chesapeake Trade, 1675–1775," *Journal of Economic History* 1 (1987): 1–43.

112. See, for instance, Henry Roseveare, ed., *Markets and Merchants of the Late Seventeenth Century: The Marescoe-David Letters, 1668–1680* (Oxford: Oxford University Press, 1987).

113. Roessingh, *Inlandse tabak*, 236. In 1705/6 John Linton, a London manufacturer of spun tobacco, noticed: "The Virginia trade seems to be in the greatest danger, the Dutch increasingly and improving their tobacco Plantations soe much in quality as well as quantity, I fear they have the assistance of some skild in the way of Planting and curing our own Plantation Tobacco." NAK, CO 5/1315/16, f. 47, cited in Roessingh, *Inlandse tabak*, 230.

"To Seeke for Justice"

Gender, Servitude, and Household Governance in the Early Modern Chesapeake

Terri L. Snyder

In the autumn of 1666, a young woman named Joan Powell boarded a ship at Bristol bound for England's North American colonies. Powell was about twenty when she made this journey, and her reasons for doing so probably were unexceptional. Like the three hundred other men and women who left Bristol that year, she likely faced few prospects in England and ventured to the Chesapeake for better opportunities. Either at port or on board Powell indentured herself to Henry Smith, and as she accompanied him to his home in Accomack County, on Virginia's Eastern Shore, her hopes may have dampened considerably. Less than two years after arriving in Virginia, in 1668, Powell stood before the local court, and, along with Smith's other bound laborers, most of them women, related a harrowing tale that encompassed servant abuse, spousal cruelty, subornation of perjury, and, most seriously, rape and homicide.[1]

Nearly forty years later, in 1703, Jane Webb, a mixed-race Virginian of about twenty-one years of age, indentured herself to Thomas Savage, a middling planter from Northampton County on Virginia's Eastern Shore. Because Webb's mother was an English servant and her father a slave, she had already been in service for most of her life. According to Virginia law, Webb had been bound out as an orphan because of her out-of-wedlock birth and mixed-race origins.[2] Shortly after gaining her liberty from this first period of service, she re-entered servitude. Webb no doubt had typical reasons for doing so, as service provided employment and the promise of material support. She also had more exceptional motives for making her indenture: by serving Thomas Savage for seven years, she was allowed to marry his enslaved man, Left. The contract between Webb and Savage generated legal proof of Jane Webb's term of service, provided a quasi-legal recognition of her marriage to the enslaved Left, and established the freedom and legitimacy of their progeny. Yet eventually its terms would be disputed, and Jane Webb, like Joan Powell before her, would also make her way to the local court to defend her rights.[3]

Timing, race, and masters channeled the experiences of Joan Powell and Jane Webb in two very distinct directions.[4] Powell typified an early generation of women servants, the majority of whom emigrated from the British Isles and, once in Virginia, were outnumbered by their male counterparts by as much as four to one. If these women survived the customary five to seven year term of service (and only 30 to 50 percent would do so), and if they did not become pregnant out of wedlock (as at least 20 percent of them did), they married late, with relative upward mobility, and bore fewer children relative to their counterparts in England and New England.[5] If Joan Powell had the good fortune to survive her term of indenture, she might indeed find the opportunity that she sought in leaving England.

But much had changed forty years later, when Jane Webb indentured herself to Thomas Savage. Virginia's mortality rates had improved and sex ratios were more balanced, but the colony's labor supply was shifting from servants to slaves. As the influx of bound laborers from the British Isles dwindled, Native American, mixed-race, and Native-born Virginians filled out the ranks of servants.[6] For mixed-race Jane Webb—who witnessed a steady circumscription in the rights of free blacks as well as the solidification of slave codes during her lifetime—the meaning of freedom was uncertain.[7] Moreover, the institutionalization of slavery, the prohibition on interracial marriage, and the small free black population circumscribed Webb's prospects for marriage. Since free black women outnumbered their male counterparts, perhaps by as much as two to one, they might more easily find their mates from the ranks of the enslaved, and at any rate, family formation for free women of color remained difficult.[8] Powell and Webb also occupied differently constituted households. In the 1660s, Powell lived and worked in or near Henry Smith's house with about thirteen other servants, all of them probably of English origins.[9] Forty years later, Thomas Savage's household reflected Virginia's transition to a slave society. It encompassed Savage's family, Jane Webb, her enslaved husband, eventually their seven children, and seven other slaves. The unfree members of the Savage household may have lived and worked in quarters separate from the master.[10]

Despite the years that separated Joan Powell and Jane Webb, their location on the Eastern Shore of early modern Virginia played a meaningful role in their experiences of indentured servitude. This was the case partly because the Shore was physically separated from the mainland and partly because it was home to a sizable free black population. By 1663 two counties, Accomack and Northampton, comprised the whole of the lengthy spit of land that separates the Chesapeake Bay from the Atlantic Ocean.[11] The Shore held about 8 percent of Virginia's population from the 1650s forward; by the end of the seventeenth century, the total population numbered approximately five thousand.[12] The geographical isolation of the region may have made it a lacuna of some official oversight; local legal institutions developed a regard for customary law over statute or English common law. Especially when it came to servants, Shore practices deviated from English models in ways that favored masters.[13] Outside the rarified ranks of the wealthiest planters, employment of white servants was the rule for most of the seventeenth century. Free blacks also filled out the ranks of the servant class, particularly because, from the colonial period through the eve of the Civil War, the Eastern Shore was also home to Virginia's largest population of free blacks.[14] Even after transatlantic slave shipments began to arrive in the colony with greater frequency, only about 20 percent of middling households claimed ownership of slaves.[15]

While these demographic markers gauge the changing structures of servitude for women, they reflect little about the dynamics of household governance or of women's experiences as servants in early modern Virginia. Regardless of whether women arrived in Virginia as emigrants from the British Isles, like Joan Powell, or were born of mixed-race or mixed-status parentage in Virginia, like Jane Webb, they constituted a class of bound female workers that existed at the very legal and social margins of the early Chesapeake. And all too little is known about what it meant for women to survive in these circumstances. This essay corrects that neglect by focusing on governance in the typically small and middling households of early modern Virginia, where masters and their female servants were engaged in face-to-face exchanges and negotiations over issues ranging from provisioning and disciplinary violence to those fundamentally concerning the immediate outcomes of women's lives and the prospects for their futures. In these households, masters, servants, and by the century's end, slaves, too, engaged in a complicated, sometimes perilous, and often high-stakes dance of mastery and subordination that was choreographed along lines of gender and race.

A close focus on the dynamics of household governance from the perspective of servant women alters our understanding of servitude, mastery, and resistance in early modern Virginia households in key ways. First, unpacking the minutiae of household governance allows us to comprehend the legal consciousness of servant women. Female servants had a clear understanding of their right to "seeke for justice" and an early modern sensibility of the entitlements accorded to their rank.[16] Joan Powell and Jane Webb knew as servants—as opposed to slaves—and as free subjects of the Crown that their masters ought to accord them "lawful courses," as Joan Powell phrased it.[17] Women demanded the few privileges of their rank and—increasingly as Virginia evolved to a slave society—their status as free persons. Servant women asserted their lawful privileges and used the legal system to structure negotiations over household governance. Their legal strategies ranged widely. Most commonly, they availed themselves of their right to complain before the bar in order to air their grievances against their masters. Such an endeavor often pitted their words against those of their masters and met with mixed success. Yet servant women also availed themselves of the written remedies of petition and contract in their attempts to obtain justice from their masters and from the courts.

Second, fixing our sights on the dynamics of household governance allows us to historicize the practices of mastery in early modern Virginia. Both Henry Smith (Joan Powell's master) and Thomas Savage (Jane Webb's master) were of middling rank.[18] Their practices of mastery stood in contrast to those observed by elite planters like William Byrd II or Landon Carter. By the mid-eighteenth century, such planters more readily carried the authority of their rank, distanced themselves from corporal punishment, and envisaged mastery as part of the rational science of plantation management.[19] Middling masters in the seventeenth- and early eighteenth-century Chesapeake, like Smith and Savage, were more improvisational in their mastery, perhaps as a result of their inexperience in mastering others or from a lack of confidence in their authority to master. Still, patriarchy was their model for household governance, and, despite their middling rank, they had no difficulty asserting a hierarchy that placed masters and mistresses over servants and slaves, husbands over wives, and parents over children.[20] Despite their similarity in status, however, Smith and Savage embodied different styles of mastery and illustrate divergent approaches to governing households. Smith was an extreme outlier and mastered his dependents with often unparalleled brutality: he ruled through violence, fear, and intimidation. In contrast, Thomas Savage was an exemplar of legal mastery. He governed his servants before the bar, so to speak, enforcing his will through contract, the interstices of legalities, and the legal privileges of whiteness. Despite these divergent approaches, however, both Smith and Savage relied on the local court to shore up their authority over their household dependants.

Third, this essay also explores the extralegal strategies of resistance resorted to by plebian women in their efforts to shape the character of domestic governance. Unfree women brought their own understandings of domestic justice to the households that they occupied, and they sought fair treatment. When denied this, they resisted their masters in various ways: they acted alone and collectively, evasively and confrontationally, and their efforts were on occasion impulsive and at other times choreographed. Women were much more unlikely than their male counterparts to abscond, strike their masters, or even join in efforts of collective revolt.[21] That they did not resort to these avenues of resistance, however, does not mean that women did not attempt to shape the contours of their lives or moderate the governance of their masters, and it does not mean that they were powerless or lacked agency.[22] Women had their own means of resisting the style of mastery they encountered. Often their strategies were aimed directly at their masters and sought changes in their styles of household management. On other occasions women used disorderly speech to shame their masters and mistresses and to shape community perceptions of them. These, too, were highly effective forms of resistance in the small, insular early modern society of the Eastern Shore of Virginia.

Household governance and, more particularly, the negotiations and exchanges that typified relations between servant women and their masters in early modern Virginia are best comprehended through the methods of microhistory. The contours of these exchanges are especially evident in the relatively well-documented legal complaints initiated by Joan Powell and Jane Webb. The words of these complaints and the dynamics they reveal come to us at a remove and are filtered through legal procedure, the tolerance of the sitting justices for the effusions of witnesses, the abilities of the court clerks who recorded their testimony, and the fact that onlookers at court would have included the masters against whom women offered testimony. Despite these limitations, however, the legal documents tell us much about the women's legal consciousness, the exercise of mastery, and the nature of resistance within these households. A close textual reading of their cases reveals the small cache of legal and cultural tools possessed by servant women, implements that they used in brokering with their masters and shaping the outcomes of their lives. Masters usually held the dominant position, but they were not impervious to community shame or legal censure that resulted from the testimony and resistance of the women who served in their households. Local courts and customary legal practices buttressed the powers of masters, but when confronted with the lack of legal remedies, servant women found alternative strategies of resistance. Excavated from the records, the experiences of Joan Powell and Jane Webb make more visible the pathways of power, the dynamics of interchange between masters and servants, and the struggles, conflicts, and compromises that typified household governance in early Virginia.

Lawful Courses

Both Joan Powell and Jane Webb understood that as free subjects, they were entitled to legal protections from the Crown's officials. Barely two years after disembarking in Virginia, Joan Powell stood before the local Accomack County court, complained of abuse at the hands of her master, and demanded that the justices provide her with a legal remedy. Henry Smith, she claimed, had repeatedly beaten her, fed her a diet of hominy and salt, and kept her without shoes and adequate clothing in the winter. She did not speak only for herself. Powell also bore witness to Smith's contractual infringements, cruelty to servants, abuse of his wife, mistreatment of his children, and most egregiously, to his torture, rape, and murder of her fellow servants.[23] Powell's was the first of many complaints: eventually nine women and four men joined her before the Accomack County court, either as fellow complainants or as witnesses. However, Powell and four other unfree women dominated the court proceedings.[24]

The women's testimony reflects both their understanding of lawful courses to which they were entitled and their comprehension that abuses of customary mastery were regular in their household. Virginia law obligated masters to provide adequate food, clothing, and lodging for servants; it also prohibited masters from immoderate correction and cruelty toward their servants. But what was adequate or moderate? Such questions lay at the heart of servants' understanding of abuse. It was up to local courts to determine case by case, on the basis of servant complaints, when, for instance, provisioning was inadequate or correction shaded into abuse. Some of the mistreatments described by Joan Powell—cruelty, poor provisioning, sexual coercion—were endemic to bound servants wherever they were found in the Atlantic world, but in Virginia the remedies for servants with violent masters were slimmer than in England or New England. In the British Isles, service contracts were often temporary and renewed yearly, and servants could simply leave masters whom they found not to their liking. Hiring out or apprenticeship in England was often done locally, allowing for parental or familial supervision. In urban areas like London, wages were competitive and servants more dear, circumstances that might bring them better treatment. And if a servant decided to abscond, there were more places to which they could escape and more persons who could harbor them.[25] Given Joan Powell's relatively recent arrival in the Chesapeake, her understanding of lawful courses was probably informed by her knowledge of the English system. What she may not have understood was that while Virginia law provided protections for servants, local courts held sway in determining the appropriate remedies, and, for the most part, local justices were not moved or persuaded by the testimony of servants.[26] In theory, this oversight by the court was consistent with English practice, but Powell may not have fully apprehended the disadvantages entailed by the absence of her kin and community. In England, those groups could bring pressure to bear on recalcitrant masters and reluctant justices. In Virginia, she had no such assistance.

For his part, Henry Smith may have been well aware that local courts on the Eastern Shore customarily favored masters over their servants. Only slightly more than half of servants bringing complaints in the Chesapeake were successful in obtaining redress, and they obtained only slow and often ineffectual remedies from justices.[27] It was probably the case on the Shore as elsewhere in the Chesapeake that servant women like Joan Powell were more likely than men to bring complaints of abuse. In Maryland, for instance, 38 percent of the complaints made by female servants were for physical or sexual abuse, compared with 8 percent for men.[28] This was the case because women were more susceptible to multiple forms of abuse than were men: they were more vulnerable to sexual coercion and more likely to be victims of physical violence from both male and female masters. Local justices and local custom did not favor providing remedies to servants, regardless of sex, but their decisions had a decidedly gendered dimension in that they were willing to disregard the very kinds of complaints of abuse that women servants typically brought to court.

The Eastern Shore preference for local legal custom trumped the protections of English common or statute law when it came to the rights of servants. The Accomack justices heard remarkably detailed testimony from Joan Powell and other female servants about Smith's broken contracts, mismanagement, physical cruelties, spousal and child abuse, rape, and homicide. The court then debated whether or not Powell—or any of Smith's servants—should be "sett free from so Cruel a Master." The evidence of abuse was overwhelming; the justices ordered Smith into custody, censured him for acting as "judge, party, and executioner" to his servants, and remanded him on felony charges to the General Court at Jamestown. In the end, however, they concluded that "servants are mens Estates and the pre[ce]dent" of setting them free from even such a master as Smith "might be of worse Consequence than intended."[29] Although they ordered Smith not to further strike any of his servants, it is plain that, in this Virginia jurisdiction at any rate, the full weight of customary practice supported the legal prerogatives of mastery, which superseded nearly all of the legal rights of servants. The justices admitted that Powell and her female compatriots had good reasons to "seeke for justice," but the court provided no remedies for their complaints. The ruling at the local court mirrored Smith's treatment at Virginia's General Court, where all charges against Smith were dropped. He was cleared by proclamation of the rape charges; the servant women who accused him were ordered to serve double the time of their absence, but he quickly sold their indentures. Apparently, both local leaders and colonial officials were unlikely to rely on the testimony of female servants to find against a master of the middling class, no matter how despicable.[30]

Yet the Henry Smith case also demonstrates that early modern justice on the Eastern Shore varied according to considerations of both rank and gender. While the justices discounted Smith's abuses of his servant women, they took more seriously the plight of his wife, Joanna Matrum Smith.[31] The legal doctrine of coverture stressed the unity of spouses and the reciprocal obligations of husband and wife; the court found Henry Smith much at fault in this regard. He had "beat, maimed, and ill-used" his wife, engaged in "frequent" acts of adultery, allied himself with his "whore," and took all manner of actions that led to the "breaking of his wife's harte." The Accomack justices provided her with several legal remedies: they granted a divorce *a mensa et thoro*, enforced it with articles of pacification, and ordered a division of property for her support.[32] Joanna Matrum Smith's status as a free woman of middling rank merited a greater consideration than did the complaints of her female servants. Ironically, however, thanks to those servant women, the cruelty of her husband had an ample hearing in court: the testimony of Joan Powell and other servant women bore witness to the brutality that Joanna Matrum Smith had suffered at the hands of her husband.[33] Aside from the remedies provided to Smith's wife, the only other individuals who benefited from the court's justice were the bound men in his household. When contracting with these men, Smith had promised to provide them with tools and Saturdays to devote to blacksmithing. The justices ordered Smith to give the men "Liberty to worke for their own advantage" as he had originally agreed. Ironically, again, it was Joan Powell who recited the exact terms of the agreements between the men and Smith as she had witnessed them in Bristol.[34] Yet the lawful courses understood by Joan Powell and her compatriots, while acknowledged by the local court as legitimate, were not redressed.

Forty years later, when Jane Webb sought aid from the Northampton County justices, she was still entitled to the same legal protections as Joan Powell or any other servant who was a subject of the British Crown. However, Webb understood that for nominally free blacks such as herself, those legal protections were increasingly at odds with customary practice in Virginia. And that is why in 1703, when Webb wanted to marry an enslaved man known from the records only as Left, she approached Left's owner, Thomas Savage, struck a bargain, and had it recorded in a written contract.[35] From this point forward, Jane Webb was recognized as both married to Left and the head of their household. It probably was not immediately clear to anyone what the doctrine of coverture meant for Webb. She was a *feme sole* and married, a *feme covert* and the head of the household, and a free woman of color legally married to a man who had no personhood under the law. She was also the legal face of her household; it was up to her to pursue legal strategies that would protect and sustain her progeny in the increasingly racialized environment of early modern Virginia. Webb made the contracts for the family, she brought suit on behalf of family members, and all of her children took the surname "Webb" as their own. Jane Webb was a "fictive widow," for although she was not high ranking, she shouldered the public face of the family throughout her life.[36]

Jane Webb attempted to use the legal system in an effort to carve out lawful courses that would ensure a certain future of freedom for her children. In early modern Virginia race mattered, and their status as free persons was too precarious to trust to oral recollection, so Webb chose a written contract to counteract the weight of customary disadvantage.[37] The contract she made with Thomas Savage had four key provisions. First, in order to marry Left, Jane Webb re-entered indentured servitude and agreed to serve the Savage household for seven years, until 1711. Second, she stipulated that any children born to the marriage during those seven years would be similarly indentured to Savage until the age of eighteen. Third, when Jane Webb's indenture ended in 1711, Left would be freed from slavery. And finally, any children born subsequently would bear no obligation to Savage. Webb's motives seem clear. Since as a slave Left had no legal right to marry, any children born to Jane Webb and Left risked being accounted mixed-race, out-of-wedlock offspring.[38] And, according to her version of the contract, her children were obligated to serve shorter terms of service than was typical for such children.[39] Moreover, by indenturing herself and future progeny specifically to Savage, Jane Webb kept her children free, legitimate, and together on the Eastern Shore.

Jane Webb and Left had three children before 1711 and four children thereafter.[40] Yet as that year came and went, Webb remained in the Savage household, Left remained a slave, and year by year Thomas Savage successively bound to his service every one of the Webb children, even those born after the terms of the contract. This was possible because in Virginia, as in England, it was perfectly acceptable to compel free individuals, if they were poor, to labor.[41] When Savage sought to indenture Webb's two youngest children and she refused, he then complained to the Northampton County court that he had the "best right" to the Webb children, since their mother had "no visible means to support [them]." As a consequence, he argued, "they may be induced to take ill courses."[42] The justices agreed: because of Webb's poverty, the master's right to her children superseded her own. Moreover, despite the fact that Jane Webb's indenture formally ended in 1711, her husband and children remained tethered to Thomas Savage, and that meant that Webb was herself effectively in service to him through the mid-1720s.

In 1725 Webb initiated a suit in chancery and made one last attempt to force Thomas Savage to honor the terms of the original agreement. Savage claimed that he had lost the original contract; indeed, if we may judge from evidence in other cases in Northampton, contracts were not always formally recorded.[43] He disputed the terms of the contract, however, and produced two witnesses (his daughter and son-in-law) who claimed to have seen (and apparently could read) the contract. They swore that "therein it was agreed that the said Jane was to serve seven years and all her children born in the life time of her husband Left should serve the said Savage ... and that the said Indenture had the approbation of the Court."⁴⁴ In rebuttal, Webb brought an unidentified free black to testify on her behalf. Statute law did not yet expressly debar the legal testimony of free blacks.⁴⁵ The Northampton justices deliberated on precisely this matter, the court being "divided" on whether or not to accept the testimony of free blacks.⁴⁶ Four months later the justices declined her witness, a decision that reflected how customary treatments of mixed-race individuals like Webb would anticipate statutory law. And with that decision, Webb's direct remedies at court to ensure lawful courses in the treatment of her children were exhausted.

Mastery

In early modern Virginia as elsewhere, mastery was intimately linked with disciplinary violence. The ability to physically correct one's dependents was a defining feature of patriarchal privilege in early modern households.⁴⁷ On the colonial frontier of the Chesapeake, with its reliance on bound labor and particularly with the evolution of slavery, the powers accorded to heads of household expanded, and, correspondingly, the disciplinary violence used by masters against their unfree workers moved beyond traditional limits.⁴⁸ British ideals of manhood may have emphasized moderation, restraint, and authority, but those standards sometimes translated imperfectly to small and middling planters in early modern Virginia.⁴⁹ Some historians have suggested that those men and women who began their lives as servants in the Chesapeake and survived to move up into the ranks of small planters revisited the poor treatment they had received as servants on their own bound laborers or that such experiences fostered a kind of unfettered aggression.⁵⁰

The legal system that was theoretically supposed to regulate masters like Henry Smith and enforce ideals of moderation buttressed rather than restrained masters' propensities to impose their authority. Legal definitions of disciplinary violence were vague. Masters like Smith acted at the interstices of legalities, governing their servants in ways that, while seemingly in violation of the common or statute law, were accepted in local jurisdictions like the Eastern Shore. For instance, Michael Dalton's *Countrey Justice* specified that laborers who were misused or had cause to be "grieved" were to make complaints to justices. Dalton did not define misuse, however, nor did other legal manuals prescribe the exact limits of disciplinary violence.⁵¹ Masters might employ, in the terms of Dalton, "injurious force" to implement their will, but too much force could become "opposed to the law."⁵² More ambiguity came from Virginia statute, which warned "cruell" masters against "barbarous usage" of servants, but it also described those potentially victimized servants as "unruly," "stubborne," and "incorrigible."⁵³ The reliance on community standards and custom in local jurisdictions like those of the Eastern Shore expanded the powers of masters. Justices might have defended such an expansion in the powers of masters because of their fears over unrest among unfree laborers and even outright revolt by servants and slaves.⁵⁴

Many masters altered their use of disciplinary violence depending on the sex of their targets. Henry Smith is a case in point. While male servants outnumbered their female counterparts at Smith's Oake Hall plantation, only women made complaints of physical violence. Smith did not hesitate to whip or beat his wife, stepchildren, or female servants, all of whom were under the age of twenty-five, nor did he refrain from employing sexual violence against selected servant women in his household. Domestic handbooks discouraged masters from beating their female servants, but if the latter turned "stout and mannish," it was acceptable for masters to "beate downe" their "rebellion." Prescriptive literature and realities rarely mesh, however, and servant women's complaints of violence suggest that they were routinely "beate downe."⁵⁵ For instance, Smith's female dependents testified to his numerous physical "cruell blows." Additionally, women's testimony gives ample evidence that their male counterparts were present on the scene, but not one of them explicitly suggests that the men were beaten. Nor do the male servants in their own testimonies make specific mention of physical correction. Given their respective ages, Smith may have practiced an expedient mastery: he might have avoided fighting men whose physical prowess matched or exceeded his own out of fear of retaliatory assaults.⁵⁶ It was also possible that the male servants understood disciplinary violence differently than their female companions. If disciplinary violence was a regular aspect of the experience of plebian males, as probably was the case, they may not have found it remarkable enough to mention and may have chosen to view it stoically.⁵⁷ Still, Smith, like other masters, did not hesitate to beat those he understood to be less physically able than him: women, children, and the aged.

Mastery in the early modern world also encompassed a psychological ability to intimidate one's dependents to force them into obedience if necessary. Like disciplinary violence, this form of mastery also had a gendered component. One method of emotional bullying was through a lack of provisioning, and the servants at Oake Hall testified that women were more deprived of supplies than were men.[58] Masters used food, clothing, and shelter to control servants, and in the Smith household, women consistently complained of being scarcely clothed (no shoes in winter), badly sheltered (sleeping on the dirt floor of the tobacco barn), and barely fed (a diet of hominy or raw oats and salt). Smith also intimidated women through his temper.[59] His "refractory and angry courses" along with his "discontented humours" and "unnatural disposition" inspired "feare and dread" in his servants. One swore that his brutality was so great it made her "desert her reason," while a neighbor testified that his looks were "so Devillish and fierce" that she "feared for her life."[60] This intimidation was profound: all of the servants watched Smith whip an elderly servant, and although they counted over forty-nine blows, they did not intercede, although afterward, when the servant was too weak to work, they clandestinely made up his share of the labor to prevent further beating.[61] Smith's servants did not run away or strike back, as many servants in the Chesapeake did, and surely this, too, is another measure of his power to overawe them. And then there was Virginia law to reinforce mastery: servants would only be penalized with more service if they ran or retaliated, so that, even in the face of Smith's violence, resistance might make matters worse. Smith's style of mastery effectively discouraged individual or collective action on the part of his servants, and, given local legal custom on the Eastern Shore, he had little reason to fear that the court would intercede on behalf of his servants, despite the fact that his actions distressed his contemporaries.

Two generations later, Thomas Savage, the master of servant Jane Webb and her enslaved husband, Left, also relied on Eastern Shore legal custom to buttress his authority over the unfree members of his household. Yet Savage's actions illustrate an approach to mastery that contrasted dramatically with that of Henry Smith. In part this reflects the evolution of the legal system itself: by the 1720s, both remedies at the bar and judicial oversight were more obtainable for both masters and servants. Rather than relying on violence and intimidation, which was clearly Smith's personal and idiosyncratic predilection, Savage used legal privilege and legal custom to control Jane Webb and her family. Savage's style may reflect a rising paternalism in the practice of mastery, a more removed style of wielding authority that, given Virginia's transition to a slave society, had more currency when it came to the treatment of servants. Savage was no doubt eager to obtain the labor of the Webb children, and that, too, shaped his exercise of mastery.⁶² The lack of reference to household violence in Webb's case most likely simply indicates that, when it came to persons of color, free or enslaved, the use of corrective discipline, whether excessive or quotidian, was neither culturally remarkable nor legally actionable. It is in this regard instructive that neither Jane Webb nor any of her children—who regularly brought complaints to the Northampton County court in the first three decades of the eighteenth century—never once cited immoderate correction or the overuse of disciplinary violence at the hands of any of their various masters.

Thomas Savage may not have needed to use disciplinary violence because he could very effectively use the legal system to control Jane Webb. He owned her husband. He owned her labor, at least temporarily. He had legal possession of her children. He also held advantages in the local court, some of which were procedural. For instance, when Webb petitioned the court in 1722 to enforce the terms of the contract she and Savage had made in exchange for her indenture, Thomas Savage stalled his appearance at court—and therefore a judgment—for over six months. At courts held from August or September 1722 through January 1723, he failed to appear, pleaded sickness, and requested more time; all of these were routine excuses for not appearing. In one instance, the sheriff neglected to serve Savage with the court's order to appear, but the justices censured neither Savage nor the sheriff. Savage may have been delaying deliberately. In 1723, new legislation went into effect that stipulated thirty years of service for children, like those of the Webbs, who were born to free black or mixed-race women who were themselves serving indentures of thirty years. This legislation did not in theory apply to Jane Webb or her children, but the language of her petition suggests that she feared that it could be applied to them. Savage may indeed have hoped that such extended terms might be retroactively applied, with the local court's help, to the Webb children. Jane Webb's petition sought to prevent exactly that from happening. When Savage finally appeared, Webb demanded to know if the court was "intending to enslave" her children, a reference to the possibility of increasing their terms of service. The justices dismissed her petition as "frivolous" but did not otherwise comment on the specific amount of time that the Webb children were to serve Savage.⁶³

Savage also had the advantage over Webb in terms of legal evidence. In 1725, Webb brought a suit against Savage in chancery in an attempt to get the court to enforce the terms of their original contract. In her recollection their contract had stipulated that Left would be freed after 1711, and only the children born before that would be bound to Savage for terms of eighteen years. Savage testified that although he had "lost" the original agreement, it never freed Left and encompassed all of the Webb children, although he could not remember the terms of service stipulated.[64] Did Savage purloin and destroy the original contract? Webb complained that Savage had "taken the Indenture or Instrument of writing into his custody" and that she could not "come to the sight thereof."[65] If Webb was correct about its terms, Savage would have had good reason to "conceal" the document, as Webb charged. If Savage was motivated originally by the prospect of decades worth of labor he would receive from the Webb children, he would have been equally moved to keep all of them laboring for him for as long as possible. Since the last three Webb children were born in 1713, 1716, and 1720, if Savage prevailed, they would be in service to his household through the 1740s.[66] The prospect of a future supply of less expensive labor might have seemed worth destroying the document. If Savage's recollection of the document was correct, however, he would have few reasons to destroy the document and very good reasons to ensure its safekeeping. Alternatively, did Webb misconstrue the terms of the original contract, or were they misrepresented to her? She never claimed to possess a copy of the contract, which seems curious, given its importance to her family's future. Finally, the original contract possessed the "approbation of the court." While not all contracts were recorded, as noted above, the loss of this document is puzzling.

Ultimately, however, the vanished contract gave the Northampton County justices no pause. When it came to presenting evidence of the original terms of the now lost contract, Savage had the upper hand. He summoned white witnesses and their testimony was accepted, but when Webb brought another free person of color to testify in her behalf, the court, after delaying to consider whether or not to accept the evidence brought by "free negroes," ruled that "none such ought to be allowed."[67] Seven years later, in 1732, the Virginia General Assembly would remake this local custom into statute law when it barred free blacks from witnessing except in trials of slaves.[68]

Thomas Savage may have acted as a paternalistic master in his household by allowing the marriage between Left and Jane Webb and thereby ensuring legitimacy for Jane and Left's children. He was, however, the primary beneficiary of this paternalism because, despite Jane Webb's free status, his legal rights over her children were extensive. Savage viewed himself as entitled to the labor of those children and to mastery over their futures into adulthood, and the legal system aided him in enforcing a state of decades-long ownership over them. He relied on local custom to give him the legal edge in procedure and evidence and won the case. Just as surely as Henry Smith controlled his dependents through disciplinary violence, Thomas Savage's legal advantages over Jane Webb and her family made him no less effective as a governor of his household.

Resistance

What alternatives were there for women like Joan Powell and Jane Webb who, in pursuit of the legal protection they were entitled to in theory, found that too little of it could be obtained in customary practice in local Virginia jurisdictions? In measuring the resistance of unfree workers in Virginia, historians have largely relied on court complaints made by masters against servants who struck them, ran away, or in some way challenged masterly authority, actions that were more readily undertaken by unfree men.[69] The resistance of servant women, however, cannot be completely comprehended through such direct measures. Instead, their resistance was indirect and covert and often—although not always—stayed within the boundaries of legality.[70]

Verbal resistance by servant women could take several forms. On occasion, they might warn their master of the illegality of his actions and implicitly threaten to expose him to the court or the neighborhood. Joan Powell and her compatriots attempted to curb their master's brutality with just such warnings. For instance, when Smith beat Powell, she reminded him that he had no "lawful courses" to do so; under similar circumstances another female servant warned him that she would "seeke for justice" unless he stopped. A third servant pleaded with Smith as he raped her that he would "undo" her, a commentary both on the effect of sexual violence and on the legal penalty she would pay if she became pregnant; he clearly understood the latter plea and replied that if he did "undoe" her, he would be able to "maintaine" her. These kinds of verbal negotiations—improvised under threats of physical and sexual violence—were used by unfree women to underscore their access to the legal system, even if their masters chose to trust, rightly as it turned out, that custom would protect them.[71]

Indentured women also generated witnesses to their own abuse. After Smith had raped Mary Hewes, she asked a fellow servant if he had heard her cry out. When he answered in the negative, she went to Smith's stepchildren and asked them if "they did not remember they heard her cry out in the morning"; they replied that "they did heare her cry and thought their father had beat her." The children could have offered testimony in court, but Hewes generated even further evidence by prompting their recollection of hearing another servant in order to reinforce her base of witnesses.[72]

As witnesses, servant women could potentially play pivotal legal roles in the local courts of early modern Virginia. Their gossip about Henry Smith created a "common fame" of his violence and brutality; their testimony in court would similarly confirm this reputation and challenge his authority in an attempt to exert some degree of social control in their community.[73] Because oral testimony was the basis of most evidence in early modern courts, bearing witness could prove to be a valuable asset, and indentured servants were conscious that they held the right to testify. They watched events unfold and committed those events to memory. Their listening was of necessity deeply purposeful if they were to prevail as moral arbiters and align the community and the court against the likes of Henry Smith. As omnipresent plantation workers, inside and outside of houses, servant women were in a position to observe the events in and around the household, and they reported on this to the court. They noted Smith's mismanagement of his estate, recalling that their master ordered a steer to be killed to provision the household but failed to salt it so that the meat rotted, that he chose an unsuitable plot for planting grain, and that he allowed the cattle to eat the germinating seedlings.[74] More to the point, they aided other members of their household. For instance, Joan Powell testified to Smith's abuse of his wife; she also recounted the terms of unfulfilled contracts made between Smith and other servants.[75] Based on Powell's testimony, the justices granted a divorce to Smith's wife and ordered him to fulfill his promises to the men. Despite Powell's failure to remedy her own grievances, bearing witness had an important legal impact in the local legal culture of the Eastern Shore.

Forty years later, it was much more difficult for Jane Webb to generate witnesses whose testimony would be accepted by the court. Webb understood that the written word enjoyed precedence over the spoken word, especially where contracts or wills were concerned. The court would not trust her testimony over that of her master. Similarly, the circle of witnesses on which Webb relied were drawn from the ranks of the free black community, and, as we have seen, by 1725 they were by law debarred from testifying in the local courts on the Eastern Shore.

Yet Jane Webb did embrace some tactics of verbal resistance that paralleled those of Joan Powell. For instance, she reported on the mismanagement of the masters of her children and grandchildren. When those masters failed to list them as tithables or detained them beyond the period of their service, Webb reported it to the court. Like indentured women throughout the colonial period and enslaved women during the antebellum era, Webb engaged in verbal sparring with her master and local legal authorities. When her chancery case against Savage was dismissed and she lost all hope of enforcing the desired terms of service for her children, Webb reproached the court for its injustice. Her verbal condemnation, however, was understood to be a serious matter because the criticism came from a mixed-race woman and was directed at the magistrates themselves. The day after the justices dismissed her case in chancery against Savage, Webb railed at them, declaring that if all "Virginia negroes had as good a heart as her they would all be free." Despite her appeal to her own good character and arguably because of her expression of racial consciousness (the "Virginia Negroes ... would *all* be free" intentionally provoked the county's ruling elite), the local justices took these to be "dangerous words" that violated the king's peace, and Jane Webb was repaid with ten lashes "well laid on" at the common whipping post.[76]

Beyond verbal accusations, however, the most meaningful example of resistance for servant women at the legal margins of early Virginia came in the form of household alliances. For Joan Powell and other indentured women at Oake Hall, fragile yet collective strategies of resistance involved other indentured women as well as free women. For instance, one of Joan Powell's fellow servants, Elizabeth Nork, described Henry Smith's attempts to rape her, and her testimony reveals that deliberate, well-choreographed aid from three other women prevented the rape from occurring. Her master, she testified, called her into the middle room of the great house and threw her down on the bed; she wrestled away and ran outside. He followed her out to the quarter and grabbed her again, but Joan Powell interrupted him; somewhat later, he again laid hold of Nork's arm, but this time he was interrupted by another young female household worker. Yet a fourth time he had Nork in his grip, and this time his wife approached.[77]

Such alliances could cross lines of rank as well. After Henry Smith had beaten his wife, Joan Powell sat up with her mistress through the night. Smith kept badgering Powell, repeatedly asking her why she stayed. "To keep my mistress company," she steadily replied. Smith rejoined that the two should keep company at the whipping post, but she calmly stated that it would not be "handsome or civill" to leave her mistress in "such a condition." Even Henry Smith recognized these alliances and accused his wife and servants of attempting to "combine" against him.[78] And he was right to suspect that the women in his household were acting as one community. In doing so, they revealed their shared plebian and gendered understandings of mastery. Having failed to obtain the protection of the law, they joined together to regulate the household patriarch.

The legal margins on which Jane Webb lived necessitated indirect resistance. At least once she "decoyed" one of her children away from the Savage household.[79] After she lost her suit against Savage, however, Webb never again directly challenged him in court. She did, however, inform the court when he—or other masters of her children—failed to list them as tithables.[80] And, instead of combining with other unfree workers, Jane Webb cemented alliances within her family, particularly with her daughters. Webb petitioned the court twice in the early 1720s, both times unsuccessfully, to remove her daughter Dinah from Savage's service because Dinah had reached the age of eighteen. When Dinah herself brought a note from the parish register attesting to the date of her birth, however, the justices had no choice but to free her.[81] When Webb's daughter Elizabeth sought, like her mother before her, to marry an enslaved man, she obtained legal recognition of the union.[82] Similarly, in the early 1730s when the Savages attempted to detain Jane Webb's grandchildren, their mother, Nanny Webb, filed a complaint in court, and the justices ordered the children to be removed from the Savage household.[83] Other free black women on the Shore made similar marriage contracts; despite the attendant difficulties, doing so was the only means of ensuring the freedom of their children. For a while, the daughters of Left and Jane Webb stayed on the Eastern Shore and on the legal margins of their freedom. Dinah married a mixed-race indentured man but did not live with him in his household, perhaps to prevent her children from suffering the same fate as she and her siblings in the Savage household.[84] Eventually she, along with one of Jane and Left Webb's sons, left the region.[85]

Lawful Courses, Mastery, and Women's Resistance in Early Modern Virginia

What can we learn from Joan Powell and Jane Webb? Despite their differences, both were part of a class of unfree women who lived on the legal margins of early Virginia. Their legal consciousness, experiences at the local courts, and strategies of resistance reflect the ways in which gender, race, and the law shaped structures of servitude. As Lois Green Carr and Lorena Walsh have argued, compared with their counterparts in England and New England, women like Joan Powell were more degraded and exploited; these adjectives apply to Jane Webb as well. Given the predilections of the local magistrates, whether or not these women experienced relatively more power and independence (the other two terms in Carr and Walsh's characterization of women in the early Chesapeake) is less apparent. If Joan Powell and Jane Webb are any indication, the rights of indentured women as *femes soles* and subjects of the Crown were abrogated by Virginia legal custom.[86]

The experiences of Joan Powell and Jane Webb also provide us with a comparative vantage point from which to understand women's experiences as servants and the nature of household governance in early modern Virginia. Despite the limits of customary law in local jurisdictions, unfree women brought their own understandings of legalities at the bar and, failing relief, they enacted alternative strategies of resisting the injustices of their masters. Joan Powell and her compatriots formed household alliances that, although improvised and temporary, constrained Henry Smith's ability to master his household without limits, challenged his attempts to subordinate them, and protected their bodies and lives. Jane Webb worked through the law for the first three decades of the eighteenth century and challenged Thomas Savage's attempts to master herself and her family.

These stories also reflect the dynamics of household governance and the complex interplay between female servants and their masters in early modern Virginia. Boundaries between acceptable and unacceptable violence were increasingly blurred, while those between free and enslaved were made increasingly clear.[87] As the colony began to replace its labor force of white servants with enslaved individuals of African decent, acceptable limits of disciplinary violence extended far beyond traditional bounds. In fact, just as Joan Powell was challenging Henry Smith before the local Accomack court, the General Assembly at James City passed a statute regarding the "casuall killing of slaves" that declared that if a slave died as a result of disciplinary correction, it would not be accounted a felony.[88] Slavery altered relations of mastery precisely because slaves were outside the protections of the law. Concomitantly, servants understood that they should be mastered differently than slaves. The women at Henry Smith's Oake Hall, for instance, understood that they were entitled to lawful courses that were not extended to slaves, and they used that knowledge to attempt to regulate Smith's mastery. One servant pleaded with Smith that he "would make her worse than a Negro by whoreing her." Pregnancy would extend her service for two more years (which might have seemed like a lifetime with Henry Smith as master), but her comment also tacitly recognized that the sexual exploitation of enslaved women was a regular feature of mastery.[89]

While Joan Powell received meager legal remedies from the court (as opposed to Joanna Matrum Smith and Henry Smith's male servants), she may have had some vindication for her efforts. In 1670, Henry Smith left Accomack County and decamped north to Maryland. Although he had successfully faced down felony rape and homicide charges at Virginia's General Court, he moved north to escape his reputation and make a new start. Perhaps it was just far enough: thanks to the unfree women of Oake Hall, his reputation followed him, but it did not in itself prevent him from ascending to political office.[90] Once in Maryland, he served as a legislator, militia captain, and justice on the county bench, an ironic ending for a man who, as his estranged wife had said, "no law could order."[91] He may have been legally free, but the community of servant women led by Joan Powell made it impossible for him to remain in Accomack, and some if not most of his servants did not accompany him to Maryland. Henry Smith was a master who could not be regulated by law, but his reputation mattered in the local realm, and his female servants did it considerable damage. That, perhaps, was their greatest act of resistance.

Jane Webb was focused on the long term, and her alliances were within the family, for the family, and for the future. The force of customary law and the drive to create a slave society in Virginia rendered legal protections for free blacks often meaningless and, at best, unpredictable. Still, like their mother, Jane Webb's daughters tried to enforce their own notions of customary practice by challenging the local courts, generating legal evidence of the freedom of their children, and avoiding the households of those who would attempt to master them. These strategies were tangible counterweights to those who would pull the Webbs and similar families back into a state of near slavery.

In matters of household governance, unfree women like Joan Powell and Jane Webb had to reckon with local courts, individual masters, and statute law. As impoverished women, they remained on the margins of lawful protections and social hierarchies, and for such women, to "seeke for justice" was an uncertain endeavor that met with mixed success at best. Still, their consciousness of lawful courses, their legal acumen, and their skills of resistance reflect the power that even such women on the margins might bring to bear on the households and courts on the Eastern Shore of early modern Virginia.

Notes

1. Joan Powell is listed in the patent Henry Smith received for importing servants and family members into the colony. Nell Marion Nugent, *Cavaliers and Pioneers: Abstracts of Virginia Land Patents and Grants*, 3 vols., (Richmond, 1977–1992) 2:24. According to the Bristol Registers, which do not record the total numbers of individuals bound for service in Virginia, Joan Powell was one of 67 women and 171 men who left England bound for the Chesapeake that fall. The total number of servants departing from Bristol that year numbered 302: 225 men and 77 women made the journey. The vast majority, and nearly all of the women, headed for Virginia, with the remainder going to Nevis, Barbados, St. Kitts, Maryland, and New England. See "Labor Contracts," Virtual Jamestown, accessed September 10, 2007, http://www.virtualjamestown.org/servantcontracts.html. Other treatments of Joan Powell's master, Henry Smith, include Julie Nock Jeffrey, "'More Like a Monster Than a Man': The Case of Henry Smith and the Accomack County Court," *Delmarva Settlers* (2006), accessed December 15, 2006, http://nabbhistory.salisbury.edu/settlers/profiles/smith.html; John C. Coombs, "Building 'The Machine': The Development of Slavery and Slave Society in Early Colonial Virginia" (Ph.D. diss., College of William and Mary, 2004), 24–26; Irmina Wawrzyczek, "The Women of Accomack versus Henry Smith: Gender, Legal Recourse, and the Social Order in Seventeenth-Century Virginia," *Virginia Magazine of History and Biography* 105 (1997): 5–26; J. Douglas Deal, *Race and Class in Colonial Virginia: Indians, Englishmen, and Africans on the Eastern Shore during the Seventeenth Century* (New York, 1993), 107, 117–19; and Richard B. Morris, *Government and Labor in Early America* (New York, 1946), 491–96.

2. Several statutes governed Jane Webb's status. Despite her mixed-race parentage, her free status was determined by a law enacted in 1662 that stipulated by the legal doctrine of *partus sequitur ventrem* (progeny follows the womb) in determining slave or free status. See William Waller Hening, *The Statutes at Large* (Philadelphia, 1819), 2:170. Until 1691, Virginia followed English practice for all out-of-wedlock children, even those of mixed-race parentage: males had to serve until twenty-four, while females served until twenty-one or the age of their marriage. However, beginning in 1691, children like Webb (with white mothers and black fathers) had to serve until thirty years of age; this was extended to thirty-one years in 1705. Ibid., 87–88, 452–53. For the binding out of infants born out of wedlock and useful comparisons of the English and the Virginia system, see John Ruston Pagan, *Anne Orthwood's Bastard: Sex and Law in Early Virginia* (New York, 2003), 105–9.

3. The story of Jane Webb has been reconstructed by several historians. See Deal, *Race and Class in Colonial Virginia*, 399–405; see also Deal, "A Constricted World: Free Blacks on Virginia's Eastern Shore," in Lois Green Carr, Philip D. Morgan, and Jean B. Russo, eds., *Colonial Chesapeake Society* (Chapel Hill, NC, 1988), 275–305; and Terri L. Snyder, "Jane Webb," in Henry Louis Gates Jr. and Evelyn Brooks Higginbotham, eds., *African American National Biography*, vol. 8, (New York, 2008), 186–87. For the Webb genealogy, see Paul Heinegg, *Free African Americans of Virginia, North Carolina, South Carolina,*

Maryland, and Delaware, 4th ed., 2 vols. (Baltimore, 2001), also at http://www.freeafrican americans.com (accessed October 10, 2009).

4. The major, now classic interpretative statement on women's experience as servants comes from Lois Green Carr and Lorena S. Walsh, "The Planter's Wife: The Experience of White Women in Seventeenth-Century Maryland," *William and Mary Quarterly*, 3rd ser., 34 (1977): 542–71. Other contributions that address the experiences of servants include Mary Beth Norton, *Founding Mothers and Fathers: Gendered Power and the Forming of American Society* (New York, 1996); Kathleen M. Brown, *Good Wives, Nasty Wenches, and Anxious Patriarchs: Gender, Race, and Power in Colonial Virginia* (Chapel Hill, NC, 1996); and Terri L. Snyder, *Brabbling Women: Disorderly Speech and the Law in Early Virginia* (Ithaca, NY, 2003). Surprisingly, Julia Cherry Spruill devotes little space to indentured women in *Women's Life and Work in the Southern Colonies* (Chapel Hill, NC, 1938) except to discuss their crimes and out-of-wedlock pregnancy in particular.

5. The parenthetical statistics are taken from the following: on mortality rates, James Horn, *Adapting to a New World: English Society in the Seventeenth-Century Chesapeake* (Chapel Hill, NC, 1994), 420; on sex ratios, Edmund S. Morgan, *American Slavery, American Freedom: The Ordeal of Colonial Virginia* (New York, 1975), 407–8; on the risk of pregnancy, Carr and Walsh, "The Planter's Wife," 547–48.

6. On Virginia's evolution to a slave society, see Ira Berlin, *Many Thousands Gone: The First Two Centuries of Slavery in North America* (Cambridge, MA, 1998); Anthony S. Parent, *Foul Means: The Formation of a Slave Society in Virginia, 1660–1740* (Chapel Hill, NC, 2003); Morgan, *American Slavery, American Freedom*; and T. H. Breen and Stephen Innes, *"Myne Owne Ground": Race and Freedom on Virginia's Eastern Shore, 1640–1676* (New York, 1986). On free blacks and indentured servitude, Brown, *Good Wives, Nasty Wenches*; and Breen and Innes, *"Myne Owne Ground."* On Native American servants on the Eastern Shore, see Helen C. Rountree and Thomas E. Davidson, *Eastern Shore Indians of Virginia and Maryland* (Charlottesville, VA, 1997), 76–83; and Susie M. Ames, *Studies of the Virginia Eastern Shore in the Seventeenth Century* (Richmond, 1940), 72–108.

7. See Deal, "A Constricted World," 276–79; Michael L. Nicholls, "Passing through This Troublesome World: Free Blacks on the Early Southside," *Virginia Magazine of History and Biography* 92 (1984): 50–70; Ira Berlin, *Slaves without Masters: The Free Negro in the Antebellum South* (New York, 1974); John H. Russell, "The Free Negro in Virginia, 1619–1865," *Johns Hopkins University Studies in Historical and Political Science* 31 (1913): 349–542.

8. On black family formation, see Breen and Innes, *"Myne Owne Ground"*; Allan Kulikoff, *Tobacco and Slaves: The Development of Southern Cultures in the Chesapeake, 1680–1800* (Chapel Hill, NC, 1986); and Philip D. Morgan, *Slave Counterpoint: Black Culture in the Eighteenth-Century Chesapeake and Lowcountry* (Chapel Hill, NC, 1998), 10–17. The ratios and numbers of free blacks in the pre-Revolutionary South are difficult to determine, but there is little doubt about the predominance of women among the free black population in early republican and antebellum America. Most historians agree that the disproportionate manumission of women in the post-Revolutionary years was largely responsible for this ratio, but my research suggests that, while post-Revolutionary manumission was of course important, the disproportion was part of a much longer trend that began in the colonial period. See, for instance, Suzanne Lebsock, *The Free Women of Petersburg: Status and Culture in a Southern Town, 1784–1860* (New York, 1984), 99 (sex ratios), 87–111 (on free women of color); and Tommy L. Bogger, *Free Blacks in Norfolk, Virginia, 1790–1860: The Darker Side of Freedom* (Charlottesville, VA, 1997), 109.

9. I have ascertained this number from the depositions given in the charges against Henry Smith made in the Accomack County court from 1668 and 1670; the depositions mention thirteen servants—eight men and five women. For the multiple complaints against Henry Smith, see Accomack County Orders (hereafter ACO), (1666–1670), especially ff. 3–5, 81–120, 176–85, Library of Virginia.

10. The physical nature of Thomas Savage's estate is not entirely clear. It is possible that Webb and Left lived with their children on the main Savage estate, but it is also possible that they lived on a distant quarter. The number of unfree workers in Savage's household has been determined by the size of Left and Jane Webb's family, as well as by the terms of Savage's will when he died in 1728. See Northampton Deeds and Wills (1725–1733), f. 229, Library of Virginia.

11. On the history of the Eastern Shore, see Rountree and Davidson, *Eastern Shore Indians*; Breen and Innes, *"Myne Owne Ground"*; James R. Perry, *The Formation of a Society on Virginia's Eastern Shore, 1615–1655* (Chapel Hill, NC, 1990); and Ames, *Studies of the Virginia Eastern Shore*.

12. John Ruston Pagan, "Law and Society in Restoration Virginia" (Ph.D. diss., Oxford University, 1996), 416–34; Morgan, *American Slavery, American Freedom*, 414–15, table 4.

13. Pagan, *Anne Orthwood's Bastard*, 20–25, 68–70, 105–12, 125–27, 148–50.

14. One tithable list taken in the mid-seventeenth century listed 29 percent of Northampton's black population as free; see Pagan, "Law and Society," 416–34; see also Morgan, *American Slavery, American Freedom*, 414–15, table 4; and Breen and Innes, *"Myne Owne Ground,"* 68–69. Up through the eve of the Civil War, the free black population on the Eastern Shore outstripped other Virginia counties by as much as 2–6 percent. See Eva Sheppard Wolf, *Race and Liberty in the New Nation: Emancipation in Virginia from the Revolution to Nat Turner's Rebellion* (Baton Rouge, 2006), 43, table 1.

15. On the labor composition of early Chesapeake households, see Carole Shammas, "Black Women's Work and the Evolution of Plantation Society in Virginia," *Labor History* 26 (1985): 5–28 (percentage of Tidewater households that owned servants and slaves can be found on 8, table 1); David W. Galenson, *White Servitude in Colonial America: An Economic Analysis* (Cambridge, 1981); and Russell R. Menard, "From Servants to Slaves: The Transformation of the Chesapeake Labor System," *Southern Studies* 16 (1977): 355–90; John C. Coombs, "Beyond the Origins Debate: Rethinking the Rise of Virginia Slavery," in the present volume. Useful descriptions of early modern Chesapeake households can also be found in Carr, Morgan, and Russo, *Colonial Chesapeake Society*; Thad W. Tate and David L. Ammerman, eds., *The Chesapeake in the Seventeenth Century: Essays on Anglo-American Society* (Chapel Hill, NC, 1979); Horn, *Adapting to a New World*; Kulikoff, *Tobacco and Slaves*; and Morgan, *American Slavery, American Freedom*.

16. Peter Thompson, "The Thief, the Householder, and the Commons: Languages of Class in Virginia," *William and Mary Quarterly*, 3rd ser., 63 (April 2006): 269.

17. Deposition of Mary Hewes ("seeke for justice"), deposition of Joan Powell ("lawful courses"), ACO (1666–1670), ff. 72 and 83, respectively.

18. Henry Smith was born in England; he may have lived in Barbados prior to coming to Virginia. By the mid-1660s, he had patented a couple thousand acres of land, possessed roughly a dozen servants, and lived in a multichambered dwelling called "Oake Hall," with a glass window, beds, chests, tables, and chairs. See the inventory of his estate made by the Accomack justices upon his divorce from Joanna Matrum Smith, ACO (1666–1670), f. 100. My assessment that Smith was at least of middling planter status is based on a com-

parison of the inventory with the data from James Horn, "Adapting to a New World: A Comparative Study of Local Society in England and Maryland," in Carr, Morgan, and Russo, eds., *Colonial Chesapeake Society*, 152–64, especially, 158–59, table 4. For details on Henry Smith, see Edward C. Papenfuse et al., *A Biographical Dictionary of the Maryland Legislature, 1635–1789*, vol. 2 (Baltimore, 1985), 734; Clayton Torrance, *Old Somerset on the Eastern Shore of Maryland* (Richmond, 1935), 424–26; and Ralph T. Whitelaw, *Virginia's Eastern Shore* (Richmond, 1951), 2:1313, 1319, 1388. Thomas Savage was, like Jane Webb, a native Virginian and had inherited the "home plantation" from his father. The latter had patented nine thousand acres in Northampton County but had sold or leased much of it during his own lifetime, and upon his death, the properties were divided among his children, with Thomas receiving a share roughly equal to the rest of his siblings. John Savage also served as a local justice, but neither he nor his son rose into ranks of the powerful. See Whitelaw, *Virginia's Eastern Shore*, 1:218–20; and Nugent, *Cavaliers and Pioneers*, 1:524–25.

19. On William Byrd II and Landon Carter, see Kenneth A. Lockridge, *On the Sources of Patriarchal Rage: The Commonplace Books of William Byrd and Thomas Jefferson and the Gendering of Power in the Eighteenth Century* (New York, 1996); and Rhys Isaac, *Landon Carter's Uneasy Kingdom: Revolution and Rebellion on a Virginia Plantation* (New York, 2004).

20. For patriarchy and household governance in early Virginia, see Carole Shammas, *A History of Household Government in America* (Charlottesville, VA, 2002), 1–52; Holly Brewer, *By Birth or Consent: Children, Law, and the Anglo-American Revolution in Authority* (Chapel Hill, NC, 2005), especially 17–44; Norton, *Founding Mothers and Fathers;* and Brown, *Good Wives, Nasty Wenches*, 3–5, 13–17; see also Parent, *Foul Means*, 197–236.

21. On discontent and resistance by servants in the early Chesapeake, see, for instance, Brown, *Good Wives, Nasty Wenches*, 139–79; Norton, *Founding Mothers and Fathers*, 132–36, 157, 416, 434; Deal, *Race and Class in Colonial Virginia*, 115–28; Morgan, *American Slavery, American Freedom*, 216–18. For the Atlantic world context of resistance, see Peter Linebaugh and Marcus Rediker, *The Many-Headed Hydra: Sailors, Slaves, Commoners, and the Hidden History of the Revolutionary Atlantic* (Boston, 2000).

22. This essay is mindful of Walter Johnson's caution that "agency" encompasses an Enlightenment emphasis on individual choice and determination that would have been far afield for the early modern subjects discussed here. That caveat notwithstanding, as Cornelia Hughes Dayton has argued, the concept of agency is elastic enough to encompass those individuals who possessed "cultural tools" that allowed them to attempt to shape "important life outcomes." See Walter Johnson, "On Agency," *Journal of Social History* 37 (Fall 2003): 113–24; and Cornelia Hughes Dayton, "Rethinking Agency, Recovering Voices," *American Historical Review* 109 (June 2004): 827–45.

23. The complaints and charges against Henry Smith can be found in ACO (1666–1670), especially ff. 3–5, 81–120, 176–85.

24. These included Joan Powell, Elizabeth Nork, Rachel Moody, Mary Jones, and Mary Hewes, servants; Joanna Matrum Smith, Henry Smith's wife; Ann Cooper and Elizabeth Carter, formerly servants to Henry Smith; Ruth Bundick and Bridgett Savage, neighbors. Richard Chambers, William Nork, Griffith Savage, and Roger Myles offered corroborating or joint statements, but their testimony is extraordinarily brief in comparison with that offered by the women; see ACO (1666–1670), ff. 81–120 and 176–85.

25. See, for instance, Bernard S. Capp, *When Gossips Meet: Women, Family, and Neighbourhood in Early Modern England* (Oxford, 2003), 150–55.

26. A 1662 statute required masters to provide adequate food, clothing, and lodging and prohibited "cruelty" or immoderate correction. The statute stipulated no penalty for offending masters. See Hening, *Statutes at Large*, 2:117–18.

27. According to Mary Beth Norton, complaints brought by servants against masters in southern colonies were more likely to be dismissed, with 57 percent succeeding in their complaints; see *Founding Mothers and Fathers*, 115–16, 433n46; and Coombs, "Building 'The Machine,'" 24.

28. Christine M. Daniels, "'Liberty to Complaine': Servant Petitions in Maryland, 1652–1797," in Christopher L. Tomlins and Bruce H. Mann, eds., *The Many Legalities of Early America* (Chapel Hill, NC, 2001), 238 and 241, table 7.

29. See the Complaint of Joan Powell, ACO (1666–1670), f. 60; and the justices' summation of charges, ACO (1666–1670), f. 176. The Accomack justices also suggested that servants' complaints were "rash." ACO, (1666–1670), ff. 73–74, 178.

30. H. R. McIlwaine, ed., *Minutes of the Council and General Court of Virginia* (Richmond, 1924), 212 (grand jury's decision on rape), 217 (sale of servants). The homicide charges were apparently dismissed; see also Wawrzyczek, "The Women of Accomack County," 20–21.

31. Alexandra Shepard also notes that English courts provided better remedies to mistreated wives than to servants; see her *Meanings of Manhood in Early Modern England* (New York, 2003), 137.

32. Justices summation, ACO (1666–1670), f. 104. One of the Accomack justices eventually paid for Joanna Matrum Smith's passage back to England.

33. On the importance of the neighborhood consensus in policing the actions of household heads, see Lorena S. Walsh, "Community Networks in the Early Chesapeake," in Carr, Morgan, and Russo, eds., *Colonial Chesapeake Society*, 238–41.

34. ACO (1666–1670), f. 128.

35. The contract is referred to in the records as an indenture, but for clarity's sake in this essay, I refer to it as a contract, by which I simply mean a written agreement. Although the document later disappeared, Webb, Savage, and two witnesses testified to its existence. For the description of the contract given by Jane Webb, see *Webb v. Savage* (1725/26), Northampton County Judgments, Library of Virginia; for Thomas Savage's version, see Northampton County Order Book (hereafter NCO), (1722–1729), f. 247, Library of Virginia.

36. Norton, *Founding Mothers and Fathers*, 140.

37. Webb was effectively attempting to purchase Left's freedom with her labor and that of her children. However, by the terms of a Virginia law enacted in 1691—a law certainly in force in 1703 when Webb made her bargain with Savage—no slave could be freed unless the person freeing them paid for their transport out of the country. Left's freedom was within Webb's means, but her indenture, the prospect of transporting both of them out of the country, and the need to leave behind some of their children with Savage was a hefty price to pay indeed. For the 1691 law, see Hening, *Statutes at Large*, 3:87–88.

38. For a description of the contract, see *Webb v. Savage*.

39. As noted above, female children born out of wedlock typically served until the age of twenty-one or until marriage, and males until the age of twenty-four, about three to six years longer than the terms of the Webb children. Those born to white women and fathered by black, Indian, or mixed-race men were to serve until thirty years of age, about

nine years longer than Jane Webb served as a penalty for her own mixed-race parentage. Neither law would have applied to the Webb children because their parents were married and both were mixed race or African Virginian, but they do contextualize the indentures of the Webb children. On these and other statutes, see Hening, *Statutes at Large*, 3:87–88, 453–54, 4:133, and 8:134–35.

40. The Webb children included Dinah (b. 1704), Daniel (b. 1706), Frances (b. 1708), Ann (b. 1711), Elizabeth (b. 1713), Lisha (b. 1716), and Abimelech (b. 1720). See Deal, *Race and Class in Colonial Virginia*, 399–405; and Heinegg, *Free African Americans*, for the genealogy.

41. Brewer, *By Birth or Consent*, 12, 273; Linda K. Kerber, *No Constitutional Right to Be Ladies: Women and the Obligations of Citizenship* (New York, 1998), 52–53; Hening, *Statutes at Large*, 3:447, 1:336, 255.

42. Petition of Thomas Savage, February 10, 1725, Free Negro and Slave Records, Northampton County, Library of Virginia.

43. See, for instance, Coombs, "Building 'The Machine,'" 157; and *Doll v. Gascoinge*, NCO (1689–1698), f. 182.

44. Webb noted in her suit that Savage had "taken the Indenture or Instrument of Writing into his Custody and ... Concealed the same" and that she could not "come to the sight thereof"; see *Webb v. Savage*. On Savage's statement and the witnesses' testimony, see NCO (1722–1729), f. 247.

45. In 1725, the prevailing law stipulated that "negroes, mulattoes and Indian servants, not being Christians" could not be witnesses at trials; this seems to have been variously interpreted and did not always exclude free blacks; see Hening, *Statutes at Large*, 3:298. However, it would not be until 1732 that free blacks were by statute explicitly prevented from witnessing except in trials of slaves. The 1732 statute stipulated that "no negro, mulatto, or Indian, either a slave or free, shall hereafter be admitted in any court of this colony, to be sworn as a witness, or give evidence in any cause whatsoever, except upon the trial of a slave, for a capital offence; in which case they shall be allowed to give evidence." Ibid., 4:327.

46. *Webb v. Savage*. The indication that the justices were "divided" is on the docket on the reverse of the complaint; see NCO (1722–1729), f. 28.

47. On disciplinary violence as a masculine prerogative, see Shepard, *Meanings of Manhood*, 130–31; Anne S. Lombard, *Making Manhood: Growing Up Male in Colonial New England* (Cambridge, MA, 2003), 120–21; Norton, *Founding Mothers and Fathers*, 103–36; Terri L. Snyder, "'As If There Was Not Master or Woman in the Land': Gender, Dependency, and Household Violence in Virginia, 1646–1720," in Christine Daniels and Michael V. Kennedy, eds., *Over the Threshold: Intimate Violence in Early America* (New York, 1999), 219–36; and Susan Dwyer Amussen, "Punishment, Discipline, and Power: The Social Meanings of Violence in Early Modern England," *Journal of British Studies* 34 (1995): 1–34.

48. Shammas argues that the powers of the heads of households in the North American colonies expanded over the course of the colonial period. See *A History of Household Government*, 51. Norton demonstrates that the powers of southern householders exceeded those of their northern counterparts; see *Founding Mothers and Fathers*, 51, 291–92.

49. For discussions of the multiple styles of manhood at work in early modern England and caution against seeing men as one gender, see Shepard, *Meanings of Manhood*, 1–10. For a discussion of styles of manliness in early New England, see Lombard, *Making Manhood*.

50. On the "hybrid" and brutal mastery of early Virginia, see Breen and Innes, *"Myne Owne Ground,"* 48–50, 67.

51. Instead, those who consulted Dalton—one of the favored law books among seventeenth-century Virginia justices—might have profitably turned to his discussion of "the Peace." Here, Dalton begins generally, explaining to his readers that disturbing any "amity, confidence, and quiet between men" is tantamount to breaking the peace. A few sentences below, he is more precise, defining any "injurious force" or "violence" and that included "threatening words," "furious gesture[s]," and "force of the body, or any other force used *in terrorem.*" See Michael Dalton, *The Countrey Justice* (London, 1630), 9 (definitions of *Peace* and *Breach of Peace*), 78 (on battery).

52. Ibid., 77 (on laborers).

53. Hening, *Statutes at Large*, 2:117–18.

54. See, for instance, Brown, *Good Wives, Nasty Wenches*, 139–79; and Morgan, *American Slavery, American Freedom*, 215–36.

55. On domestic handbooks, see Shepard, *Meanings of Manhood*, 138. For female servants and disciplinary violence in the early Chesapeake, see Norton, *Founding Mothers and Fathers*, 115–16; Snyder, *Brabbling Women*, 89–116; and Daniels, "'Liberty to Complain,'" 219–49.

56. Retaliatory violence by male servants was fairly regular in the early Chesapeake. See Daniels, "'Liberty to Complain'"; and Snyder, "'As If There Was Not,'" 219–36.

57. For a parallel example on gendered responses to violence among antebellum slaves, see Stephanie M. H. Camp, *Closer to Freedom: Everyday Resistance in the Plantation South* (Chapel Hill, NC, 2004), 42–43.

58. The joint deposition of Richard Chambers, Elizabeth Nork, William Nork, and Joan Powell states that the men were better provisioned than were the women. See ACO (1666–1670), f. 133.

59. Summation of Charges against Henry Smith, ACO (1666–1670), f. 126.

60. For complaints of women in Henry Smith's household see ACO (1666–1670), depositions of Joanna Matrum, f. 69; Mary Hewes, f. 72; Elizabeth Carter, f. 75; Mary Jones, ff. 99–100; and Mary Hewes, ff. 112. For the neighbor, see deposition of Marrion Fruin, f. 131.

61. Deposition of Richard Chambers, Elizabeth Nork, William Nork, and Joan Powell, ACO (1666–1670), f. 135. Although this is a joint deposition, the individual testifying is often clear.

62. Pagan, *Anne Orthwood's Bastard*, 109.

63. For Savage's delaying tactics, see NCO (1719–1722), ff. 179, 185, 191, 198. For the dismissal, see NCO (1722–1729), f. 46. For the petition itself, see Petition of Jane Webb, October 5, 1722, Free Negro and Slave Records, Northampton County, Library of Virginia.

64. NCO (1722–1729), f. 260.

65. *Webb v. Savage.*

66. The statutes governing the Webb children could be construed in various ways. Prior to the 1690s, Virginia followed English law: out-of-wedlock offspring female servants served terms of twenty-one years, and male servants served to age twenty-four. A statute enacted in 1691 lengthened service for out-of-wedlock mixed-race children to thirty years, if their mothers were white and their fathers black. Hening, *Statutes at Large*, 3:86–88. In 1723, the law decreed that any—not just out-of-wedlock—children born to "female mulatto or Indian" servants in lengthy terms of indenture (thirty years) would serve a similar

thirty-year term to the same master as his or her mother. See Hening, *Statutes at Large*, 4:133. While the 1691, 1705, and 1723 legislation did not expressly apply to the Webb children, it certainly gave them ample reason to be concerned over the exact length of their terms, perhaps especially because Jane Webb's two terms of service totaled thirty years.

67. NCO (1722–1729), f. 278.

68. Emphasis mine. For the 1705 statute preventing "negros, mulattoes and Indian servants, not being Christians" from being witnesses, see Hening, *Statutes at Large*, 3:298. On the 1732 statute that debarred free blacks from witnessing, except in trials of slaves, see ibid., 4:327.

69. See Daniels, "'Liberty to Complain,'"; Deal, *Race and Class in Colonial Virginia*, 115–28; Morgan, *American Slavery, American Freedom*, 216–18.

70. For the resistance of unfree women in the early Chesapeake, see Norton, *Founding Mothers and Fathers*, 132–36, 157, 416, 434; Morgan, *Slave Counterpoint;* Camp, *Closer to Freedom;* Hillary Beckles, *Natural Rebels: A Social History of Enslaved Women in Barbados* (Rutgers, NJ, 1989); and Deborah Gray White, *Ar'n't I a Woman? Female Slaves in the Plantation South* (New York, 1985).

71. Deposition of Joan Powell, ACO (1666–1670), f. 83 ("lawful courses"); deposition of Mary Hewes ("seeke for justice"), f. 72; deposition of Mary Jones (rape), f. 99. By law, women who became pregnant before their indentures were finished served their masters for two additional years. See Hening, *Statutes at Large* 2:166–77.

72. Deposition of Mary Hewes, ACO (1666–1670), f. 130. On testifying by children, see Brewer, *By Birth or Consent*, 137.

73. The Accomack justices referred to the "common fame" of Smith's abuse when Joan Powell made her first complaint against him in June 1668; this suggests his servants had been gossiping about their treatment. See Complaint of Joan Powell, ACO (1666–1670), f. 60.

74. ACO (1666–1670), depositions of Elizabeth Nork, f. 87; Jane Pearce, f. 88; Marion Fruin, f. 81.

75. ACO (1666–1670), joint deposition of Joan Powell and Rachel Moody, f. 128; depositions of Elizabeth Nork and Ann Cooper, f. 101.

76. That Jane Webb uttered "dangerous words" is entered as the information of Colonel George Harmanson, NCO (1722–1729), ff. 247–48.

77. Deposition of Elizabeth Nork, ACO (1666–1670), f. 131.

78. Deposition of Joan Powell, ACO (1666–1670), ff. 84–85. This incident might be read as a "mosaic of different interests" that occasionally brought together women of different classes and races in Virginia households rather than as an example of collective action, as I regard it. See Brown, *Good Wives, Nasty Wenches*, 307.

79. Petition of Thomas Savage, February 10, 1725, Free Negro and Slave Records, Northampton County, Library of Virginia; see also Deal, *Race and Class in Colonial Virginia*, 400, 404n11.

80. NCO no. 20 (1732–1742), f. 6.

81. Petition of Dinah Webb, NCO (1722–1729), f. 179.

82. Elizabeth Webb offered to serve Elizabeth Harmanson sixteen years "under Condition that the said Elizabeth will admit her to be married to her Negroe fellow Ezekiel Moses." See NCO (1732–1742), f. 382. Moses is described as a slave elsewhere; see Heinegg, "Moses Family," in *Free African Americans*.

83. Petition of Nanny Webb, NCO (1732–1742), f. 7.

84. This is also Douglas Deal's suggestion. See *Race and Class in Colonial Virginia,* 400.

85. Her eldest son left the Eastern Shore for North Carolina, where he prospered. See Heinegg, *Free African Americans.* Her youngest son, Abimelech, was convicted in 1750 for asserting that the "Negroes ... would be free" and that "with their one [e]ndeavour and godalmightys assistance or blessing" they might "go though the County in one night's time." For this he received fifty lashes, perhaps at the same whipping post where, a quarter century earlier, his mother received her own punishment. Abimelech's expression of race consciousness strongly suggests that, while he was a servant, by 1750 he understood his condition to be more intimately linked with that of slaves than of free persons and that race was becoming important as laws increasingly took away the rights of free blacks. See NCO (1748–1751), ff. 271–272; and Deal, *Race and Class in Colonial Virginia,* 402.

86. Carr and Walsh, "the Planter's Wife," 542–43.

87. Alexandra Shepard offers a useful corrective to Americanists by suggesting that mastery in England went largely unregulated during this period as well. See *Meanings of Manhood,* 132–39.

88. Hening, *Statutes at Large,* 2:270–71. As Edmund S. Morgan points out, this law is the foundation for unrestrained treatment of slaves; later legislation only extended the principle laid down by this law; see *American Slavery, American Freedom,* 312–13.

89. Deposition of Mary Hewes, ACO (1666–1670), f. 112.

90. Other scholars have suggested that Smith went free from all charges, and while it is true that the felony charges were dismissed, the local justices did make some attempt, however unsuccessfully, to control his behavior through legal mechanisms. See n. 1, above.

91. Deposition of Joanna Matrum, ACO (1666–1670), f. 177.

Deference, Defiance, and the Language of Office in Seventeenth-Century Virginia

ALEXANDER B. HASKELL

In 1794, the Reverend Devereux Jarratt looked back nostalgically on his childhood in New Kent County, Virginia, recalling the "regard and reverence" that people then "paid to magistrates and persons in public office." Unlike the "high republican times" of the 1790s, when Jarratt believed there was "more leveling than [was] ... consistent with good government," settlers in the 1730s and 1740s knew their places better and were more apt to give respect where respect was due, especially when an office was held by a recognized gentleman. "We were accustomed to look upon what were called gentle folks as being of a superior order," Jarratt said. "For my part, I was quite shy of them, and kept off at a humble distance." Indeed, because gentlemen were most easily distinguishable by the periwigs that they commonly wore, Jarratt recalled responding viscerally any time he saw "a man riding the road, near our house, with a wig on." The sight "would so alarm my fears, and give me such a disagreeable feeling, that, I dare say, I would run off, as for my life."[1]

Jarratt's bashful flight from bewigged gentlemen has come to serve in many histories of early America as the example par excellence of deferential behavior. Jarratt's unhesitating belief that a vast social gulf lay between gentlemen and more ordinary settlers, his assumption that "simple" folk (like his carpenter father) had a duty to defer to gentlemen in the exercise of their offices, and his view that "magistrates and [other] persons in public office" deserved not just respect but even something approaching reverence for the contributions they were making to the polity, all have made Jarratt's autobiographical musings particularly useful for historians who want to stress the persistence of traditional valuations of order, authority, and hierarchy among settlers, thereby highlighting the novelty of the more democratic and egalitarian world that began crystallizing in the wake of the American Revolution.[2]

But precisely the aspect of Jarratt's narrative that makes it so useful in this regard—his self-conscious sense of humility, even obeisance, in the mere presence of gentlemen—has also made him something of a lightning rod for another group of historians with a rather different, though equally valuable, scholarly agenda. These historians, whose aim has been primarily to recover ordinary settlers' political behaviors in all their rich complexity and to describe the colonial political order in a way that pays equal attention to the will of the governed and the ideals of governors, have tended to discount Jarratt's memory as romantic and grossly unrepresentative of the bold and often defiant attitude that settlers often displayed in the face of governing authority.

Several distinguished scholars, including Michael Zuckerman and Greg Nobles, have gone so far as to propose discarding the concept of deference entirely because of its failure to accommodate fully the "unruliness of the rabble." Zuckerman says flatly that Jarratt was "indisputably wrong" in believing that his own "ideas about the difference between gentle and simple" folk were "universal among all of my rank and age." "So far from fearing the gentry or even from being intimidated by constituted authority," Zuckerman says, "commoners all over the Virginia of Jarratt's youth boldly imposed themselves on their self-styled betters." Indeed, settler defiance (the "unruliness of the rabble") was so pronounced in Zuckerman's view that he proposes that we replace the prevailing assumption of widespread colonial deference with a depiction of early America as filled with the "bumptious egalitarianism and antiauthoritarianism" that Alexis de Tocqueville and Frederick Jackson Turner once regarded as the colonies' defining political characteristics. Nobles does not go quite so far as Zuckerman in proposing a return to a view of early America as egalitarian, but his treatment of Jarratt's account similarly downplays the significance of deference. For Nobles, deference functioned mainly as a facade. It was a form of role-playing, an act of "artful misdirection, deception, or display, a personal performance that puts on the appearance of acceptance and submission but masks another, more resistant pose altogether." Some persons, like Jarratt, might have internalized this act of resistance to the extent that they "accepted their own lowliness" (to use Gordon Wood's phrase), but Nobles proposes that most people simply donned this mask of deference from time to time whenever they regarded it as a useful "tactic of negotiation" in the "incessant, if often implicit, effort to redefine their lives."[3]

This essay seeks to find a middle ground between these two positions, not by discarding the concept of deference or by denying the existence of settler defiance, but rather by shifting the discussion in such a way as to show that deference and defiance in the early modern Anglo-American world were not contradictory or mutually exclusive categories in quite the way that we have sometimes imagined. I make this case by relying upon the political scientist Conal Condren's recent investigations into a widespread early modern European vocabulary of office holding and its abuse, a form of argumentation and way of conceiving of the world that Condren persuasively shows was "pervasive" in early modern England and that he proposes underlay virtually all discussion of authority and moral responsibility from the sixteenth to the mid- to late eighteenth century, when a number of factors (which I discuss toward the end of this essay) contributed to the vocabulary's diminishing resonance.[4] Although Condren's own focus is not on deference per se, his demonstration of the way in which the vocabulary of office worked in everyday as well as more philosophical argumentation suggests some intriguing possibilities for reconsidering the meaning and dynamics of early modern Anglo-American deference, precisely by situating it in relationship to persistent and often highly complex and open-ended arguments about when people were or were not fulfilling the requirements of their respective offices. By examining such arguments as they occurred in colonial Virginia courts and within Virginia's developing rural neighborhoods, and as they were uttered by ordinary settlers as well as by their ostensible betters, I try to recover the complexities of an emerging colonial political world in which deference and defiance were not opposites but were rather flip sides of the same conceptual coin.[5]

Let us turn again to Jarratt's autobiography but focus, for now, not on his famous flight from gentlemen scene but rather on a much less studied passage that on first glance might appear to have very little to do with the theme of deference. The passage, like the rest of the autobiography, was addressed to Jarratt's fellow Episcopal minister John Coleman, whom Jarratt had charged with the task of publishing his autobiographical letters after his death. In the passage, Jarratt set forth his view of why the deists were wrong in denying Jesus's divinity. His argument rested explicitly upon the assumption that Jesus was above all an officeholder, in particular the only fit person to perform the office of shepherd of God's human flock. Jarratt was especially eager to make the (decidedly circular) case that Jesus's possession of the qualities needed for the office and the office's requirement of those qualities were mutually supporting:

> I see in my shepherd every perfection requisite for the office he sustains, and every qualification necessary to enable him to take care of such needy, oppressed, frail creatures as we are. He is perfectly acquainted with every individual of his flock—he is intimately near them—his eye is upon them, and his ear is open to the prayers of all, equally as to the prayer of any particular one; his arm supports, leads, guides and protects them at all times, in all ages and in all places.... Such, my friend, is our shepherd—and could I be induced to suppose, for a moment, that he is not possessed of every attribute of divinity, supreme, and incommunicable, my hope would sink, my heart faint, and my soul despair. But the very nature of his office requires that he should be possessed of these divine perfections, and the holy scriptures assure us that he is possessed of them.[6]

In short, Jesus's identity as God's son and the duties of his office (outlined by scripture) were so interchangeable that the one effectively proved the existence of the other.

Several aspects of this passage are relevant for our understanding of the vocabulary of office and its relationship to deference. The first observation to make is simply the readiness with which Jarratt turned to a vocabulary of office to make his complex theological case. Condren has argued that, in England, the language of office was just that, a vocabulary for moral discourse rather than a particular ideology or even a singular concept.[7] Particular shared presuppositions arose from the vocabulary, making it far more than simply random talk; indeed, because it was almost universally accepted, the language effectively gave rise to the world of offices that it described. But its power rested fundamentally in its universality and, as we will see in more detail below, its profound adaptability. Jarratt used this language, in other words, not only because it could accommodate diverse, even contradictory, moral claims but also because it offered a mutually acceptable basis for conversation on matters that were otherwise extremely divisive.

As is also clear from Jarratt's passage, the vocabulary of office by no means concerned itself solely with the political offices that are the usual stock-in-trade of political and institutional historians. While magistrate, minister, sheriff, and monarch were all offices, so too were subject, mother, master, servant, and Son of God.[8] The language of office presumed not the existence of a Weberian bureaucratic state but rather the existence of a God-ordained world in which capacities, duties, and offices were all mutually interconnected. One possesses an office because one possesses the capacities, or qualities, to perform it; in turn, the possession of that office imposes duties that nobody, not even Jesus, can ignore without falling into the grievous sin of office abuse. Within this logic, virtually any element of the natural world could be described as occupying an office. Jarratt even assigned such a place to his molars. With old age, he complained, one's teeth become few and "the grinders cease to perform their office of mastication."[9]

That this reasoning sounds much like that associated with the conception of the calling, a notion with which early Americanists are generally more familiar than they are with the concept of office, is not accidental. Condren finds a wide range of terms that, while not always synonymous with office, nevertheless were often interchangeable with it. In this list, he includes the terms "calling, vocation, trade, sphere, role, condition, profession, sometimes power, often care."[10] Jarratt, in addition to "calling" and "office," also used the words "station" and "place" as rough synonyms for office, such as when in the autobiography he thanks Jesus for raising him "from the depths of obscurity, and the lowest walks of life" to the "distinguished place and station" of minister.[11] The conflation of all these terms reflected in part the importance of the common ideas that they communicated and in part the way in which classical and Christian terminology had fused over time. Office, after all, had conspicuous classical origins. Many English people would have encountered the idea of office as sphere of duty in Cicero's *De officiis*, a staple of early modern English school curricula. The association of just rule with the office of the shepherd, an analogy that became a favorite of the eighteenth-century Virginia gentry, appears in Plato's *Republic*. But by the early modern era all of these classical concepts had become so bound up with analogous Christian terms like *calling* and *vocation* that they became virtually indistinguishable. Ciceronian office, the Platonic shepherd, and the New Testament conception of calling had blurred into one.[12]

Jarratt made one other crucially important dimension of the language of office clear in his discussion of Jesus's divinity: office's duplex nature. The vocabulary of office always presupposed that offices existed in interrelationship.[13] For Jarratt, Jesus's performance of the office of shepherd implied that those persons under his care also occupied an office, that of the sheep of his flock, and the two offices had meaning only in relationship with one another. Indeed, Jarratt took this sense of official interrelationship so much for granted that he used it to buttress his claim of Jesus's divinity; Jarratt's capacity to fulfill his own duties served as evidence that Jesus must have the proper qualifications to fulfill his own. "If I am one of his people, and of the sheep of his pasture," Jarratt said, "then I am an individual of a very numerous flock—a flock wide diffused and scattered on a thousand hills throughout the habitable world" and thus in danger of being "overlooked amidst the multiplicity of objects and concerns which must engage his [i.e., Jesus's] attention." So how was Jarratt to perform his own sheep-like duty of feeling absolute comfort and trust in Jesus's protection? He could do so only if Jesus truly possessed divinity: "If Jesus, my Shepard, be the omnipotent, omniscient, and omnipresent Jehovah, as David's shepherd was, then my fears depart—suspicious glooms disperse, and [my own] cheerful hopes of safety and protection dawn and revive."[14]

Here we might appear to be quite far from any meaningful discussion of deference. But what I want to suggest is that it was precisely in this extraordinarily intricate sort of reasoning about office—in this case, Jarratt's tightrope-like reckoning that one individual's office could most appropriately be judged on the basis of another person's own official capacities—that we come closest to understanding early modern deference in practice. For deference was, strictly speaking, the performance of a duty of office by one officeholder toward his or her official other. To adopt Jarratt's language, the "due submission" that he regarded as owed to "gentle folks" rested upon his assumption that gentlemen did indeed possess capacities that automatically conferred upon them a particular kind of office—what Condren calls an "office of rule"—that "simple" persons, the governed, were bound (by their own office) to respect.[15] But this assumption of gentlemen's superior capacities did not in and of itself foreclose all possibility of independent judgment and even "defiance" on the part of the governed. On the contrary, it actively invited such judgment because of the language of office with which the duty of deference itself was understood.

To grasp this logic, we might usefully consider one last passage in Jarratt's autobiography. This was a withering critique of his childhood parish minister, a critique that seems so much more the province of the "boldly" imposing commoners of Zuckerman's account than of the obsequious boy with whom Jarratt is usually associated that we are immediately struck by how different Jarratt's own understanding of "due subordination" must have been from the one that we usually read into such accounts. The critique went as follows. The minister "was but a poor preacher—very unapt to teach or even to gain the attention of an audience," Jarratt said. "Being very nearsighted, and preaching wholly by a written copy, he kept his eyes continually fixed on the paper, and so near, that what he said seemed rather addressed to the cushion than to the congregation."[16]

To us, the force of this criticism is easy to miss. But in Jarratt's narrative the attack on the minister as a lackluster preacher serves to reveal a profound failure of office. The minister's poor delivery is far from simply a laughable defect in ministerial aptitude; it is, on the contrary, one of the principal reasons Jarratt himself failed to attend church as a child and thus for so long "followed the way of my own heart" and "walked in the sight of my own eyes" without ever "considering, as every one ought, *that for all these things God would bring me into judgment.*"[17] In other words, the minister's failure of office had an inevitable effect on Jarratt's capacity to fulfill his own offices, including that most vital one of service to God. The minister's behavior, therefore, did not just deserve criticism; it demanded it.

Our own impulse in encountering this critique only a few short pages after Jarratt's harangue about Americans' lamentable loss of esteem for "persons in public office" is to accuse him of hypocrisy; after all, was not the minister a public officer requiring deference? But whereas we tend to think in modern sociological terms (especially in the language of "class") and thus assume that status is a fairly stable thing that is uninfluenced by conduct, Jarratt saw the world in early modern official terms. For him, poor conduct in office, especially an egregious lack of capacity like the minister's, effectively denied his station as minister and thus dissolved any obligation of respect that his ministerial office might otherwise have demanded. To be sure, people did not lose their offices left and right in the early modern Anglo-American world just because their rivals happened to accuse them of misconduct; such an outcome was extremely rare. The point is rather that, because office abuse implied an absolute failure of moral obligation and, therefore, in extreme cases, as Condren says, "erased, sometimes almost by definition, moral identity and social standing," the language of office opened up considerable moral room for legitimate criticism of officials.[18] As a result, someone like Jarratt, who evidently regarded due "respect and reverence" for officeholders as the linchpin of an orderly and moral universe, nevertheless also apparently felt little, if any, compunction about singling out abuses of office, even when they were committed by "gentle folks"—in part, because an abuse of office signaled, in and of itself, that a gentleman was not really a gentleman.

This latter point deserves further explication because it contrasts so sharply with the presumptions about class that we still almost automatically read into the seventeenth and eighteenth centuries that hopelessly cloud our understanding of deference. To put it crudely, our impulse is to look back into the colonial past and to attempt to identify where everyone stood in relation to everyone else in terms of certain material markers, especially wealth. We then, on the basis of that assessment of the society's makeup, judge the strength or weakness of deference on the basis of whether one "class," ordinary settlers, deferred to another "class," grandees; if they did not, then we regard deference as weak, nonexistent, or for show rather than genuine or heartfelt. But in a world conceived of in terms of office, where the distinguishing characteristic of a "gentleman" was not only that he had the wealth to support such a charge but also that he fulfilled the duties that the office of gentleman required, then suddenly the test of whether deference was strong or weak becomes much more complex, for it requires that we examine in any individual case of seemingly "undeferential" behavior whether it was the office or its erstwhile occupant who was being condemned.

That offices and persons were potentially distinguishable was a vital presupposition of office, although it should not be confused with Nobles's conception of artful role-playing. The language of office did indeed envision officeholders (that is, everyone, the governed and governors alike) as *personae* rather than persons. This assumption helped open up room for criticizing officials; one could claim to condemn the person while still according due respect to the *persona* and office itself. Alternatively, a critic of an officeholder could deflect blame by claiming that his own *persona* was momentarily disrupted, for instance by drink or by the seductive assurances of a demagogue, thus rendering his act the mere conduct of his imperfect person rather than his far more duty-bound *persona*. The same idea also proved useful in preserving the continuity of offices during troubled times; most famously, the idea of the king's two bodies, one the *persona* of office and the other the corporal body that inhabited it, proved highly appealing in England because of the perceived insecurity of the monarchy. But the notion of *persona*, as Condren takes special pains to show, is quite different from the notion of social role-play that is associated with writers such as Erving

Goffman and, more recently, James C. Scott, Nobles's own model and an increasingly popular one for students of "negotiated power" in early modern Britain.[19]

Whereas the idea of social role-play invites endless speculation about the "artful misdirection, deception, or display" that Nobles urges us to see behind settler deference, *persona* had different implications.[20] It was, again to quote Condren, "a manifestation, or realization and representation of a character, or type, such as a young slave, an old man, a free woman."[21] One could easily add to these examples Jarratt's own characters of "gentle and simple" folk. Sometimes, in some circumstances, one occupied the office of a "simple" man, especially when a gentleman was present. But that did not boil down to the playing of a part in quite the way that Nobles imagines it, nor did it exhaust one's *personae*. To use another example from Jarratt's autobiography, he described his parents as persons who dutifully acted in ways that were "suitable to their humble station." They "lived in credit among their neighbors ... and above the frowns of the world," and they provided Jarratt and his siblings with basic educations and church teachings so that they too could take up "some honest calling, that we might earn our bread by the sweat of our brow, as they did."[22] But in some instances, Jarratt's father undoubtedly asserted his *persona*, not as "humble" man, but as father of the household or as freeman or as tradesman, just as Jarratt's mother likely occasionally asserted her *persona* as goodwife rather than "simple" woman. These were richly suggestive character types that communicated a world of assumptions about not only one's duties but also what one was owed. They were not simply masks that one tried on at will, nor were they statuses that were straightforwardly linked to class. Although wealth contributed to one's capacity to make a credible claim to any number of these *personae*, ultimately they were hashed out in the crucible of local opinion. One fought for one's reputation as a goodwife or honest yeoman or even subject because these *personae* defined one's moral being.

They also inevitably placed people in the position of facing multiple, even conflicting, obligations simultaneously. Indeed, if anything defined a world of offices, it was this, the dilemma—and certainly sometimes the opportunity—created by competing duties. The centrality of this dilemma of competing duties, as Condren shows, made casuistry a far more vital element of early modern English culture than has generally been recognized, so vital in fact that Condren suggests that "much of what we inadvertently reclassify as political theory" in this period was actually "pervasively casuistical."

Casuistry is a method for adjudicating conflicting moral claims when no definitive code of acceptable behavior exists, or to use Condren's preferred description, which moves beyond seeing casuistry as a singular doctrine, it was a "constellation of propensities sharing the recognition that principles under-determine conduct." Casuistry figured significantly in areas like the law and religion because the welter of values in play in such disciplines required delicate navigation. The political and religious uncertainties of post-Reformation Europe made casuistry in this regard especially relevant because cases of conscience, casuistry's raison d'être, became so pronounced. This form of casuistry, which involved mediating among different moral imperatives within a single general office, Condren calls *presumptive casuistry*. But the array of *personae* presumed by the vocabulary of office required an additional form of casuistry as well, one that allowed a person to navigate the "persistent tension between the ethical demands of adjacent offices." This form of casuistry, which involved adjudicating the different moral imperatives of alternative *personae*, Condren calls *modal casuistry*. The modal casuistic defense was "that, in a given case, one sort of duty [by a particular *persona*] took precedence over another. What the servant could not say, the counselor must; what the woman could not steal, the mother might. What the subject must accept, the citizen, or the patriot, might stand against."[23] Or to use Jarratt's example, what a parishioner feared to allege about his minister the neglected child of God had a duty to expose.

In short, office talk envisioned deference not as a duty incumbent upon persons in every circumstance of their lives but rather as a duty required only in those very particular situations when no other pressing obligation, no other duty to one's *personae*, could credibly be seen as having precedence. Another way of putting the same point is that, in a world of often conflicting offices, deference and defiance existed less as hard-and-fast behaviors than as propositions. The aggrieved target of a charge of office abuse might condemn his accuser of defiance (an immoral violation of duty), but the accuser in turn had every incentive to assert that the opposite was true: her criticism was entirely consistent with deference (a due regard for duty) because it was her adversaries' violated office, not her own, that was on trial. The reality of the situation, that is, who in fact was guilty of office abuse, depended ultimately on how other members of the community, the putative judges in all such confrontations over duty and authority, viewed such conflicting claims of individual propriety.

This involvement of the community as the vital monitors and judges of these negotiations over obligation is perhaps the most important point to make in regard to the relationship between deference and defiance. Too often scholars have evaluated the strength or weakness of deference on the basis of individual acts of contempt viewed in isolation of the context in which they were made. But if I am right that the language of office created far more maneuvering room for criticizing officeholders within the bounds of communal norms of propriety than usually thought possible in a "deferential political culture," then we need to pay more attention than we traditionally have done, not just to individual acts of contempt, but to the complex deliberations and judgments that such acts inevitably triggered within the community at large and that to a great extent determined how those acts were to be interpreted: as instances of deference, or of defiance.

In what follows, I examine two confrontations over authority that came before Virginia courts in the seventeenth century. I have chosen these two cases from roughly a hundred such examples that I have drawn from the seventeenth- and eighteenth-century records of Virginia county courts and the colony's General Court that might have served equally well to show the dynamics of the language of office in action. These two cases stand out, not because they are anomalous (in fact they are highly representative of other cases I have examined), but rather because their records are sufficiently complete to permit a greater glimpse than is sometimes available at the community deliberations that accompanied these negotiations over authority.[24] The two cases are interesting as well because they cover a range of different scenarios. The first case, for instance, occurred very early in the colony's history, in the mid-1620s, when county courts had not yet emerged or supplanted the General Court at Jamestown as the primary arenas for negotiating over authority, and involved an ordinary male settler (or "poor" man, as he characterized his own *persona* at one point) challenging the authority of some of the colony's most prominent officeholders, including the governor himself. I suggest as one reason for the sheer audacity of his challenge the unusually precarious political circumstances that prevailed in Virginia in the mid-1620s, circumstances that greatly affected how other members of the community were likely to judge his particular casuistic arguments. The second case, in contrast, considers a very different scenario. The accuser in this case was not a man but a female parishioner, a planter's wife who took a great interest in the state of her local church in mid-seventeenth-century Marston Parish, a parish that overlapped with York County. Her challenge to authority was more limited than her predecessor's. Rather than accusing the entire government of office abuse, she directed her contempt only at two very particular local church officials. Although her gender clearly affected how other community members judged her accusations, what is more conspicuous is simply how the greater density of kin and neighborhood networks that existed in local Virginia communities by midcentury held everyone, accusers as well as the accused, to greater scrutiny—a state of affairs that while limiting in certain ways the maneuvering room for accusing persons of office abuse also worked the other way and subjected officeholders to higher expectations. It is perhaps this state of affairs that we most have in mind when we speak of deference as "growing" as colonial societies gradually cohered.

On August 16, 1624, Virginia's fledgling General Court considered an elaborate defamation suit. The plaintiff in the case, John Utie, accused William Tyler of defaming him by calling him a "fidlinge Rogue and Rascall" and by alleging that he had stolen Virginia Company tobacco. As details of the case came to light, it turned out that the tensions between the two men arose from a subtle contest over status. According to one deponent, the controversy began over the most mundane of subjects, a fishing hook. Yet Utie, someone who bore the appellations "Ensign" and "Mr." in court and who thus was striving at least to be seen as a gentleman, had taken offense at Tyler's presumptuousness and asserted that he had "growne very high and loftie." It was at this point that Tyler apparently shot back that Utie was a fiddler and a thief, but, as he explained later to the court, these were not undeferential remarks; he really had seen Utie play "A violl at sea" and had heard "other[s] say [that] he was a musitione in England," and he knew for a fact that Utie carried the company's tobacco at night to the houses of certain high-ranking Virginia officials.[25] In short, Tyler was denying any failure of duty on his part, and he was doing so precisely by framing his action as an honorable instance of exposing Utie's own abuse of office. Rather than failing to show Utie the deference that he deserved, Tyler was exposing the man for the faux gentleman that he really was.

How the court might have handled this allegation of Utie's masqueraded status on its own is impossible to say, for Tyler's hint that certain of the colony's leading officials were recipients of Utie's stolen tobacco suddenly gave the case a whole new dimension. In particular, Tyler had said that one of Utie's accomplices was Ralph Hamor, who was not only a member of the governor's council but also, by virtue of that office, a member of the General Court itself. Thus, the case now implicated another, far more prestigious officeholder and therefore gave the question of Tyler's deference new, more pointed relevance.

At this point, it is worth stepping back momentarily to consider the unusually precarious political circumstances that prevailed in Virginia at this early stage in settlement, for that precariousness helps to explain both Tyler's startling audaciousness in defying Hamor's authority and Hamor's own curious caginess in responding to Tyler's defamation. In the fall of 1624, the Virginia polity teetered on the brink of implosion. The surprise deadly assault on the young settlement by a confederacy of local Indian groups led by the Powhatan ruler Opechancanough two years earlier had left settlers stunned and uncertain about what the colony's ultimate fate would be. Rumors about the possible revocation of the Virginia Company's charter added to the confusion. Exploiting these uncertainties, several powerful settlers, including most prominently Captain John Martin, a wealthy planter and former councilor whom the colony's current oligarchy had shunted aside in earlier years, began maneuvering for position in an effort to enhance their own political power. Martin especially sought to undermine the legitimacy of the prevailing oligarchy, and he did so, naturally, by declaring that Governor Sir Francis Wyatt and the councilors around him (including Hamor) were guilty of office abuse. They were, he said, "Rebels," persons defiant of all duties, and as a result, under the colony's new royal government, they would surely find themselves supplanted by a "new Governor and Counsell" who were more respectful of their offices.[26]

Thus, in making his own accusations against local leaders, Tyler was merely adding his critical voice to a rising chorus of others. Whether or not Tyler was directly allied with Martin is difficult now to determine, but at the very least it seems likely both that Tyler was emboldened by this higher-ranking settler's own defiance of local leaders and that Hamor himself recognized that Tyler's slander was only the most immediate manifestation of a broader show of discontent that went so far as to question whether the current government still possessed the legitimacy to govern at all. That Martin and, by extension, Tyler were able to invoke the king's new authority in the colony to further reinforce their own position only enhanced the threat posed to Hamor and his associates. Thus, the confrontation between Tyler and Hamor that occurred in the General Court, before an audience that probably included sizable numbers of ordinary settlers as well as more elite officials, was less a clear-cut case either of settler defiance or of impugned magisterial pride than an intricate political dance in which both individuals, as well as the audience watching them, recognized that a great deal indeed was open for contestation, including the very question of whether criticism of the government was justifiable or not.

Hamor, despite his indisputable elite status, felt the burden of this tense confrontation no less acutely than did his humbler rival. As a result, rather than simply charging Tyler with defamation, Hamor seems to have pursued another, more ambitious tack: he attempted to portray Tyler as a man who was so unmindful of his duties, so disrespectful of his office as a member of the governed, that he recklessly disregarded all magisterial authority whatsoever. Relying on no fewer than four witnesses, Hamor sought to neutralize the allegation that he was a thief by painting Tyler as an indiscriminate condemner of authority who dangerously attempted to introduce class rifts into the already fragile polity. Hamor began this attack by testifying himself that Tyler had made shockingly bold accusations against the government as a whole. According to Hamor, Tyler said in his presence that neither "the Governor nor Counsell could or would doe any poore men right, but that they would shew favor to great men and wronge the poore." Another deponent, Ryse Watkins, related Tyler's speech in somewhat greater detail:

> William Tyler said to Captain Hamer that [even] if hee [i.e., Tyler] were A man of meanes ... hee would nott be one of the Counsell, Captain Hamer asked Tyler why, To which Tyler answered that his Conscyence would not suffer [it] because he could doe noe righte, To which Captain Hamer said *doe you know any of the Counsell that doe any man wronge,* Tyler answered that poore men could hardly gett any righte and that the great men wold hold all together, and fourther said that he did not see that the Governor could doe any man right.

Watkins went on to relate certain of Tyler's other assertions "concerning ye awthorytie ... [that] ye Governor and Counsell had to punishe men," an apparent reference to controversial powers left over from the colony's military regime of earlier years that Governor Wyatt and his council continued to wield over the objections of a number of settlers.[27]

That Hamor and his allies would introduce these scandalous statements at all in the trial suggests that they took for granted that Tyler's words were already common knowledge. Ignoring the words could therefore be more dangerous than presenting them as evidence of Tyler's lack of credibility. Yet the tension in the court must have been palpable, for nobody could have known the consequence of introducing the statements in this context when the verdict of local settlers—their popular judgment on the issue of where legitimacy lay—was so uncertain. Would settlers agree with Tyler that the entire colonial government was guilty of office abuse, a profound accusation that if accepted would, in one fell swoop, strip away whatever legitimacy the current government still possessed? Or would settlers accept the implication by Hamor and his witnesses that Tyler's assertions were, even if not entirely groundless, nevertheless so threatening to order in precarious times as to justify making an example of Tyler through some public punishment?

In this intensely delicate moment, the issue of deference per se took a backseat to the broader matter of office abuse. Who was the real abuser of office in this case? Hamor and his fellows, embracing the *personae* of recklessly defamed magistrates, sought to cast Tyler as standing outside the pale of civil conduct. They did so, however, not from a position of strength but rather from a clear-eyed recognition that Tyler's statements might tar them as the true abusers of office, self-interested magistrates whose partisanship for their fellow wealthy elites made them incapable of the justice toward all subjects that their offices demanded. Tyler made such an assertion not only in his *persona* as a "poor" man, someone who knew firsthand the government's neglect in this regard, but also in his *persona* as one of God's children, someone endowed, as all persons were, with conscience and thus capable of cutting through mere human artifices about what was right and wrong by consulting the original moral source. Under the colony's fraught circumstances of the mid-1620s, these latter *personae* could easily trump in moral authority the magisterial *persona* that Hamor and his fellows asserted, *even though* under most circumstances this magisterial *persona* was owed deference. Indeed, in the political confusion of this period, when it was not even clear whether accepting the authority of Wyatt's government was in keeping with the king's own desires (a possibility that Martin especially insinuated), the charges that Tyler directed against Wyatt and his fellows could appear to be the very essence of deference, not a stark violation of it.

Thus, moments of pronounced political uncertainty like that which the colony faced in the mid-1620s gave the language of office a particular edge, plunging settlers into those profound (and probably for many persons, deeply disquieting) casuistic moments in which every individual, consulting his or her conscience or engaging in whatever other form of self-justification was available, had to determine whether he or she agreed that an entire body of officials was guilty of office abuse rather than deserving of deference. Similarly profound casuistic moments occurred in seventeenth-century Virginia in 1635 (during the "thrusting out" of Governor Sir John Harvey), in the mid-1670s (during Bacon's Rebellion), and in 1682–83 (during the so-called Plant-Cutting Riots, a referendum on the official misconduct of the long-absent governor Lord Thomas Culpeper). That so many powerful, soul-searching confrontations between settlers and their government occurred in Virginia's first century suggests the difficulty that the colony experienced in this time in reaching an acceptable equilibrium between governing magistrates' official behavior and settlers' own expectations of what that behavior should be. But, of course, even in this prolonged "sorting out" period, moments of profound instability were periodic and short lived rather than continuous.[28] In between such sudden and sporadic political nadirs, people settled down, seeking out as much normalcy and order as they could find.

The second case we will consider took place during one of these "settling down" periods. The case came before the local court of York County, Virginia, on October 26, 1658, in the form of another defamation suit. The plaintiff in the case, Robert Cobb, a Marston Parish churchwarden, complained that he, Thomas Bromfield (a parish vestryman), and their wives had been the targets of a well-organized libel campaign. Three women in the parish, Elizabeth Woods, the campaign's apparent ringleader, and Johannah Poynter and Elianor Cooper, had dropped notices inside and outside the church that were addressed to the "Gentlemen" of the congregation and that announced a supposed scandal. Allegedly, the Bromfields and Cobbs had manufactured a merkin, a pubic wig traditionally worn by prostitutes, and then sent it to a couple in the neighborhood, perhaps as a bawdy joke or maybe as a coarse rebuke for perceived illicit conduct. According to the libel, Bromfield purportedly followed up the gesture by encouraging another neighbor to inquire of the couple "how they like itt." The libel ended by asking its "beholders" whether on the basis of such behavior Cobb and Bromfield "are fitt to beare office in the Church."[29]

Here then was another instance in which abuse of office was the explicit charge, and once again we encounter the elaborate maneuvering that inevitably accompanied such accusations. But Woods's accusations against Bromfield and Cobb took place in a very different context than that which had framed Tyler's accusations against Hamor. By the 1650s, Virginia society was more settled and diverse than it had been three decades earlier. A network of county courts radiated out from the General Court in Jamestown to serve a settler population that numbered now around forty thousand rather than the paltry twelve hundred or so persons who had inhabited the colony in the mid-1620s. The volatility of that earlier era had given way to a sustained political calm that even the disruptions caused by the English Civil War did little to disturb. Although men still greatly outnumbered women, the ratio between them had begun to narrow, and county and parish jurisdictions now marked out a communal geography that, while not identical to England's, was sufficiently so to reassure settlers that Virginia was an ever more orderly and civilized world.

These relatively tranquil circumstances by no means foreclosed the possibility of ferreting out official misconduct, but they did significantly complicate the problem of convincing other community members to regard such an agenda as beneficial rather than disruptive to the neighborhood. Elizabeth Woods knew these limits well—hence her decision to address the libel to the gentlemen members of the congregation. These were the members of the community who ultimately needed convincing if real pressure were to be brought to bear on church officials, for it was their *persona* as gentlemen that gave them moral authority over the conduct of other gentlemen serving as churchwardens and vestrymen. What about her own *personae* as a goodwife and a female parishioner? Did those *personae* potentially have moral leverage in a parish confrontation like this one? Intriguingly, Woods seems initially to have believed that they did, for at first she signed her name to the libels and only desisted after her husband, alarmed at learning of her involvement in the libel campaign, "spake to hir to cut hir ... name out."[30] In an emerging parish like Marston, the question of what role, if any, the voice of female parishioners would play in constituting that community was evidently sufficiently in flux that the issue could become a matter of controversy even at the level of the household.

What John Woods's confrontation with his wife more immediately reveals, however, is, not any significant concern about female moral authority in the parish per se, but rather the more mundane pressure that increasingly dense kin and community networks placed upon individuals as they contemplated how to interpret charges of office abuse. John Woods's concern about his wife's involvement, after all, seems to have related mainly to his fear about how his own reputation would fare once her authorship of the libel came to light. During the trial, both he and fellow planter Thomas Poynter, Johannah's husband, denied involvement in the libel campaign, asserting that they had been in Jamestown when the libels were being written and had only learned about them when they returned home. When John Woods urged his wife to remove her name from the libels, she apparently interpreted his request as a further effort to avoid being incriminated himself, for she allegedly snapped back that if "your name" was on the libel she would "rent [i.e., tear] it but if my name were Thrise as formerly [she] would not."[31]

Moreover, Woods's husband was not the only person to react uneasily to her libel campaign. Neighbors, too, expressed uneasiness, indicating the tensions that must always have accompanied such confrontations, as community members deliberated whether the benefit that such confrontations might elicit outweighed their possible disruptions to order and neighborly relations. In Marston Parish, the community appears to have been divided on the issue. After all, Woods was able to find two other female parishioners, Poynter and Cooper, willing to join her campaign, and people speculated at the possible involvement of "Deafe" John Moore, suggesting that discontent with the church officials was fairly widespread.[32] On the other hand, other neighbors openly discredited the disparagement of Cobb and Bromfield. Without knowing of Elizabeth's role in the affair, for instance, one member of the parish, Francis Hall, told both of the Woodses that he considered the libel-dropping campaign "basely" done.[33]

That Hall used the explicitly moral term "base" to convey his disagreement with the campaign is significant, because it reveals the degree to which these deliberations over how to interpret charges of office abuse were ultimately deliberations over who was acting dutifully and who was not. The challenge for Woods was to make the case that she was acting within the bounds of duty and that Cobb and Bromfield were not. But as she well knew, this was not an easy case to make in a culture in which attacks on neighbors and authority figures were automatically viewed with suspicion because of their potential disruption to hard-won order. One neighbor, Adam Straughan, made this logic explicit when, upon receiving a "scolding" from Elizabeth Woods, he retorted, "Mrs Wood are you not ashamed to scold & brawle & feud ... among the neighbours as you doe saying further that hee ... heard shee dropt four Lybells" in church.[34]

Ultimately, the York County court accepted the interpretation that Woods's campaign was disorderly rather than beneficial; it placed both John Woods and Thomas Poynter under obligation to pay ten thousand pounds of tobacco on demand if their wives did not "behave" themselves in relation to "any neighbour or any other person or persons in this Countrey" until the following Whitsuntide. Elizabeth's own guarded assessment of her behavior, which she expressed in response to Straughan's and Hall's accusations against her, was that whoever had led the libel campaign "need not be ashamed of it."[35] The comment significantly fell short of accepting responsibility for the campaign herself; evidently she did not see divulging her own part in the affair as helpful in convincing these particular critics. But her assertion that the act was perfectly consistent with a clear conscience was important. It expressed her view, which she was strenuously attempting to convince the broader parish to accept, that exposing Cobb's and Bromfield's violations of office overrode whatever obligations her own offices, as goodwife, neighbor, and parishioner, placed upon her. In this regard, her action was basically identical to Tyler's three decades earlier; he too had invoked conscience to justify his complaints about the governor and council and to assert where he believed propriety truly lay. What most separated Woods's assertion from Tyler's was less the logic of those assertions than the context in which they were made. Whereas Tyler spoke at a moment of profound instability in which the capacity to interpret the bounds of propriety anew was suddenly greatly expanded, Woods made her allegations in the more confining environs that were probably the norm during the colony's sustained "settling down" periods, when people happily avoided controversy and looked warily upon those neighbors who might scrutinize officials' performance of office too severely.

Deference, therefore, was inevitably the product of negotiation, or rather of the myriad negotiations that took place in courthouses, rural neighborhoods, and households all over Virginia as the society took shape and as people worked out the mutual duties of office that in this new environment met their expectations of a civil and just polity. Because the language of office was the one to which these persons naturally turned in order to conduct such complex negotiations, criticism of officeholders was always an intrinsic part of the mix. To assert that one had a duty to defer to "great" men was necessarily to invite the corresponding assertion that deference was only due to those men who were truly "great." Although there was inevitably an implicit tension between the two claims, such that community disputes like the one that concerned Woods almost automatically devolved into conflicts that seemed to pit the upholders of "order" against those willing to stand up against abusive officials, in fact the line between the two sides was always far more porous than their often heated rhetoric suggests. This ambiguity resulted not just from the fact that the defender of "order" one day could easily become an officeholder's critic the next. It resulted far more fundamentally from the fact that everyone, the critic of officials and the defender of "order" alike, claimed to be arguing from precisely the same moral vantage point, that is, an imagined world in which everyone fulfilled the duties of his or her office.

The appeal of that basic conception of the moral order, or at least the absence of any significant alternative vision to which an interlocutor might turn, meant that complex negotiations over office like those we see in the cases of William Tyler and Elizabeth Woods were destined to play out over and over again in the colony, simply because they were the mode by which people exerted some control over the larger communities of which they were a part. To the extent that we can chart the "growth" or "decline" of deference, a task that, as I have suggested, is more difficult than we have sometimes imagined because of the countless individual casuistic calculations about duty that ultimately composed it, the sheer accretion of social and kin networks that occurred as the population grew and as the colony matured does seem to have contributed to deference's growth, if for no other reason than that there were simply more people policing the boundaries of moral behavior.

But that act of moral policing worked in more ways than one, and this brings us to the final point to make about the interrelationship between criticism of officeholders and deference. Although charges of office abuse by a William Tyler or an Elizabeth Woods against the officials in their midst rarely forced those officials to step down and might not even have had much of an impact on their individual conduct, nevertheless the sheer utterances, and especially the *accumulated* utterances, of those charges influenced the moral landscape. By accusing "great" men of neglecting the poor or of engaging in other behaviors unsuitable for their positions, people like Tyler and Woods were actively helping to define the duties of those "great" men's offices. No precise checklist of duties existed for any given office. Its parameters, therefore, required definition, and in their ongoing negotiations over where "shame" truly lay in the community the Tylers and the Woodses of this world and the increasingly dense networks of people around them were gradually working those parameters out. On the one hand, this process defined the offices of the governed, as we saw occurring in York County as Marston Parish residents determined where they stood in relation to Elizabeth Woods's bold attack on Cobbs and Bromfield. On the other hand, the same process shaped the offices of rule, as officials like Cobbs and Bromfield confronted judgments of their own conduct that indicated which behaviors in government were likely to encourage order and which ones were not.

In other words, deference was likely to grow not only as members of the governed became more ensconced in neighborhood and kin networks that exerted negative pressure on perceived antisocial behavior but also as government officials themselves bowed to those pressures by adhering ever more closely to the expectations of the governed. Jack Greene has demonstrated some of the ways in which the colony's legislators became more competent at governing Virginia society over time, and arguably a similar growth in competence occurred in numerous other offices, from justices of the peace and ministers to county clerks and constables.[36] This was an uneven process and one that was bound to differ from county to county, let alone from colony to colony, because of the wide range of variables that might influence how a given community judged its own needs and hence the duties that leaders were expected to perform. But as long as a vocabulary of office remained the dominant mode by which people negotiated authority, officials almost certainly never assumed that they were immune from criticism, even when they most took for granted the deference of the governed.

Which brings us, finally, back to Jarratt. What accounts for his perception that late-eighteenth-century Americans no longer adhered to the duty of deference, even though, as Jarratt's own office talk suggests, the language of office still possessed some resonance? Here I proceed in admittedly very speculative fashion, but I want to conclude by considering briefly Thomas Jefferson's famous letter to John Adams in 1813 about "natural aristocracy," a concept that I suspect accounts not only for some of deference's lost ground at the time but also for some of the scholarly confusion about deference that has since led historians like Zuckerman and Nobles to throw their hands up in their air and to call for discarding the concept altogether.[37]

In the letter, Jefferson noted his agreement with a concept that Adams had advanced earlier in their correspondence, the idea "that there is a natural aristocracy among men" distinguished not by wealth and birth alone, the markers only of "artificial" aristocrats, but rather by superior "virtue and talents." Jefferson proposed a possible historical account of the rise of such a natural aristocracy: initially "bodily powers gave place to the aristoi," he suggested, but then the invention of gunpowder leveled differences between the weak and strong, making "bodily strength, like beauty, good humor, politeness and other accomplishments" merely the "auxiliary ground for distinction," while virtue and talents became the real determination of elite status. But a natural aristocracy founded upon virtue and talents also arose from another source, God's grand scheme: "The natural aristocracy I consider as the most precious gift of nature for the instruction, the trusts, and government of society. And indeed it would have been inconsistent in creation to have formed man for the social state, and not to have provided virtue and wisdom enough to manage the concerns of the society."[38] God expected humans to be sociable; therefore, certain persons had to possess superior virtue and wisdom in any given society in order to help it govern itself.

Adams's concern was that it was not this natural aristocracy but the artificial or "pseudo-aristoi" who would seize power in government, and he pondered the possibility that perhaps such pseudoaristocrats could be corralled into a chamber of government reserved just for them, both to hinder them "from doing mischief" (as Jefferson characterized Adams's position) and to preserve their wealth from poorer legislators' efforts to equalize property. Jefferson, however, considered Adams's concerns misplaced and possibly a result of the peculiar political circumstances of his New England home, where Jefferson suspected that certain pseudoaristocratic families really had developed a hereditary lock on governmental offices, in part because earlier generations in those families did in fact possess virtue and talents and in part because New England's "strict alliance of church and state" had "canonised" such families "in the eyes of the people" to the extent that the families' progressive decline in merit did little to diminish their power. Based on his own experiences in Virginia, Jefferson did not believe that such an artificial corralling of pseudoaristocrats was necessary. Instead, he believed that the "best remedy" was already supplied by all of the present state constitutions, namely, "to leave to the citizens the free election and separation of the aristoi from the pseudo-aristoi, of the wheat from the chaff." In short, the people themselves were the best judges of the qualities of their leaders and thus could be counted upon to know a genuinely superior superior when they saw him: "In general they will elect the real good and wise. In some instances, wealth may corrupt, and birth blind them; but not in sufficient degree to endanger the society."[39]

To a great extent, Jefferson's notion of the populace's capacity to distinguish truly superior men from their pretenders has lain at the center of the scholarly definition of deference upon which most early Americanists rely. But consider the subtle way in which Jefferson's focus had in fact changed from conceptions of deference that prevailed before. Here, for instance, is how Governor Sir William Berkeley explained deference to his councilor Nathaniel Bacon Jr. in 1675, at a time when Bacon and others were beginning to question Berkeley's capacity to fulfill his office: "Sir the king hath committed cheyfely the care of the Country to mee and though you and diverse with you may thinke mee unable to manage soe greate a Trust, yett whilst I hold the place I thinke all will say that some defference was to bee shewed to mee in soe important an affaire of the Country espetially those that know I doe nothing but by advice of the Councell."[40]

Berkeley's understanding of deference was one that was highly consistent with presuppositions of office. Deference was due to Berkeley not because of his person but because of his *persona* as the king's appointed governor. This *persona* was indelibly attached to office, for which Berkeley used three different designations that we have seen before: "care of the Country," "Trust," and "place." Within his office, Berkeley was due the "defference" of a lesser officer like Bacon, but partly that respect was owed because Berkeley faithfully performed his own official duties, including that most important one that was expected even of the king himself, to abide "by the advice" of his "Councell."

Jefferson was not so distant from this understanding of deference that he had lost all sense of the duties that any leader must perform in order to preserve the people's esteem. As he said in regard to the "great" families of Adams's Massachusetts, "I presume that from an early period of your history, members of these families happening to possess virtue and talents, have honestly exercised them for the good of the people, and *by their services* have endeared their names to them."[41] But Jefferson's perspective on deference *had* changed in the extent to which he no longer distinguished between *persona* and person. Instead, the two had become one; the "natural aristocrat" won the deference of ordinary citizens not because he was presumed to have qualities that made his habitation of a particular *persona* simply plausible but because his actual singular moral person was, in itself, recognizably superior to that of everyone else's, period.

This conception was new, and it almost certainly related to a cultural shift of massive proportion that Jarratt associated with "leveling" and that Jefferson similarly associated with the age's enthusiasm for the "equal rights of men." Condren offers his own characterization and interpretation of this shift in explaining how office talk in England became ever more circumscribed until its resonance was restricted mainly to those two arenas in which it is most often encountered today, bureaucracies and the professions. In part, the change had to do with the ways in which the logic of office talk itself invited overextension and abuse. The fact that arguments of office could be used to legitimize just about any conduct meant that by the eighteenth century the ethics of office had become a ripe target for parody in England and there was a growing appetite for alternative ethical theories that, although they still had one foot in presuppositions of office, nevertheless also departed self-consciously from certain aspects of it. Kant's frustration with the potential moral looseness of casuistry led him to theorize precisely the same singular moral person, bound to a universal principle of conduct, that arguably underlay Jefferson's complacent view of the "natural aristocrat" as a kind of oversized vessel for the selfsame virtue that filled everyone else's much smaller cups. At the same time, natural law theory, which until the middle of the eighteenth century had consistently regarded rights as inextricably tied to duties and so had identified rights as meaningless outside a world of offices, now began to posit the isolated rights-bearing individual as the true agent of God's will.[42]

These broad philosophical changes, which the Revolution undoubtedly helped to broadcast and popularize in the American context, arguably had two countervailing tendencies that quickly converted deference from a seemingly healthy holdover from the colonial era to an invalid whose days were suddenly numbered. On the one hand, armed with a Kantian epistemology that invited them to conflate person and *persona*, the Jeffersons (and perhaps too the Jarratts) of the world began to understand the respect due to them in ways that placed an almost hopeless burden on their ability to pull off the ideal of their inherently superior personal qualities. On the other hand, armed with an equally heady rhetoric of male equality and of rights strangely divorced from duties, Americans high and low were far more willing to regard their former official duty of deference as incompatible with their newfound "freedom," which no longer depended upon a language of office to define.

The inevitable clash of these two tendencies helps to explain why deference in America could seem to Jarratt to have died almost overnight. What had died, of course, was not Jefferson's view of a deference due to the persons of the truly virtuous few; it had barely even lived. But there was indeed a body on the table. The deference owed to *personae* performing their duties of office had lived a long and significant life, and we would gravely misunderstand the colonial British American world if we failed to recognize it.

Notes

The author thanks the American Historical Association for a Littleton-Griswold Research Grant, which supported his research in the Virginia county court records.

1. [Devereux Jarratt], *The Life of the Reverend Devereux Jarratt, Rector of Bath Parish, Dinwiddie County, Virginia. Written by Himself, in a Series of Letters Addressed to the Rev. John Coleman, One of the Ministers of the Protestant Episcopal Church in Maryland* (Baltimore: Warner and Hanna, 1806), 14–15.

2. Gordon S. Wood, *The Americanization of Benjamin Franklin* (New York: Penguin, 2004), 35; Wood, *Radicalism of the American Revolution* (New York: Knopf, 1991); Rhys Isaac, *The Transformation of Virginia, 1740–1790* (Chapel Hill, NC: Published for the Institute of Early American History and Culture at Williamsburg, Virginia, by University of North Carolina Press, 1982), 43, 46, 48.

3. Michael Zuckerman, "Tocqueville, Turner, and Turds: Four Stories of Manners in Early America," in "Deference or Defiance in Eighteenth-Century America? A Round Table," *Journal of American History* 85, no. 1 (June 1998): 13–42. Quotations are from pp. 17 and 42. See also Zuckerman, "Authority in Early America: The Decay of Deference on the Provincial Periphery," *Early American Studies* 1, no. 2 (Fall 2003): 1–29; and Zuckerman, "Endangered Deference, Imperiled Patriarchy: Tales from the Marchlands," *Early American Studies* 3, no. 2 (Fall 2005): 232–52. Gregory H. Nobles, "A Class Act: Redefining Deference in Early American History," *Early American Studies* 3, no. 2 (Fall 2005): 286–302. Nobles's piece and the latter piece by Zuckerman appeared in a special issue of *Early American Studies* focused on the theme "Deference in Early America: The Life and/or Death of an Historiographical Concept." The other essays in that volume can also be read with profit.

4. Conal Condren, *Argument and Authority in Early Modern England: The Presupposition of Oaths and Offices* (Cambridge: Cambridge University Press, 2006). See also Condren, "The Office of Rule and the Rhetorics of Tyrannicide in Medieval and Early Modern Europe: An Overview," in Robert von Friedeburg, ed., *Murder and Monarchy: Regicide in European History, 1300–1800* (New York: Palgrave Macmillan, 2004), 48–72; and Condren, "Liberty of Office and Its Defence in Seventeenth-Century Political Argument," *History of Political Thought* 18 (1997): 460–82.

5. Nobles similarly addresses the dichotomy commonly posed between deference and defiance, but his solution to this dichotomy is different from mine. He recommends that we see these categories as the extreme ends of a spectrum of human behaviors and relations that are best understood as differential modes, or tactics, of negotiation, most of which fell somewhere between outright deference and defiance. In contrast, I am proposing that we see deference and defiance, not as fixed ends on a spectrum of behaviors and relations, but rather as the rival interpretations that hung *simultaneously* over *every* confrontation (or negotiation) over authority in early modern Anglo-American political culture and that were not resolved one way or the other until the community as a whole, or major segments within it, reached some consensus about who, the accuser or the accused, was most guilty of an abuse of office, or duty. For a study of early modern English political culture that advocates an approach similar to the one I am proposing here, see Ethan Shagan, *Popular Politics and the English Reformation* (Cambridge: Cambridge University Press, 2003).

6. *Life of the Reverend Devereux Jarratt*, 199–200.
7. Condren, *Argument and Authority*, especially 3–6.
8. Ibid., throughout.
9. *Life of the Reverend Devereux Jarratt*, 7.
10. Condren, *Argument and Authority*, 25.
11. *Life of the Reverend Devereux Jarratt*, 11.
12. Condren, *Argument and Authority*, 15–20.
13. Ibid., especially 26–29.
14. *Life of the Reverend Devereux Jarratt*, 199.
15. On "office of rule," see Condren, *Argument and Authority*.
16. *Life of the Reverend Devereux Jarratt*, 21–22.
17. Ibid., 20.
18. Condren, *Argument and Authority*, 6.

19. Erving Goffman, *The Presentation of the Self in Everyday Life* (New York: Doubleday Anchor Books, 1959); Goffman, *Frame Analysis: An Essay on the Organization of Experience* (New York: Harper and Row, 1974); James C. Scott, *Domination and the Arts of Resistance: The Hidden Transcript of Subordinate Groups* (New Haven, CT: Yale University Press, 1992); Condren, *Argument and Authority*, 6–9. The concept of the king's two bodies is most commonly associated with Ernst H. Kantorowicz, *The King's Two Bodies: A Study in Medieval Political Theology* (Princeton, NJ: Princeton University Press, 1957). For an example of the use that historians of early modern Britain have made of Scott's work, see Michael J. Braddick and John Walter, *Negotiating Power in Early Modern Society: Order, Hierarchy, and Subordination in Britain and Ireland* (Cambridge: Cambridge University Press, 2001).

20. Nobles, "Class Act," 290.
21. Condren, *Argument and Authority*, 6–7.
22. *Life of the Reverend Devereux Jarratt*, 13–14, 16.
23. Condren, *Argument and Authority*, 172–85. Quotations are, respectively, from pp. 173, 172, 174, and 182.

24. I culled these examples while explicitly looking for instances in which persons contemned the authority of others in the conduct of their duties. Cases of this sort include a broad array of defamation suits; complaints of contempt of magistrates, sheriffs, and constables; and any depositional evidence that might shed unusual light on the negotiations over status and authority that took place within communities.

25. H. R. McIlwaine, ed., *Minutes of the Council and General Court of Colonial Virginia*, 2nd ed. (Richmond: Virginia State Library, 1979), 18–19.

26. Wesley Frank Craven, *Dissolution of the Virginia Company: The Failure of a Colonial Experiment* (Gloucester, MA: Peter Smith, 1964); McIlwaine, *Minutes of the Council*, 21.

27. McIlwaine, *Minutes of the Council*, 19–20.

28. My view of seventeenth-century Virginia as a persistently unstable political world, though one in which moments of real political uncertainty were brief and short lived and surrounded by more sustained periods in which settlers sought and attained a degree of normalcy and order, is my own compromise position between the rival views on seventeenth-century political stability. For one side of this debate, see Jon Kukla, "Order and Chaos in Early America: Political and Social Stability in Pre-Restoration Virginia," *American Historical Review* 90, no. 2 (April 1985): 275–98. For the other side, generally, see Bernard Bailyn, "Politics and Social Structure in Virginia," in James M. Smith, ed.,

Seventeenth-Century America: Essays in Colonial History (Chapel Hill, NC: Published for the Institute of Early American History and Culture at Williamsburg, Virginia, by University of North Carolina Press, 1959), 90–115; Jack P. Greene, "The Growth of Political Stability: An Interpretation of Political Development in the Anglo-American Colonies, 1660–1760," in Greene, *Negotiated Authorities: Essays in Colonial Political and Constitutional History* (Charlottesville: University Press of Virginia, 1994), 131–62; and T. H. Breen, "'Looking Out for Number One': Conflicting Cultural Values in Early Seventeenth-Century Virginia," *South Atlantic Quarterly* 78 (1979): 342–60.

29. York County Deeds, Orders, and Wills (hereafter York DOW) 3 (1657–1662), 38, John D. Rockefeller Jr. Library, Williamsburg, VA.

30. Deposition of Stephen Royston, ibid.

31. Ibid.

32. Ibid.

33. Deposition of Francis Hall, York DOW 3 (1657–1662), 38.

34. Deposition of Adam Straughan, York DOW 3 (1657–1662), 38.

35. Ibid.; Deposition of Francis Hall, York DOW 3 (1657–1662), 38.

36. See, for instance, Greene, "Growth of Political Stability." See also "Legislative Turnover in Colonial British America, 1696–1775: A Quantitative Analysis," in Greene, *Negotiated Authorities*, 215–37; and Greene, "Society, Ideology, and Politics: An Analysis of the Political Culture of Mid-Eighteenth-Century Virginia," in ibid., 259–18.

37. The relationship of the theory of "natural aristocracy" to conceptions of deference has rarely been scrutinized but has instead been accepted largely without question, very likely because much of the scholarly work on deference in the 1960s and 1970s coincided with interest in classical republican ideology. As articulated by James Harrington in the mid-seventeenth century and by Thomas Jefferson in the late eighteenth, classical republicanism does indeed seem to have melded the two theories, but as I suggest below, I have considerable doubts about the strength of the theory of "natural aristocracy" in the colonies before the Revolution. For influential studies that are very sophisticated in their treatment of deference yet arguably err in viewing it too much through the lens of the particular ideal of "natural aristocracy," see J. G. A. Pocock, "The Classical Theory of Deference," *American Historical Review* 81, no. 3 (June 1976): 516–23; Wood, *Radicalism of the American Revolution*; and Richard R. Beeman, "Deference, Republicanism, and the Emergence of Popular Politics in Eighteenth-Century America," *William and Mary Quarterly*, 3rd ser., 49 (July 1992): 401–30; and Beeman, *The Varieties of Political Experience in Eighteenth-Century America* (Philadelphia: University of Pennsylvania Press, 2004).

38. Thomas Jefferson to John Adams, October 28, 1813, in Lester J. Cappon, ed., *The Adams-Jefferson Letters: The Complete Correspondence between Thomas Jefferson and Abigail and John Adams*, vol. 2 (Chapel Hill, NC: Published for the Institute of Early American History and Culture at Williamsburg, Virginia, by University of North Carolina Press, 1959), 387–92.

39. Ibid., 388–89.

40. Sir William Berkeley to Nathaniel Bacon Jr., September 14, 1675, in Warren M. Billings, ed., *The Papers of Sir William Berkeley, 1605–1677* (Richmond: Library of Virginia, 2007), 486–87.

41. Jefferson to Adams, 389.

42. Condren, *Argument and Authority*, 343–52.

Middle Plantation's Changing Landscape

Persistence, Continuity, and the Building of Community

PHILIP LEVY

Over the winter of 1609–10 the English colonists of James Fort fell on the hardest times possible. All manner of social collapse, chaos, and even man eating became the norm in the small settlement. In the end, they buried their possessions (as well as their less delectable fellows) and took to the sea. They were stopped by a newly arrived English resupply fleet, whose leadership re-established the outpost and returned to colonizing. Gradually the repaired fort developed anew, grew to be a town, and in time became as thriving a colonial city as one could expect in a salty swamp.[1]

The colorful story of the so-called starving time and Jamestown's growth from its ashes is understandably an oft-retold staple of seventeenth-century Virginia's narrative. But dramatic as it is, this disaster is famous beyond the weight of its long-term consequences, except perhaps for the Virginia narrative it helped to establish.

The Jamestown-to-colony story is one of colonists pulling victory from the jaws of defeat—if not from the jaws of fellow colonists. The story's horrors serve to show how Jamestown began in chaos and gradually moved to order and even success. That story line—failure to success, chaos to order, mob to society—is one with deep roots in how historians have seen Virginia's first century. In that story line, the seventeenth century's foment, disorder, and constant reinvention yielded to the eighteenth century's settled establishment of dynastic families, stately homes, and a rather sudden golden age by the second decade of the eighteenth century. We only have to look at Bernard Bailyn's "veritable anarchy" or Jack Greene's "profoundly unstable world," filled with T. H. Breen's "highly individualistic" settlers, who, as the Chesapeake School has shown, died readily and married rarely, to see the seventeenth century serving as a sort of prolonged "starving time"—a century-long social dung heap that in time produced beautiful roses.[2]

There has been some dissent from this narrative along the way, though. Jon Kukla most notably, for example, strenuously objected to the "chaos to riches" narrative in his 1985 essay "Order and Chaos in Early Virginia." Kukla's forceful assertion of Virginia's political stability and even typicality in light of English and European trends offered an often-overlooked counterpoint to the prevailing model of a century of disorder. Recent work on Virginia is taking that call to heart, and many of the essays in this volume follow Kukla's implicit call to move away from the powerful pull of the chaos-to-order framework.

This essay looks at change in a seventeenth-century Virginia landscape—the area then known as Middle Plantation, but better known as Williamsburg after the 1699 founding of the new capital. This landscape has been under continuous archaeological study since the 1930s. Even though that work has focused mostly on understanding the eighteenth-century capital, it nevertheless resulted in older Middle Plantation being the most comprehensively excavated 1600s rural neighborhood in the colony. Archaeology usually comes in site-sized units. After all, digging a site is difficult, expensive, and time-consuming work. Also, numerous uncontrollable variables determine which sites survive and which do not, as well as which get excavated and which do not. The archaeological record can be idiosyncratic, in the sense of being riddled with site-specific considerations. Furthermore, sites have been studied under a range of excavation regimes, making meaningful intersite comparisons a long-standing challenge. But the Colonial Williamsburg Foundation's work on sites dating to the period of Middle Plantation—particularly excavations conducted over the 1990s—offer a rare chance to look at not just a single site but a series of related proximate sites excavated with the same techniques and data-recording regimes. The result is the archaeology of a community seen through its varied sites. This material text provides a narrative of how this somewhat poorly documented community grew over the century.

Most material-based scholarship has held, at least tacitly, to the chaos-to-order narrative. Dichotomies of frontiers and centers, cores and peripheries, and, particularly, impermanence and permanence are all frameworks created in light of the century-of-disorder premise.[3] But Middle Plantation's narrative as reconstructed here tells a different story. Buildings came and went, but the community grew, evolved, and adapted—often atop of what came before and on occasion even to the point of housing members of the same families.

Rather than showing chaos and reinvention, this landscape reveals steady progress over time, with each new development resting in its way on what came before it. Rather than a set of disjunctures, what we see is order begetting order, the logic of one moment's development creating conditions that enabled the next—not so much chaos and reinvention as a flow of changing orders reflecting local manifestations of far larger British and even global trends. Much of this change was generational, with settlers of the 1630s building as they needed and then those of the 1660s absorbing and recontextualizing that changed setting only to have their own world absorbed and again recontextualized in their wake.

Each of the places discussed here sat close to one another. If the night breeze was right, voices on one could be heard at others. The people who lived at Middle Plantation would have seen these various sites on a daily basis, and these buildings and places would have defined residents' spatial world. The circumstances that went into the construction of one went into the others. There is something profoundly local, something intimate and closely linked about these places, while at the same time the influence of far wider nonlocal trends is also evident.

What follows, then, is an examination of three episodes in the history of Middle Plantation's landscape and built environment. The first is a brief review of the story of how a 1630s military palisade became the founding spine of the community and how that wall itself melted into the rural neighborhood it helped create. The second episode is the story of how local elite planters reflected their urban sensibilities in their homes and home lots in and around the 1660s. The third episode shows how two proximate and related buildings reflected a local community and artisanal sophistication in the 1680s and 1690s, on the eve of the founding of Williamsburg. These buildings show the extent to which local building vocabularies and options had developed and how these served as a sort of community tie. Seen this way, the 1699 platting is not the disjuncture or starter's gun it is understood to have been. Instead, it marks the next small step in a long local story of a gradually changing landscape.

By 1699 a small part of Middle Plantation was beginning its transformation into the eighteenth-century city of Williamsburg. This experiment in urban planning was never a complete success. Slow to develop, modest measured against the hopes of its planners, and quick to fade after the capital moved to Richmond, Williamsburg nevertheless enjoyed over eighty years as the center of Virginia's political and social life.[4] But the Revolutionary War capital was hardly cut out of the wilderness. Instead, it took shape on one corner of what for over six decades had been a growing and thriving rural neighborhood. The process of creating an appropriately usable and English landscape began well before anyone imagined bringing the capital up to the plateaus between the James and York Rivers. Middle Plantation was born in the dark brutal years of Virginia's second Anglo-Indian conflict.[5]

Shocked and badly damaged by Native leader Opechancanough's March 22, 1622, surprise attack, Virginians retaliated and took measures to see that the "trecherie of the salvages" would never again catch them unawares.[6] The task of organizing first revenge and then protection fell primarily to Governor Sir Francis Wyatt, who, though a political casualty of the war, nevertheless outlined an ambitious plan to secure colonial territory and provision an army that could "wholie exterpat" Opechancanough and his people. What Wyatt envisioned was nothing less than a major landscape transformation. At the center of the plan was a large "palizado" or extended fortified paling wall, which would secure a "rich circuit of ground" to be divided up into small private holdings.[7] Once the land was securely walled and apportioned, settlers could stock the acres with horses and cattle and line the wall with fortified garrisons manned by squads of soldiers who would be fed by the cattle and ride the horses. Virginia would be defended by its own version of a Roman frontier.

Of course much of the plan was little more than bravado and ambition. But the wall did come into being, erected by Wyatt's successor, Sir John Harvey. By order of the General Assembly, in February 1632 a labor force assembled through a levy of "every fourtyth man" was to meet at a newly constructed plantation between the heads of Queen's and Archer's Hope Creeks (a few miles west of the originally proposed Martin's Hundred–Chiskiak line) and begin the work of "securinge that tract of land lyinge betweene the sayd creekes."[8] As an incentive, the assembly promised fifty acres and a temporary exemption from all "taxes and publique chardges" for new settlers whose shoulders would have to bear the burden of local security and of westward-aimed firearms.[9] The motivation worked, and soon corvée crews had dug the palisade's twin trenches and set its heavy posts in the ground.

Almost as soon as the wall was up, new English plantations began to spring up on either side of the creek-to-creek palisade.[10] Middle Plantation was born as Virginians began to mark and map tracts along the palisade's length. Acre by acre and field by field, the land along the wall began to fill with English plantations. The one hundred acres Edward Whitaker patented in 1638 sat "joining upon the Pallisadoes of the middle plantation." Whitaker's land was "without the forrest," meaning that it lay west of the wall enclosing the Kent-sized forest.[11] The following year John Saines used headrights to patent one hundred acres also "upon the Pallisades of the middle plantation, without the forrest," and Lieutenant Richard Popeley filed claim for 1,250 acres "at the Midle Plantation upon the Pallisadoes."[12] By the early 1640s Secretary of the Colony Richard Kemp had seated his plantation on Archer's Hope Creek (now College Creek) on land that bounded "part of the Palisadoes of the middle plantation."[13] In 1645 George Wyatt took up 250 Middle Plantation acres "along the Palisadoes."[14] Thomas Hill's deed of the same year noted that his land was adjacent to that of Francis Peale "and the palisades," and Henry Tyler's deed of the following year described his land as "situate on the Midle Plantation pale."[15] In 1646, Nicholas Brooke's land was "bounded S.W. upon the Pallisadoes," while Lewis Burwell deeded two hundred acres that lay "within the Pallisado at Middle Plantation" in 1652.[16] George Reade's land in 1655 sat "butting upon the Pallizadoe" when John Page took possession of it and began to compile a string of "parcels of land bounding on the pallizado at Middle Plantation."[17]

By the mid-1650s, though, the overgrown remains of the wall and ditches were showing their age, and the land records began to reflect the effects of time. The land John Bates purchased in 1655 was "butting e[aster]ly upon the *old* paile," and when the aging John Page ordered a survey of his Middle Plantation holdings in 1683, the surveyors made mention not only of a "corner red oak" and a "marked white oak" but also the "trench where the old pales stood."[18] As late as 1747 a deed for what had once been John Page's palisade-bordered property, now in the possession of one Thomas Penman, used the "end of a ditch," quite possibly the old palisade trench, to re-mark the edge of the property.[19]

The land records from this part of Virginia are fragmentary, but what survives reveals how central (both literally and figuratively) was the line of the "old pales" to the shape of Middle Plantation.[20] Williamsburg was from its inception a place of grids, right angles, and intentional vistas. Its planners hoped to make the new capital a showplace and thus built into the landscape the boulevards and vistas befitting the great town they envisioned.[21] But Middle Plantation was a different animal altogether. No planner's hand directed the growth of this rambling rural community. Instead, its patchwork of patents gradually spread between the heads of Archer Hope and Queen's Creeks in an organic fashion. But there was some small logic to their ramble: they clung to the run of the old pales. The wall was the pioneering tendril opening up the land between the rivers. Before the wall, Virginia was a place of waterfront settlements spreading mostly along the James River, with a few colonists living on other shores or inland. But the palisade changed that by becoming the physical and cartographic catalyst for a new line of inland settlements. In this way, the wall served as a sort inland river wicking colonial plantations into the peninsula and away from the real riverfronts.

The wall originally envisioned as a barrier to Indians and a vehicle for their displacement gradually became something more quotidian and rural—a marker between tobacco fields and private property. But in this transformation lay the wall's real achievement. As a line of rotting pales and silted ditches, the wall was admittedly not the most intimidating barrier. But as its run became part of an English-style rural landscape of fences, homes, fields, and gardens, the wall became a far more effective barrier and marker of a permanent English presence, as the onetime "forrest" became forever changed and denativized. The old wall facilitated, and was then enveloped by, a new wall of English settlements, which themselves fully achieved the goals Wyatt and company originally envisioned.

The palisade went up because it served an immediate, largely military purpose, and it came down thanks to the forces of time and nature, but not before it left an enduring mark on the land. What developed along its run was an inland Virginia community. The first wave of Middle Plantation settlers included men like George Menefie, Richard Popley, Robert Higginson, John Clarke, and Henry Tyler.[22] By midcentury, though, Middle Plantation had become a collection of about twenty plantations—and was home to a new wave of prosperous and prominent colonists, including Secretaries of the Colony Richard Kemp and Thomas Ludwell, Ludwell's brother Philip, Sir Thomas Lundsford, local merchant and member of the House of Burgesses John Page, and merchant-planter and later member of the Governor's Council James Bray.[23] Other prominent men included burgesses Otho Thorpe, Francis Page, and Thomas Ballard, all of whom lived in substantial homes clustering along the run of the old palisade.

As these men moved into the neighborhood, by the 1660s Middle Plantation became an enclave of elite settlement. Many of these settlers' homes would have been within sight of each other on a clear day with the right wood lots being cleared. An English visitor would have noted how familiar looking was this landscape of country homes (though modest by English standards) and farm fields. To be sure, the fences, the crops, and much of the labor force would have been unique to the colony, but nevertheless the overall effect was distinctly English in organization and direction.[24] By the 1660s the heart of the community had shifted from a wall to a road, specifically the so-called Horse Path, which snaked its way between ravine fingers. Probably tracing a similar route to precontact Native trails, the Horse Path would have been wider and muddier in the rain than its Native antecedent. But it tied together the homes of Middle Plantation and served as the anchoring point for new buildings including, in time, the College of William and Mary's Wren Building, an arsenal for the public protection, a church, and a few smaller plantations. (See map 6.1.)[25]

There was much that unified the cadre of gentlemen who lived along this road and the remains of the wall that preceded it. They shared ambitions and business interests and sometimes married each other's widows. They also shared important ties to urban England, and these ties took form in the Middle Plantation landscape, making it at once a place of both rural living and metropolitan sensibilities. This meant that while much of the white labor force consisted of displaced country folk, the owners of land and resources were originally city folk who looked back to urban contacts for commercial and personal reasons.[26] Despite these commercial and personal connections to urban England, seventeenth-century Virginia was noted for its lack of towns, though if towns failed to materialize, it was not for any lack of laws, exhortations, and best wishes of colonial planners. But elements of the English town, and particularly the English capital, found their way into the otherwise distinctly nonurban plantation landscape.

Rich Neck Plantation offers some clues about the relationship between the English town and the Virginia tobacco plantation. Rich Neck stood on a rise of ground a few miles into Virginia's Lower Peninsula from the James River floodplain. Between the early 1640s and about 1700 it was home to men who typified the post–English Civil War gentry. Secretary of the Colony Richard Kemp lived at Rich Neck until his death in 1649. His wife, Elizabeth Wormely Kemp, remarried Sir Thomas Lundsford in 1650, and the two resided principally in Lancaster County near Elizabeth's family and Lundsford's old English Civil War cronies. In 1665, Elizabeth and her

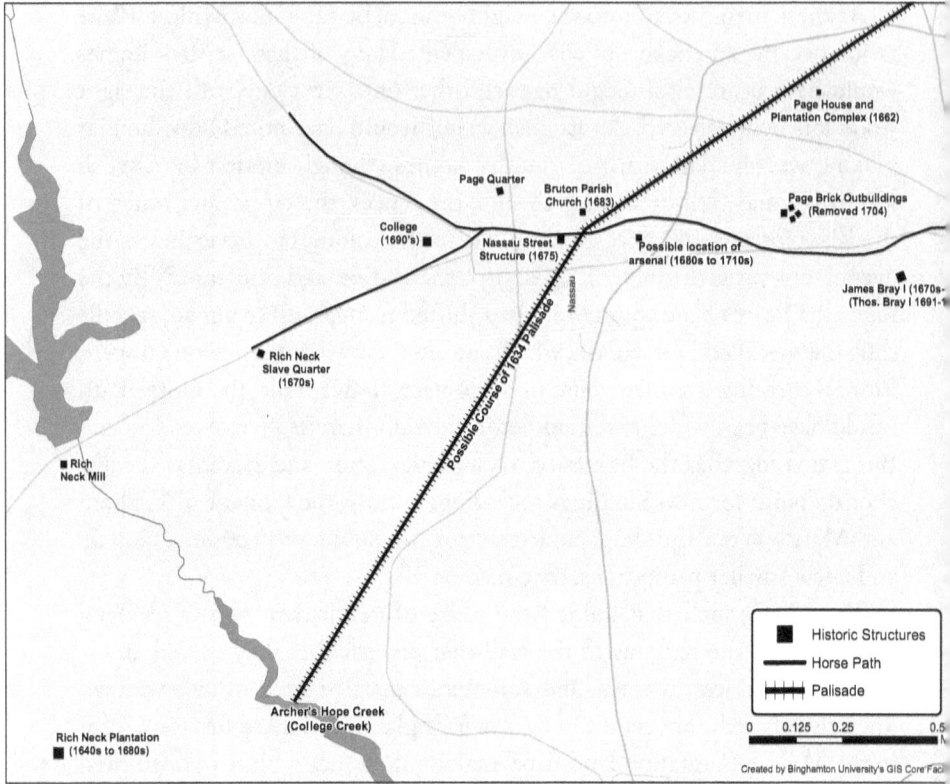

Selected Middle Plantation sites and course of 1634 palisade, with present-day Williamsburg streets. (Map by Kevin Heard, GIS Core Facility, Binghamton University)

third husband, Major General Robert Smith, sold Rich Neck to Thomas Ludwell, who was one of Governor Berkley's favorites and secretary of the colony since King Charles II's restoration in 1660.[27]

In the 1630s Richard Kemp built a brick home in Jamestown. Kemp's digs won high, if not unbiased, praise as being the "fairest that was ever knowne in this countrye" from Kemp's principal benefactor, Governor Sir John Harvey. Archaeological examination of the site revealed that the secretary's home, once thought to be part of a magnificent U-shaped building, in fact had a two-room, hall-and-parlor floor plan and measured twenty-five feet by thirty-four feet.[28] A double line of bricks along the south wall may have been part of an H-shaped hearth dividing the rooms and giving each a fireplace. Part of the home's noted "substance and uniformitye" stemmed from its being built of brick, although only the dry course at the base of the wall and some brick flooring has survived in the ground.[29]

The house was also significant in that sometime in the early 1640s Kemp built a nearly exact copy of it on his newly acquired land near Archer's Hope—the acres laid out along the palisade and named "The Secretary's Land" but later known as Rich Neck. Rich Neck's dwelling measured thirty-five feet by twenty feet and had the Jamestown building's hall-and-parlor layout divided by a central hearth. The homesite also boasted a large square kitchen. Both the home and the kitchen were built of brick. Juxtaposition of the secretary's Jamestown and Rich Neck houses allows the one to answer architectural questions about the other but also raises the question of why Kemp built the same structure in both town and plantation settings.

Kemp's Jamestown home was part of Governor Harvey's attempts during the 1620s and 1630s to beef up the town's cityscape and industrial base. In England by this time, timber shortages had forced builders to abandon the late-sixteenth-century fashion for externally framed buildings. Although brick had been common as nogging, filling the gap between fashionably blackened framing members, relatively few English buildings were brick stand-alones. All that changed during the reign of James I as tastes shifted toward brick, often with a Low Countries flare. By building in brick—especially in a colonial setting that reversed England's reliance on little timber but lots of labor—Kemp demonstrated his fashionableness as well his awareness of trends in the metropole. If he made a statement of status, it lay in his knowledge of and ability to reproduce English fashions and only secondarily in the solidity or permanence of the edifice. Just as Kemp's Jamestown home inspired Harvey's commendation of its "substance," its fashionably built, roughly symmetrical plan inspired Harvey's praise of its "uniformitye."[30]

Kemp transferred this town-based sensibility to his Rich Neck land by building an equally up-to-date style of home away from town. Although Rich Neck's dwelling lacked the impressive Dutch brick flooring of its city cousin, the country home was no bumpkin. Four brickbat-wide dry footers reveal a one-and-a-half-story building whose loft may have been lighted by dormers as so often seen in contemporary English homes.[31]

But what was current in the early 1640s was no longer adequate in the 1660s. When Thomas Ludwell purchased Rich Neck in 1665, he undertook a major renovation of the property. Ludwell's expansion was due in part to an expansion of the plantation's population, including the arrival of Ludwell's brother Philip. But an increase in residents cannot account for the shape and style of the changes. Part of Ludwell's drive to change what had been impressive before the English Civil War stemmed from a different vision of what constituted appropriate elite housing during the Restoration's cultural upheaval. Nor were the Ludwell brothers alone in overseeing these changes, as noted by numerous scholars of seventeenth-century architecture. Like many other planters, the Ludwells removed the central hearth and replaced it with two end hearths. They also added two room additions off the back of the home and a cellar wing at the corner of the northern addition. These ultimately changed the hall and parlor structure into a five-room structure (excluding loft space) whose plan approximated that of a much larger dwelling with both front and back rooms.[32]

When Kemp built his twin homes, there were four basic house types common in London. Two of these were multistory townhouses, which soon became the mainstay of the capital's architecture. The other two were older rural types, which would soon be all but gone from the metropolis.[33] These were the courtyarded house and the small home of four or five rooms. Kemp's homes only counted four rooms if one included the loft spaces. But the fact that by the last quarter of the sixteenth century most English homes had enclosed lofts means that Kemp's structures fit the bill as this rural/urban form of London home.

By the late 1660s these rural house types were gone from London streets—casualties to changing building fashions and a whopping great fire. Rebuilding after the 1666 conflagration provided an opportunity to apply new thinking to London's streets and structures. Although ambitious plans for new streets and vistas were thwarted by old property rights, one of the fire's legacies was a marked division between the capital's architecture and that of the countryside.

As men with London connections, the Ludwells would have been in the middle of these shifting ideas. Their Rich Neck revision, contemporaneous with the aforementioned changes in London, changed Kemp's former London rural/city home into one distinctly non-London in plan. In other words, the Ludwells brought their new home in line with the style of the times—a style that had changed from Kemp's day. The Ludwell plantation was a country home and now reflected it. Similarly, Ludwell properties in Jamestown were exclusively urban-style row houses, reflecting the Ludwells' awareness of these new divisions between urban and rural architecture.

But while bringing current rural style to Rich Neck, they ironically employed two important urban elements. The first was the home's pantile roof. Sometime during the renovation process, a spread of rounded pantiles replaced the earlier roof. These tiles were new to the English building scene, with Charles II issuing an early patent for their manufacture in 1663. Most of these tiles came from the Netherlands and soon became a Restoration roofing fad. But this fad was restricted to the capital and a few towns in southeastern England well connected to commerce with the Low Countries. These tiles did not make it into the hinterlands until the eighteenth century and did not appear in the Ludwells' home county of Somerset until the nineteenth century. Thomas and Philip covered their newly countrified home with the most up-to-date fashion in urban roofs.[34]

Another high style connection at Ludwell's Rich Neck manifested itself in the home's increasing number of small single-purpose rooms. Most Virginians lived in small post-in-ground homes of one or two multipurpose rooms, often with a half loft affording more space overhead. Indeed, the average number of rooms in Virginia homes remained stable or, according to some studies, decreased as the seventeenth century neared an end. But in both urban and rural gentry homes on both sides of the Atlantic, the number of small specialized rooms increased dramatically.[35] William Fitzhugh boasted of thirteen rooms in his Stafford County home, while John Custis's Northampton seat, called Arlington, probably had no fewer than twelve. Nathaniel Bacon's York County home had a minimum of eight rooms, and Lancaster County justice David Fox's home had six. Also worth noting is that many of these fancy homes had multiple stories, making them as visually impressive and stylish as they were roomy.[36]

At Middle Plantation, Ludwell's Rich Neck—a rambling maze of over eight rooms—and John Page's nearby cruciform home comprising a minimum of eight rooms, both exemplify local versions of this larger trend. This proliferation of rooms occurred in contemporary England as well and grew out of a variety of changes. Shifting family ideals from an expansive network of kin, allies, and retainers to a closely connected domestic unit tied together by affective bonds shifted how a gentry family would live within their now more numerous walls.[37] Likewise, a growing practice of shifting servile labor out of the main home and into separate quarters—a trend commented on by at least one late-seventeenth-century architectural observer—would have disrupted the ideal flow of life in older homes.[38] This trend has special significance in Virginia, taking place when many elite Virginia planters added Africans to their labor forces. For homes like Rich

Neck this meant that what worked well in one time was no longer sufficient in another. By 1700 or so Rich Neck had fallen into tenantage and ultimately abandonment and careful demolition so that its building materials could be reused elsewhere. Likewise, John Page's highly fashionable Restoration-period cruciform home underwent a similar slide from elite home to rental property. Sometime in the 1720s the now somewhat down-in-the-mouth Jacobean structure burned, and its ruins were demolished. These two Middle Plantation homes rose as part of establishing a community, housing what would become prominent dynastic families and serving as a platform for their participation in metropolitan style trends. They disappeared along with much of the rest of the seventeenth century's constructed landscape, victims less of nature than of changing ideals of domestic life, labor, and the relationships between them.

Middle Plantation continued to develop into the 1680s. Even in the wake of Bacon's Rebellion and the 1682 Plant-Cutting Riots—a time usually understood as one of considerable disarray—Middle Plantation was quietly maturing.[39] An armory rose near the Horse Path—a sure sign that Middle Plantation was understood as a community of some worth. Soon thereafter builders erected the only still-visible part of the landscape. Sitting almost midway between the Ludwell's and John Page's already proximate homes, the College of William and Mary's Wren Building was immediately a deeply significant marker of the community's substance.[40] In addition to these symbols of state and learning was a brick church that stood for a short time near the Horse Path and midway between the creeks—almost at the physical center of Middle Plantation.

The emerging village received its first church in 1658 when the General Assembly ordered that its parish join with Harrop and the two become one new parish named Middletown, later changed to Bruton.[41] By 1660, the newly incorporated vestry had constructed its first church—a structure about which we know almost nothing. In 1677, though, the vestry agreed that "neither the Upper Church, nor the lower Church should be repaired, but that a New Church should be built in brick, att the Middle Plantation."[42] It is unclear whether these older churches from the two merged parishes (including, presumably, the 1660 church), were simply rotting away on their own timetable or were damaged in the "late troubles" of Bacon's Rebellion to which the vestrymen referred.[43] But by the fall of 1678, the vestry began to collect donations large and small for a new church building fund. Local elites offered a substantial part of the needed sum.[44] Most notable of these was merchant and planter John Page. Like many of their class, the Pages had their fingers in many commercial pies. But this family and its extensive brickmaking resources would prove instrumental in one of the most distinctive aspects of Middle Plantation and its built environment: the large presence of brick buildings. The family had in place by the 1660s all of the resources needed to make fashionable brick buildings and the tiles to cover their roofs. The story of the construction and early demise of the second Bruton Parish Church brings into focus the operations of the Pages and the functioning of brick as a building medium at Middle Plantation.

John Page donated "land sufficient for the Church and Church yard" from his own acres as well as twenty pounds sterling for the building's construction.[45] But before the church was built, the parish had to raise far more money. Locals stepped up and offered their aid in the form of subscriptions ranging from five to twenty-five pounds sterling. Each of the surviving subscriptions makes specific reference to the "building of a brick church" for which the subscribers offered their donation.[46] The subscriptions served as a sort of contract whereby the donors offered set sums for a set project. Making clear that the new church would be, unlike others, built of brick, established that the donation was for a well-defined project—a *brick* church. Likewise, keeping the building material in focus would have helped the vestry raise the needed money, by emphasizing that this church project was something distinctive and worthy of patronage.

After the needed money was in hand, the vestry hired George Marable to erect the church. But that relationship soon turned sour—a common enough occurrence between Virginia vestries and their contractors—and it fell to Francis Page to oversee the project's completion.[47]

The choice of Page to oversee the construction after Marable was no accident. Francis was the son of land donor John Page and, like his father, resided in another of Middle Plantation's brick structures. Given his family's local prominence and connection to brick architecture, it is reasonable to surmise that the Page family masonry operation kicked into gear to build the church. Masons associated with the family would have been well aware of where to find the best stocks of usable clay for bricks and where to collect and dig up supplies of oyster shell for mortar. The large kiln near John Page's house showed that local brickmakers were able to build efficient multiuse firing facilities capable of producing bricks as well as other items like roofing tiles. This infrastructure was initially a product of Middle Plantation's prominent residents' desire to build in brick and the area's proximity to Jamestown, where such skills were also prized. But once in place, it also created local conditions that enabled other less well-off residents to also have brick buildings. Viewed this way, Middle Plantation's planters' choices to build in brick not only reflect the individual concerns of class-conscious planters but also reveal the presence of local building conditions that were themselves shaped by the architectural decisions of a few prominent residents.

Under Francis Page's watch, the vestry saw its brick church erected. On November 29, 1683, the vestry recorded that the "Brick Church at Middle Plantation is now finished."[48] Soon, though, numerous structural problems emerged, and by 1714 the vestry had contracted builder James Morris to erect a new church. By December 2, 1715, Morris had completed his work, and the new church still stands to this day.

The church project was a challenge all along the way. But local commitment to the *idea* of Middle Plantation having this church was strong enough to sustain the several attempts to maintain the 1684 building and, when it became necessary, to build all over again. Middle Plantation's first brick church proved to be no more permanent than an average earthfast structure. But the needs and desires of the enduring community that built it were far from fleeting. Furthermore, the brick churches themselves were products of a growing and complicated infrastructure that shaped Middle Plantation.

In the 1680s a brick dwelling sat about one hundred yards southwest of the church. Like its public neighbor, it did not stand long. Three Colonial Williamsburg Foundation excavations provide the sum total of what we know about this building near the corner of Nassau and Duke of Gloucester Streets, and all the evidence points to its having been another short-lived brick building.

The Nassau Street site had been assumed to be the home of vestryman Francis Page, which after his death, had been rented out as a tavern.[49] But a 1999 Colonial Williamsburg excavation concluded that belief was wrong.[50] This opened up a question about who in fact owned this brick dwelling.

In 1654, Francis Peale patented a fifty-acre tract, which local historians believe was in the vicinity of the Nassau Street site. By 1662 this land was in the hands of Robert Weeks, and by 1690 it had been folded into the large landholdings of the locally prominent Bray family, who owned a considerable number of acres on the southern side of Williamsburg.[51] The Nassau Street building may have been associated with any one of these owners. But the archaeologically derived post-1676 construction date cast doubt on the possibility that this was the Peale-Weeks dwelling. Likewise, the late date rendered Bray ownership unlikely, as the family was already well established at another Middle Plantation residence by 1676. Rather than clarifying who may have owned this dwelling, the 1999 excavations only left the issue in greater doubt than before by ruling out all of the main contenders as well as eliminating the possibility that this was Page's tavern.[52]

Though the owner of the Nassau Street structure remains anonymous, we can infer a few key details about him. All of the local members of the gentry are accounted for, meaning that the owner was not among their number. What we do know, then, is that the owner had some resources but was not among the colony's uppermost social strata. While we may never know who commissioned the Nassau Street structure, we can be sure of at least one thing: whoever he was, he did not rise high enough in colonial society to pierce the veil of anonymity that hides most colonists from our view. What we see at Nassau Street is the property of a middling sort of planter who built in brick, quite in contrast to what we understand the regional norm to be and at a time of not only considerable social and political upheaval but supposedly economic distress as well.[53]

The Nassau Street structure reflects individual choice, the unique norms of a particular community, and how economic considerations may have affected both. The structure's owner was most likely the sort of colonist who, had he lived in another part of the colony, would have built a post-in-ground dwelling or some other lower-investment home. But in Middle Plantation, planters had other options. Here, the possibility of masonry architecture was not limited to the upper orders. Even residents further down the colonial social ladder could build in brick. In Middle Plantation, masonry was a sort of local style that initially emerged in response to the architectural desires of the area's wealthiest residents and the ready availability of the right kinds of clays. In time, though, this type of building became fundamentally woven into the fabric of the community in ways more complicated than simply the desire of elites to show off their accomplishments and aspirations.[54] Masonry required the presence of skilled artisans to make the materials and maintain the buildings. Once this network was in place—as it seemed to have been as early as the 1660s—its existence facilitated building in brick. Availability of materials and skills would lower the cost of building in brick, making masonry available to the widest possible number of planters. In this way, building in brick served to reinforce the specifics of the local economy, while also entwining planters within its tendrils. The result was a self-perpetuating local preference for brick, which drew on local talents and local materials.[55]

After nearly a century of sequential change, by 1699 the core of Middle Plantation, the highland between the creeks, where the pales once ran and where the Horse Path probably passed, was again facing transformation. Jamestown had suffered yet another fire, and the effort to build a college in the heart of Middle Plantation was in full swing. Influential locals like John Page and his son Francis, among others, had long advocated moving the capital upcountry, nearer to their homes and to a place high and dry and not subject to the threat of enemy naval bombardment. Even better, Middle Plantation, already boasted an arsenal, a brick church, and soon a college. By the beginning of the eighteenth century that had happened, and the new town grew up almost literally at John Page's old doorstep.

But much of Middle Plantation did not change in tone and form—the transformation was slow. It continued to be a rural neighborhood near the capital—albeit a bit nearer than before. And while the growth of Williamsburg certainly changed parts of the area, it alone cannot account for the almost total disappearance of the golden age capital's seventeenth-century predecessor. Instead, there are many locally specific reasons Middle Plantation ultimately faded away. Conceptualized in the heat of war, those parts of it erected as a response to conflict soon faded once peace took over. Palisade pales rotted and fell and gradually became farm lot lines or property markers, often more visible on paper and in their owners' minds' eyes. Far from being a failure, the old palisade was a stunning success in establishing a British colonial community with a transformed, no-longer-Native landscape.

The material remains of Middle Plantation show something quite different from a colony suffering a century of turmoil and chronic disorder. Rather than a community remaking itself in the face of failure, we see instead families setting roots, and the community that developed along the old wall's former run featured surprisingly fashionable and urbane homes. Rich Neck and John Page's Bruton Heights home would have been as comfortable and familiar in the English home counties as they were in Virginia. Indeed, so conscious of metropolitan trends were their owners that, at least in Rich Neck's case, changes in fashionability spelled its doom as gentry styles and tastes changed. Even though the Ludwells worked hard to turn Rich Neck into an expansive, currently fashionable English-style seat, they seem to have been unable to turn it into what changing tastes most demanded, and in time they left it behind.

At Middle Plantation, seventeenth-century Virginians achieved some of their greatest success in creating their own American England. That the area finally became the colonial capital was itself part of a process of landscape transformation that began with the palisade and continued through the creation of a built environment modeled in part first on English urban buildings and then on the homes of well-to-do rural gentlemen—essentially what many of these merchant-planters saw themselves as being. Far from reflecting "rude simplicity" or a prolonged period of chaos and reinvention, Middle Plantation was a British Atlantic settlement in which the feats of each generation set the stage for the generation that followed.

The landscape itself reflected this episodic character of development. It was made in one moment, worked for its time, and then faded into successive landscapes that local inhabitants fashioned by using some of what came before and discarding the rest. Each episode rested on what preceded it, and in time became in turn the baseline for what followed. Viewed at the ground level, the change that made Middle Plantation was not chaotic, violent, or the result of failure atop failure. Instead it was local, gradual, and remarkably steady.

Notes

1. I appropriate this opening device from Jon Kukla, "Order and Chaos in Early America: Political and Social Stability in Pre-Restoration Virginia," *American Historical Review* 90, no. 2 (April 1985): 275–98. A very small and recent sample of Jamestown narratives includes Bill Kelso, *Jamestown: The Buried Truth* (Charlottesville: University of Virginia Press, 2008); James Horn, *A Land as God Made It: Jamestown and the Birth of America* (New York: Basic Books, 2006); and Karen Ordahl Kupperman, *The Jamestown Project* (Cambridge, MA: Belknap, 2009).

2. Bernard Bailyn and Jack Greene quoted in Kukla, "Order and Chaos," 275; T. H. Breen, "Looking Out for Number One: Conflicting Cultural Values in Early Seventeenth-Century Virginia," *South Atlantic Quarterly* 78 (Fall 1979): 345. For the work of the Chesapeake School and their contemporaries on mortality rates and marriage patterns in the region, see Russell R. Menard and Lorena S. Walsh, "Death in the Chesapeake: Two Life Tables for Men in Early Colonial Maryland," *Maryland Historical Magazine* 69 (1974): 211–27; Carville V. Earle, "Environment, Disease, and Mortality in Early Virginia," in Thad W. Tate and David L. Ammerman, eds., *The Chesapeake in the Seventeenth Century: Essays on Anglo-American Society* (Chapel Hill: Published for the Institute of Early American History and Culture by University of North Carolina Press, 1979), 96–125; Darrett B. Rutman and Anita H. Rutman, "Of Agues and Fevers: Malaria in the Early Chesapeake,"

William and Mary Quarterly, 3rd ser., 33 (1976): 31–60; Rutman and Rutman, "'Now Wives and Sons-In-Law': Parental Death in a Seventeenth-Century Virginia County," in Tate and Ammerman, *The Chesapeake in the Seventeenth Century*, 153–82.

3. The most recent restatement of this perspective can be found in Willie Graham et al., "Adaptation and Innovation: Archaeological and Architectural Perspectives on the Seventeenth-Century Chesapeake," *William and Mary Quarterly*, 3rd ser., 64 (July 2007): 451–52. Very little survives of Virginia's seventeenth-century landscape—a fact that lends itself to the chaos-and-disorder narrative framework. Post-in-ground architecture no doubt accounts for the largest part of this loss, as demonstrated by Cary Carson et al., "Impermanent Architecture in the Southern American Colonies," in Robert Blair St. George, ed., *Material Life in America, 1600–1860* (Boston: Northeastern University Press, 1988). The data set has changed a bit, but the framework has not. Scholars have been slower to understand the scale and implications of brick architecture. See David A. Brown, "Domestic Masonry Architecture in 17th-Century Virginia," *Northeast Historical Archaeology* 27 (1988): 85–120; and Philip Levy and John Coombs, "To Build in Brick: Seventeenth-Century Brick Architecture and Colonial Virginia Society, a Reappraisal," paper presented at the 10th Annual Omohundro Institute for Early American History and Culture Conference, Northampton, MA, June 2004. Analyses of the meanings of these buildings have almost universally stressed their significance as markers of elite status. See Dwayne Pickett, "The John Page House Site: An Example of the Increase in Domestic Brick Architecture in Seventeenth-Century Tidewater, Virginia" (master's thesis, College of William and Mary, 1996); Brown, "Domestic Masonry Architecture"; and Ann Markell, "Solid Statements: Architecture, Manufacturing, and Social Change in Seventeenth-Century Virginia," in Paul Shackel and Barbara Little, eds., *Historical Archaeology of the Chesapeake* (Washington, DC: Smithsonian Institution Press, 1994), 51–64. For deviations from this emphasis on status, see Julia King and Edward Chaney, "Lord Baltimore and the Meaning of Brick Architecture in Seventeenth-Century Maryland," in Geoff Egan and R. L. Michael, eds., *Old and New Worlds* (Oxford: Oxbow Books, 1999), which emphasizes brick as a vehicle for elite competition; and David Muraca, "The Aspirations, Ambience, and Actualities of Middle Plantation," paper presented at the 28th Annual Society of Historical Archeology Conference, Washington, DC, 1995, emphasizing the use of brick in Middle Plantation to advertise the community as a possible capital.

4. The best study of Williamsburg's early development remains Cathleene Hellier, "Private Land Development in Williamsburg, 1699–1748: Building a Community" (master's thesis, College of William and Mary, 1989).

5. This discussion of the palisade is a brief distillation drawn from my larger discussion of the wall and its role in Virginia settlement patterns. See Philip Levy, "A New Look at an Old Wall: Indians, Englishmen, Landscape, and the 1634 Palisade at Middle Plantation," *Virginia Magazine of History and Biography* 112, no. 3 (2004): 226–65.

6. Samuel Purchas, *Hakluytus Posthumus; or, Purchas his Pilgrimes, Contayning a History of the World in Sea Voyages and Lande Travells by Englishmen and Others* 26 vols. (New York, 1906), 19:210; Susan Myra Kingsbury, ed., *The Records of the Virginia Company of London*, 4 vols. (Washington, DC: Government Printing Office, 1935), 4:11.

7. "Wyatt to Privy Council," Millie G. Cook, editor, "Sir Thomas Wyatt, Governor, Documents, 1624–26," *William and Mary Quarterly*, 2nd ser., 3 (July 1928), 165.

8. William Waller Hening, ed., *The Statutes at Large: A Collection of the Laws of Virginia*, 13 vols. (New York: R., W., and G. Bartow, 1823), 1:208.

9. Hening, *Statutes at Large*, 1:199, 208–9.

10. Levy, "A New Look at an Old Wall." Previous scholarship has seen the palisade as a quaint failure at best. See Edmund Morgan, *American Slavery, American Freedom: The Ordeal of Colonial Virginia* (New York: Norton, 1975), 136–37; Frederic W. Gleach, *Powhatan's World and Colonial Virginia: A Conflict of Cultures* (Lincoln: University of Nebraska Press, 1997), 170; Gleach, "'Where the Pales Ran': Sir Thomas Dale's Palisades of Seventeenth-Century Virginia," *Quarterly Bulletin of the Archaeological Society of Virginia* 41, no. 3 (September 1986): 160–68; Michael Puglisi, "Revitalization or Extirpation? Anglo-Powhatan Relations, 1622–1644" (master's thesis, College of William and Mary, 1982), 37; Virginia DeJohn Anderson, "Animals into the Wilderness: The Development of Livestock Husbandry in the Seventeenth-Century Chesapeake," *William and Mary Quarterly*, 3rd ser., 59 (April 2002): 377–408.

11. Nell M. Nugent, ed., *Cavaliers and Pioneers: Abstracts of Virginia Land Patents and Grants*, 3 vols. (Baltimore: Genealogical Publishing, 1963), 1:106.

12. Ibid., 1:110, 1:113.

13. Ibid., 1:105.

14. Ibid., 1:161.

15. Ibid., 1:159; York County Deeds, Orders, and Wills, Etc., 2 (1645–1649), 122.

16. Nugent, *Cavaliers and Pioneers*, 1:224, 266.

17. York County Deeds, Orders, Wills, Etc., 1 (1633–1694), 174; Deeds Order, Wills, Etc., 6 (1677–1684),128.

18. Nugent, *Cavaliers and Pioneers*, 1:316, 2:261, author's emphasis in quote.

19. As quoted in John Metz et al., *"Upon the Palisado" and Other Stories of Place from Bruton Heights* (Williamsburg: Colonial Williamsburg Foundation, 1998), 24.

20. Martha McCartney has done the most work toward recreating the patchwork of land holdings in this part of Virginia. She has collected much of her work in *James City County: Keystone of the Commonwealth* (Virginia Beach: Donning, 1997).

21. Hellier, "Private Land Development."

22. Lyon Gardner Tyler, "Williamsburg—the Old Colonial Capital," *William and Mary Quarterly* 1st ser., 1 (July 1907): 3–6. Bernard Bailyn describes these men, the second generation of Virginia elites, as "tough, unsentimental, quick tempered" and "crudely ambitious." Bailyn, "Politics and Social Structure in Virginia," in Stanley Katz, John Murrin, and Douglas Greenberg, eds., *Colonial America: Essays in Politics and Social Development* (New York: McGraw Hill, 1993), 22.

23. For more on the John Page site and its role in Middle Plantation, see Metz et al., *"Upon the Palisado" and Other Stories*. For an old but still very useful review of who was in the community, see Tyler, "Williamsburg—the Old Colonial Capital," 6.

24. Cary Carson et al., "New World, Real World: Improvising English Culture in Seventeenth Century Virginia," *Journal of Southern History* 74(February 2008), 31–89.

25. Colonial Williamsburg Foundation archaeologist and architectural historian James Knight speculated with some effect that Williamsburg's Duke of Gloucester Street runs along the line of the Horse Path. See Philip Levy, *Nassau Street Site Summer 1999 Excavations* (Williamsburg: Colonial Williamsburg Foundation, 2000), appendix A, "James Knight's 1942 Report." The Virginia Historical Society has a land plat for Richard Kemp's Rich Neck Plantation that shows a segment of the course of the Horse Path.

26. Martin Quitt has identified important ties between London and the members of Bailyn's third gentry group who migrated to Virginia between 1644 and 1666. The Byrds

and the Carters were members of prosperous London trading families, while many other important Virginians spent time in the capital before settling in the colony. Martin Quitt, "Immigrant Origins of the Virginia Gentry: A Study of Cultural Transmission and Innovation," *William and Mary Quarterly*, 3rd ser., 3 (1998): 635. Quitt estimates that more than one-third of Virginia's gentrymen spent significant time along the Thames, while James Horn concludes that servants migrating to the Chesapeake were mostly rural folks passing through English urban centers. James Horn, *Adapting to a New World: English Society in the Seventeenth-Century Chesapeake* (Chapel Hill: University of North Carolina Press, 1994).

27. See David Muraca, Philip Levy, and Leslie McFaden, *The Archaeology of Rich Neck Plantation* (Williamsburg: Colonial Williamsburg Foundation, 2003). See also Levy, "A Planter's Urbanity: City Living in the Colonial Virginia Countryside" *Journal of Middle Atlantic Archaeology* 21 (Winter 2005): 63–70, for a more preliminary, less contextualized discussion of Rich Neck and the Page house.

28. Audrey Horning, "'A Verie Fit Place to Erect a Great Citie': Comparative Contextual Analysis of Archaeological Jamestown" (Ph.D. diss., University of Pennsylvania, 1995).

29. Sir John Harvey to the Privy Council, in "Virginia under Governor Harvey," *Virginia Magazine of History and Biography* 3 (July 1895): 29; Kathleen Bragdon, Edward Chappell, and William Graham, "A Scant Urbanity: Jamestown in the Seventeenth-Century," in Theodore Reinhart and Dennis Pogue, eds., *The Archaeology of 17th-Century Virginia* (Courtland, VA: Archaeological Society of Virginia, 1993), 223–50.

30. Harvey to the Privy Council, in "Virginia under Governor Harvey."

31. Muraca, Levy, and McFaden, *Archaeology of Rich Neck Plantation*.

32. Ibid. The replacement of the central hearths with end hearths has been the object of considerable speculation, with some suggesting that perhaps the loss of central hearths afforded planters better surveillance within the home at a time when the labor force was in flux. See Fraser Neiman, "Temporal Patterning in House Plans from the Seventeenth-Century Chesapeake," in Reinhart and Pogue, *Archaeology of 17th-Century Virginia*, 251–84. Indeed, an enslaved African labor force was well in place at Rich Neck as well as other Middle Plantation settings by midcentury. See John C. Coombs, "Building 'The Machine': The Development of Slavery and Slave Society in Early Colonial Virginia" (Ph.D. diss., College of William and Mary, 2004), 24–26. But gable-end hearths were one of many architectural options at play in England during the period, and similar house-plan shifts occurred there without a commensurate demographic change in the labor force. What's more, at Rich Neck at least, the removal of the hearth left the view-obstructing wall still in place, therefore doing little to enhance surveillance. See also Eric Mercer, *English Vernacular Houses* (London: Her Majesty's Stationery Office, 1975).

33. Maurice Barley, *The House and Home* (London: Vista Books, 1963), 44.

34. Lyndon Cave, *The Smaller English House* (London: Robert Hale, 1981). See also April Lee Hatfield, *Atlantic Virginia: Intercolonial Relations in the Seventeenth Century* (Philadelphia: University of Pennsylvania Press, 2004), 48–51; and Victor Enthoven and Wim Klooster, "The Rise and Fall of the Virginia-Dutch Connection in the Seventeenth Century" in the present volume for a discussion of the timing of the Dutch trade into Virginia.

35. Ursula Priestly and P. J. Canfield, "Rooms and Room Use in Norwich Housing, 1580–1730," *Post-Medieval Archaeology* 16 (1982): 93–123; R. Machin, "The Great Rebuilding: A Reassessment," *Past and Present* 77 (1977): 33–56; Alan Dyer, "Urban Housing: A

Documentary Study of Four Midland Towns, 1530–1700," *Post-Medieval Archaeology* 15 (1981): 207–18. See also Coombs, "Building 'The Machine,'" 180–210, for another discussion of the phenomenon.

36. Levy and Coombs, "To Build in Brick"; Coombs, "Building 'The Machine,'" 199–202.

37. Lawrence Stone, *The Family, Sex and Marriage in England, 1500–1800* (New York: Harper and Row, 1977), 225–29.

38. Howard Colvin and John Newman, eds., *Of Building: Roger North's Writings on Architecture* (Oxford: Clarendon, 1981), 68.

39. Wesley Frank Craven, *The Colonies in Transition, 1660–1713* (New York: Harper and Row, 1968), chap. 5, "A Time of Trouble"; Morgan, *American Slavery, American Freedom*.

40. Susan Godson et al., *The College of William And Mary: A History* (Williamsburg: King and Queen Press, Society of the Alumni, College of William and Mary in Virginia, 1993), vol. 2.

41. Dell Upton, *Holy Things and Profane: Anglican Churches in Colonial Virginia* (Cambridge, MA: MIT Press, 1986), 12.

42. Quoted in Rev. John McCabe, "Churches in Virginia," *American Ecclesiastical History* (January 1856), 591. The vestry book was lost during the American Civil War. But fortunately Reverend McCabe wrote a brief history of the church the decade before the war using the then still extant vestry book as his guide. Therefore, we have two types of references to the lost text: a few direct quotations and McCabe's paraphrasing. It is impossible to assess the closeness or accuracy of McCabe's paraphrasing, but his direct access to the now lost original is encouraging. Direct quotations from the vestry book are identified as such in the notes that follow.

43. Vestry book, quoted in McCabe, "Churches in Virginia," 591. See also Upton, *Holy Things and Profane*, 31. Upton quotes the Christ Church Parish Vestry Book in noting that this Middlesex County, Virginia, parish planned its 1665 church "in every respect to be done and Finished according to the Middle plantacon Church." This, and the fact that the Bruton Parish vestry chose to abandon this church in 1677 is all we know of this structure.

44. The second Bruton Parish Church was built at a low point in Virginia church-related construction and just before a large increase in the number of newly built churches. The period 1607–99 saw the erection of 28 new churches, while 1700 to 1790 saw 166 new churches built. Of these 66 were in brick and 113 were framed. Upton, *Holy Things and Profane*, 12–13.

45. McCabe, "Churches in Virginia," 592.

46. Muraca, "Aspirations, Ambience, and Actualities"; Muraca, "The Development of Middle Plantation: The Community That Preceded Williamsburg," paper presented at the Council for Northeast Historical Archaeology, annual meeting, Williamsburg, VA, 1994.

47. Upton, *Holy Things and Profane*, 17–19.

48. Vestry book, quoted in McCabe, "Churches in Virginia," 594.

49. James Knight, "1942 Report," in Levy, *Nassau Street Site*, 39–40.

50. Artifacts from the structure's builders' trenches (dug to set the brick foundation) revealed a construction date of sometime after 1676, consistent with Francis Page's dates, but there are other problems with this attribution. The most notable is that Page's 1692 will mentioned the presence of a brick barn and malt house near his brick home. Excavations in the area yielded no sign of these dependencies. Likewise, the site's artifact assemblage

was not consistent with the quantity and quality of refuse usually associated with tavern sites. Levy, *Nassau Street Site*, 29.

51. Colonial Williamsburg Foundation, Department of Archaeological Research, "Middle Plantation Map," Daughters of the American Revolution Office, Williamsburg, VA, 2000. This valuable though unpublished map was created by Colonial Williamsburg staff and Martha McCartney, the area's reigning expert in regional landholdings. Much of McCartney's work is collected in *James City County: Keystone of the Commonwealth* (Virginia Beach: Donning, 1997).

52. Levy, *Nassau Street Site*, 28–34.

53. See Douglas Bradburn and John C. Coombs, "Smoke and Mirrors: Reinterpreting the Society and Economy of the Seventeenth-Century Chesapeake," *Atlantic Quarterly* 3, no. 2 (October 2006): 131–57.

54. Most scholars have interpreted these buildings as conveyors of status. The most recent statement of this idea is Graham et al.'s assertion that a biological evolutionary imperative drove elites to build in brick. The authors see the use of brick as analogous to animal behavior, as a means of "costly signaling" through which colonial elites could show that they were "formidable competitors or valuable social allies" ("Adaptation and Innovation," 475, 484). In contrast, though, I am not suggesting that bricks were somehow artifacts of social harmony but quite the contrary. Common vocabularies and shared systems could be vehicles for conflict as well as felicity, and brick was no different. See King and Chaney, "Lord Baltimore and the Meaning of Brick Architecture." See also Virginia Price, "Constructing to Command: Rivalries between Green Spring and the Governor's Palace, 1677–1722," *Virginia Magazine of History and Biography* 113, no. 1 (2005): 2–45, for another example of elite architecture as a vehicle for gentry conflict.

55. Architectural historian Henry Glassie saw this kind of focus on local production as a key defining trait of vernacular technology. In light of Glassie's criteria, Middle Plantation's brick buildings were a true vernacular architectural tradition in that residents relied principally on the specific skills and resources found in the area. See Henry Glassie, "Vernacular Architecture and Society," in Daniel Ingersoll Jr. and Gordon Bronitsky, eds. *Mirror and Metaphor: Material and Social Constructions of Reality* (Latham, MD: University Press of America, 1987), 232.

"Scatter'd upon the English Seats"

Indian Identity and Land Occupancy in the Rappahannock River Valley

Edward DuBois Ragan

Attachment to place was and remains the core of Rappahannock Indian identity. The Rappahannock's sense of place along the Virginia river that bears their name shaped their sense of themselves, their community, and their place in the world. When external forces threatened the Rappahannock, they typically responded with varying degrees of accommodation and resistance. For example, before English settlement, the Rappahannock participated with other Tidewater Algonquians in a broad shared regional culture, just as they resisted Powhatan's efforts to dominate them socially and politically. After English settlement, the Rappahannock continued to seek balance between accommodation and resistance, just as English settlement threatened the Rappahannock's commitment to place. This central tension centered on the Rappahannock's commitment to remain mobile within their ancestral homeland and to resist the fixity that Virginia's provincial authorities tried to impose. Provincial authorities wanted mapped, bounded Indian towns, which opened frontier land for English settlement and consolidated "neighbor" Indians as a frontier defense for settlers against "foreign" Indians who lived beyond the frontier. The Virginia General Assembly further insisted that it approve tribal chiefs and councilors and that Indian children be sent to live and work as servants in English homes. The Rappahannock refused these conditions. Instead, they secluded themselves in the remote uplands of those "English Seats," where they avoided fixed towns and having their community leaders approved. By the eighteenth century, Anglo-Virginian observers often interpreted Indians' flexible communities as "scatter'd," which then became evidence of indigenous decline and disappearance. But the Rappahannock did not disappear. Instead, they continued to live as they had before English settlement. The Rappahannock passively resisted outsiders and only accommodated colonial Indian policy when absolutely necessary.[1]

For as long as Algonquian people lived along the Rappahannock River, they modified their settlement patterns in response to changing environmental conditions. When the climate was warm and the rains regular, extended families built their towns and planted their crops in the alluvial soils along the banks of tidal creeks and rivers. During droughts, Algonquians relocated to the ridgelines between the tidal rivers and dispersed into settlements of from one to three families.[2] The clay soil of the ridge accommodated drier climates by retaining more moisture so that during droughts, the Rappahannock could continue to plant their corn and feed their families. These dispersed settlements did not diminish the group, and when environmental conditions improved, the people returned from the ridgeline to the river and re-established their larger villages. Throughout the Middle and Late Woodland Periods, or from A.D. 200 to 1600, settlement sizes and locations in the Tidewater continued to ebb and flow as groups' residential patterns fluctuated in response to periodic environmental and human stress.

Around A.D. 200, settlements consisted of both small and intermediate-sized sites. These sites typically contained from one to six households and were located both along rivers and in the interior along the ridges of elevated necklands, where freshwater springs fed the brackish tidal rivers. These intermediate-sized sites functioned as base camps during the fall and winter and perhaps into the early spring. Then populations dispersed to smaller sites to exploit particular resources. Some of these smaller, single-household settlements were located in the interior uplands, where each person performed his or her gender-specific job. Men and older boys hunted bear, fowl, and deer. Women and children foraged for nuts and medicinal herbs and collected firewood and building materials, such as saplings and elm bark for houses and cedar bark for cordage. Other families dispersed along marshes, rivers, and creeks. There, men foraged for shellfish and caught fish, such as shad, herring, and sturgeon. Women collected reeds for mats and foraged for starchy tubers like tuckahoe. These settlement and subsistence patterns were adaptations to a cooler, drier climate, so that living in small and intermediate-sized settlements was one response to environmental stress.[3]

Beginning about A.D. 645, warmer temperatures and more rain seem to have stimulated a growth in settlement sizes. The remains of larger villages have been found on the necklands near coves and along the embayments of tributaries.[4] Men, women, and children still went out to occupy and exploit smaller, seasonal sites, but there seems to have been a core of people who occupied a single, large village throughout the year. This trend toward larger villages continued until about A.D. 900, when the majority of people once again dispersed.

Two significant events forced this human shift and social adjustment: the climate became markedly drier, and women began to cultivate corn, beans, and squash.[5] This dry period lasted about three hundred years and undoubtedly slowed the development of settled horticulture in the Tidewater. Large settlements disappeared from the archaeological record, replaced by semipermanent, intermediate-sized settlements and temporary small camps located near specific resources such as fish or game. During this adjustment to settled horticulture, there is no evidence of large settlement sites in the Rappahannock or Potomac River valleys or, for that matter, anywhere in the Chesapeake.[6] Even after this drier period ended, another hundred or so years passed before new technologies and perhaps new belief systems reconnected people by bringing on the return to larger, more permanent "village communities."[7]

Such fundamental change occurred unevenly across the Chesapeake. On the James River, the transition to large "village communities" began around A.D. 1200.[8] Further north, on the Rappahannock River, the growth of "village communities" came later and continued well into the sixteenth century.[9] Taken together, these settlement trends suggest that Tidewater Algonquians required several centuries to accommodate horticulture, both environmentally and culturally. After centuries of adjustment, corn, beans, and squash provided as much as 50 to 75 percent of the peoples' total subsistence needs. Given more ample sustenance from cultivated crops, larger villages, which covered perhaps five acres, replaced the mix of small and intermediate sites, though small sites, like fishing and oystering camps, continued to support the larger villages.[10]

Alongside the fluctuations in settlement patterns and the emergence of corn-based horticulture, the archaeological record suggests other important material and ideological transformations. Both the bow and arrow and secondary burial customs arrived in the Chesapeake around A.D. 900. During this significant period of change in Algonquian material culture, ideological changes no doubt followed. The Okeus deity may have joined the Algonquian pantheon at this time, as people incorporated new rituals to encourage the corn and deer to return each year. Our current understanding of the archeological record indicates that it took some four hundred years after the arrival of bows and burials for Native communities to incorporate and master these new ways. Significantly, these changes were as revolutionary as the technologies, customs, and ideologies that arrived in 1607 with the English and their deity.

As part of Tidewater Algonquians' cultural evolution, the political chiefdom emerged as a social solution to the challenges of material and ideological change. The archaeological record supports the so-called Big Men cycle of leadership at different places across the Chesapeake throughout the Woodland era, and Powhatan seems to have been the first person to attempt a panregional paramount chiefdom with a centralized political authority. To build his paramount chiefdom, Powhatan incorporated nearby groups, like the Kecoughtan, the Piankatank, and the Opiscopank. He destroyed those he could not dominate politically or incorporate socially, like the Chesapeake peoples at the mouth of the bay.[11]

To resist the expanding authority of Powhatan, neighboring peoples distanced themselves both from Powhatan and from one another. They began to organize their kin groups around the chiefdom model. Many even palisaded their towns for defense. However, most were unsuccessful at resisting Powhatan's dominion. When English explorers first documented Powhatan's paramount chiefdom, the Chickahominy were the only people in Powhatan's heartland who had managed to retain complete political independence.

Other groups relied on geography to keep themselves on Powhatan's fringe. One need only look at settlements along the Rappahannock River to see peoples' determination to retain their independence. By the end of the sixteenth century, Powhatan's paramount chiefdom extended north from the James River to the southern shores of the Rappahannock River. Powhatan had questionable control between the Rappahannock and Potomac Rivers. Those who wished to avoid Powhatan's dominion tended to live on the north side of the Rappahannock River. In fact, by the early seventeenth century, there were some thirty-four towns on the north bank of the river, compared with five on the south bank. The river's north shore was the most densely settled region of the Tidewater.[12] (See map on p. 000.)

In the summer of 1608, when John Smith mapped the Rappahannock River, he recorded the populations of the groups he encountered there. Beginning at the river's entrance, he noted that "on the North side are seated a people called Cuttatawomen, with 30 fighting men. Higher on the river are the Moraughtacunds, with 80 able men. Beyond them Toppahanock with 100 men. Far above is another Cuttatawomen, with 20 fighting men. On the South, far within the river [upstream] is Nantaughtacund having 150 men."[13] These 380 warriors translate to roughly 1,900 people who lived along the Rappahannock River from the fall line to the Chesapeake Bay. Of that total, some five hundred, or roughly 25 percent, were Rappahannock.[14]

In these northern reaches, the Rappahannock Indians and their riverine neighbors maintained a tenuous balance between independence and domination by Powhatan. The Rappahannock's principal villages stretched along the northern shores of the river. Their location kept them just beyond Powhatan's dominion, though they interacted with Powhatan in limited ways through shared hunting grounds south of the river, communal feasts, and limited exchange networks.[15] From their experience avoiding Powhatan's complete dominion, Algonquians like the Rappahannock learned how to live with the presence of an expanding authoritarian political chiefdom, so that when the English began to settle in the Rappahannock River valley, the Rappahannock people had a cultural framework for dealing with aggressive neighbors.

In the winter of 1607 and the summer of 1608, when John Smith visited and mapped the Rappahannock homeland, their capital town, Tappahannock, straddled the nearly mile-wide river. Since waterways were the principal thoroughfares, Tidewater Algonquians often built their towns on both sides of creeks and rivers, so that the river joined the Rappahannock's capital town at Tappahannock and connected the lesser Rappahannock towns to each other.[16] Smith dubbed those lesser towns "ordinary houses."[17] We might think of them as hamlets, or family settlements, of from one to four single-family dwellings. Since Smith based his map on his summer 1608 observations, the "ordinary houses" he mapped may have been seasonal residences where men and boys fished while women and girls tended fields of corn, beans, and squash and foraged for local foods and herbs. Or these settlement sites may have been semipermanent places that identified and defended the Rappahannock's homeland.

After Smith's departure from Tappahannock in the summer of 1608, Rappahannock River people disappeared for a time from the historical record. The periodic absence of Rappahannock peoples from the narrative of Anglo-Indian Virginia is suggestive of the Rappahannock's peripheral place in the English field of vision. Because beaver in the area were thin-pelted, the fur trade did not develop on the Rappahannock as it did along the Potomac and upper Chesapeake Bay. As the Rappahannock River valley remained unsettled by Englishmen into the 1640s, there were no occasions for Anglo-Indian violence to mobilize Native warriors.[18]

Instead, the English built their settlements along Virginia's Lower Peninsula, between the James and York Rivers, where they tried to reconstruct Indian identity. After a year of curious interaction and only minor violence, the English attempted to assert their sovereignty over local Algonquians through a traditional, distinctly European, coronation ceremony. In October 1608, Captain Christopher Newport presented Powhatan with a crown, ostensibly a gift from King James I. Newport, however, had great difficulty convincing Powhatan to kneel to accept his crown, both parties understanding all too well the symbolism conveyed by bowing the head or lowering oneself in the presence of others. John Smith, who was present at Powhatan's English coronation, wrote that only after "leaning hard on his shoulders, he a little stooped."[19] Newport crowned Powhatan and claimed that the Indian chief recognized King James's dominion over Virginia and its people. Once subjugated, efforts to gain Algonquians' compliance, and thus remake the Indian, extended to Native peoples across the Virginia Tidewater.

In 1609, the Virginia Company of London laid out this policy for Sir Thomas Gates when he assumed control of the Jamestown plantation. The company instructed Gates to convert Virginia's Indians to tributaries of the English Crown. This process involved three components: an English claim of sovereignty over the land, the education of Indian children as a means to break the superstitious influence of Native priests, and the incorporation of Native trading practices into the English mercantile economy.[20] Through these means, the English believed they could remake Native religion, society, and economy. In reality, the plan was overly ambitious. The settlers at Jamestown, who struggled for survival themselves, could do little to act on policy statements from London.

The English failed to appreciate that dispossessed Indians would be militant against Christianity and English social customs. The Virginia Company's unrealistic goals reflected prevailing English attitudes about how the Indians ought to be treated as humans. Some people like the Reverend George Thorpe (who was sent to the colony in 1620) maintained that Indians were human beings worthy of a place in English society.[21] But many in the colonies and in London remained generally ambivalent about how to deal with the natives, encouraging both dominion and civility:

> Wee praie you also to have especiall Care that no injurie or oppresion be wrought by the English against any of the natives of that Countrie, whereby the present peace may bee disturbed and ancient quarrels (now buried) might bee revived. Provided nevertheless that the honor of our Nation and safety of our people bee still preserved and all manner of Insolence committed by the natives be severely and sharpelie punished.[22]

Such was the dilemma of the Virginia Company. What would be the balance between "oppression" and "honor"? And in Virginia, despite the pleas from London for benevolence toward Indians, settlers more frequently showed contempt. Reverend Thorpe summarized the real attitude of Virginians when he said, "There is scarce any man amongst us that doth soe much affoord them a good thought in his hart and most men with theire mouthes give them nothinge but maledictions and better execrations."[23] In this instance, Thorpe vocalized the frustration of trying to effect the company's Indian policy in the face of continued ambivalence both in England and among the English settlers around him.

Though both Indians and Englishmen suffered, there were too few English in Virginia to either convert or destroy the local Algonquian population. In 1608, Captain John Smith estimated 2,400 Algonquian warriors in the Virginia colony, or 13,000–15,000 total inhabitants.[24] By 1624, the indigenous population had declined to 5,000.[25] During roughly the same time, approximately 6,000 people migrated to Virginia. A 1625 census recorded 1,232 colonists.[26] In this setting, Tidewater Algonquians felt little need to acquiesce to English demands. The vast majority did not send their children to live among the English, and they continued to resist English culture. But the English appropriated Indian land, and they segregated Indians from white settlement. In 1622, Opechancanough led his warriors against the English to check the expansion of new settlements on the Lower Peninsula. Of approximately 1,200 English Virginians, Algonquian warriors killed 347.[27]

In response, the English declared "perpetual enmity" against all Indians.[28] The colonial militias launched annual attacks and seized Indian corn. During the 1620s and 1630s, the colonists supplemented their own corn production with stolen Indian corn. To defend against future attacks, the General Assembly at Jamestown ordered that a line of settlement be extended across the Lower Peninsula.[29] In 1632, the assembly offered fifty acres to any man who settled along this defensive line. When completed in 1634, a six-mile palisade stretched from the James River to the York River. This "pale" formalized a pattern of Indian segregation from white settlement.[30]

In 1644, Opechancanough led a second uprising to check English expansion up the Lower Peninsula. This time, the Algonquian warriors killed nearly four hundred colonists; however, there were over ten thousand settlers in Virginia, and the effect was greatly diminished.[31] For the next two years, the English struck back with a vengeance. They attacked Indian towns, seized crops, and displaced Indians from their traditional lands. Greatly reduced in number, the separate Algonquian groups could not withstand continued attacks by the English. Defeated militarily, the remnant of Powhatan's paramount chiefdom concluded a general peace with Virginia.

In 1646, the Englishmen in Virginia succeeded in their thirty-seven year effort to reduce the Tidewater Algonquians to tributary status. The treaty of October 1646 asserted English rights of conquest over all Virginia Indians.[32] Opechancanough's successor, Necotowance, now held his dominions as a vassal of the English king. He acknowledged the sovereignty of the English crown and agreed to pay an annual tribute of twenty beaver skins. While not a substantial tribute, it was an annual recognition of English dominion. Implicit in this treaty were both the responsibilities and the rights conveyed through tributary status. Among the responsibilities, the English now required all tributaries to gain English approval for tribal leaders. More important, the English required all Indians to vacate the land between the James and York Rivers from the fall line to Kecoughtan, the tip of the Lower Peninsula.

The English were now the sole occupants of the Lower Peninsula. No Indian could "repair to or make any abode upon the said tract of land, upon paine of death, and ... it shall be lawfull for any person to kill any such Indian."[33] The treaty established points of entry at Fort Royal for the north side at the Pamunkey River and Fort Henry for the south side at the Appomattox River. Indian messengers had to obtain a permit and a striped coat, which verified the authority of the permit, to travel within this section. In effect, only authorized Indians could enter the area of English settlement. This is significant because it expanded the cultural and legal segregation of Indians from Anglo-Virginia. As Virginians settled around the individual tributaries, these tribes maintained communities that were separate from the English. The English required that Indians return all prisoners, slaves, and weapons that they had captured during the uprising. By contrast, captured Indians became slaves to be returned to their masters if they ran away. In other words, the English maintained complete freedom to enter Indian territory. Lastly, Necotowance was to encourage the Indians to send their children "not above twelve yeares old" to live with the English.[34] Tributary children were especially desired as servants. This demonstrates the extent to which English dominion penetrated Indian culture. By assimilating the children, Virginians could break traditional Powhatan social influences, particularly religious influences, and thus remake Indians in English ways.

Of course these responsibilities were not without rights. The English guaranteed the tributaries military support against their enemies. The proximity of white and Indian settlements meant that it was in the colony's interests to defend the tributaries from attacks by foreign Indians. The principal right given to the tributaries was the freedom to inhabit the north side of the York River without interference from the English, except the parts of that peninsula that were already settled (from Poropatanke downward, or Gloucester County, the southern tip of the Middle Peninsula).[35] Thus, the provisions of the 1646 treaty are important, for they reveal the pattern of expanding white settlement and demonstrate English desires to ensure that settlement continued in a peaceable manner. The year 1646 corresponds roughly to the period in which the population of the Virginia colony began to grow through natural increase (in addition to continuing immigration).[36] This makes the 1646 treaty all the more significant because Virginia obtained increased military security at a time when the colony could benefit from expanding English settlement among tributary Indians.

Indians could inhabit lands north of the York River, where the English were prohibited from going except to recover their property. The treaty with Necotowance was Act I of the 1646 session of the General Assembly. Act VI, presumably passed not much later, opened, with the governor's permission, settlement north of the York River.[37] Certainly this raises questions as to the assembly's sincerity and suggests that its actions were never intended to be permanent. Thus, the pattern was confirmed. Military defeat and political subjugation gave way to greater expropriation of Indian land by Virginians who were not content to remain south of the York River or, for that matter, south of the Rappahannock River.[38]

As English settlement washed up the Rappahannock River like a tidal wave, once again the Rappahannock Indians had to alter their settlement patterns to accommodate their new neighbors. The occupation of so much Rappahannock land by English planters restricted the Rappahannock's mobility and access to their favorite fields and habitual hunting grounds.

The principal strategy that the Rappahannock Indians employed to ensure their survival was to accommodate the English when absolutely necessary and to avoid them whenever possible. To counteract the imbalance and breakdown that English colonization presented to Algonquian society, groups like those in the Rappahannock area retreated to survive. They secluded themselves within the interior of their ancestral homelands along freshwater creeks, marshy thickets, and wooded uplands. The Rappahannock often addressed their own grievances but did not join with nearby Algonquian groups to confront the greater threat that English colonization posed. Instead, the Rappahannock remained independent from outsiders.

As proof, the Rappahannock had avoided entirely the first two Anglo-Powhatan wars, which lasted from 1609 to 1614 and from 1622 to 1632, and they did not join Opechancanough in the third Anglo-Powhatan war (1644–46). Instead, the Virginia Council solicited Rappahannock warriors as guides against Opechancanough.[39] Even after 1646, when the General Assembly approved English land patents in the Rappahannock River valley, it was another five years before English settlement reached the Rappahannock people. By then, continually closer contact between English settlers and Rappahannock people made the threat of conflict real and the need for accommodation constant.

Then, on April 4, 1651, Moore Fauntleroy, a former burgess from Upper Norfolk County, presented the Rappahannock *weroance* (chief), Accopatough, and his council with "ten fathom [sixty feet] of peake and goods, amounting to thirty arms'-length [approximately ninety feet] of Rohonoke," in exchange for roughly one-third of the Rappahannock homeland on the north side of the Rappahannock River "so long as the sun and moon endureth."[40] According to the conveyance, the Rappahannock lived in two towns, each situated some two miles inland along freshwater creeks that fed the Rappahannock River: "great Rappahannock Town," which was two miles up Rappahannock Creek, and "Totusha," also known as "Tanks ['little'] Rappahannock Town,"[41] located three miles up Totuskey Creek. It remains unclear why the Rappahannock had retreated from their riverfront residences. Perhaps these were fishing villages. After all, it was April, and the shad and herring had spawned in these creeks. Similarly, those dispersed towns in the Rappahannock River floodplain mapped by Smith in the summertime may have been seasonal farming communities.[42] However, the conveyance made no mention of a single capital town called Tappahannock. By 1651, Tappahannock may have been abandoned, perhaps in response to epidemic diseases that undoubtedly reduced Rappahannock numbers in the first half of the seventeenth century. Maybe it was drought or the threat of attack by the English after Opechancanough's assaults on English settlements in 1622 and 1644. Each of these tensions that English colonization presented resulted in a changed settlement pattern for the Rappahannock. (See map 7.1.)

Fauntleroy purchased roughly forty square miles from the Rappahannock Indians and settled at Farnham Creek, the midpoint of the grant. His patent included seven miles of riverfront property between Totuskey and Morattico Creeks that extended inland from the river, perhaps six miles in some places, "unto the bounds of the Potowmack River," that is, the headwaters of the Potomac's tributaries, which issued from the ridgeline of the Northern Neck and bounded the Rappahannock territory.[43]

The language of the agreement suggested a hopeful relationship between Fauntleroy and the Rappahannock. However, hope and Anglo-Rappahannock accommodation soon degenerated into an ongoing squabble over land, livestock, encroachment, and nonpayment. The brotherly love that the Rappahannock first acknowledged for Fauntleroy soon turned to contempt as other Englishmen followed Fauntleroy onto Rappahannock land. The Rappahannock River valley quickly became some of the most prized tobacco land in Virginia.[44] This pattern of disillusion and dispute was replicated across the Middle Peninsula and Northern Neck of Virginia as Native communities and English settlers collided.

In November 1652, to quell the mounting frontier violence between Englishmen and displaced Indians, the Virginia General Assembly ordered that there would "be no grants of land to any Englishman whatsoever ... until the Indians be first served with the proportion of fiftie acres of land for each bowman." The measure demonstrated the attempt by provincial authorities both to reduce the amount of Indian land and to protect what remained from English encroachment. Significantly, the English defined the Indians' apportionment in English terms: fifty acres was the headright that planters received for each individual they imported into the colony. By apportioning land at the same rate for Indians and Englishmen, the assembly created an Indian headright and began a process to transform Tidewater

218 / Edward DuBois Ragan

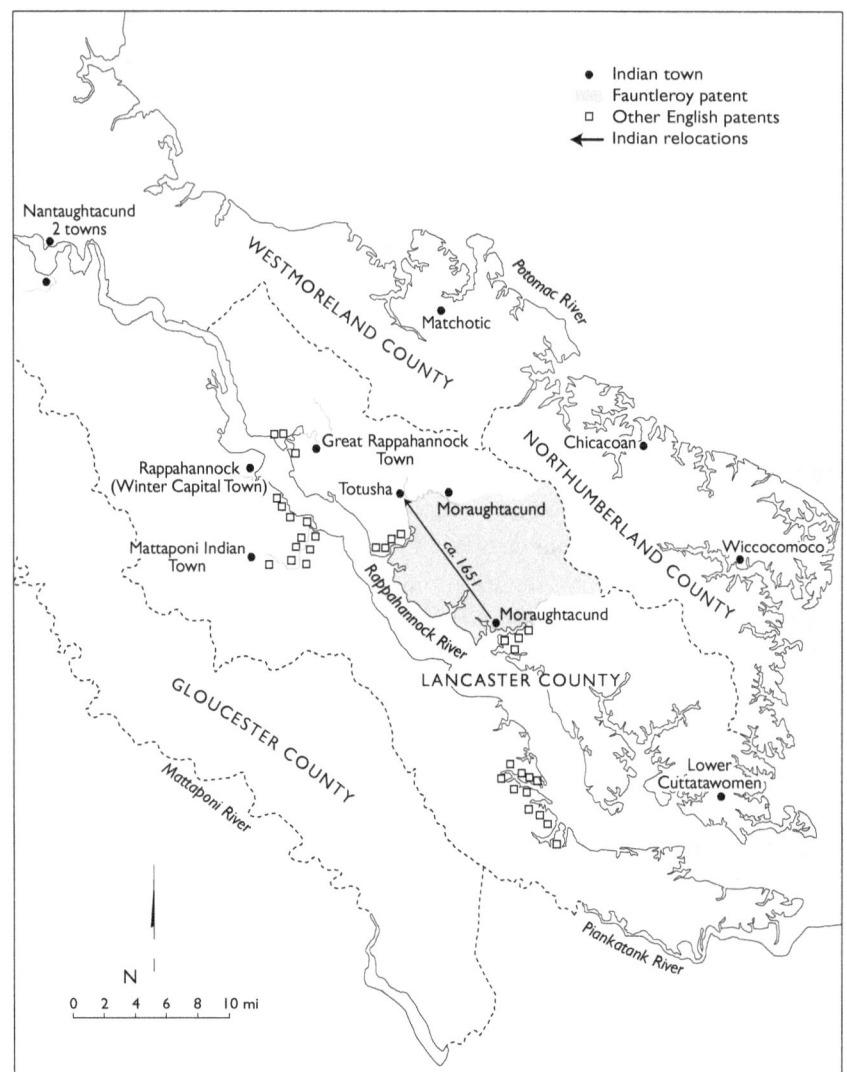

Map 7.1. Rappahannock River Valley, ca. 1653. (Map by Bill Nelson)

Algonquians into subsistence farmers. Control of land and the drastic reduction of Indian territory became a primary means through which the English tried to change Indian identity. To prevent an uprising by rapidly displaced Native communities on the Northern Neck, in the summer of 1653 the General Assembly specifically directed Lancaster County, which now bounded the Rappahannock's homeland, to comply with the colony's Indian land act.⁴⁵ On September 14, 1653, Lancaster County, "by an order of the last Assembly required to settle the Indians Inhabiting within this countie," concluded a treaty with the "Rappahannocke nation" that described and bounded the Rappahannock's homeland and afforded Indians the "rights of Englishmen" in court.⁴⁶

To this and similar acts, the Rappahannock were not entirely passive. As they learned what it meant to have English neighbors, to be alienated from ancestral lands, and to have what remained mapped and bounded, Rappahannock men retaliated frequently against the property of individual Englishmen. They killed the Englishmen's free-roaming hogs and cattle that ate Indians' corn, and they took English tools—axes, picks, and shovels—whenever they needed them. For these and other reasons, on November 20, 1654, the General Assembly ordered a "defensive" march against the Rappahannock. In the ensuing encounter, the Rappahannock's weroance, Toweren, was killed.⁴⁷ This was the second Rappahannock weroance to die in five years (Accopatough had died on his way to Jamestown in 1651 to confirm Fauntleroy's patent) and the third for whose death the English were directly responsible. Toweren's death marked the end of armed Rappahannock resistance to English settlement. The Rappahannock continued to lose ground with every accommodation they made, but they avoided a militant response. Even as Native communities around them rose up in succession against the English intrusion, the Rappahannock did not join them.

These were difficult adjustments to make for the Rappahannock. Alien laws and customs had circumscribed where they could hunt, fish, oyster, plant, or gather. The Rappahannock weroance had agreed to provisions that he may have understood poorly. In 1651, when Fauntleroy made his original purchase, Accopatough had given Fauntleroy and his agents permission "to punish, correct, beat, or kill any Indian, ... which shall ... presume to molest, harm, or offer any manner of harm, wrong, injury, or violence upon the said land, or any part of it, unto the said Fantleroy ... or any whomsoever he or they shall seat, place, or put upon any part or parcel of the abovesaid land."⁴⁸ Efforts by the Rappahannock to continue to live on the land deeded to Fauntleroy may have been the source of earlier Anglo-Indian friction that had brought out the militia and resulted in Toweren's death. The Rappahannock intended to remain on their ancestral land. Doing so meant that they had to learn how to accommodate their English neighbors. As they looked around to their Native neighbors on the Northern Neck, they could see the effect of resisting English settlement.

To limit frontier violence and make more land available to English settlement, the English tried to assign Indians to particular towns. When groups occupied more than one town, colonial officials treated the residents of each town as a separate group, but Indians continued to live as they always had: they relocated, combined, and dispersed their communities to suit their needs.[49] These competing notions of group identity and land ownership and occupancy caused the conflict that often landed Indians and Englishmen alike in court.[50]

In early March 1656, to address these and other issues, the Virginia Council put forward its plan for civilizing local Indians. A central component of this plan was the introduction of Indian severalty, or separate property, to tributary Indians. First, to combat the wolves that threatened settlers and livestock alike, the assembly granted to the tributaries one cow for every eight wolf heads delivered to county officials. The councilors asserted that "this will be a step to civilizing them and making them Christians."[51] The connection between cattle and Christianity seems odd at first; however, the intended outcome of this policy sought to reconstruct Indian economies along English lines, and part of this re-creation required Indians to adopt settled agriculture, which included animal husbandry.[52]

The second part of this plan restated the education policy of the 1646 tributary treaty. While colonial officials were content to influence adult Indians through economic means, they sought to remove Indian children from their native environment and educate them as Englishmen. The assembly maintained that if "the Indians shall bring in any children as gages of their good and quiet intentions to us and amity with us, then the parents of such children shall choose the person to whom the care of such children shall be intrusted and the country by us their representatives do engage that we will not use them as slaves, but do their best to bring them up in Christianity, civility and the knowledge of necessary trades."[53] In effect, these children were hostages ("gages of their good and quiet intentions") designed to ensure the tributaries' good behavior. The reality was that Indian children became servants, a source of labor.

Concurrently, the colonial legislature enacted measures to ensure some form of protection for Indians against unscrupulous land deals. All sales of Indian land had to be approved by the General Assembly.[54] In general, the English never doubted the eventual demise of Indian land titles. Fair legislation both ensured the peaceful transfer of land and kept tributary Indians within Virginia's settled boundaries, a defensive measure necessary for Virginia's survival. According to the 1646 treaty, the tributaries and the English entered a military alliance, and despite efforts to segregate Indians from the English, the tributaries, their reduced numbers notwithstanding, remained an essential component of frontier settlement and defense.

The Virginia General Assembly had ordered planters in the Rappahannock valley to "purchase the said land of the Indians or relinquish the same," but frequently settlers did neither.[55] Moore Fauntleroy continued to claim Rappahannock land even though his new patents violated the Rappahannock's treaty rights. Fauntleroy did not pay the Rappahannock for his subsequent patents, and when the Rappahannock weroance complained to the Virginia Council, Fauntleroy ignored the council.[56] To add insult to injury, in early 1662, the Rappahannock weroance, Wachicopa, and his councilors were on their way to Jamestown with "the Roanoake" to pay their annual tribute to the governor when Fauntleroy captured and imprisoned the Rappahannock leaders. Fauntleroy claimed the governor's tribute as "ransome" for Wachicopa's release and then took his prisoners to Jamestown, where he accused them of not paying their tribute to the governor. At Jamestown, Wachicopa complained that Fauntleroy had not only stolen their tribute and imprisoned him and his councilors unfairly but that Fauntleroy had yet to pay for the land he had patented.[57]

The Rappahannock did not suffer alone. That same month another illegal detention and tribute confiscation occurred on the Potomac River between the Patawomeck weroance, Wahanganoche, and four Englishmen: Captain Giles Brent, Colonel Gerard Fowkes, Captain George Mason, and John Lord.[58] Provincial authorities sided with the Rappahannock and Patawomeck, fined all five Englishmen, and barred them from holding provincial office, yet the penalties remained unenforced. Without real provincial punishment, English settlers continued to push their way onto Indian land and abuse community leaders.[59] Similar "violent intrusions" at Chicacoan, Wiccocomico, Machodoc, Moraughtacund, and Mattaponi increased the likelihood that the Rappahannock River frontier would erupt in Anglo-Indian violence.[60]

To quell the potential for violence, in 1663, the General Assembly passed an act addressed to "Northerne Indians." This specific measure was aimed at the Patawomeck, but the message was clear for the Doeg, Piscattaway, and Susquehannock, all of whom lived north of the Rappahannock River and continually raided and threatened English expansion on the Northern Neck.[61] The language in this measure was harsh and precise:

> Deliver such hostages of their children or others as shall be required; and if they or any of them shall refuse to deliver such hostages as shall be required, ... the nation [shall] be declared as an enemy and proceeded against accordingly.... And as we have endeavoured for the future to provide for the safety of the country that such hostages be delivered as shall be required, soe it is also enacted that the hostages to be delivered shall be civilly used and treated by the English to whose charge they shall be delivered, and that they be brought up in the English literature (soe far as they are capable).[62]

Contrast this with the language used regarding the tributaries in 1656, where Indian children were "gages" of their parents' "good and quiet intentions."[63] The images are similar in that children were seen as the means through which Indian society must be re-created. The differences arise in how each was conveyed. For the tributaries, children were "gages"; for hostile Indians, children were "hostages" who would be educated "soe far as they are capable." Despite this apparent distinction in degrees of perceived enmity, colonial legislators agreed that Indians should have equal justice with whites.[64] The English understood that civilizing Indians was a process. Anglo-Virginians afforded Indians legal rights equivalent to those of whites because Virginians conceived of Indians more in ethnic-class terms than in racial ones. That is, Indians had equal access to English law, even if Englishmen treated them unequally before that law.

Just as Virginians moved to secure the legal rights of Indians generally, they reinforced their dominion over the tributaries. In October 1665, the General Assembly passed a series of measures designed to further regulate tributary actions. The assembly appointed Indian commissioners for each county with orders to enforce the law. At the same time, it limited tributary sovereignty and eliminated tributaries' power "to elect or constitute their owne Werowance or chief commander."[65] This differed from the 1646 provision. In the earlier instance, the tributaries retained the power to nominate leaders who were then approved or rejected by the governor of Virginia. The 1665 measure arbitrarily transferred the power of appointment to Virginia's governor, who was to "authorize such person in whose fidelity they may finde greatest cause to repose a confidence to be the commander of the respective townes."[66] And so the English continued their attack on Indian sovereignty.

The Rappahannock, who refused to have their weroance approved by provincial authorities and resisted provincial efforts to confine them to bounded, mapped towns, decided to sell their towns on Rappahannock and Totuskey Creeks to escape this increased oversight that threatened their families and their freedom. They may have been overwhelmed as well by the violence that surrounded them and decided to further remove themselves from the English settlements. Or the Rappahannock decision to relocate may have been influenced by the fierce storms that ravaged the Chesapeake. In April 1667, "a most p[ro]digeous Storme of haile many of them as bigg as Turkey Eggs" damaged crops, livestock, and homes across the colony. That summer, the crops that had survived the hailstorm drowned in a rainstorm that "continued for 40 dayes." In August, "the most Dreadfull Hurry Cane that ever this Collony groaned under" swept through the Tidewater. The hurricane destroyed "at least 10000 houses ... [and] all the Indian Graine laid flatt upon the grownd, all the Tobo[acco] in the fields torne to pieces ... the fences about the Corne fields either blown downe or beaten to the grownd by trees w[hi]ch fell upon them." The rains flooded rivers and creeks well beyond their banks.[67] Natives would have interpreted the violent intrusions of Englishmen and the divine manifestations of floods, hailstorms, and hurricanes as omens of travails to come and punishment for past transgressions.[68] After twenty years of steady intrusion by English settlers, the Rappahannock had been devastated psychologically as well as physically. That October, they sold their town on Totuskey Creek and moved to the south bank of the Rappahannock River.[69]

It may have been this year of devastation that forced the Rappahannock to seek refuge on higher ground. The highest elevation in their ancestral homeland was on the south side of the Rappahannock River along the ridge between the Mattaponi and Rappahannock Rivers. The midreaches of the Middle Peninsula were the Rappahannock's ancestral hunting ground. After the fall harvest, the Rappahannock hunted the ridgeline along the south side of the Rappahannock River. It was also along these peninsular ridgelines where Native peoples had secluded themselves in earlier eras of stress that predated English colonization. (See map 7.2.)

By 1669, the Rappahannock lived in two settlements along the ridgeline of the Middle Peninsula. That fall, when the General Assembly recorded its first Indian census since 1608, seventy "bowmen," or approximately 350 people, lived in the two towns listed as "Rappahannocks" and "Totas Chees."[70] These communities appear to be direct transplants from the Northern Neck towns on Rappahannock and Totuskey Creeks. How-

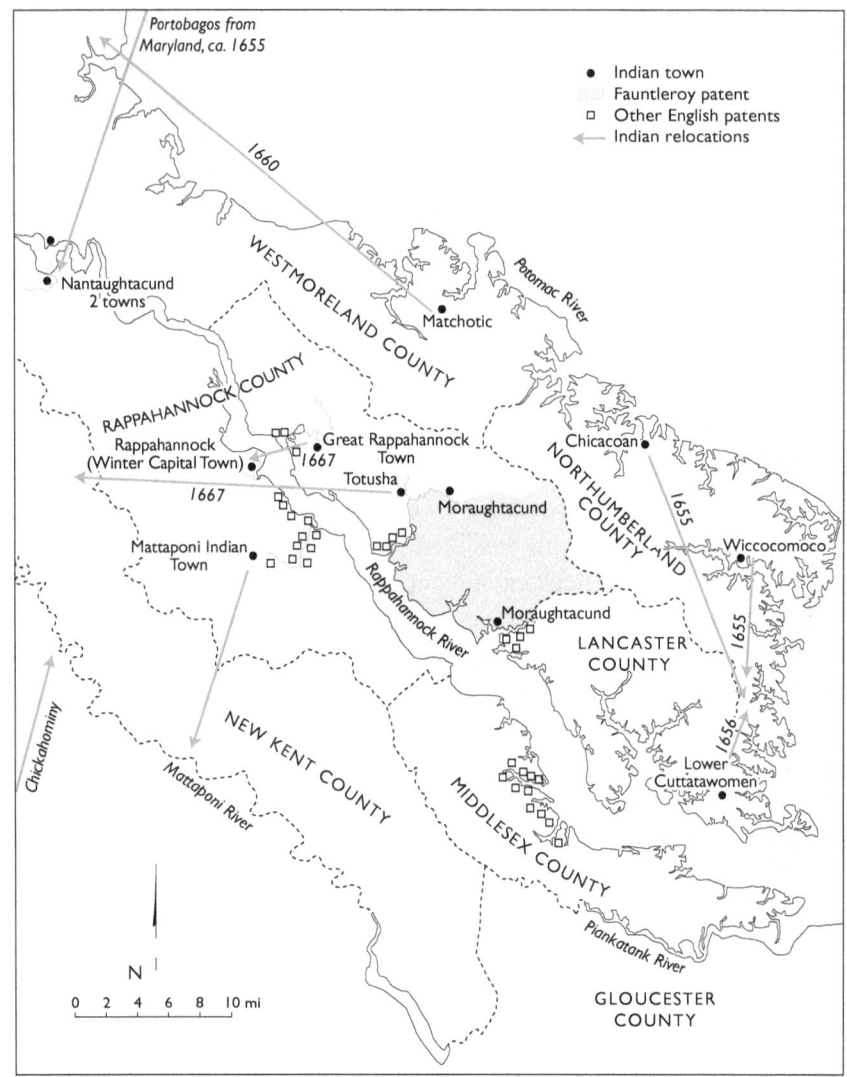

Map 7.2. Relocation of Native groups in Rappahannock River Valley, 1655–67. (Map by Bill Nelson)

ever, the census did not include a map of the new villages, so it is difficult to locate these communities precisely on the Middle Peninsula.

Though the people of Rappahannock and Totuskey lived centrally in large towns of between 150 and 200 people, seasonal mobility and periods of village dispersal remained important cultural and survival practices.[71] This traditional pattern of transience would have remained possible on the south side of the Rappahannock River because English settlement there grew at a slower rate than it did on the north side of the river. It was more difficult to grow tobacco on the south side, where lowland areas flooded easily and the sharp escarpment was close to the river. In the upland interior of the Middle Peninsula, numerous shallow waterways cut deep ravines across the clay loam soil, which made both cultivation and transportation quite difficult. In short, most of the land in Rappahannock County, south of the river, was considered unproductive by English standards.[72]

Under Virginia governor Sir William Berkeley's Indian policy, the English wanted their tributary Indian neighbors to reside in surveyed Indian towns, bounded by English planters, and controlled by provincial Indian regulations. The English believed that these "neighbor" Indian towns would increase the settlers' security. The town's residents provided a physical buffer between English settlers and "foreign" Indians, those nontributary Indians who might attack English settlements along the frontier. Mapped Indian towns could also be easily located and those that lived there held accountable for frontier violence.[73] However, not all Indians remained in their towns. In the late 1660s and early 1670s, the Rappahannock people, along with the Mattaponi and Chickahominy, moved their towns away from English encroachment and worn-out fields, often without new surveys or patents. At the same time that these "neighbor" Indians flouted English law, English settlers felt more threatened by the return of "foreign" Indians, like the Doeg and Susquehannock, to the Rappahannock frontier.[74] English settlers on the Rappahannock frontier did not trust these "foreign" Indians and could not, or did not, always distinguish "foreign" from "neighbor" Indians.

When Bacon's Rebellion erupted in the fall of 1675, some English settlers conflated "foreign" Indians and "neighbor" Indians and began to see all Indians as a unified threat.[75] The innocent Rappahannock understood the Virginians' confusion and "left theire townes wth in 4 days" after the Susquehannock attacked English settlements along the Rappahannock River. Contrary to what the English expected, the Rappahannock and other Algonquian communities in the Rappahannock, Mattaponi, and Pamunkey River watersheds did not scatter along the fall line frontier. They retreated to the swamps and thickets of the Middle Peninsula where few Englishmen dared go.[76] By the summer of 1676, perhaps as many as a thousand "neighbor" Indians from the Pamunkey, Mattaponi, Chickahominy, Rappahannock, Totuskey, Portobacco, and Nanzatico towns had hidden themselves in the Dragon Swamp, the most secluded and protected area on the Middle Peninsula.

Even after the rebellion ended and peace was restored between Indians and Englishmen, many of those Algonquians who lived on the Pamunkey Neck and the Rappahannock River frontier remained secluded in the Dragon Swamp. By May 1677, the Pamunkey and Nanzatico had come out of their seclusion to sign the Treaty of Middle Plantation; meanwhile, the Rappahannock, Chickahominy, and Mattaponi remained secluded. The Rappahannock did not sign the treaty, and they rejected the Pamunkey's claim of dominion over Tidewater Algonquian peoples.[77]

The Rappahannock demonstrated their independence from the Pamunkey chiefdom and from English governance, though not through active protest to the Pamunkey weroansqua, Cockacoeske, or to the Virginia governor, Herbert Jeffreys. Instead, the Rappahannock disregarded all authority and continued to do as they pleased. In where they chose to live and to whom they agreed to submit, the Rappahannock exhibited a passive, stubborn determination. Their tendency was to withdraw from threat or oversight so that they could make their own decisions without interference. The few extant records that shine light on tribal communities in the late 1670s and early 1680s suggest the separation from the Pamunkey. The Rappahannock and Totuskey communities, who had lived separately before the war, now settled together at the former Rappahannock town on the ridgeline of the Middle Peninsula.[78]

Meanwhile, Englishmen continued to patent land around the Rappahannock's town. In 1681, English settlers and speculators patented 3,030 acres near the town. In 1682, they patented another 8,166 acres.[79] It seems that speculators claimed much of this land, which often meant that the patents remained unseated. Still, the increased presence of English settlers and African slaves placed new restrictions on Rappahannock mobility. The Virginia Council wanted to clear the way for more English settlement on the Middle Peninsula, but first the council had to survey and bound the Rappahannock in a "tribal" town so that the rest of the Middle Peninsula could be opened for English settlement. On November 25, 1682, the council "directed that 4,000 acres of land should be laid out for the Rappa' Indians about the town where they dwelt."[80]

This was the first survey of a Rappahannock town since September 1653.[81] As noted previously, surveyed and bounded Indian towns had been one goal of Virginia's Indian policy. While some groups, like the Chickahominy, did have their land surveyed, it had been thirty years since the Rappahannock had a provincial confirmation of their land. During those three decades, the Rappahannock had moved several times throughout their homeland. This degree of mobility had afforded the Rappahannock considerable flexibility in how they fed and protected their families and how they accommodated English settlement. The Rappahannock moved by choice and by need both for sustenance and for security. In each instance, the Rappahannock's "tribal" town broke apart according to circumstances. When the Rappahannock lived dispersed, their kin networks, and thus their group, remained connected. The Rappahannock "tribal" and kin group was fluid and always in some state of removal or return. The bounding of the Rappahannock's town threatened the group's flexibility and jeopardized the people's mobility. In 1683, the same year that the Virginia Council surveyed the Rappahannock's town, eleven Englishmen patented 13,322 acres around the town.[82] By the end of that year, English encroachment and attacks by "foreign" Indians once again jeopardized the Rappahannock's residence.

In March 1683, the Virginia Council received a report that Seneca, Cayuga, Onondaga, and Oneida warriors from Iroquoia had threatened to come south that spring to raid the Piscataway and Nanticoke tribal towns in Maryland and the Pamunkey and Portobacco/Nanzatico towns in Virginia.[83] Throughout the summer and fall, Virginians waited for the alarm. Then, on November 21, 1683, Iroquoian warriors attacked Indian towns across Rappahannock and New Kent Counties. Heading down the Mattaponi River, Oneida war parties had "reduced and taken ye Mattopny Indian Town." The Mattaponi ran for the Chickahominy's fort downriver. No sooner had the Mattaponi arrived at Chickahominy than the Iroquois "beseiged ye Chickahominy fort" as well.[84]

The following week, the Virginia Council decided to act to protect "our neighboring Indians (whom by Articles of Peace wee are obliged to defend)," specifically the people who lived at the Rappahannock and Nanzatico towns. After some discussion, the councilmen decided "it absolutely necessary, for ye preservation of our Indians, that either Rappa: & Nanzattico Indians be united & incorporated (ye Nanzatticos being willing) or that ye Rappa: Indians remove to their new fort."[85] The Virginia Council intended to concentrate tributary peoples to resist Iroquoian assaults. The council condescended to allow the Rappahannock weroance and his councilors to decide whether to move to a new fort or join the intertribal Portobacco/Nanzatico town. Both options put the Rappahannock closer to the

Rappahannock River fall line, where the western Iroquois entered the Tidewater. Selecting a new fort might have placed the Rappahannock in a more vulnerable location, while a merger with Nanzatico would create a sizable Native community at the Portobacco/Nanzatico town. The Virginia Council reasoned that "tribal" consolidation strengthened the Native buffer designed to absorb Iroquoian raids on English seats along the Rappahannock River frontier.[86]

To carry out the Virginia Council's plan to place the Rappahannock between English settlers and Iroquoian raiders, Henry Awberry, the Rappahannock's closest English neighbor and the translator of messages from the council to the community, made the arrangements with the Rappahannock.[87] He presented the council's ultimatum and waited for the Rappahannock to decide whether to move to Nanzatico or to a new fort. In early January 1684, the Rappahannock decided to be "united and incorporated" with the Portobacco/Nanzatico Indian community.[88]

The Rappahannock's relocation was a major undertaking for colonial defense. The Rappahannock, who had run away from the frontier during Bacon's Rebellion, were now relocated to its edge. Portobacco/Nanzatico was the largest Indian town on the Rappahannock River and, hence, the obvious target for Iroquoian raiders. The Rappahannock had to realize that this removal placed them in harm's way. The Rappahannock's leaders may have felt they had little choice in the matter. They contented themselves to accommodate the council's plan and avoid conflict with the English.

These were hard times for the Rappahannock and all of the other Indians who lived at the Portobacco/Nanzatico town. They were reluctant to embrace English culture and colonial dictates about where they could live. Inevitably, Rappahannock families left the worn-out fields of Portobacco/Nanzatico to find fresh farmland elsewhere in their ancestral hunting grounds. They traveled south along the Portobacco-Chickahominy path, which crossed the Middle Peninsula from the Rappahannock River to the Mattaponi. It is not known just how soon after the Rappahannock's arrival at Portobacco that they began to leave. It was a slow exodus of perhaps two or three families per year. Contemporary Indian population estimates bear out this migration. In 1697, a tributary Indian list showed just two communities with 40 bowmen, or 200 people, living on the Rappahannock River.[89] Five years later, only 30 bowmen, or roughly 150 Indians, lived at Portobacco/Nanzatico.[90] There is a single piece of evidence to document these early Rappahannock departures from Portobacco. In 1699, the Virginia Council gave Gawin Corbin, collector of the Rappahannock River, permission "to allow some Rappahannock Indians to live upon his land."[91]

It is possible that in addition to settling on Corbin's land, some Rappahannock returned to the vicinity of their 1682 fort, although in June 1699, William Leigh, a King and Queen County burgess, had patented that tract of land.[92] The Rappahannock had been removed from this fort in January 1684, and their land had remained vacant for fifteen years afterward. There is no indication that Leigh seated or improved the 3,474-acre grant.[93] Nor is there evidence that Henry Awbrey, William Smith, or Stephen Benbridge seated their patents around the Rappahannock's former town.[94]

While the Rappahannock were at Portobacco/Nanzatico, Robert Beverley Jr. had moved onto his father's six-thousand-acre plantation, Beverley Park, in upper King and Queen County, not far from Gawin Corbin's property.[95] In 1705, when Beverley published his *History and Present State of Virginia*, he noted that colonial policy and Indian realities were at odds. As he described a persistent, though changed, Native culture, he concluded that the "Indians of Virginia are almost wasted," but then he listed twenty "Towns, or People as retain their Names, and live in Bodies." Collectively, these communities "can't raise five hundred fighting men. They live poorly, and much in fear of the Neighbouring [Iroquois] Indians." Most of the communities listed were "decreased" in some capacity. Smallpox had struck one town on the Eastern Shore. Others there had "joyn'd with a Nation of the Maryland Indians." On the Western Shore the story was the same. There were seven Appomattox families living in "Collonel Byrd's Pasture." There were "four or five families" here, "thirty Bow-men" there. A few communities had increased. The Chickahominy, with "about sixteen Bow-men, but lately increas'd," may have had Mattaponi families living with them and perhaps some Rappahannock too. Beverley reported that the Rappahannock in Essex County were "reduc'd to a few Families, and live scatter'd upon the English Seats." At Portobacco/Nanzatico, "about five Bow-men" and their families remained.[96] In the spring of 1706, the Essex County militia, led by Colonel Richard Covington, removed the rest of the residents from the Portobacco/Nanzatico town. Militiamen escorted the Indians south along the Portobacco path "through Essex to King and Queen" County.[97] The county line to which Covington escorted the Indians followed the ridgeline of the Middle Peninsula and, in places, the Portobacco path. It was also within a mile of the eastern boundary of Beverley Park, though Beverley never mentioned whether any Indians lived in the distant reaches of his plantation.

In his history, Beverley recognized the diversity of Algonquian settlement patterns. He understood that the Rappahannock, like other Indians in Virginia, "retain their Names, and live in Bodies" even though they dispersed their communities across their ancestral homelands. The Rappahannock community was "scatter'd upon the English Seats," yet the families maintained kin and place connections and, hence, a group identity. The Rappahannock's flexibility to adapt their settlement patterns and their willful commitment to stay on their land became clear in the last three decades of the seventeenth century. For the Rappahannock, fixed Indian towns were no longer the settlement norm. Though surveyed Indian towns remained a goal of Virginia Indian policy, the Rappahannock paid little attention to these dictates when they could be ignored. The Rappahannock never patented or requested land from the colony and never acknowledged local, provincial, or imperial government dominion over the land. They lived where they could and moved when they had to. Even after the Rappahannock's removal to the Portobacco/Nanzatico town, the county did not survey the town. Portobacco/Nanzatico was never surveyed. Even though the population there doubled when the Rappahannock arrived, there is no record that the Rappahannock requested more land or that the Virginia Council made additional apportionments. Even had land been provided, it is doubtful that the Rappahannock would have stayed. The evidence in the local record suggests that the Rappahannock community on the south side of the Rappahannock River was characterized more by mobility than by fixity.

The Rappahannock's efforts to maintain their mobile, dispersed settlements and English efforts to either consolidate Indian groups or destroy them were recurrent. English settlers and foreign Indians repeatedly threatened the Rappahannock and forced their relocation. Then, in 1705, the Virginia General Assembly passed a new consolidated slave law that restricted Indians' rights to resist English settlement and abuses.[98] After each removal, Rappahannock families returned to the place on the ridgeline of the Middle Peninsula that their ancestors had occupied since time immemorial. According to Rappahannock oral tradition, this area became known as "Stumptown."[99] But the Rappahannock's settlement patterns remained fluid. Families lived dispersed within or near their ancestral homelands. The Rappahannock did not subscribe to the English concept of fee simple land ownership, nor were they constrained by the bounds of "Indian towns." Thus, they were able to resist the fixity that Virginia governments tried to place upon them.

From the colony's perspective, once the Essex County militia expelled Rappahannock and Portobacco/Nanzatico families into King and Queen County, the Virginia colony no longer recognized the Rappahannock's existence as a "tribe." The Rappahannock were without status in Virginia. Without an identifiable town, local and provincial government no longer acknowledged or approved the Rappahannock's community or its leaders. Without recognized leaders and group status and without individual rights, the Rappahannock could no longer petition the county court or the colonial council. In short, there was no redress for the Rappahannock.

The demise of political recognition for the Rappahannock diminished the influence of their chiefs and councilors alike. The political survival of these leaders depended on their ability to mediate forces outside the community that included both colonial governments and foreign Indians. Instead, the Virginia Council intruded into intertribal diplomacy and confiscated the Rappahannock's belts of peak. Without access to either councilmen or council fires, rulers ceased to have a role outside their community.[100]

Unfortunately, this emphasis on the political structure and survival of the tribal chiefdom has overshadowed the deeper, structural foundations of Algonquian life in the Tidewater that began long before and continued long after the era of Algonquian political chiefdoms. For English contemporaries and their historians, the political chiefdom has been the most recognizable evidence of group structure. Observers then and now have focused on this component of Algonquian society and concluded that in the absence of clear, uninterrupted political leadership, the group could not survive.

Of less concern to the English were the Rappahannock's ties of community and kinship that kept them in their homeland and cultivated their sense of place. When the Rappahannock people operated within the Virginia tributary Indian framework, the Rappahannock "tribe" appears in the historical record. When Rappahannock people lived according to their own cultural dictates and, hence, outside the tributary Indian structure, the Rappahannock "tribe" is absent from the historical record. However, an absence of evidence is not evidence of absence, and the fact that seventeenth- and eighteenth-century colonists failed to record or acknowledge the persistence of the Rappahannock's communal and kin structures does not diminish in any way the significance of community and kin for the Rappahannock people. It is a testament to the power of place and family that the Rappahannock remained on their ancestral land with intact families.

Most groups were not so fortunate. Of the more than thirty tribal communities in Tidewater Virginia mapped by John Smith, few survived into the modern era. The rest were killed or expelled by the English or incorporated into nearby groups. In every instance, the survivors clung together in their Native neighborhoods. Some, like the Pamunkey and Mattaponi, managed to retain a provincially protected land base. Others, like the Rappahannock, either lived on the periphery of English plantations or squatted on unseated English land. Life remained a struggle for the Rappahannock people. When the group remained dispersed for decade after decade through the eighteenth century, it must have been difficult to stay in regular contact with kin who lived on the periphery of the community. Still, the close kin connections survived, and those who remained created new kin relations. We know this is true because in the early nineteenth century when Rappahannock families reappear in the historical record, the deep interconnectedness of their families across the ancestral Rappahannock homeland is immediately obvious. These communities of kin are what have always been important for the people who live, and have lived, where the water ebbs and flows.

Notes

1. James Carson, "Ethnogeography and the Native American Past," *Ethnohistory* 49 (Fall 2002): 769–88; Jean M. O'Brien, *Dispossession by Degrees: Indian Land and Identity in Natick, Massachusetts, 1650–1790* (Lincoln: University of Nebraska Press, 1997); Keith H. Basso, *Wisdom Sits in Places: Landscape And Language among the Western Apache* (Albuquerque: University of New Mexico Press, 1996).

2. Stephen R. Potter, *Commoners, Tribute, and Chiefs: The Development of Algonquian Culture in the Potomac Valley* (Charlottesville: University Press of Virginia, 1993), 100–110.

3. According to Potter, this Sub-Atlantic climate episode lasted from A.D. 210 until 645. Ibid., 100. For the ebb and flow of settlement sizes, see Martin Gallivan, *James River Chiefdoms: The Rise of Social Inequality in the Chesapeake* (Lincoln: University of Nebraska Press, 2003), 86.

4. Potter, *Commoners*, 100.

5. Ibid., 100–102, 144–45. According to Potter, "pollen samples taken from this period contain high ratios of plants that prefer drier conditions (oak, hickory, and pine) to those which grow best under wet conditions (river birch, sweet gum, and black gum)" (101).

6. Michael J. Klein and Douglas W. Sanford, "Analytical Scale and Archaeological Perspectives on the Contact Era in the Northern Neck of Virginia," in Julia King and Dennis Blanton, eds., *Contact in Context: New Archaeological, Anthropological, and Historical Perspectives on Natives and Europeans in the Mid-Atlantic*, (Gainesville: University of Florida Press, 2004), 47–73, especially 55–58.

7. Gallivan, *James River Chiefdoms*, 83–87.

8. Ibid., 3, 50–51, 156–58.

9. Klein and Sanford, "Analytical Scale," 58.

10. Richard J. Dent Jr., *Chesapeake Prehistory: Old Directions, New Traditions* (New York: Plenum, 1995), 250; Potter, *Commoners*, 85, 102, 144–45; E. Randolph Turner, "The Virginia Coastal Plain in the Late Woodland Period," in Theodore R. Reinhart and Mary Ellen Hodges, eds., *Middle and Late Woodland Research in Virginia*, 97–136 (Richmond: Council of Virginia Archaeologists, 1992), 107; William Ritchie and Robert Funk, *Aboriginal Settlement Patterns in the Northeast* (Albany: New York State Museum, 1973), 359–68.

11. William Strachey, *The Historie of Travell into Virginia Britannia* (1612), ed. Louis B. Wright and Virginia Freund, Works Issued by the Hakluyt Society, 2nd. ser., no. 103 (Cambridge: Hakluyt Society, 1953), 43–44, 67, 104; Potter, *Commoners*, 177.

12. John Smith, *A Map of Virginia*, in Philip Barbour, ed. *The Complete Works of Captain John Smith*, 3 vols. (Chapel Hill: University of North Carolina Press, 1986), 1:119–289; Klein and Sanford, "Analytical Scale," 58; James D. Rice, "Escape from Tsenacommacah: Chesapeake Algonquians and the Powhatan Menace," in Peter C. Mancall, ed., *The Atlantic World and Virginia: 1550–1624*, (Chapel Hill: University of North Carolina Press, 2007), 96–140; E. Randolph Turner, "A Reexamination of Powhatan Territorial Boundaries and Populations, ca. A.D. 1607," *Quarterly Bulletin of the Archeological Society of Virginia* 37 (1982): 56–57.

13. Smith, *Map of Virginia*, 1:146.

14. Ibid., 1:147. For coastal Virginia as a whole, the Algonquian population estimate is at least 14,000. For verification of these conservative population estimates, see Christian F. Feest, "Seventeenth Century Virginia Algonquian Population Estimates," *Quarterly Bulletin of the Archeological Society of Virginia* 28 (1973): 66–79; Turner, "A Reexamination," 45–64; Douglas Ubelaker, *Reconstruction of Demographic Profiles from Ossuary Skeletal Samples*, Smithsonian Contributions to Anthropology, no. 18 (Washington, DC: Smithsonian Institution Press, 1974), 69; and Potter, *Commoners*, 32–40.

15. Helen C. Rountree, *The Powhatan Indians of Virginia: Their Traditional Culture* (Norman: University of Oklahoma Press, 1989), 15.

16. John Smith, *A True Relation*, in Barbour, *Complete Works of John Smith*, 1:52–53. See also "Zuñiga Map [of Virginia, 1608]," in Philip L. Barbour, ed., *The Jamestown Voyages under the First Charter*, Works Issued by the Hakluyt Society, 2nd. ser., no. 136, (Cambridge: Hakluyt Society, 1969), 102–4, which traces the captivity of John Smith and locates the Rappahannock capital town of Tappahannock on the south side of the river. Smith's *Map of Virginia*, published in 1612, places the Rappahannock capital town on the north side of the river.

17. Notation of village types taken from the key to John Smith's map in *Map of Virginia*.

18. The patchwork of English settlements along the Atlantic seaboard meant intense contact between Englishmen and Algonquians in some places while elsewhere Native groups continued to live in relative isolation. See Peter A. Thomas, "Cultural Change on the Southern New England Frontier, 1630–1665," in William W. Fitzhugh, ed., *Cultures in Contact: The European Impact on Native Cultural Institutions in Eastern North America, A.D. 1000–1800*, (Washington, DC: Smithsonian Institution Press, 1985), 131–32, 133; James Horn, *Adapting to a New World: English Society in the Seventeenth-Century Chesapeake* (Chapel Hill: University of North Carolina Press, 1994), 163, 174; O'Brien, *Dispossession*

by Degrees, 6; Peter A. Thomas, "Contrastive Subsistence Strategies and Land Use as Factors for Understanding Indian-White Relations in New England," *Ethnohistory* 23 (1976): 14–15.

19. Smith, *A Map of Virginia,* 1:237; Smith, *Generall Historie,* in Barbour, *Complete Works of John Smith,* 2:184.

20. Wesley Craven, "Indian Policy in Early Virginia," *William and Mary Quarterly,* 3rd ser., 1 (January 1944): 65–82. For Sir Thomas Gates's 1609 instructions to reduce Indians to tributary status, see "Instructions Orders and Constitutions to Sir Thomas Gates Knight Governor of Virginia," May 1609, in Susan M. Kingsbury, ed., *The Records of the Virginia Company of London,* 4 vols. (Washington DC: Library of Congress, 1906–35), 3:12–24.

21. This position is referred to as the "metropolitan" view. For attitudes about the treatment of natives, see Michael Leroy Oberg, *Dominion and Civility: English Imperialism and Native America, 1585–1685* (Ithaca, NY: Cornell University Press, 1999).

22. "Instructions to the Governor and Council of State in Virginia," July 24, 1621, in Kingsbury, *Records of the Virginia Company,* 3:469.

23. Thorpe quoted in Helen C. Rountree, "The Powhatans and the English: A Case of Multiple Conflicting Agendas," in Rountree, ed., *Powhatan Foreign Relations, 1500–1722* (Charlottesville: University Press of Virginia, 1993), 188–89.

24. Feest, "Seventeenth Century Algonquian Population"; Rountree, *Powhatan Indians,* 15.

25. Helen Rountree, *Pocahontas's People: The Powhatan Indians of Virginia through Four Centuries* (Norman: University of Oklahoma Press, 1990), 78–79.

26. John Camden Hotten, *The Original List of Persons of Quality . . . and Others Who Went from Great Britain to the American Plantation, 1600–1700* (London, 1874), 201–65, quoted in Wesley Craven, *Red, White, and Black: The Seventeenth-Century Virginian* (Charlottesville: University Press of Virginia, 1971), 3.

27. J. Frederick Fausz, "The Powhatan Uprising of 1622: A Historical Study of Ethnocentrism and Cultural Conflict" (Ph.D. diss., College of William and Mary, 1977); Frederic W. Gleach, *Powhatan's World and Colonial Virginia: A Conflict of Cultures* (Lincoln: University of Nebraska Press, 1997), 148–58.

28. H. R. McIlwaine, ed., *Minutes of the Council and General Court of Colonial Virginia, 1622–1632, 1670–1676,* 2nd ed. (Richmond: Virginia State Library, 1979), 184–85; William W. Hening, ed. *The Statutes at Large, Being a Collection of all the Laws of Virginia from the First Session of the Legislature,* 13 vols. (Richmond: Samuel Pleasants Jr., 1809–23), 1:153, 177, 202; Craven, "Indian Policy," 73.

29. The Lower Peninsula lies between the York and James Rivers and is bounded on the west by the rivers' fall line and on the east by the Chesapeake Bay.

30. Hening, ed., *Statutes at Large,* 1:139–40, 199, 208; "Virginia in 1632–33–34," *Virginia Magazine of History and Biography* 8 (1900): 157–58; Philip Levy, "A New Look at an Old Wall: Indians, Englishmen, Landscape, and the 1634 Palisade at Middle Plantation," *Virginia Magazine of History and Biography* 112 (2004): 226–66.

31. For more detail on the 1644 uprising, see J. Frederick Fausz, "Fighting Fire with Firearms: The Anglo-Powhatan Arms Race in Early Virginia," *American Indian Culture and Research Journal* 3 (1979): 33–50; Fausz, "Opechancanough: Indian Resistance Leader," in David G. Sweet and Gary B. Nash, eds., *Struggles and Survival in Colonial America* (Berkeley: University of California Press, 1981), 21–37; Fausz, "Patterns of Anglo-Indian

Aggression and Accommodation along the Mid-Atlantic Coast, 1584–1634," in Fitzhugh, *Cultures in Contact,* 229, 238, fig. 3; Fausz, "'An Abundance of Blood Shed on Both Sides': England's First Indian War, 1609–1614," *Virginia Magazine of History and Biography* 98 (1990): 3–56; Gleach, *Powhatan's World,* chaps. 5 and 6; and Oberg, *Dominion and Civility,* 59–65, 74–78, 176–78.

32. Rountree (*Pocahontas's People,* especially chap. 5, "A Declining Minority," 89–127) asserts that 1646 marks the beginning of Powhatan's decline. For Virginia Indian policy through 1662, see Craven, "Indian Policy," 65–82. For the legal status of Virginia Indians, see W. Stitt Robinson, "The Legal Status of the Indians in Colonial Virginia," *Virginia Magazine of History and Biography* 61 (July 1953): 247–59; and Robinson, "Tributary Indians in Colonial Virginia," *Virginia Magazine of History and Biography* 67 (January 1959): 49–64.

33. Hening, *Statutes at Large,* 1:323–24.

34. Ibid., 1:326.

35. The Middle Peninsula lies between the Rappahannock and the York Rivers.

36. The best account of this demographic shift is Edmund Morgan, *American Slavery, American Freedom: The Ordeal of Colonial Virginia* (New York: Norton, 1975), 133–57. For greater use of quantitative data, see Richard S. Dunn, "Servants and Slaves: The Recruitment and Employment of Labor," in Jack P. Greene and J. R. Pole, eds., *Colonial British America: Essays in the New History of the Early Modern Era* (Baltimore: Johns Hopkins University Press, 1984) 157–94; and Craven, "Indian Policy," 76–77.

37. Hening, *Statutes at Large,* 1:323–29; Rountree, *Pocahontas's People,* 87.

38. Despite continued English encroachment north, there was relatively little movement west. This is due to at least two factors. First, the Indians who lived west of the fall line were notably more hostile. Their warring ability explains, in part, why Powhatan had not extended his empire beyond the fall line. Second, numerous rivers and creeks facilitated expansion northward, and English expansion around the bay essentially recreated earlier English settlement patterns.

39. McIlwaine, *Minutes of the Council,* 501–2, 563.

40. "Land Conveyance from Rappahannock Weroance Accopatough to Moore Fauntleroy, April 4, 1651," copied in Bishop William Meade, *Old Churches, Ministers, and Families of Virginia,* 2 vols. (Philadelphia: J. B. Lippincott, 1857; reprint, 1910), 2:478–79. Meade is the only source for this land transfer between the Rappahannock and Fauntleroy. Meade published *Old Churches* in 1857 and probably copied the document around that time. During the Civil War, fire destroyed the original document. The corroborating source is Fauntleroy's obituary, which details his public life, genealogy, and land purchase from the Rappahannock. This "purchase was confirmed by 'ACT I. The Grand Assemblie at James Cittie, Va., the 23rd March 1660–1 Sir Wm. Berkeley, his Majestie's Governor, 13th year of Charles II.'" See "Fauntleroy Monument at Naylor's Hole," *Virginia Magazine of History and Biography* 35 (April 1927): 204–5.

41. William Strachey translates tanks as "little." See Strachey, *Historie of Travell,* 203.

42. Nell Marion Nugent, *Cavaliers and Pioneers: Abstracts of Virginia's Land Patents,* 7 vols. (Richmond: Virginia State Library, 1934–79), 1:259; Meade, *Old Churches,* 2:478. Without further archaeological research, the size and function of these residences will remain uncertain.

43. Meade, *Old Churches,* 2:478–79.

44. Warren M. Billings, "Some Acts Not in Hening's Statutes: The Acts of Assembly,

April 1652, November 1652, and July 1653," *Virginia Magazine of History and Biography* 83 (January 1975): 68, 72–73. For the wave of Rappahannock River valley patents, see Nugent, *Cavaliers and Pioneers*, 1:132.

45. Billings, "Some Acts," 71.

46. "Indian Affairs in Lancaster County," *William and Mary Quarterly*, 1st ser., 4 (July 1895): 178–79.

47. Lancaster County, Deeds, Etc., no. 1 (1652–1657), 95.

48. Meade, *Old Churches*, 2:478.

49. For Algonquian tendencies to resist fixity, see O'Brien, *Dispossession by Degrees*, 17, 21, 69.

50. [Old] Rappahannock County, Records (1656–1664), 42; Nugent, *Cavaliers and Pioneers*, 2:366; Rountree, *Pocahontas's People*, 94. For other Indian communities on the northern neck, see Hening, *Statutes at Large*, 2:13–14, 34, 35, 39.

51. The following year (March 1658), the colony-funded wolves-for-cows plan was scrapped in favor of a county-funded wolves-for-tobacco plan. See Hening, *Statutes at Large*, 1:456.

52. Virginia DeJohn Anderson, "Animals into the Wilderness: The Development of Livestock Husbandry in the Seventeenth-Century Chesapeake," *William and Mary Quarterly*, 3rd ser., 59 (April 2002): 377–408; Anderson, *Creatures of Empire: How Domestic Animals Transformed Early America* (New York: Oxford University Press, 2006), 147–48; Craven, "Indian Policy," 78.

53. Hening, *Statutes at Large*, 1:396. This measure first appeared in the 1646 tributary treaty and had been reintroduced in March 1655. See ibid., 1:410.

54. Ibid., 1:396.

55. Ibid., 1:456–57.

56. Ibid., 2:14–15, 37.

57. Ibid., 2:152–53; William Montgomery Sweeney, "Gleanings from the Records of [Old] Rappahannock County and Essex County, Virginia," *William and Mary Quarterly*, 2nd ser. (July 1938), 18:298.

58. "Col. Gerard Fowkes and the Indians," *William and Mary Quarterly*, 1st ser., 8 (July 1899), 23–24; Hening, *Statutes at Large*, 2:149–52; H. R. McIlwaine, ed., *Journals of the House of Burgesses*, 13 vols. (Richmond: Colonial Press, E. Waddey, 1905–15), 2:14–15; Rountree, *Pocahontas's People*, 121.

59. Oberg, *Dominion and Civility*, 189–90. The Patawomeck weroance was forbidden to hold council "with any strange nation without knowledge of the aforesaid officers of the militia." Hening, *Statutes at Large*, 2:194.

60. Sweeney, "Gleanings," 298; Hening, *Statutes at Large*, 2:155.

61. The Northern Neck is the peninsula that lies between the Potomac and Rappahannock Rivers.

62. Hening, *Statutes at Large*, 2:193–94.

63. Ibid., 1:396.

64. Ibid., 2:194.

65. Ibid., 2:219.

66. Ibid.

67. Thomas Ludwell to Lord Bartley Berkeley of Stretton, November 7, 1667, British Public Records Office, Colonial Office, class 1, vol. 21, f. 282 (Virginia Colonial Records Project, Richmond, Library of Virginia, microfilm).

68. Strachey, *Historie of Travell*, 89; Samuel Purchas, *Purchas his Pilgrimes* (London: William Stansby, 1617), 954–55; Smith, *Map of Virginia*, 168–69.

69. William Montgomery Sweeney, "Some References to Indians in Colonial Virginia," *William and Mary Quarterly*, 2nd ser., 16 (October 1936): 599. There is no extant record for the sale of the town on Rappahannock Creek.

70. Hening, *Statutes at Large*, 2:274–75.

71. The best account of Native efforts to resist fixity, even within a tightly bounded space, is O'Brien, *Dispossession by Degrees*, 6, 17–18, 21, 69, 194, 211–12. See also Daniel Mandell, *Behind the Frontier: Indians in Eighteenth-Century Eastern Massachusetts* (Lincoln: University of Nebraska Press, 1996), 49, 60–62.

72. David Hardin, "'Alterations They Have Made at This Day': Environment, Agriculture, and Landscape Change in Essex County, Virginia, 1600–1782" (Ph.D. diss., University of Maryland, 1995), 59, 66–67, 117–18. Hardin notes that those upland "areas remained largely untouched by farming even through Virginia's agricultural revival prior to the Civil War" (118).

73. For the October 1665 law that made whole communities answerable "with their lives or liberties" for "any murthers [that] be committed upon the English," see Hening, *Statutes at Large*, 2:218–20. Though this law was repealed in October 1666 because it "seemes too full of severity and rigour" (ibid., 2:237), such harsh measures are indicative of Virginians' efforts to control tributary Indians.

74. Oberg notes that the Doeg and Susquehannock "were caught in a vise between the Maryland English, the Virginia frontier, and the Iroquois" (*Dominion and Civility*, 195). See also Stephen Saunders Webb, *1676: The End of American Independence* (New York: Knopf, 1984), 4; and Hening, *Statutes at Large*, 2:153.

75. H. R. McIlwaine, *Minutes of the Council*, 361, 515; Rountree, *Pocahontas's People*, 89, 93, 96, 112; Oberg, *Dominion and Civility*, 194, 200.

76. "[Sir William] Berkeley to [Thomas] Goodrich," May 15, 1676, Longleat House, Sir Henry Coventry Papers, Papers Relating to Virginia, Barbados, and other Colonies, vols. 77–78, Virginia Colonial Records Project (Richmond, Library of Virginia, microfilm), 77:85; "Causes of Discontent in Virginia, 1676 [Sittenbourne Parish Grievances]," *Virginia Magazine of History and Biography* 3 (July 1895): 36–37; Commissioners [Herbert Jeffreys, Sir John Berry, and Francis Moryson], "Review, Breviary and Conclusion," Virginia Colonial Records Project, British Public Records Office, C.O. 5/1371, 416; Wilcomb E. Washburn, "Bacon's Rebellion: 1676–1677" (Ph.D. diss., Harvard University, 1955), 298–99.

77. "Articles of Peace between the most Mighty Prince . . . Charles the II . . . And the severall Indian Kings and Queens &c . . . the 29th day of May: 1677," *Virginia Magazine of History and Biography* 14 (1906): 289–96.

78. The Mattaponi and Chickahominy peoples settled together along the upper Mattaponi River as well. See Rountree, *Pocahontas's People*, 114–15.

79. For the English land patents near the Rappahannock's town, see Nugent, *Cavaliers and Pioneers*, 2:195, 199, 211, 212, 219, 224, 225, 228, 229, 236, 244, 245, 251, 252, 253, 257.

80. Louis des Cognets, comp., *English Duplicates of Lost Virginia Records* (Princeton, NJ: privately printed, 1958), 63. For the metes and bounds of this town, see Virginia Land Office Patents and Grants, Patent Book no. 9 (1697–1706) (Richmond, Library of Virginia), 214.

81. The September 1660 survey was a verbatim restatement of the September 1653 sur-

vey. For that survey, see John Philips, "Indian Affairs in Lancaster County," *William and Mary Quarterly*, 1st ser., 4 (January 1896): 177–78.

82. Nugent, *Cavaliers and Pioneers*, 2:254, 255, 256, 259, 262, 267, 267.

83. Noel Sainsbury, ed., *Calendar of State Papers, Colonial Series*, 60 vols. (London: Longman, Green, and Roberts, 1860–1901), 11:206 (hereafter cited as *CSPC*).

84. H. R. McIlwaine, ed., *Executive Journals of the Council of Colonial Virginia*, 5 vols. (Richmond: Virginia State Library, 1925), 1:53. Rountree says that the Mattaponi merged with the Chickahominy and are not mentioned in the records again until the early nineteenth century (*Pocahontas's People*, 114).

85. McIlwaine, *Executive Journals*, 1:54.

86. Rountree, *Pocahontas's People*, 104.

87. For Henry Awberry's 5,100-acre patent on the ridgeline near the Rappahannock's town, see Nugent, *Cavaliers and Pioneers*, 2:165–66.

88. McIlwaine, *Executive Journals*, 1:54; Sweeney, "References," 594–96.

89. Sainsbury, *CSPC*, 15:546.

90. "List of.... Tributary Indians," Virginia Colonial Records Project, British Public Records Office, C.O. 5/1312, pt. 2, ff. 221–22, printed in *Virginia Magazine of History and Biography* 1 (1893): 363.

91. Sainsbury, *CSPC*, 17:576.

92. For the metes and bounds of Leigh's patent, see Land Office Patents, no. 9, 1697–1706, 2 vols. (Richmond, Library of Virginia), 1:214, microfilm, reel 9.

93. Des Cognets, *English Duplicates of Lost Virginia Records*, 62–63.

94. Nugent, *Cavaliers and Pioneers*, 2:165, 251, 279, 302, 320.

95. For the original patent by Robert Beverley Sr., dated July 12, 1669, see Nugent, *Cavaliers and Pioneers*, 2:56.

96. Robert Beverley, *History and Present State of Virginia*, ed. Lewis B. Wright (Chapel Hill: University of North Carolina Press, 1947), 232–33.

97. Essex County, Orders, no. 3 (1703–1708), 245. Thomas Warner, *History of Old Rappahannock County Virginia 1656–1692* (Tappahannock, VA: privately printed, 1965), 39.

98. Hening, *Statutes at Large*, 3:251, 289, 449–50, 453–54, 459.

99. Bud Nelson, personal communication to author, July 9, 1999.

100. The situation in New England developed differently but ended much like the Rappahannock's story. In Massachusetts, the colony concentrated Indians into "Praying Towns" and, after 1719, created a proprietary system that apportioned the towns' lands to individual Indians. By the end of the eighteenth century, Englishmen owned most of the land in these "Praying Towns." As Jean O'Brien notes, "Indian communities had become minority clusters dotted throughout southeastern New England" (*Dispossession by Degrees*, 212). The significant difference is that the Rappahannock did not remain in their bounded towns for long, and they did not pass through a phase of "land ownership" before becoming landless.

# Beyond the "Origins Debate"

Rethinking the Rise of Virginia Slavery

JOHN C. COOMBS

In a series of lectures delivered during the fall of 1970, Wesley Frank Craven offered an insightful critique of the already extensive historiography then available on the development of slavery in seventeenth-century Virginia. "In my own review of the literature, old and new," the great scholar of the colonial South observed, "I am struck by the thought that American historians have been so largely concerned with the question of the Negro's status, with the origins of the institutions of slavery, as to be indifferent to other questions they might have investigated."[1]

Although Craven was addressing the state of inquiry as it existed at the time, the analytical single-mindedness he alluded to in his comments would continue to shape scholarly discussion of the subject for decades to come. The scope of interest in this "origins debate," as historian Alden Vaughan would later call it, widened somewhat in the 1970s, expanding beyond a narrow concern with when and why Virginians first began enslaving blacks (and whether racism prompted or followed their decision) to include a distinct, though related, dialogue about when and why the colony's planters ultimately turned to slavery as their predominant form of bound labor.[2] But by seeking to identify a critical turning point of change and the reasons behind it, contributors to this offshoot thread of the origins debate essentially adopted the same framing of the historical problem as their predecessors had in the 1950s and 1960s. Consequently, much as Craven had suggested of that earlier work, the heavy emphasis given to issues of timing and causality marginalized numerous other questions relevant to the examination of slavery's establishment in Virginia—such as the conduct of the colony's seventeenth-century slave trade, patterns of slave ownership, and the shifting demography of the enslaved population to name just a few—which were only vaguely addressed in the published literature.[3]

The last thirty years have brought little change. With the notable exceptions of two oft-cited studies of the Eastern Shore (one by J. Douglas Deal and the other by Timothy Breen and Stephen Innes), Darrett and Anita Rutman's pioneering demographic work on Middlesex County's black inhabitants, and information about early slave trading to the colony presented in the opening chapter of a recent book by Linda Heywood and John Thornton, the various topics listed above have received remarkably limited attention.[4] And yet despite the paucity of new research, or perhaps because of it, the major findings of the origins debate continue to exert a powerful sway over how historians think and write about the initial growth of slavery in Virginia. This persistent influence is clearly evident in the arguments and endnotes of important books published over the last decade or so by Kathleen Brown, Ira Berlin, and Anthony Parent, which when read together give the impression that virtually all of the fundamental issues associated with this crucial transformation "have been laid to rest," and that only the application of heretofore underutilized perspectives such as gender or class is needed to flesh out our collective knowledge of its course and consequences. Indeed, constant repetition of the prevailing consensus by such accomplished historians has made it seem as though the available evidence has been more or less exhausted and that by extension new research is unlikely to change the basic story of how the colony's conversion from servant to slave labor unfolded.[5]

This essay contends not only that there is great deal more to learn about the rise of Virginia slavery but that much of what we think we know about it is the product of insufficient attention to socioeconomic and geographic differences, unwarranted extrapolation from limited data, or just plain unsupported assumption and assertion. New information derived from a comprehensive study of Virginia probate records, along with additional material—some of it well known, some not—compiled during a systematic examination of extant county court books and other sources, reveals a quite different story than what has heretofore been presented in the published literature and demonstrates that even some of the most fundamental and widely accepted notions about slavery's early development should either be revised significantly or abandoned altogether.

The most important of those notions had their genesis in the scholarship of the origins debate. As Alden Vaughan noted twenty years ago, despite some lingering disputes, by the late 1980s historians studying Virginia's conversion from servants to slaves had reached a broad consensus on several core issues. All of them maintained that Virginia's transition to slave labor occurred slowly and gradually and that slavery was of little economic or demographic importance in the colony until the number and size of arriving slave shipments rose sharply around 1680. They also generally accepted that the legal standing of slavery remained unsettled until the 1660s and that well into the 1670s permanent, hereditary enslavement was a relatively permeable condition, with a significant percentage of those sold into lifetime bondage gaining their freedom through manumission, self-purchase, or challenging their status in court. Finally, they widely concurred that in the last quarter of the seventeenth century the trade in slaves to Virginia shifted from small, coastwise shipments from other colonies—particularly in the Caribbean—to larger direct deliveries from Africa and that this change resulted in the arrival of slaves whose cultural differences with the majority white population were more pronounced than those of earlier black immigrants.[6]

The enduring influence of these "points of agreement," as Vaughan called them, would be difficult to overstate. Incorporated into virtually every study of Virginia's shift from servant to slave labor for a generation, they have acquired the status of immutable facts around which any explanation of it must necessarily be constructed. Yet, regardless of their historiographical longevity, these tenets of consensus are useful only if they further understanding of the existing documentary record, and by that measure they have significant flaws. To state this is not to belittle the contributions of the origins debate, which undeniably generated scholarship of the highest quality—including several seminal works in the field of early American slavery—that continues to be relevant and informative. Indeed, this essay employs some of the very same analytical techniques pioneered during these years. As with all history, however, the consensus that emerged from the origins debate reflected the limits of research at the time, and those limitations played a critical role in shaping the conclusions its participants drew about key aspects of slavery's development. The discussion that follows is intended to elucidate this connection between evidence and argument in their work, with the ultimate goal of building the case for a more systematic approach in future inquiry.

One of the most important blind spots in the books and articles Vaughan examined (and in subsequent work) is the absence of detailed examination of the socioeconomic distribution of slaves and how it changed over time. Edmund Morgan's assertion that it was the Byrds, Carters, Wormeleys, and "a host of others" like them "who brought slavery to Virginia," for example, clearly suggested that wealthy elites played a leading role in transforming the colony's labor force after 1660. But he provided no specifics about when such men first began purchasing slaves, the numbers they eventually obtained, or how large a percentage of the total enslaved population they controlled. Nor did he offer much comment about how their labor investments compared with those of earlier members of the gentry or exactly when and how slave ownership spread to planters of more limited means.[7] While a few accounts had the same limited precision as Morgan's—Robert McColley observed that almost all slaves mentioned in early records belonged to "the wealthiest, the most powerful, and the most resourceful people in the colony"—the majority were far more vague, attributing the growing use of enslaved workers to the actions and attitudes of "Virginians," "planters," or a "planter class."[8]

Discussion of geographic differences in slavery's growth was also circumscribed. Some historians noted, of course, that the enslaved population was unevenly spread across the colony. Morgan's analysis of extant tax lists led him to contend that the proportion of slaves "must have been larger" in wealthy areas along the York River than in less prosperous counties such as Surry, where by 1700 they still only comprised about half of all tithable-age laborers. Russell Menard's "impression" from working with naval office returns and probate inventories was that the distribution of the slave population followed the "geography of tobacco cultivation," with the affluent sweet-scented tobacco growing zone between the James and Rappahannock Rivers having the highest density of slaves, marginal staple-producing counties of the Southside and Eastern Shore the lowest, and those areas that grew better-quality grades of oronoco leaf somewhere in between. But both Morgan and Menard were describing how things stood at the turn of the eighteenth century, when slavery had become much more established. Although more specific than their contemporaries, most of whom limited their analyses to total population figures, neither considered whether similar subregional differences had been evident during the period of transition, with respect not only to how slaves were spatially dispersed but also to the timing, pace, and character of the conversion itself.[9]

How contributors to the origins debate treated these two issues, when they dealt with them at all, was largely a reflection of the sources they utilized. Extensive research in family papers, official correspondence, and the surviving institutional records of the colonial government, while sufficient for discerning the broad outlines of the shift from servant to slave labor, simply did not produce the kind of evidence that lent itself to parsing along socioeconomic and geographic lines. Achieving a more finely grained understanding of the conversion required compiling and collating the mass of information scattered throughout the surviving deed, order, and will books of Virginia's county courts. Menard, for one, was well aware of the need for such work, remarking that "a systematic study" of probate materials "should permit a more precise description of regional variations in the distribution of slaves." Yet that was a task only a few historians such as Menard himself and the Rutmans accomplished for Virginia, and even they focused their efforts on individual counties rather than examining multiple localities in a comparative framework.[10] In most published accounts, references to local records were limited to anecdotal examples employed chiefly for illustrative purposes and were often culled not from the original manuscripts but from excerpts published (often in support of genealogical inquiries) in older issues of the *Virginia Magazine* and *William and Mary Quarterly* or the transcriptions and secondary works of older scholars like Philip Alexander Bruce and Susie M. Ames.[11]

It was no mere happenstance that Menard noted the untapped potential of Virginia's county records. Along with other members of the Chesapeake School, he was already combining deep research in similar Maryland sources with innovative analytical techniques to garner new insight into myriad aspects of the region's plantation society, including slavery.[12] However, the significant achievements of the Chesapeake School reflected the coordinated efforts of several historians and the St. Mary's City Commission, which provided them with essential institutional support. The comparative aspects of their work simply would not have been possible without this cooperation, since in what was (at least by today's standards) the technological dark ages of the 1970s and 1980s, gathering data for multiple counties and processing it into usable form would have been a prohibitively expensive and time-consuming undertaking for any one scholar. The Rutmans' research notes on the single county of Middlesex, for example, fill fifty-two large binders, each one packed with alphabetically arranged sheets of information on individual settlers that was initially recorded by hand and then laboriously transferred onto punch cards for computer-assisted analysis. When one considers the practical challenges that confronted contemporary practitioners of the "new social history" and the lack of a collaborative venture akin to what existed north of the Potomac, it is not surprising that much of the material in Virginia's local records remained inaccessible and unused.[13]

Without the systematic collection of the evidence contained in those records, however, the origins debate scholars could not devise a nuanced chronology of how the transformation of Virginia's labor force unfolded. Instead, what emerged from their work was a generalized "date" for the transition to slavery that strongly implied it was relatively homogenous and temporally compressed. In a string of books and articles published during the 1970s that cited differing combinations of official population estimates, census and tithable list figures, and data drawn from Maryland and York County, Virginia probate inventories, Timothy Breen, Edmund Morgan, Russell Menard, Gloria Main, David Galenson, and Richard Bean and Robert Thomas all pointed to the last quarter of the seventeenth century as when the shift began in earnest, a period that coincided with what other sources suggested was the advent of more consistent direct slave shipments from Africa. Breen and Morgan both focused exclusively on the Old Dominion and were notably less precise on the question of timing. Yet even the quantitatively rigorous analyses of probate materials put forward by the other, regionally oriented historians suffered from two important deficiencies. First, as Menard noted, the data they used came mostly from Maryland, the younger and less wealthy of the two Chesapeake colonies, since at the time only scattered evidence was available for Virginia counties other than York. Second, their dating method heavily emphasized aggregate trends by equating "conversion" with the point at which the total number of slaves surpassed the total number of servants among all inventoried bound workers, thus eliding variations in timing among different localities and socioeconomic groups, as well as the more subtle expansion of slavery earlier in the century.[14] Galenson touched on this last point in a 1991 essay, remarking that concentration on the changing makeup of the region's workforce after 1680 had led to the "relative neglect" of the more "gradual growth of slavery" in preceding decades. Still, even though the evidence he presented suggested that slaves already comprised over a third of York County's bondsmen by the 1670s, Galenson did not question the accepted dating of the transition and instead devoted much of the remainder of his essay to reconciling the "significant problem" of early investment in slave labor with what by then had become the established periodization.[15]

By dating the transition to slavery in the last quarter of the seventeenth century, historians presented themselves with the problem of explaining why Virginians turned so rapidly to black labor after six decades had passed since they first landed on tobacco as a successful staple crop. Two schools of thought on this apparent conundrum developed during the 1970s. The first, led by Morgan, Breen, and Theodore Allen, saw the conversion as stemming from social instability. By the latter decades of the century, they asserted, destitute and discontented ex-servants and smallholders kept the colony "continually on the brink of rebellion." After Nathaniel Bacon led this "giddy multitude" in armed resistance against the government in 1676, however, "Virginians" finally began to eliminate the threat they posed "by buying slaves instead of servants," thereby curtailing growth in that segment of the colony's population, poor freemen, who had "flocked to Bacon's standard."[16]

Within only a few years, Menard, along with Gloria Main and David Galenson, forwarded an alternative explanation that contended changes in labor markets, not social and political strife, was the principal reason for the shift. Noting that the number of servants emigrating to the Chesapeake began to wane in the 1660s and dropped precipitously around 1680 as potential settlers found more attractive opportunities at home or in other colonies, they argued that the region's planters reluctantly turned to African slave shipments—and other "less desirable" workers such as convicts, Irishmen, and Indians—only when the onset of a regional labor shortage forced them to seek alternative sources of bound workers. In other words, the declining availability of white bondsmen led to the rise of slavery rather than the other way around, or as Menard succinctly put it, "Chesapeake planters did not abandon indentured servitude; it abandoned them."[17]

As Vaughan pointed out, although these two event-driven conceptualizations of the conversion seem contradictory, they were not wholly incompatible, and subsequent work tended to blend them together.[18] This trend has continued in more recent scholarship. In his description of a "Tobacco Revolution" that transformed the Chesapeake's labor force and society, for example, Ira Berlin's allusion to "the thunder of canons and the rattle of sabers" that accompanied Bacon's Rebellion evoked the interpretations of Morgan, Breen, and Allen, while his noting that a decline in the supply of European servants led the region's "great planters" to look increasingly to Africa for workers offered a nod to the labor market school. Anthony Parent's chapter on "the labor switch" in his 2003 monograph *Foul*

Means closely followed the interpretations put forward by the proponents of a market-driven explanation. Yet in his introduction he insisted that the emergence of racial slavery in Virginia was not the product of an "unthinking" response to "market and labor forces" but rather a deliberate choice made by a "powerful planter class, acting in their short-term interest," a statement that Allen in particular would have agreed with wholeheartedly.[19]

The explanations postulated by both schools, however, prompt the same question: what "Virginians" or "planters" are we talking about? The colony's householders, almost all of whom were planters in the sense that they engaged in raising tobacco or other crops for sale, possessed widely varying amounts of wealth, particularly in the essential forms of land and labor, and the use of such vague descriptors not only glosses over these important differences but also obscures crucial aspects in the chronology of slavery's development. While distinguishing between the large mass of ordinary settlers and the more affluent inhabitants who occupied positions of leadership solves much of this problem, it is also misleading to portray elites as a single, undifferentiated "class" of "great planters." Like the larger society of which they were a part, levels of wealth among the gentry were far from uniform. Some county elites, those who held the more important local offices of justice of the peace and sheriff and were elected to serve in the House of Burgesses, had only slightly larger estates than their more prosperous non-elite neighbors, while others were much richer and possessed considerably more extensive holdings in land and laborers. As the century progressed, commercial diversification led to geographic differences among the gentry as well, further complicating any collective portrait. Yet before the early eighteenth century, only a small percentage of this already small group achieved the degree of affluence and influence that the term "great planter" suggests. During the 1680s and 1690s, no more than forty or so families—from whom the governor selected his nominees to the Council of State—could boast a member of this exclusive cohort at any given time.[20]

However, in the first half of the century Virginia lacked any men of such signal significance. The colony, of course, did have some settlers whose relative wealth and access to political office set them apart. But economic differences between the early gentry and the rest of society were far less notable than they would later become. Although the largest operators in this period, such as Major George Colclough of Northumberland County, had upwards of forty laborers, the typical county officeholder only controlled around a half dozen. The holdings of some local elites were even more mod-

TABLE 4
Aggregate rates of bound labor ownership among non-elite Virginia decedents, 1640–1700

	No. non-elite planters[a]	% with bound labor[b]
1631–50	101	25.7
1651–60	139	30.9
1661–70	181	31.5
1671–80	350	24.9
1681–90	417	23.5
1691–1700	600	21.8

Source: Data from Virginia Probate Files.
[a]Number of non-elite planters for whom inventories survive.
[b]Percentages include information drawn from wills as well as inventories.

est. Philip Taylor and William Andrews of Northampton County, for example, each had just three workers; Lieutenant Colonel Cornelius Lloyd of Lower Norfolk had five. As unimpressive as these figures are, the mere ownership of labor separated the gentry from most ordinary planters. (See table 4.) Among non-office-holding decedents of the 1640s and 1650s who had accumulated enough property to have an inventory taken of their estate, 70 percent possessed no bound workers whatsoever and another 10 percent had just one.[21]

While on the whole even the gentry's labor forces remained small throughout these decades, slave ownership was already widespread among their ranks. Between 1630 and 1660, no fewer than one hundred officeholders claimed land for the importation of blacks in patents awarded by the provincial government or certificates issued in the county courts, and nearly half of the surviving officeholder inventories taken during these years included at least one slave. County elites not surprisingly had only a few. The two "Negroes" belonging to Lower Norfolk justice Captain John Sibsey in 1652 was typical. Among the more affluent planters who had achieved membership on the council, however, the level of commitment was considerably greater; most, if not all, had built up holdings of at least ten slaves, and some owned more than twice that number. If the anonymous visitor who called at the Warwick County plantation of Samuel Mathews in the late 1640s was not exaggerating, the wealthy and well-connected councilor was perhaps the largest slave owner in the colony, with "forty Negroe servants."[22]

Investments in slave labor, already evident across a broad spectrum of the Virginia gentry at midcentury, steadily expanded in the 1660s and early 1670s. In the forty-three surviving inventories of county-level officeholders that were recorded between 1661 and 1675, well over half (58 percent) owned slaves, and slaves either equaled or outnumbered servants in the labor forces of more than a third (39 percent). Moreover, subregional differences in the size and makeup of plantation workforces also became increasingly evident around this time. In the best tobacco-growing areas along the James, York, and Rappahannock Rivers, some local gentry, such as Lancaster commissioner David Fox, assembled surprisingly large numbers of slaves. Fox's purchases seem to have begun sometime in the mid-1650s, when he received a land certificate from the county court for importing six blacks. He would claim fifteen more such "headrights" in 1663 and an additional one in 1668. At the time of his death the following year, twenty-nine of his thirty-two bondsmen were slaves. By comparison, the thirteen blacks George Colclough owned when he died in 1662 was the largest number recorded for a local elite in the extant records of the Potomac River counties during the 1660s, while Lower Norfolk justice John Okeham's eight slaves exceeded the known holdings of all other Southside county-level gentry.[23]

However, it was deepening investment by great planters, the first meriting that description in the colony, that transformed the wealthier areas of the mainland Tidewater into an emergent "black belt." Though Fox was clearly a wealthy man, he was not even the largest slave owner in his county. His neighbors Sir Henry Chicheley and Colonel John Carter operated on an even larger scale, employing workforces twice as large. In 1665, Chicheley and Carter together controlled more taxable laborers than all of Northampton County's elites combined and probably double the number of slaves as well. When he died in 1669, the same year as Fox, Carter owned a total of seventy-seven laborers, forty-three of them enslaved blacks and mulattoes.[24]

Although the number of slaves in Virginia was undeniably small in these decades, the 2,000 that Governor Sir William Berkeley estimated were living in the colony by 1671—and who by his account made up a quarter of all bound laborers—were highly concentrated in the hands of the roughly 250 planters who occupied the coveted positions of county commissioner, burgess, and councilor. In every source that can be used to measure the social distribution of labor through the mid-1670s—land patent and certificate records, inventories, and tax lists—officeholders controlled between two-thirds and three-quarters of all enslaved bondsmen. Blacks already made

TABLE 5
Slave ownership trends in Virginia officeholder inventories

	No. officeholder inventories with labor	% officeholders with slaves[a]	% officeholders' bound laborers enslaved
1651–60	17	47.1	32.0
1661–70	26	53.8	48.8
1671–80	38	89.5	54.3
1681–90	23	69.6	76.2
1691–1700	45	91.1	90.9

Source: Data from Virginia Probate Files.

[a]Percentages include cases in which decedents' inventories did not list slaves but one or more were mentioned in their wills.

up a significant majority of the bound laborers owned by great planters and some wealthier county elites, while in the second half of the 1670s slaves would surpass servants in the workforces of almost all members of the gentry.[25] These were not men on the verge of turning to slavery; they already had. And neither Bacon's Rebellion nor the steep decline in the availability of white servants that occurred in the years after the revolt had anything to do with it.[26]

Even in the aftermath of these two supposedly transformative events, ownership of enslaved labor remained almost exclusively the prerogative of elites, who continued to own a majority of slaves in the colony despite the arrival in the Chesapeake of nearly ten thousand slaves in direct deliveries from Africa over the last third of the century.[27] Between 1670 and 1700, officeholders claimed 70 percent of all black headrights awarded in land certificates and controlled 60 percent of slaves listed in inventories. Over three-quarters of inventoried elite decedents owned slaves in these decades, with a substantial minority of local officeholders accumulating over ten enslaved workers and some more than thirty. (See table 5.) Improving access to slaves also helped fuel the development of the colony's first truly large enslaved labor forces. The 107 blacks and mulattoes working the fields of Colonel John Carter II's Lancaster plantation when he died in 1690, for example, was more than twice the number his father had owned twenty years before. The holdings of Councilor Ralph Wormeley II were perhaps even more extensive, since the eighty-seven slaves named in a 1701 appraisal of his estate represented only the workforce of his home plantation in Middlesex and did not include bondsmen located on quarters in other counties.[28]

Most Virginians, by contrast, derived little benefit from the rising frequency of transatlantic shipments. While the gentry's bound workforces were made up almost entirely of slaves by the 1690s, somewhere between 25 and 40 percent of ordinary planters' laborers were still white servants at the turn of the eighteenth century. (See table 6.) The relative rarity of slaveholding among planters of lesser means further illustrates the socioeconomic disparities in the conversion. Just 12 percent of non-elite inventories recorded between 1675 and 1700 list slaves—only a marginal increase from 6 percent in the 1660s—and while the frequency of slave ownership among those possessing some form of bound labor grew from 20 percent to 70 percent during the same period, the number of small and middling decedents with bound workers of any kind shrank by a third. Unable to acquire slaves in numbers sufficient to offset the growing scarcity of white bondsmen that Menard and Galenson described, ordinary Virginians suffered from a labor shortage that continued to persist well into the second decade of the eighteenth century.[29]

However, these aggregate figures mask a more complex subregional story. The labor crisis that began in the Chesapeake around 1660 hit Virginia with full force in the last quarter of the seventeenth century and was pervasive despite increasing slave deliveries, both directly from Africa and via intercolonial trade. But the crisis did not affect every part of Virginia with equal severity, and ordinary planters throughout the colony did not cope with the problem in the same way. When surviving inventories are divided into the three economic subregions referenced by Menard and described more thoroughly by Lorena Walsh, settlers in the oronoco-growing zone along the Potomac River had the most obviously aberrant response. (See map 8.1.) Although the available evidence is admittedly sparse—less than 150 estate accounts dating to the last third of the seventeenth century survive for Westmoreland and Stafford Counties and only a handful for Northumberland—even when combined with a much larger number of inventories from Maryland counties located directly across the river, the data clearly suggest that planters in this area were well behind their counterparts elsewhere in converting to slavery and continued to rely heavily on white servants through the end of the century. This delay was probably owing to the subregion's relatively weak connections with larger London-based tobacco importers who could extend the credit necessary to arrange for contract slave shipments by the Royal African Company, the principal means through

TABLE 6
Labor ownership in the inventories of non-elite Virginia planters, 1651–1700

SUBREGION	1651–70	1671–80	1681–90	1691–1700
Sweet-scented				
Total inventories	118	171	239	328
% all inventories with bound labor	39.8	31	27.2	23.5
% all inventories with slaves	10.2	7.6	12.1	16.5
% labor owners with slaves	25.5	24.4	44.6	70.1
% labor owners with servants	91.5	90.6	72.3	51.9
% bound labor force enslaved	11.1	32.7	52.4	73.8
Oronoco				
Total inventories	80 (193)	38 (301)	27 (279)	61 (402)
% all inventories with bound labor	25.0 (36.3)	26.3 (37.5)	14.8 (31.2)	18.0 (22.1)
% all inventories with slaves	1.3 (5.2)	2.6 (9.0)	0.0 (8.6)	4.9 (8.5)
% labor owners with slaves	5.0 (12.9)	10.0 (23.9)	0.0 (27.6)	27.3 (38.2)
% labor owners with servants	100.0 (98.6)	90.0 (94.7)	100.0 (96.6)	81.8 (83.1)
% bound labor force enslaved	9.4 (14.8)	10.0 (16.3)	0.0 (22.0)	37.9 (41.8)
Provisioning				
Total inventories	122	141	151	211
% all inventories with bound labor	27.0	17.0	19.2	20.4
% all inventories with slaves	4.9	3.5	11.3	16.1
% labor owners with slaves	18.2	20.8	58.6	79.1
% labor owners with servants	87.9	87.5	62.1	41.9
% bound labor force enslaved	16.9	23.3	74.7	78.3
All subregions				
Total inventories	320 (433)	350 (613)	417 (669)	600 (941)
% all inventories with bound labor	31.3 (34.6)	24.9 (31.0)	23.5 (27.1)	21.8 (22.2)
% all inventories with slaves	5.9 (6.5)	5.4 (7.3)	11.0 (10.5)	15.2 (13.0)
% labor owners with slaves	19.0 (8.7)	21.8 (23.7)	46.9 (38.7)	69.5 (58.4)
% labor owners with servants	92.0 (94.0)	89.7 (92.6)	70.4 (82.3)	51.1 (63.2)
% bound labor force enslaved	12.7 (13.8)	28.8 (22.2)	58.0 (41.9)	72.6 (61.2)

Source: Data from Virginia Probate Files.

Note: Values in parentheses are totals or percentages including probate data from the Maryland Potomac River counties of St. Mary's, Charles, and Prince George provided by the Historic St. Mary's City Commission. Labor ownership figures include information drawn from wills as well as inventories.

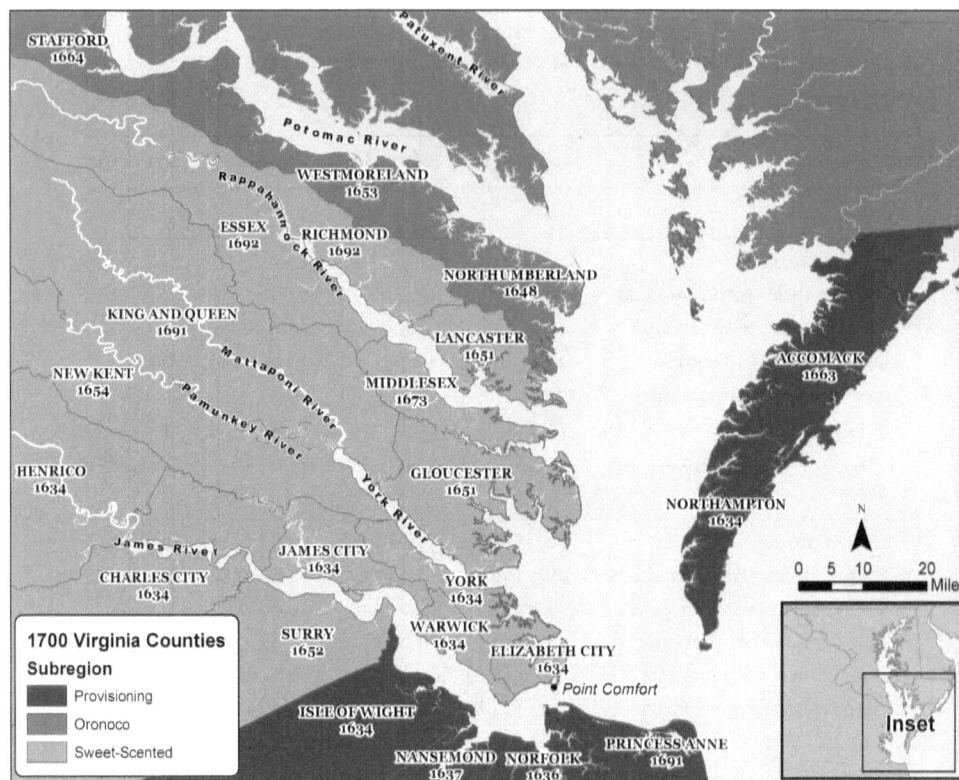

Map 8.1. Chesapeake economic subregions, ca. 1700. (Drawing on Lorena S. Walsh, "Summing the Parts: Implications for Estimating Chesapeake Output and Income Subregionally," *William and Mary Quarterly*, 3rd ser., 56 (January 1999): 53–94. Map by Kevin Heard, GIS Core Facility, Binghamton University)

which the Chesapeake received transatlantic slave deliveries throughout the duration of monopoly control. Even wealthy Potomac inhabitants such as Stafford grandee William Fitzhugh seem to have experienced difficulty in acquiring black workers during these years, since on several occasions he sought out slaves for purchase in better-supplied areas further south.[30]

Closer scrutiny of the data reveals significant variation even within subregions. Considering its higher overall levels of wealth, concentrations of great planters with strong ties to the leading London tobacco firms, and consequent status as the primary receiving destination for transatlantic shipments, the more intense commitment to slavery evident in the sweet-scented area is not surprising. Yet it was localities on the upper James River, not the affluent York and Rappahannock Counties where these advantages were most pronounced and most direct deliveries arrived, that exhibited the greatest frequency of slaveholding among ordinary planters. The combined rate of slave ownership among small and middling decedents with some bound labor along the York and Rappahannock was 47 percent, compared with 62 percent for all counties on the upper James and three-quarters for Henrico County alone. At first glance the probate statistics would seem to make little sense, since gentry planters on the upper James claimed 70 percent of the black headrights awarded in land patents and certificates between 1670 and 1700. However, the availability of Indian slaves, who made up almost 40 percent of all enslaved bondsmen employed by ordinary decedents in Henrico, and for whom no headright could be claimed, resolves this apparent discrepancy. If we assume that those who only had Indian slaves would not have owned slaves at all if blacks alone had been available, the rate of slave ownership among non-elite planters falls to 52 percent in Henrico and 50 percent for the upper James as a whole, much more in line with other parts of the sweet-scented subregion. While the evidence base is again somewhat slight, it is highly probable that access to the Indian slave trade helped to somewhat assuage the labor shortage in Virginia's southwestern counties.[31]

Economic diversification seems to have played a similar role in alleviating the crisis in the provisioning subregion. Counties on the Southside and Eastern Shore had only limited soils suitable for tobacco cultivation, and by the 1670s their inhabitants were increasingly abandoning the staple in favor of producing foodstuffs, naval stores, and wood products such as staves and heading for colonial markets, particularly the West Indies. Even with the weaker connections to transatlantic trading networks in these areas, however, the probate evidence exhibits an even greater frequency of slaveholding among labor-owning decedents than in the sweet-scented subregion. Particularly high rates of non-elite slave ownership in Lower Norfolk and Princess Anne Counties, where the coastwise trade with the Caribbean was centered, appears to have been the cause. Ordinary planters were credited with 46 percent of the black headrights awarded in land certificates issued in these two counties and owned over half (53 percent) of slaves listed in inventories, suggesting a more equitable distribution of enslaved workers than existed in other parts of the colony.[32]

So instead of occurring as a widespread "shift" confined largely to the last two decades of the seventeenth century, the initial growth of slavery in Virginia unfolded as a complex process, with multiple phases and significant subregional diversity, in which the timing and extent of investments in slave labor varied widely according to wealth, location, and economic need. In an initial phase, which lasted into the 1650s, English participation in transatlantic slaving was still in its infancy and for much of the period was confined mainly to raiding the vessels of other European powers. Consequently, access to slaves was limited to those Virginians—many of them members of the council—who had the right connections, first to privateering interests, and later to Dutch traders or the emerging English "new merchants" involved in early African slave-trading ventures. A broad segment of the gentry acquired at least a few slaves in this phase, and by its end most councilors likely had more slaves than servants in their workforces.[33] The period from the late 1640s to the late 1670s constituted a second phase, in which the growth of intercolonial slave trading, supplemented with limited direct deliveries from Africa, facilitated expanded access to slaves among county-level elites, and slaves first achieved a majority in the labor forces of all strata of the gentry. A third phase, lasting from the 1670s to the end of the seventeenth century, was marked by the emergence of the colony's first large, fully enslaved labor forces and the extension of slaveholding to a sizable percentage of non-elite Virginians for the first time, though change would not reach the mass of ordinary labor-owning planters until the first decades of the eighteenth century. There was no "trigger" cause for the conversion. Rather, the rise of slavery began in the first decades of settlement and steadily grew in concert with the development of England's empire, the expansion and maturation of English involvement in commercial slave trading, and Virginia's integration into the Atlantic economy, where slave-based plantation labor had become firmly established long before the colony's founding, and throughout which the traffic in enslaved men and women had become commonplace.

Discussion concerning the legal status of slaves and their prospects for securing freedom suffered from a similar, though somewhat different, evidentiary shortcoming than the timing and causality question. While this topic had been the focus of the initial strain of the origins debate and had generated a series of heated exchanges during the 1950s and 1960s, by the 1970s most historians conceded that even before passage of Virginia's first slave laws, some blacks were held in permanent bondage, some were servants for a term, and some were free; what remained at issue was the relative size of each group. However, in addressing this question, scholars relied far too heavily on the admittedly rich records of Accomack and Northampton Counties, the earliest volumes of which were made readily available through Susie Ames's excellent transcriptions. This was not so much of a problem with Timothy Breen and Stephen Innes's *"Myne Own Ground"* or Douglas Deal's doctoral dissertation. Although both works dealt exclusively with the Eastern Shore, for the most part they refrained from using the information gathered on the area's substantial free black community to generalize about circumstances elsewhere. Deal was particularly cautious in this respect. Readily acknowledging the Shore's singular characteristics, he explicitly declined to extend his findings beyond the "one corner of Virginia" he was attempting to describe. Edmund Morgan and Ira Berlin, on the other hand, were far less reticent about engaging in aggressive extrapolation. Even though virtually all of the specific examples they offered were from Accomack and Northampton, Morgan maintained that in the early decades of the century white Virginians as a whole "were ready to think of Negroes as members or potential members of the community on the same terms as other men," while Berlin claimed that "black freemen could be found throughout the region owning land, holding servants, and occasionally attaining minor offices." Whereas Deal cautioned that until similar research was completed on other areas there was no way of knowing "how reliable and representative" the stories he related were, Morgan and particularly Berlin effectively transformed the Eastern Shore into a proxy for the entire colony.[34]

Like the chronological framework that emerged from the origins debate, the idea that in the initial decades of slavery's growth the legal status of slaves remained fluid and permeable has persisted in more recent scholarship, with the most notable example being Berlin's influential 1998 study *Many Thousands Gone*. Building on his earlier work, Berlin maintained that until Bacon's Rebellion ushered in a "Tobacco Revolution" in the mid-1670s, most Chesapeake slaves were highly adaptive "Atlantic Creoles" who came from the vicinity of European trading posts along the African coast, various colonies in the Caribbean, or the Dutch settlement of New Netherlands. Reflecting their cosmopolitan backgrounds, these early arrivals already possessed considerable familiarity with the commercial practices and languages of the Atlantic world, skills that enabled them to quickly master the complexities of Virginia's social politics. Anthony Johnson, a free black planter on the Eastern Shore, epitomized the confidence, perseverance, and cultural dexterity of these immigrants. Imported as a slave sometime in the 1620s, by the 1640s Johnson had managed to obtain both his freedom and a respectable estate. For Berlin, the circumstances of this "charter generation" stood in stark contrast to the harsher form of slavery that confronted the "plantation generations" of enslaved men and women who began flooding into Virginia after the Tobacco Revolution and the advent of direct trade from Africa. Whereas Johnson and many of his contemporaries spoke English, professed adherence to the Christian faith, acquired livestock and access to land of their own, and were often able to secure freedom for themselves and their descendants, later arrivals were "not nearly as fortunate." Drawn from the interior regions of Africa rather than littoral areas with direct connections to Atlantic trade networks, they did not speak or understand the languages of their captors, were ignorant of Christianity, were denied the ability to own property, and spent the entirety of their lives in bondage.[35]

Berlin's depiction of Virginia slavery as being initially more lenient and permeable than it would later become recently has received considerable support from Linda Heywood and John Thornton, who, while they differ with Berlin about the backgrounds of early slaves—presenting convincing evidence that through the 1630s most were native Angolans seized by English and Dutch privateers from Iberian vessels on the high seas—agree with most of the other points in his argument. Adopting Berlin's terminology, Heywood and Thornton maintain that despite their lack of New World experience, black immigrants of the charter generation often had received prior exposure to European culture, religion most importantly, and that this familiarity afforded them with substantial opportunities to improve their lot once they arrived in the Chesapeake. A significant number of "the first Africans were Atlantic Creoles," they assert, stressing that knowledge of Christianity was the key attribute that helped "a large percentage" successfully make the "transition from slavery to freedom." Yet they also go beyond Berlin to contend that the legal status of slaves was also somewhat unsettled in these decades. Although allowing that Virginians quickly came to regard *negro* and *slave* as synonymous terms in the same manner as the Portuguese, they surmise that "in English, the word *slave* did not have a fixed legal meaning," and thus while it was clearly a lifetime condition in the early seventeenth century, "even in the 1660s" the colony "still had not resolved whether it was perpetual."[36]

Despite Deal's caution that without a systematic study of other areas in the colony there was no way of knowing to what extent circumstances on the Eastern Shore were representative, Berlin again drew heavily on its free black community for examples to support his arguments. Heywood and Thornton do as well, remarking that "it is possible that the mainland had similar communities, though lack of documentation prevents a thorough examination of it."[37] But eight counties on the mainland have extant records that date to the period they and Berlin were concerned with, several having substantially long runs. A thorough examination of these sources is essential for placing the now well-known conditions on the early Shore within a broader comparative context, since it was on the Lower and Middle Peninsulas and the Northern Neck that most of Virginia's black population lived. Over 90 percent of black workers listed in inventories taken through the rebellion year of 1676 and 70 percent of those named in wills are found in mainland county records. Nearly eighty deeds conveying property rights in blacks also survive from this time frame, as do tax lists for both Surry and Lancaster Counties that overlap with many of the same years available for the Eastern Shore.[38]

There is, however, one thing notably missing from these records: evidence of sizable numbers of free blacks and mulattoes. In contrast to the nearly sixty such individuals documented as having lived on the Eastern Shore by 1676, just twenty-six can be identified in records of the mainland counties.[39] The disparity suggested by extant tax lists is even more striking. Historians have long highlighted the thirteen free black heads of household who appear in the detailed Northampton tithable lists for 1664 to 1677, and another five are named in two earlier lists for Northampton and contemporary lists for neighboring Accomack.[40] What has rarely, if ever, been remarked upon, though, is the near absence of black householders in the surviving tax lists of localities across the bay. In the seven lists available for Surry between 1668 and 1677, the only two mentioned are an unnamed "Negro woman" and "Jack Negro," probably the former slave John Daule who together with his wife, Izabell, purchased their freedom from Arthur Jordan in 1669. Although the free black John Pedro was involved in several land transactions in Lancaster and seems to have briefly owned at least one tract before removing to Maryland sometime in the mid-1650s, not a single black householder appears in the twenty-five known lists compiled in that county from 1653 to 1677.[41]

Clearly there were real differences between the mainland and the Eastern Shore. Yet looking at the evidence from all of Virginia's counties collectively affords the best possible empirical basis—given the limits of the existing documentary record—for addressing long-standing questions about the status of blacks before what Breen and Innes described as an "inexorable hardening of racial lines" in the decades after Bacon's Rebellion. Such an analysis makes clear, for starters, that even before the supposedly critical turning points of statutory recognition of slavery in the 1660s and the beginning of direct African deliveries in the mid-1670s, only a handful of blacks in Virginia were held in the capacity as servants. Among bound workers who were individually listed in inventories taken through 1676, 83 percent of white or "English" laborers had a remaining term of service included next to their names, while only 2 of 286 "negroes" did so. If this obvious indication of differing status is not convincing enough, when coupled with the higher valuations generally given persons of African descent in the inventories, the lack of a single example of their appearing in court to complain about mistreatment, and the fact that in six of the seven known instances where one brought suit for being unjustly detained beyond their term of service the master involved countered by claiming his accuser was bound for life, the case becomes overwhelming: the normative condition for "negroes" was enslavement.[42]

Of course, as Heywood and Thornton point out, lifetime service did not necessarily mean hereditary status. However, material in the court records demonstrates that slavery in Virginia was indeed perpetual even before the General Assembly began passing legislation in the early 1660s that brought greater clarity to the property rights of masters. Of the 104 blacks listed in inventories taken before December 1662, when the first such measure was adopted, 33 were under the age of sixteen and 27 were younger than twelve. With one exception, these young "negroes" did not have a length of time to serve entered next to their names and were valued at generally higher rates than English servants, clearly indicating that they were slaves. Tom, "a negro boy about 5 yeares old" belonging to Lieutenant Colonel Thomas Ludlow of York, for example, was appraised at the same value as an adult male servant named John Sayers who had four years left on his term, while two "Negro boyes" and a "Negro girle" who were part of Northampton justice Peter Walker's estate were valued collectively at 5,500 pounds of tobacco, which was 2,100 pounds more than the combined total of two adult white male bondsmen each with four years to serve and a white woman servant with two. Unless one is willing to maintain that all or most of these children were immigrants—a highly unlikely prospect considering the near balanced sex ratio between boys and girls—then the only reasonable explanation for their status is that they had inherited it from their parents.[43]

If inventory listings still leave some small room for doubt about the perpetual nature of slavery in these years, the evidence contained in wills and deeds does not. Fourteen black boys and girls were mentioned in wills promulgated before December 1662, and another thirty-four appear in deeds executed during the same period, again in both cases with no time of service stipulated. These figures, though compelling, obviously have the same limitations as the inventories, since it is not absolutely certain that the individuals named were born in the colony. But over half of the pre-1662 surviving wills and deeds that mention female slaves also convey rights to their *future* progeny. Thus in anticipation of his 1651 marriage to Rachaell Constable, York justice John Chew set aside two men and two women slaves with "all and every their increase" for George Ludlow and Richard Lee to hold in his future wife's name, and three slaves that justice Rowland Burnham of Lancaster bequeathed to his sons Thomas and John in 1656 included "a Negro woman called Joane, with what children she shall bear from this date to them & their heirs forever." These were not anomalous assertions of vague "customary" privilege. The routine use throughout the colony of this terminology and phrasing, the same that appears in transfers of livestock, constitutes unequivocal proof of hereditary enslavement in Virginia well before statutory recognition. Wills and deeds (and inventories) were legal documents, and by authorizing the inclusion of such transactions among their county's records, local justices were not only giving the property rights of slave owners official sanction but were establishing provincial common-law precedent for slavery's very existence as a legal system.[44]

It is perhaps some measure of the strength of this colonial common-law system that through the mid-1670s, over 80 percent of the free blacks whose means of achieving freedom can be determined gained their release through manumission or self-purchase or by virtue of being the child of a parent who was already free.[45] Virginia slavery was—and until the very end of the century remained—flexible enough that a few masters were willing to afford certain slaves the possibility of escaping their condition, and through a mixture of luck, talent, and struggle some managed to take advantage of the opportunity. However, even in these early decades the overwhelming majority lacked such prospects. Ambitious men seeking to increase their estates did not, after all, achieve their aims by routinely letting go of valuable property, and however much we would like to believe that slaves possessed the agency to shape their futures, manumission was the exclusive prerogative of masters. This is not to say that the authority of masters was absolute. As Berlin and other scholars have amply shown, their relations with their bondsmen, even those who were enslaved, were complex affairs marked by considerable give and take. Yet even if a slave was shrewd enough at these negotiations to gain ownership rights of some livestock or permission to occasionally work the soil on his own behalf, privileges that could enable him to eventually scrimp and save sufficient resources to purchase himself or his loved ones, he still had no legal power to compel his owner's consent to the sale.

While some slave owners clearly were willing to relinquish their rights, be it for reasons of faith, fondness, or financial gain, their numbers should not be exaggerated. Even the community that emerged on the Eastern Shore was largely created through the actions of only a few planters. Of the fifteen Northampton free blacks of tithable age in 1668, the notable year in which they made up more than a quarter of all adult blacks living in the county, one was a free immigrant from New England, and another eight had formerly belonged to just four men: Captain Francis Pigot, Lieutenant Colonel William Kendall, Captain Stephen Charleton, and Justice Richard Vaughan.[46] The distressing reality that confronted the colony's slaves was that such "reluctant masters" were exceptionally rare, particularly on the mainland, where most blacks lived. Only four of the fifty-nine extant wills of slave owners recorded in the mainland counties through 1676 included manumission clauses, which freed just 5 of 208 slaves. In pursuit of profit, all but a small number of masters adopted the same attitude as Isle of Wight justice Robert Williamson, whose 1670 will directed that the slave Great Jack he bequeathed to his son Robert should "be enjoyed" by him "and his heirs for ever."[47]

If a slave could not persuade his master to offer a grant of freedom, the courts potentially offered an alternative means of escape. But even without statutory recognition of slavery, the legal path to liberation was barred to most slaves. The best indicator of what options existed is a 1656 case in which a young mulatto woman named Elizabeth Key—the illegitimate daughter of former burgess Thomas Key—sued for her freedom in Northumberland County. Although Elizabeth won the initial trial of her suit before the local justices, two months later the General Court in Jamestown reversed this decision. Her attorney made a final appeal to the General Assembly, the colony's court of last resort at the time, which ultimately declined to offer a "determinative judgement" and remanded the case back to the county because "noe man appeared against the said Elizabeths petition." But in taking this action the assembly concurred with a committee report that recommended she be given her freedom on the grounds that "by the common law the child of a woman slave begot by a free man ought to be free," Elizabeth had "long since been christened" and was "able to give a very good account of her faith," and the fact that Thomas Key had placed contractual limitations on the terms of her service when selling her to another man two decades before. Final settlement of the dispute seems to have taken a few more years. Yet by 1659 Elizabeth was a free woman and had married her former attorney, a white man named William Grinsted, by whom she had already had two children.[48]

The details of this case yield several insights into the legal development of slavery in the first half of the century. The first concerns matters of timing. According to the deposition of Alice Larrett, Elizabeth Key was twenty-five years old in January 1656 and was therefore born around 1630. Her date of birth, combined with the committee's reference to her mother as a "woman slave," is perhaps the clearest evidence available that the practice of holding blacks in permanent bondage dated back at least to the late 1620s. Secondly, the pleas Grinsted put forward suggest that only a small minority of slaves were in a position to question the legality of their status. Elizabeth Key was a mulatto; "Negroes" were not. Thomas Key had crafted a legally binding arrangement regarding the length of her service; slaves, by definition, lacked such agreements. This left baptism as the one line of argument that a number of enslaved blacks might potentially pursue, particularly those who had perhaps acquired some degree of familiarity with Christianity in the African trading enclaves and New World colonies of the Iberian powers. But Protestant Englishmen, some of them Calvinist in doctrinal orientation and vehemently anti-Catholic, probably took a skeptical attitude toward the converts of "popish" priests and questioned the authenticity of baptisms if a slave could not offer a "good account" of his beliefs.[49] Masters could also limit their vulnerability to such challenges by refusing to christen native-born bondsmen and prohibiting their religious instruction. Finally, the different decisions reached in the case as it wound its way through the judicial system reveals the emergence of a powerful political interest in support of slavery. There is no way of ascertaining which of the various grounds cited in the committee's report were most persuasive to either the Northumberland justices or the members of the assembly. It may have been the cumulative weight of all three that led both to conclude that Elizabeth Key should be free. But the General Court's decision when presented with the same arguments is perhaps even more significant, since its verdict presaged the changes that were soon to come. Consisting of the governor and Council of State sitting in a judicial capacity, the General Court was the one body to hear the case that was probably made up entirely of slave owners. Tellingly, when presented with the same evidence of Elizabeth's white parentage, Christian baptism, and contractual terms of service, they still ruled that she was a slave.[50]

What happened in the years following the resolution of Elizabeth Key's suit is well known. Over the course of a decade, the General Assembly passed four key statutes that more clearly delineated and augmented the colony's existing common-law slave system. The first of these, adopted in 1662, clarified the status of mulattoes by holding that "all children borne in this country shall be held bond or free only according to the condition of the mother." A 1667 law that declared "the conferring of baptisme doth not alter the condition of the person as to his bondage or freedome" largely eliminated the religion loophole, while the 1669 "Act about the casual killing of slaves" granted masters nearly absolute control over the domestic management and discipline of their enslaved bondsmen. The last of these landmark measures, approved in 1672, committed the government to the burdensome task of policing slaves for the first time and established the practice of compensating owners from the public treasury if an "outlawed" slave of theirs was killed in the process of being retaken. The assembly would continue to tinker with things throughout the remainder of the colonial era, adding new laws and changing others. But these four statutes would continue to provide the legislative foundation of Virginia slavery until its abolishment after the American Civil War.[51]

The timing of these measures has never fit well with the established periodization of the conversion. Why would Virginia's leaders move on this particular range of issues before the supposed "date" of the transition, when blacks still made up an insignificant portion of the colony's total population? Even Edmund Morgan seems to have struggled with this question. With laws such as the 1669 act "already on the books," he awkwardly contended in his classic study, "Virginia was prepared to make the most of slavery when slaves began to arrive in quantity." Morgan was, in a general sense, completely correct. The acts he mentioned would indeed serve the purposes of white Virginians quite well, though it is a highly dubious proposition that the assembly was prescient enough to foresee an expansion in the supply of slaves that was still years in the future. Moreover, laws are usually, if not always, passed to meet immediate needs, not vaguely anticipated problems. Viewed within the context of an expanding commitment to slavery among all strata of the colony's elite in the 1660s and early 1670s, however, the timing of these four critical statutes makes perfect sense. By adopting them, the members of the assembly were serving the interests of their most important constituency: themselves.[52]

The last of the three "points of agreement" Vaughan described, that the background of Virginia's slaves changed as Africa replaced the Caribbean as the colony's primary source of black laborers, was also the most thinly sourced. This notion was based largely on a 1708 letter by acting governor Edmund Jennings to the Board of Trade, in which he reported that "before the year 1680 what negros were brought to Virginia were imported generally from Barbados for it was very rare to have a Negro ship come to this country directly from Africa," adding that "since that time, and before the year 1698, the trade of negros became more frequent, tho not in any proportion to what hath been of late." Historians often construed these remarks to mean that before 1680 most slaves arriving in Virginia had been taken from the resident black population of the West Indian islands and that afterward they were primarily Africans lacking any previous experience of plantation life. Citing Jennings, for example, T. H. Breen differentiated between early slaves, who "probably learned to speak some English" in the Caribbean before coming to Virginia, and later African immigrants, who "had no stopover in Barbados to learn English or to adjust either physically or mentally to an alien culture." Berlin drew the same contrast several years later, distinguishing the cosmopolitan "West Indian creoles who bore English or Spanish surnames and carried records of baptism," which he claimed made up the majority of slaves sent to the Chesapeake throughout the first three quarters of the seventeenth century, from "blacks born in Africa," who "entered the region in increasingly large numbers" during its final two decades.[53]

Yet such interpretations completely ignore the purpose of Jennings's letter, which was, as Will Pettigrew's essay in this volume clearly demonstrates, written in response to an official inquiry into the conduct of the English transatlantic slave trade. At the time, Parliament was embroiled in the highly contentious process of determining the final fate of the Royal African Company, whose monopoly on providing slaves to the colonies it had suspended a decade earlier by permitting, for a period of thirteen years, independent merchants called "separate traders" to engage in the slave traffic upon payment of a 10 percent duty on imports and exports for the upkeep of the company's African forts. To aid in its deliberations, Parliament requested that the Board of Trade instruct governors throughout the empire to provide information on "what number of negroes had been yearly imported directly from Africa" into their jurisdictions during the period of monopoly's suspension, the rates at which they had been sold, and how many had been delivered by the company and the separate traders respectively. The board further required governors "to confer with some of the principal planters and inhabitants" within their governments about "how the negro trade was carried on" before and after "1698, when that trade was laid open by Act of Parliament," and to supply some comment as to "what manner they think the said trade may best be managed for the benefit of the plantations." Jennings followed these instructions closely, and after consulting with the "proper officers" and some "ancient inhabitants" provided what was, in essence, an assessment of the company's performance in supplying Virginia with black laborers during the quarter century its monopoly was in force and how the situation had changed in the decade following passage of the 1698 act. His comments were thus restricted solely to the slave trade from Africa and had nothing to do with intercolonial shipments beyond mentioning their importance to the colony in the years before 1680, when direct deliveries seldom arrived. In short, the claims of those historians who referenced Jennings's remarks to contend that there were pronounced differences in the relative scale of the transatlantic and coastwise slave trades in the century's last two decades—or that black immigrants to Virginia were temporally divided into disparate groups of New World creoles and unacculturated Africans—are simply not supported by an informed reading of his instructions and letter of response.[54]

Even the handful of scholars who offered more empirically based interpretations of the size of the two trades after 1700—and whose work has played an important role in shaping perceptions on this question—did not pursue their research as far as they could have. Philip Curtin and Herbert Klein simply accepted at face value that all slave vessels listed in shipping returns as arriving from the West Indies had acquired their cargoes in the islands, when in fact some of those carrying larger numbers of slaves had only made a brief stop after completing the crossing from Africa. Alan Kulikoff attempted to account for this practice by assuming that all British-registered vessels carrying more than forty slaves were transatlantic slavers, an approach that significantly reduced Curtin and Klein's estimates of the size of the coastwise slave trade. Susan Westbury subsequently endorsed Kulikoff's position and, noting that most documented coastwise shipments only ranged between one and sixteen slaves, concurred with his finding that three-quarters of the blacks shipped to Virginia in the early decades of the eighteenth century were transported directly from Africa.[55]

However, close examination of Barbadian shipping returns eliminates much of the need for the kind of assumptions Kulikoff and Westbury advocated, while also demonstrating that some large shipments did indeed originate in the West Indies. It is possible to track the comings and goings of William Godfrey's *Philipa*, for example, throughout the several months preceding his 1716 slaving voyage to Virginia. The *Philipa* made four trips between Barbados and the Leeward Islands from December 1715 to February 1716, eventually re-entering Bridgetown harbor for the last time on March 29. Godfrey cleared for Virginia three weeks later, arriving in the lower James on May 11 with a cargo of seventy-seven "Negroes."[56] This cross-checking makes clear that several other sizable shipments transported in vessels with British registry, such as the 88 slaves brought to Virginia by John Jennings's *Mary* in September 1715 and another 111 delivered by James Pearce's *Maidstone* two years later, were also procured in the islands.[57]

Anecdotal evidence suggests that larger deliveries of this sort occasionally occurred in the coastwise trade during the seventeenth century as well. The London tobacco merchant William Paggen had "34 Negro's & 7 or 8 tun of rum and sugar" shipped to his Virginia factors John Pleasants and Richard Kennon of Henrico in 1684, and the following year William Byrd reported that "Paggen's concerne" had "certaine intelligence" of another "Negro ship" being sent to them that probably also embarked its human cargo in the Caribbean. Fearing that Kennon and Pleasants might lure away some of his lesser neighbors who sold him their tobacco, Byrd voiced concern that if the "designe by Barbados" planned by his own factors Micajah Perry and Thomas Lane should happen to fail, "wee shall bee fairly disappointed for without servants or slaves, no great crop is now to be purchased."[58]

Although Maryland governor John Seymour was undoubtedly correct in describing the typical coastwise slave cargo as consisting of just "seaven, eight, nine, or ten in a sloope," scholars have wrongly assumed that the small size of most West Indian shipments resulted in a low overall total of imports. A systematic analysis of surviving Caribbean shipping returns demonstrates that between 1680 and 1687 around seventy vessels annually departed from the islands for the Chesapeake colonies, a number that dropped to roughly twenty-five per year after the outbreak of the Nine Years' War in 1688.

Information contained in similar Virginia sources for the late seventeenth and early eighteenth centuries indicates that around one-quarter of these vessels are likely to have carried slaves, with a mean average cargo size of eighteen slaves per vessel. When these figures are applied to the shipping volume in the coastwise trade, the resulting estimate of the number of blacks sent to the Chesapeake between 1680 and 1700 is 3,600, and if the volume of traffic in the 1670s was comparable to the 1680s, then the total number of blacks arriving from Caribbean sources over the last third of the seventeenth century would have been something on the order of 6,200.[59]

Perhaps the most striking aspect of this estimate is its size; only one-third less than 9,900 slaves historian David Eltis has estimated were probably brought to the Chesapeake via the transatlantic slave trade over the same period. However, the available information on the growth of the Chesapeake's slave population indicates that 6,200 is a reasonably accurate number. Exactly how many blacks lived in the region at the end of the seventeenth century is uncertain. The more recent scholarly estimates range from Phillip Morgan's cautious "educated guess" of 13,000 for the Old Dominion alone to Lorena Walsh's less precise but clearly more expansive suggestion of "as many as 20,000" for Virginia and Maryland combined, with the Bureau of the Census's regional total of just over 16,000 being the most frequently cited.[60] Yet, regardless of what point on this fairly broad spectrum one chooses, there exists a considerable "immigration gap" between the quantity of Africans known to have been delivered to Virginia and Maryland via the transatlantic slave trade and the number of blacks present in the two colonies at century's end, a shortfall that can be illustrated using David Galenson's calculations of decennial net black migration for the thirty years from 1670 to 1700. After applying demographic multipliers to the Census Bureau's statistics to adjust for growth stemming from natural increase and loss resulting from "seasoning mortality," Galenson concluded that an expansion in the Chesapeake's black population from 2,000 at the beginning of the period to 16,000 at its close would probably have required imports of about 16,700 blacks. Subtracting Eltis's estimate of 9,900 slaves transported by English Atlantic shippers from Galenson's figure thus leaves a deficit of 6,800 who ostensibly came from alternative sources. Although this gap obviously would narrow or widen depending upon what set of population statistics and multipliers are used, the resulting change is unlikely to be of such magnitude that the proposed estimate for the coastwise trade would be rendered untenable.[61]

If the estimated volume of coastwise deliveries is reasonably accurate, then the notion of a pronounced shift in the sources of Virginia's slaves that has long been a fixture in the literature did not happen. Slaves disembarked from vessels arriving in the colony from the West Indies during the late seventeenth century were not drastically outnumbered by their counterparts sent directly from Africa. Of course, few of these "Caribbean" blacks were actually from the Caribbean in any meaningful sense. The transatlantic and coastwise trades were functionally equivalent, the only difference between them being that, with some exceptions, slaves sent from the West Indies had been transferred onto ships different from those in which they had endured the Middle Passage. Unless sugar planters willingly parted with more than 6,000 seasoned immigrants and native-born slaves, the large majority had probably spent only a few days or weeks in the hands of a merchant before being reloaded onto smaller vessels for the trip northward to the Tobacco Coast. The same was probably true of their predecessors in earlier decades, since a profound alteration in how the West Indians conducted their intercolonial slave trade seems equally implausible. No Virginian ever noted a marked change in the backgrounds of blacks acquired from the Caribbean, nor do extant Barbados records document such a transformation. Numerous slave sales between resident planters can be found in the island's surviving deed books from the 1640s onward, but only two mention shipments to Virginia, and neither mentions how long the blacks involved had lived there. While the rarity of such transactions does not prove conclusively that the coastwise trade was restricted largely to transshipped Africans, had creolized slaves been involved to the extent that Breen, Berlin, and numerous others have asserted, one would certainly expect to see a more substantial documentary trail. If there was a "generational" divide in the character of African American society in Virginia, it most likely did not stem from a change in the nature of the colony's slave trade but from the differing degrees of exposure to European culture that immigrant blacks had experienced in Africa, as Heywood and Thornton contend, coupled with the diminishing duration and intensity of their interactions with white servants in the Chesapeake as planters moved from employing a diverse mixture of bondsmen to a reliance on slaves alone.[62]

There is obviously much more that could be said about each one of these topics than the brief analyses offered here. The objective has been to show how further digging in the sources can controvert even the most well-established beliefs about the rise of slavery in Virginia and by so doing suggest that scholars have too readily accepted the interpretive status quo of the 1970s and 1980s when a substantial amount of the relevant evidence has yet to be thoroughly examined. But future research should not be directed solely toward reconsidering familiar arguments and conclusions. As noted at the beginning of this essay, there are numerous topics relating to slavery's establishment that contributors to the origins debate never effectively addressed and that have continued to receive scant attention in more recently published studies. We still lack detailed information about how early slave trading to Virginia fit within the broader organizational structure of the colony's export economy, for example, or to what extent the strategies planters adopted when bequeathing black laborers differed in accordance with decedent wealth, subregional access to slaves, and over time. We also know little about the seventeenth-century black population's demographic characteristics or whether the social and geographic distribution of slaves aided or inhibited the formation of African American communities. In short, a great deal more work can be done on this important subject. The development of user-friendly personal computers and software that has largely eliminated the technical difficulties that formerly hampered broad-based research—combined with old-fashioned due diligence in the archives—enables a far more comprehensive and systematic approach than the selective sampling of evidence that has heretofore underpinned analysis. When trends among different socioeconomic groups in all parts of the colony are examined closely, it will be possible to construct a new composite vision of slavery's development that highlights the importance of variation rather than subsuming it within a generalized, aggregate story. There are, admittedly, some aspects of the conversion that even the most intrepid investigator will never be able to explore. But as historians begin to move beyond the origins debate and expand the boundaries of current understanding by revisiting old answers and posing new questions, we would do well to keep in mind another nugget of wisdom that Wesley Frank Craven conveyed on that autumn day some forty years ago. "The plain fact is that the surviving record is so incomplete as to impose a decided limit on what we are ever likely to know about the Negro in seventeenth-century Virginia," he reflected. "What bothers me is that we may have been too content to have it that way."[63]

Notes

1. Wesley Frank Craven, *White, Red, and Black: The Seventeenth-Century Virginian* (Charlottesville, VA, 1971), 76.

2. Alden T. Vaughan, "The Origins Debate: Slavery and Racism in Seventeenth-

Century Virginia," *Virginia Magazine of History and Biography* 97 (1989): 311–54. Unless otherwise noted, throughout this essay, the term "origins debate" is used as a collective reference to the body of scholarship published during the 1970s and 1980s that Vaughan surveyed. Much of that work was not explicitly preoccupied with the so-called chicken-and-egg dilemma about the relationship between slavery and racism in early British America, nor is it my concern in this piece. While for a number of reasons Virginia has frequently served as a "laboratory" for exploring that issue, as Rebecca Goetz has recently noted, this focus has deflected attention from the varying ways slavery became institutionalized across the colonial South (and considering the recent work of Michael Guasco and April Hatfield, one might add throughout the English Atlantic) and the parameters of discussion should properly be much broader. It is worth noting, however, that the secondary strain of the origins debate was only tangentially related to the original question and dealt with historical phenomena much more specific to Virginia and the Chesapeake. See Rebecca Anne Goetz, "Rethinking the 'Unthinking Decision': Old Questions and New Problems in the History of Race in the Colonial South," *Journal of Southern History* 75 (2009): 599–612; Michael J. Guasco, "'Encounters, Identities, and Human Bondage': The Foundations of Racial Slavery in the English Atlantic World" (Ph.D. diss., College of William and Mary, 2000); and April Lee Hatfield, "A 'Very Wary People in Their Bargaining' or 'Very Good Marchandise': English Traders' Views of Free and Enslaved Africans, 1550–1650," *Slavery and Abolition* 25 (2004): 1–17.

3. The more important works in the debate over timing and causality produced during this period are T. H. Breen, "A Changing Labor Force and Race Relations in Virginia, 1660–1710," *Journal of Social History* 7 (1973): 3–25; Edmund S. Morgan, "Slavery and Freedom: The American Paradox," *Journal of American History* 59 (1972): 5–29; Morgan, *American Slavery, American Freedom: The Ordeal of Colonial Virginia* (New York, 1975); Theodore Allen, "'... They Would Have Destroyed Me': Slavery and the Origins of Racism," *Radical America* 9 (1975): 40–63; Russell R. Menard, "From Servants to Slaves: The Transformation of the Chesapeake Labor Force," *Southern Studies* 16 (1977): 362–90; Richard N. Bean and Robert P. Thomas, "The Adoption of Slave Labor in British America," in Henry A Gemery and Jan S. Hogendorn, eds., *The Uncommon Market: Essays in the Economic History of the Atlantic Slave Trade* (New York, 1979), 377–98; David W. Galenson, "White Servitude and the Growth of Black Slavery in Colonial America," *Journal of Economic History* 41 (1981): 39–47; and Galenson, *White Servitude in Colonial America: An Economic Analysis* (New York, 1981).

4. T. H. Breen and Stephen Innes, *"Myne Own Ground": Race and Freedom on Virginia's Eastern Shore, 1640–1676* (New York, 1980); J. Douglas Deal, *Race and Class in Colonial Virginia: Indians, Englishmen, and Africans on the Eastern Shore during the Seventeenth Century* (New York, 1993); Darrett B. Rutman and Anita H. Rutman, *A Place in Time: Middlesex County, Virginia, 1650–1750* (New York, 1984), chap. 6; Rutman and Rutman, "More True and Perfect Lists: The Reconstruction of Censuses for Middlesex County, Virginia, 1668–1704," *Virginia Magazine of History and Biography* 88 (1980): 37–74; Darrett B. Rutman, Charles Wetherell, and Anita H. Rutman, "Rhythms of Life: Black and White Seasonality in the Early Chesapeake," *Journal of Interdisciplinary History* 11 (1980): 29–53; Linda M. Heywood and John K. Thornton, *Central Africans, Atlantic Creoles, and the Foundation of the Americas, 1585–1660* (New York, 2007), chap. 1. See also April Hatfield, *Atlantic Virginia: Intercolonial Relations in the Seventeenth Century* (Philadelphia, 2004), chap. 6. One topic that has seen ongoing attention is the legal development of slavery. See Warren M. Bill-

ings, "The Law of Servants and Slaves in Seventeenth-Century Virginia," *Virginia Magazine of History and Biography* 99 (1991): 45–62; Jonathan A. Bush, "Free to Enslave: The Foundations of Colonial American Slave Law," *Yale Journal of Law and the Humanities* 5 (1993): 417–70; Bush, "The British Constitution and the Creation of American Slavery," in Paul Finkelman, ed., *Slavery and the Law* (Madison, WI, 1997), 379–418; and Thomas D. Morris, *Southern Slavery and the Law, 1619–1860* (Chapel Hill, NC, 1996). Deal completed his doctoral dissertation in 1981. My citations of his work refer to a slightly revised version printed by Garland Publishing.

5. Kathleen M. Brown, *Good Wives, Nasty Wenches, and Anxious Patriarchs: Gender, Race, and Power in Colonial Virginia* (Chapel Hill, NC, 1996), 2; Ira Berlin, *Many Thousands Gone: The First Two Centuries of Slavery in North America* (Cambridge, MA, 1998); Anthony S. Parent, *Foul Means: The Formation of a Slave Society in Virginia, 1660–1740* (Chapel Hill, NC, 2003). Several of the more prominent book-length studies of slavery in Virginia or the Chesapeake completed since 1980 focused on the eighteenth century and therefore dealt only marginally with decades before 1700, though their introductory chapters do reflect the influence of the origins debate to some extent. See Alan Kulikoff, *Tobacco and Slaves: The Development of Southern Cultures in the Chesapeake, 1680–1800* (Chapel Hill, NC, 1986); Lorena S. Walsh, *From Calabar to Carter's Grove: The History of a Virginia Slave Community* (Charlottesville, VA, 1997); and Phillip D. Morgan, *Slave Counterpoint: Black Culture in the Eighteenth-Century Chesapeake and Low Country* (Chapel Hill, NC, 1998).

6. Vaughan, "The Origins Debate," 338–39. While individual works obviously vary in detail, every examination of Virginia's conversion to slavery published over the last decade that I looked at—including full-scale monographs, specialized student readers, and survey textbooks—conforms with this chronological framework. For examples, see Berlin, *Many Thousands Gone*, chaps. 1 and 5; Parent, *Foul Means*, chap. 2; Betty Wood, *Slavery in Colonial America, 1619–1776* (Lanham, MD, 2005), 1–12; Gary B. Nash, *Red, White, and Black: The Peoples of Early North America*, 5th ed. (Upper Saddle River, NJ, 2006), 146–47, 167–68; Kenneth Morgan, *Slavery and the British Empire: From Africa to America* (New York, 2008), 25–30; Alan Taylor, *American Colonies: The Settlement of North America* (New York, 2002), 139–58; Robert A. Divine et al., *America: Past and Present*, 7th ed. (New York, 2005), 71–72; and James A. Henretta et al., *America's History*, 6th ed. (Boston, 2008), 52–54.

7. Morgan, *American Slavery, American Freedom*, 304–5.

8. Robert McColley, "Slavery in Virginia, 1619–1660: A Reexamination," in Robert H. Abzug and Stephen E. Maizlish, eds., *New Perspectives on Race and Slavery in America: Essays in Honor of Kenneth M. Stampp* (Lexington, KY, 1986), 18–19.

9. Morgan, *American Slavery, American Freedom*, 306, 420–23; Menard, "From Servants to Slaves," 382–85. For a thorough treatment of economic differences within the Chesapeake that describes these subregions more precisely, see Lorena S. Walsh, "Summing the Parts: Implications for Estimating Chesapeake Output and Income Subregionally," *William and Mary Quarterly*, 3rd ser., 56 (1999): 53–194.

10. Menard, "From Servants to Slaves," 361, 368, 383n52; Darrett B. Rutman and Anita H. Rutman, *A Place in Time Explicatus* (New York, 1984), chaps. 3 and 12; Robert A. Wheeler, "Lancaster County, Virginia, 1650–1750: The Evolution of a Southern Tidewater Community" (Ph.D. diss., Brown University, 1972), 17–25, 74–77, 108–14. The footnotes in *American Slavery, American Freedom* clearly show that Morgan also did substantial research in the surviving records of at least ten different counties. But with the exception of

tithable lists, his presentation of this material suggests he did not compile or analyze evidence in a systematic fashion as did Menard and the Rutmans. The same also seems to be true of Breen and Innes and Deal, who worked extensively with the extant records of the Eastern Shore counties.

11. Phillip Alexander Bruce, *Economic History of Virginia in the Seventeenth Century: An Inquiry into the Material Condition of the People, Based on Original and Contemporaneous Records*, 2 vols. (New York, 1896); Bruce, *Institutional History of Virginia in the Seventeenth Century: An Inquiry into the Religious, Moral, Educational, Legal, Military and Political Condition of the People, Based on Original and Contemporaneous Records*, 2 vols. (New York, 1910); Bruce, *Social Life of Virginia in the Seventeenth Century: An inquiry into the Origin of the Higher Planting Class, Together with an Account of the Habits, Customs, and Diversions of the People* (Richmond, 1907); Susie M. Ames, *Studies of the Virginia Eastern Shore in the Seventeenth Century* (Richmond, 1940); Ames, ed., *County Court Records of Accomack-Northampton, Virginia, 1632–1640* (Washington, DC, 1954); Ames, ed., *County Court Records of Accomack Northampton, Virginia, 1640–1645* (Charlottesville, VA, 1973). The point I am trying to make here is not that such material is inaccurate or somehow untrustworthy but that the use of Virginia's local records was (and has remained) haphazard or selective. As noted below, for example, the high quality and ready availability of Ames's transcriptions of Northampton records has undoubtedly influenced the excessive attention given to the character of slavery on the early Eastern Shore.

12. For a good introduction to the scholarship of the Chesapeake School in these years, see Aubrey C. Land, Lois Green Carr, and Edward C. Papenfuse, eds., *Law, Society, and Politics in Early Maryland: Proceedings of the First Conference on Maryland History, June 14–15, 1974* (Baltimore, 1977); and Thad W. Tate and David L. Ammerman, eds., *The Chesapeake in the Seventeenth Century: Essays on Anglo-American Society* (Chapel Hill, NC, 1979). For a recent assessment of the pathbreaking nature of their work, see Bernard Bailyn, *Atlantic History: Concepts and Contours* (Cambridge, MA, 2005), 36. For examples of their innovative use of local records in examining slavery, see Russell R. Menard, "The Maryland Slave Population, 1658–1730: A Demographic Profile of Blacks in Four Counties," *William and Mary Quarterly*, 3rd ser., 32 (1975): 29–54; Gloria L. Main, "Maryland and the Chesapeake Economy," in Land, Carr, and Papenfuse, *Law, Society, and Politics*, 134–52; and Main, *Tobacco Colony: Life in Early Maryland, 1650–1720* (Princeton, NJ, 1982), chap. 3.

13. Darrett Bruce Rutman and Anita Helen Rutman, comps., Research materials concerning *A Place in Time: Middlesex County, Virginia, 1650–1750*, Mss1 R9375a, Virginia Historical Society, Richmond.

14. Breen, "A Changing Labor Force," 16–18; Morgan, "Slavery and Freedom," 24–27; Morgan, *American Slavery, American Freedom*, chap. 15; Menard, "From Servants to Slaves," 360–62; Main, "Maryland and the Chesapeake Economy," 139–41; Galenson, *White Servitude in Colonial America*, 151–54; Bean and Thomas, "Adoption of Slave Labor," 377–98.

15. David W. Galenson, "Economic Aspects of the Growth of Slavery in the Seventeenth-Century Chesapeake," in Barbara L. Solow, ed., *Slavery and the Rise of the Atlantic System* (New York, 1991), 267, 268. Robert McColley had made a similar observation about the lack of attention given to earlier decades five years before Galenson. See McColley, "Slavery in Virginia," 11.

16. Morgan, "Slavery and Freedom," 22–27; Morgan, *American Slavery, American Freedom*, 295–97; Breen, "A Changing Labor Force," 14–15; Allen, "'They Would Have De-

stroyed Me.'" Breen and, particularly, Morgan were much more subtle than Allen in their articulation of this position. Morgan, for example, allowed that declining mortality rates played an important role in prompting wealthier Virginians to begin investing in black laborers, albeit on a limited basis, from around 1660, while also contending that their substitution of slaves for servants was undertaken without "any apparent consciousness of the social stability to be gained thereby." Still, the overall arrangement of his and Breen's arguments strongly suggested that Bacon's Rebellion marked a decisive turning point in slavery's rise.

17. Menard, "From Servants to Slaves," 362–71, 389; Main, "Maryland and the Chesapeake Economy," 139–41; Main, *Tobacco Colony*, 97–106; Galenson, "White Servitude and Black Slavery," 40–41; Galenson, *White Servitude in Colonial America*, chap. 8. A version of this interpretation later put forward by Bean and Thomas differed somewhat in that they asserted that changes in the price differential between servant and slave labor, which made the latter a more attractive option by the 1680s, was the likely reason for the shift. However, they did not fully consider that the rising relative cost of servants was perhaps reflective of their declining availability in the face of continuing expansion of demand. Thus their explanation was entirely consistent with that originally outlined by Menard.

18. Vaughan, "The Origins Debate," 333–37. Morgan, for example, explicitly acknowledged that declining availability of servants possibly played a role in the shift. See *American Slavery, American Freedom*, 299.

19. Berlin, *Many Thousands Gone*, 110–26; Parent, *Foul Means*, 2, 55–79.

20. For an overview of leading families of Virginia in these decades, see Emory G. Evans, *A "Topping People": The Rise and Decline of Virginia's Old Political Elite, 1680–1790* (Charlottesville, VA, 2009), 1–22. It is worth noting that Menard, Main, and Galenson all used total estate value (TEV) to parse their inventory evidence rather than the kind of socioeconomic groupings I am suggesting here. While the method they employed demonstrated effectively the distribution of slaves among planters of differing wealth levels, their selection of an upper "cut point" of £150 elided early investments in slaves by the gentry. Main, for example, noted that before 1684 less than half of all planters worth £150 or more in York County, Virginia, owned even one slave. However, the mean average TEV of local officeholders in the county during that period was £380 with a median of £321, more than double the figure she selected, and the frequency of slave ownership was 68.4 percent. Still, their work clearly demonstrated the value of paying attention to not only economic but also geographic variation in slave distribution patterns, something that was not done in works focused solely on Virginia's transition to slavery. See Main, *Tobacco Colony*, 97–106; Galenson, "Economic Aspects," 281–87; Menard, "From Servants to Slaves," 385–88; and Menard, "Maryland Slave Population," 34–38.

21. Northumberland County, Record Book (1658–1666), 82–83; Northampton County, Wills, Deeds, Etc., no. 3 (1645–1651), ff. 77–78; Northampton County Deeds, Wills, Etc., no. 5 (1654–1655), ff. 103–4; Lower Norfolk County, Will and Deeds C (1651–1656), ff. 168–69; Virginia Probate Files. This database, at the time of writing completed up to 1700, comprises information compiled from all wills, estate appraisals, and inventories found in the surviving court records of Virginia counties established by 1730, which are available on microfilm at the Library of Virginia in Richmond. The mean average number of laborers listed in the inventories of county-level elites taken between 1640 and 1660 is 5.94, with a median of 5.50.

22. Virginia Black Headright Files; Virginia Probate Files; Lower Norfolk County, Wills and Deeds C (1651–1656), ff. 53–55; Anonymous, "A Perfect Description of Virginia (1649)," in Peter Force, ed., *Tracts and Other Papers Relating Principally to the Origin, Settlement, and Progress of the Colonies in North America from the Discovery of the Country to the Year 1776*, 4 vols. (1836–46; reprint, Gloucester, MA, 1963), 2: no. 4, 15. The raw number of elite inventories including slaves is ten of twenty-four. However, five of the inventories did not list any laborers whatsoever, and if these are eliminated from consideration, the percentage rises to 52.6 percent. By comparison, of the 241 inventories of non-elite decedents that survive for these years, only 16 (6.6 percent) listed slaves. The black headright database is compiled from a systematic examination of the seventeenth-century entries in Nell M. Nugent, *Cavaliers and Pioneers: Abstracts of Virginia Land Patents and Grants*, 3 vols. (Richmond, VA, 1977–1992), and land certificates recorded in surviving county court books. From very early in Virginia's settlement individuals could claim fifty acres of land for transporting either themselves or someone else to the colony, and until 1699 they could claim such "headrights" for any blacks so imported. For a concise explanation of headright records and some of the problems involved in using them, see Edmund S. Morgan, "Headrights and Headcounts: A Review Article," *Virginia Magazine of History and Biography* 80 (1972): 361–71.

23. Virginia Probate Files; John C. Coombs, "Building 'The Machine': The Development of Slavery and Slave Society in Early Colonial Virginia" (Ph.D. diss., College of William and Mary, 2004), 80–83, 98–99; Lancaster County, Deeds, Wills, Etc. (1652–1657), 285; Lancaster County, Orders (1655–1666), 213, 359–62; Lower Norfolk County, Wills and Deeds E (1666–1675), 81.

24. Lancaster County, Orders (1666–1680), 80, and Fiduciary Records, box 1, folder 1670–71; Northampton Record Book, no. 9 (1664–1674), ff. 14–15. In 1665, Chicheley and Carter were taxed on 109 tithables, while that same year Northampton County's officeholders paid levies for a total of 104 workers, of whom 24 were blacks. In 1669, 29 of Carter's slaves were of tithable age.

25. Of the 23 local officeholder inventories that are extant for the years 1676–80, nineteen list slaves. The mean percentage of enslaved workers was 52.4 percent, with a median percentage of 53.8 percent.

26. William Waller Hening, ed., *The Statutes at Large; Being a Collection of all the Laws of Virginia . . .* , 13 vols. (Richmond, Philadelphia, and New York, 1809–23), 2:515. Between 1635 and 1670, officeholders were credited with 67 percent of all black headrights claimed in provincial land patents and 74 percent in land certificates issued at the county level. Nearly 80 percent of the slaves listed in inventories taken over the same period also belonged to members of the gentry, while between 1664 and 1668 the commissioners of Northampton County—the only county with extant tax lists that can be analyzed for distribution trends in this period—controlled between 59 percent and 65 percent of enslaved tithables.

27. David Eltis, *The Rise of African Slavery in the Americas* (New York, 2000), 208; Eltis et al., *Voyages: The Trans-Atlantic Slave Trade Database*, http://www.slavevoyages.org (accessed October 1, 2009). According to this updated version of the Du Bois Slave Trade Database, nine Atlantic slavers delivered cargoes to the Chesapeake during the 1670s, eleven in the 1680s, and five in the 1690s. Another five arrived in the single year of 1700.

28. Virginia Black Headright Files; Virginia Probate Files; Lancaster County, Wills, Etc., no. 8 (1690–1709), ff. 21–28; Middlesex County, Will Book A (1698–1713), 113–32.

29. Virginia Probate Files.

30. Ibid.; St. Mary's City Commission Inventory Files; Lorena S. Walsh, "The Chesapeake Slave Trade: Regional Patterns, African Origins, and Some Implications," *William and Mary Quarterly*, 3rd ser., 58 (2001): 147; Jacob M. Price and Paul G. E. Clemens, "A Revolution of Scale in Overseas Trade: British Firms in the Chesapeake Trade, 1675–1775," *Journal of Economic History* 47 (1987): 6–8; Coombs, "Building 'The Machine,'" 80; K. G. Davies, *The Royal African Company* (New York, 1957), 294–95; William Fitzhugh to Ralph Wormeley, June 19, 1681, and Fitzhugh to John Withers, June 5, 1682, in Richard Beale Davis, ed., *William Fitzhugh and His Chesapeake World: The Fitzhugh Letters and Other Documents* (Chapel Hill, NC, 1963), 93, 119–20; Stafford County, Record Book (1686–1694), f. 47. For the importance of credit in the Chesapeake's transatlantic slave trade, see Jacob M. Price, "Credit in the Slave Trade and Plantation Economies," in Solow, *Slavery and the Rise of the Atlantic System*, 293–339; Lorena S. Walsh, "Mercantile Strategies, Credit Networks, and Labor Supply in the Colonial Chesapeake in Trans-Atlantic Perspective," in David Eltis, Frank L. Lewis, and Kenneth Sokoloff, eds., *Slavery in the Development of the Americas* (New York, 2004), 89–119; Coombs, "Building 'The Machine,'" 215–20.

31. Virginia Probate Files; Walsh, "The Chesapeake Slave Trade," 149; Coombs, "Building 'The Machine,'" 96–98; Douglas M. Bradburn and John C. Coombs, "Smoke and Mirrors: Reinterpreting the Society and Economy of the Seventeenth-Century Chesapeake," *Atlantic Studies* 3 (2006): 144–45. Between 1675 and 1700, 154 slave children are recorded as being brought before the courts of upper James counties to have their ages judged, of whom 38 were of African descent and 116 were Indians. Although nonofficeholders owned just 40 percent of the black children presented, they owned 86 percent of the natives, suggesting that the trade in Indian slaves was largely directed toward ordinary planters. Extrapolations from surviving Charles City records to account for missing order books indicate that a total of 190 Indian children were brought into the upper James commercial zone over the last quarter of the seventeenth century, while the adult-to-child ratio among enslaved natives listed in extant inventories is .25. Taken together, these figures yield a rough estimate of 240 Indian slaves imported into the upper James zone during these years, a number just under the mean average shipment size (250.20) of contemporary slave cargoes arriving in Virginia via the transatlantic trade.

32. Virginia Probate Files; Walsh, "Summing the Parts," 59; Bradburn and Coombs, "Smoke and Mirrors," 139–43. Rather than use Walsh's term "periphery" to describe this area, a term that emphasizes its marginal connection to the transatlantic tobacco trade (the subject of her article), I have adopted the more neutral label "provisioning subregion" to reflect its emergence in the late seventeenth century as an increasingly divergent economic area with a different system of labor organization than what prevailed in those parts of the colony that remained committed to the regional staple.

33. Heywood and Thornton, *Central Africans, Atlantic Creoles*, chap. 1; Hatfield, *Atlantic Virginia*, 140; P. E. H. Hair and Robin Law, "The English in Western Africa to 1700," in Nicholas Canny, ed., *The Origins of Empire: British Overseas Enterprise to the Close of the Seventeenth Century*, vol. 1 of William Roger Louis, ed., *The Oxford History of the British Empire* (New York, 1998), 249–55; Robert Brenner, *Merchants and Revolution: Commercial Change, Political Conflict, and London's Overseas Traders, 1550–1653* (New York, 1993), chap. 4.

34. Vaughan, "The Origins Debate," 316–33, 339–41; Deal, *Race and Class*, x–xii; Mor-

gan, *American Slavery, American Freedom*, 154–57; Ira Berlin, "Time, Space, and the Evolution of Afro-American Society on British Mainland North America," *American Historical Review* 85 (1980): 67–71.

35. Berlin, *Many Thousands Gone*, 17–46, 95–108; Berlin, "From Creole to African: Atlantic Creoles and the Origins of African-American Society in Mainland North America," *William and Mary Quarterly*, 3rd ser., 53 (1996): 276–79. For criticism of Berlin's treatment of the experiences of slaves shipped directly from Africa in the early seventeenth century, see Robin Law and Kristin Mann, "West Africa in the Atlantic Community: The Case of the Slave Coast," *William and Mary Quarterly*, 3rd ser., 56 (1999): 307–34, esp. 310; and James H. Sweet, "African Identity and Slave Resistance in the Portuguese Atlantic," in Peter C. Mancall, ed., *The Atlantic World and Virginia, 1550–1624* (Chapel Hill, NC, 2007), 225–47.

36. Heywood and Thornton, *Central Africans, Atlantic Creoles*, 25–33, 242–48, 312–23, 327. For a similar interpretation, see Tim Hashaw, *The Birth of Black America: The First African Americans and the Pursuit of Freedom at Jamestown* (New York, 2007). Though they never discuss it explicitly, Heywood and Thornton redefine Berlin's concepts of "Atlantic creoles" and "charter generation" along geographic lines by applying them to slaves and free blacks of West Central African origin exclusively. Similarly, they apply Berlin's term "plantation generation" solely to West Africans, regardless of when they arrived.

37. Heywood and Thornton, *Central Africans, Atlantic Creoles*, 246. All but three of the specific examples Berlin put forward in his chapter on the Chesapeake's "charter generation" in *Many Thousands Gone* were drawn from Accomack and Northampton.

38. Virginia Free Black Files; Virginia Tithable Files. The first database includes every person of color recorded as being manumitted or otherwise free in the extant records of Virginia's counties and provincial government through 1730, and at the time of writing is complete up to 1700. The second database is a spreadsheet version of the various detailed tax lists that survive for Accomack, Northampton, Lancaster, and Surry Counties.

39. Virginia Probate Files; Virginia Slave Conveyance Files. The latter database, which at present is also completed up to 1700, includes information compiled from all deeds of sale, gift, trust, security, and jointure that transferred property rights in slaves from one owner to another, as well as entries in order books mentioning such transactions, found in the same records noted above.

40. Morgan, *American Slavery, American Freedom*, 430–32; Breen and Innes, *"Myne Own Ground,"* 68–69.

41. Surry County, Deeds, Wills, Etc., no. 2 (1671–1684), 148; Surry County, Deeds, Wills, Etc., no. 1 (1652–1672), 349, 374; Nugent, *Cavaliers and Pioneers*, 1:204; Lancaster County, Deeds, Etc., no. 1 (1652–1657), 45, 118, 324. Pedro might have been included among the several tithables attributed to Evan Davis, with whom he had several business dealings. The absence of black householders in the Lancaster lists is particularly notable, since foreigners such as "Epo the Dutchman" and "Richard the Irishman" are occasionally singled out. See Lancaster County, Deeds, Etc., no. 1 (1652–1657), 90, and Orders, Etc. (1655–1666), 102, 132, 163. See also a payment out of the 1673 levy to "Capt. John, an Indian" in Lancaster County, Orders, no. 1 (1666–1680), 275.

42. Breen and Innes, *"Myne Owne Ground,"* 5; Virginia Probate Files. One of the two blacks with limited terms, a three-year-old "Negro Boye" belonging to Capt. Argoll Yeardley of Northampton, was probably a manumitted slave, considering his age and that "by

witnesse of his godfathers" he was to be free at age twenty-four and receive two cows. See Northampton County, Deeds, Wills, Etc., no. 5 (1654–1655 [1656]), f. 119. For the instances of blacks alleging unlawful detention in service, see (John Baptist) Lower Norfolk County, Wills and Deeds C (1651–1656), ff. 8, 68, 71, 75; (Degoe) Lancaster County, Orders, Etc. (1655–1666), 369, and Lancaster County, Deeds, Etc., no. 2 (1654–1702), 337; (John Keratan) Charles City County, Deeds, Wills, Orders, Etc. (1655–1665), 604–5, 617–18, and Warren M. Billings, ed., *The Papers of Sir William Berkeley, 1605–1677* (Richmond, 2007), 264; (Casor) Northampton County, Deeds, Wills, Etc. (1651–1654), f. 226, and Northampton County, Deeds, Wills, Etc. nos. 7, 8 (1655 [1654]–1668), f. 10; (Philip Gowen) H. R. McIlwaine, ed., *Minutes of the Council and General Court of Colonial Virginia*, 2nd ed. (Richmond, 1979), 411, and Billings, *Berkeley Papers*, 473–74; (Edward Mozingo) McIlwaine, *Minutes of the Council*, 316. The seventh case, involving Elizabeth Key is discussed below. The disparate character of slavery on the Eastern Shore has also been noted by April Hatfield. See *Atlantic Virginia*, 164–67.

43. Virginia Probate Files; York County, Deeds, Orders, Wills, Etc., no. 3 (1657–1662), f. 108; Northampton County, Deeds, Wills, Etc., no. 5 (1654–1655 [1656]), f. 110. There were eleven boys and nine girls among the children whose sex was identified, for a ratio of 1.22. According to the Voyages transatlantic slave trade dataset, the overall sex ratio of boys to girls disembarked in the English colonies during these years was 1.72. See Eltis et al., *Slave Trade Database*. Three of the children were mentioned explicitly as belonging to resident mothers and were thus undoubtedly native born.

44. Virginia Probate Files; Virginia Slave Conveyance Files; York County, Deeds, Orders, Wills, Etc., no. 1 (1633–1694), 132; Lancaster County, Deeds, Etc., no. 2 (1654–1702), 46–49. I am agreeing here with Thomas Morris's argument about the importance of English common law of property to the legal establishment of slave ownership rights in Virginia, but I also believe that the application of these precedents to "human property" required the kind of subtle, conservative adjustment to existing practice described by John Pagan. See Morris, *Southern Slavery and the Law, 1619–1860* (Chapel Hill, NC, 1996), 38–46; and John R. Pagan, *Anne Orthwood's Bastard: Sex and Law in Early Virginia* (New York, 2003), esp. chap. 5. The precise numbers of conveyances referencing future children or "increase" are 18 of 31 deeds and 5 of 12 wills, for an overall total of 53 percent. The analysis was limited to documents mentioning female slaves, because those are obviously the only instances where the status of future progeny was in question, and excludes deeds of security, since the transfer of property rights was contingent rather than final.

45. Virginia Free Black Files.

46. Northampton County, Record Book, no. 9 (1664–1674), ff. 54–55. Of the remaining six free blacks in the 1668 Northampton tax list, two had belonged to masters who had removed from the colony and left them behind to work their holdings, one was the daughter of a black already freed, and the backgrounds of the remaining three are unknown.

47. Virginia Probate Files; Isle of Wight County, Wills, Deeds, Etc., no. 2 (1661–1719), 85. If the Eastern Shore is included, the figure changes to 10 of 79 wills including manumission clauses, freeing 19 of 267 slaves. The phrase "reluctant master" is taken from a chapter in Deal's study detailing the life stories of slaves belonging to Charleton and Vaughan, many of whom were manumitted. See *Race and Class*, 251–64.

48. Most of the documents generated by this case are transcribed in Warren M. Billings, *The Old Dominion in the Seventeenth Century: A Documentary History of Virginia, 1606–1689* (Chapel Hill, NC, 1975), 165–69. See also Billings, "The Cases of Fernando and

Elizabeth Key: A Note on the Status of Blacks in Seventeenth-Century Virginia," *William and Mary Quarterly*, 3rd ser., 30 (1973): 467–74. The original documents can be found in Northumberland County, Record Book (1652–58), ff. 66–67, 85, 115–21; Northumberland County, Record Book (1658–1666), f. 28; Northumberland County, Order Book (1652–1665), ff. 40, 49; and McIlwaine, *Minutes of the Council*, 504. For an explanation of the judicial role played by the General Assembly, see Warren M. Billings, *A Little Parliament: The Virginia General Assembly in the Seventeenth Century* (Richmond, 2004), 19, 55–58.

49. Notably, a census taken of the colony's inhabitants in early 1620 lists thirty-two "Negros in the service of sev[era]ll planters" under the heading "Others not Christians in the Service of the English," suggesting that even the earliest African immigrants who had been exposed to Catholic missionaries in Portuguese Angola were not recognized as Christians by their Virginia masters. See William Thorndale, "The Virginia Census of 1619," *Magazine of Virginia Genealogy* 33 (1995): 155–77; and Martha McCartney, "An Early Census Reprised," *Quarterly Bulletin of the Archaeological Society of Virginia* 54 (1999): 178–96.

50. Coombs, "Building 'The Machine,'" 142–45, 149–53; Billings, "The Cases of Fernando and Elizabeth Key," 468n5; Billings, *A Little Parliament*, 149. Of the twenty-three slaves recorded as bringing freedom petitions in the surviving seventeenth-century order and deed books of the county courts, the level of jurisdiction where most cases were initially contested, only three (including Key) cited baptism as grounds for their release. Moreover, all three claimants had extenuating circumstances in their backgrounds that make ascertaining the precise role of religion in the outcome of their cases impossible to determine conclusively.

51. Hening, *Statutes at Large*, 2:170, 260, 270, 299–300. For more detailed analyses of these laws, see Billings, "The Law of Servants and Slaves"; Morris, *Southern Slavery and the Law*, 42–45; Coombs, "Building 'The Machine,'" chap. 5.

52. Morgan, *American Slavery, American Freedom*, 312.

53. Elizabeth Donnan, ed., *Documents Illustrative of the History of the Slave Trade to North America*, 4 vols. (Washington, DC, 1930–35), 4:88–89; Breen, "A Changing Labor Force," 6–7, 16–17; Berlin, "Afro-American Society," 68, 71. Berlin consistently reiterated his argument that before 1670 most of the slaves imported into Virginia were "Atlantic creoles" who had spent considerable time in the West Indies, citing Jennings's letter as evidence. See Berlin, "From Creole to African," 276n60; and Berlin, *Many Thousands Gone*, 39. Although Breen acknowledged that there was no way of knowing how long blacks shipped from the West Indies had been in the Americas, to bolster his point about the cultural experience of Virginia's early black immigrants he speculated that "it is doubtful Virginia planters would have invested what little capital they possessed in expensive 'unseasoned' laborers who could easily die after a single summer in the tobacco fields." He did not, however, provide any evidence to support this contention, nor did he offer any explanation as to why this attitude changed once direct shipments became more available. See also Breen and Innes, *"Myne Own Ground,"* 70–71.

54. W. Noel Sainsbury, ed., *Calendar of State Papers, Colonial Series, America and the West Indies*, 40 vols. (London, 1860–; reprint, 1964), 23:718–19; Donnan, *Documents of the Slave Trade*, 4:88. See also William A. Pettigrew, "Free to Enslave: Politics and the Escalation of Britain's Transatlantic Slave Trade, 1688–1714," *William and Mary Quarterly*, 3rd ser., 64 (2007): 3–38.

55. Philip D. Curtin, *The Atlantic Slave Trade: A Census* (Madison, WI, 1969), 143; Her-

bert S. Klein, "Slaves and Shipping in Eighteenth-Century Virginia," *Journal of Interdisciplinary History* 5 (1975): 384–85; Allan Kulikoff, "A 'Prolifick' People: Black Population Growth in the Chesapeake Colonies, 1700–1790," *Southern Studies* 16 (1977): 392n5; Susan Westbury, "Slaves of Colonial Virginia: Where They Came From," *William and Mary Quarterly*, 3rd ser., 42 (1985): 231–32; Westbury, "Analyzing a Regional Slave Trade: The West Indies and Virginia, 1698–1775," *Slavery and Abolition* 7 (1986): 241. For a proposed solution very similar to Kulikoff's, see Menard, "From Servants to Slaves," 369n25.

56. Colonial Office 33/15, Virginia Colonial Records Project microfilm reel no. 472, Library of Virginia, Richmond; Walter Minchinton, Celia King, and Peter Waite, eds., *Virginia Slave-Trade Statistics, 1698–1775* (Richmond, 1984), 25.

57. John C. Coombs, "Seventeenth-Century Chesapeake–West Indian Commerce and the Coastwise Trade in Slaves" (working paper, Harvard University International Seminar on the History of the Atlantic World, Cambridge, MA), 9–10.

58. William Byrd to Thomas Grendon, June 12, 1684, and Byrd to [Perry and Lane?], March 29, 1685, in Marion Tinling, ed., *The Correspondence of the Three William Byrds of Westover, Virginia, 1684–1676*, 2 vols. (Charlottesville, VA, 1977), 1: 22–23, 30–31; Henrico County, Order Book (1678–1693), 163.

59. Donnan, *Documents of the Slave Trade*, 4:21–22; Coombs, "Coastwise Trade in Slaves," 4–5, 11–12.

60. Morgan, *Slave Counterpoint*, 61; Walsh, "The Chesapeake Slave Trade," 144n15; US Bureau of the Census, *Historical Statistics of the United States: Colonial Times to 1970* (Washington, DC, 1975), 1168. The revised Millennial edition of this work raises the estimate of the Chesapeake's black population in 1700 to 19,617 for the region as a whole and 16,390 for Virginia alone. See Susan B. Carter et al., eds., *Historical Statistics of the United States: Earliest Times to the Present* (New York, 2006), table Eg1-59.

61. Galenson, *White Servitude in Colonial America*, 212–17; Eltis, *The Rise of African Slavery in the Americas*, 208. For a more conservative estimate of the coastwise slave trade between the West Indies and Virginia, see Gregory E. O'Malley, "Beyond the Middle Passage: Slave Migration from the Caribbean to North America, 1619–1807," *William and Mary Quarterly*, 3rd ser., 66 (2009): 138–41.

62. Heywood and Thornton, *Central Africans, Atlantic Creoles*, chaps. 2 and 4; Coombs, "Building 'The Machine,'" chap. 4. The two Barbadian deeds that mention slave shipments to Virginia were found during a complete search of deed books covering the period between 1640 and 1700. They are RB3/17/381 and RB3/12/82–84, Recopied Deed Books, Barbados Archives, St. Michael, Barbados. See also O'Malley, "Beyond the Middle Passage," 135–37.

63. Craven, *White, Red, and Black*, 76.

Transatlantic Politics and the Africanization of Virginia's Labor Force, 1688–1712

WILLIAM A. PETTIGREW

In the early eighteenth century, a visit to London offered many opportunities for a Virginia gentleman. He could seek employment within the colonial administration, or promotion if he had already secured a position, or he could undermine rival office seekers. He could also make arrangements for receiving slave shipments to stock his tobacco plantations at home in the colony. In a 1711 letter dispatched from London to Virginian Philip Ludwell, the Reverend Stephen Fouace described how Ludwell's father, also named Philip, was "very earnest for getting you the business of negro consignments tho' he is afraid that will prevent and hinder the satisfaction of seing you in England."[1] As a prominent Virginian who recently had retired to the mother country, the elder Ludwell was well positioned to assist his son by soliciting shipments from the numerous slave traders located in the capital. Failing that, it seems, Philip junior would have crossed the Atlantic to procure such deliveries himself. Rather than attend a slave auction in Virginia, some affluent Virginians preferred to preorder their slaves with London merchants on the Royal Exchange. Yet Fouace's letter does more than illustrate the convenience of having good commercial contacts. It demonstrates the artificial nature of distinctions that historians' of the slave trade typically draw between the trade's demand and supply sides and that historians of the British Atlantic empire make between the colonies and the metropolis.[2] In the scenario Fouace describes, planter and merchant, demand and supply, colony and metropolis all converge within an integrated familial network. This convergence encapsulates an Atlantic moment that altered how the British Empire functioned at the turn of the eighteenth century, a moment that played a critical part in Africanizing the labor force of early modern Virginia.

Ambiguity and dearth of evidence, as well as the contemporary focus on racial discrimination, have made the "origins debate" about American slavery one of the most keenly fought and widely contested controversies in colonial American history.[3] The debate, which, it must be stressed, has generated some superb scholarship, divides into two overlapping disputes: the wrongly posed, circular question about whether slavery predated racism (or vice versa) and, second, the debate about why African slaves replaced white servants as the predominant labor force in the Chesapeake. This essay is concerned with the second dispute. I argue that two errors of interpretation have clouded our understanding of this critical turning point in Virginia's history. First, slavery has traditionally been an American subject, its students neglecting the importance of a transatlantic field of view. Most colonial American historians have dwelt excessively on the demand side of the trade and thus reified the distinction between an institution of slavery and a process of slave trading. They have also privileged legal turning points or local events such as Bacon's Rebellion when attempting to explain the shift from servants to slaves, neglecting to observe that the transition occurred concurrently across the mainland colonies and was therefore conditioned by transatlantic developments.[4]

Second, slavery, it was assumed, originated spontaneously without public coordination. While economic historians such as Russell Menard and David Galenson concentrated on the slave trade and the timing of the transition from white servant to African slave and necessarily sustained an Atlantic field of view, they could only partly explain the transition because they viewed the decision to purchase slaves as a series of individual and uncoordinated calculations. They dismissed any notion of planning, any sense of organization, and any role for public bodies.[5] This misconception has also permeated cultural accounts of the development of slavery. According to Winthrop Jordan, American slavery was the result of an "unthinking decision."[6] David Brion Davis agreed: "The Africanisation of large parts of the New World was the result not of concerted planning, racial destiny, or immanent historical design but of innumerable local and pragmatic choices made in four continents."[7] The existing literature neglects to consider the importance of transatlantic political changes when explaining the development of slavery in Virginia.[8] The present essay describes the thoughtful deliberations that informed a coordinated, public campaign to develop the transatlantic slave trade and American slavery.

During the seventeenth century, the Chesapeake colonies had been supplied with slaves, somewhat precariously, through intercolonial commerce with English possessions in the Caribbean. But as Galenson acknowledged, slaves did not begin to arrive directly from Africa in large numbers on a consistent basis until the ending of the Royal African Company's monopoly over the transatlantic slave trade.[9] Between 1690 and 1712, a group of politically active Atlantic merchants lobbied Parliament to end the company's monopoly. The demise of the Royal African Company's control of the English Atlantic slave trade profoundly altered the trade's dimensions. Although the company had never been able to fully enforce its monopoly, the company's demise increased the number of Africans transported, which Africans were enslaved, where they went, and who transported them. The opening up of the slave trade increased the trade's long-term capacity by at least 164 percent. In 1686, during James II's reign, when the Royal African Company's monopoly came closest to being enforceable, English slavers embarked upon thirty-nine voyages. By 1729, the open trade in slaves allowed slavers to conduct 111 voyages. During this period, the company's market share (of the legal trade) fell from 100 percent to 4 percent. This expansion in turn hastened the development of Jamaica; accelerated the slave-trading operations of provincial seaports, especially in Bristol and Liverpool; and offered a green light for merchants in the colonies to enter the slave trade. The shift to a free trade model saw the Gold Coast, popular with the mainland American planters, supplant the Bight of Benin as the most popular supplier of African slave labor.[10] Most important for our purposes, a free trade in slaves also provided the mainland American colonies with an adequate supply of slaves for the first time. The mainland colonies in particular benefited from the company's demise. In the fifteen years prior to the 1698 act, slavers transported close to five and a half thousand slaves to the American mainland. In the fifteen years after, that figure increased by nearly 300 percent to over fifteen thousand.[11] Virginian interests were at the heart of the political campaign that secured a free trade in slaves.[12]

The Royal African Company's monopoly power decreased in three stages. First, in 1688, James II's flight from England deprived the company of its governor and its best means of enforcing its monopoly. Second, in 1698, after public debates throughout the 1690s, Parliament opened the slave trade to all English subjects for thirteen years on payment of a 10 percent duty on imports and exports. Independent slave traders, formerly illegal interlopers on the company's monopoly, became known as "separate traders." During this decade-long debate over the company's monopoly position,

Chesapeake interests petitioned Parliament twice in 1696 and twice again in 1698, with Virginians taking the leading role and Virginian expatriates also representing the region's tobacco planters before the House of Lords. Third, the separate traders, including numerous suppliers of Virginia, prevented the company from gaining parliamentary recognition for its monopoly when the 1698 act expired in 1712, opening up the slave trade to all.[13]

Two related transatlantic political developments aided the Africanization of Virginia's labor force. The first was the emergence of modern political culture and institutions in England,[14] which benefited the company's opponents, and the second was a changing balance of power in Britain's Atlantic empire that allowed Atlantic interest groups, including Virginians, access to that culture and those institutions.[15] After 1688, Parliament became the undisputed arbiter of macroeconomic and, increasingly, colonial concerns. Parliament became more responsive to interest groups like the separate traders, who then played a decisive role in expanding the number of slave shipments sent from Africa directly to Virginia. The separate traders' success as an interest group also reflected a devolution of imperial initiative to colonists, including Virginians, who by the end of the seventeenth century asserted themselves politically within the metropolis to the detriment of the African company.

Prior to these political changes, Virginia had been undersupplied with African slave labor. The first African slaves arrived in Virginia in 1619, and English and Dutch privateers intermittently continued to bring slaves through the 1640s. The Navigation Acts began to force the Dutch out of the Virginian trade after 1650, and independent English slavers began to sporadically supply slaves to the Old Dominion. The majority of the English slave trade dispatched slaves to English holdings in the Caribbean, especially Barbados, and accordingly most slaves arrived in Virginia after first experiencing the slave auctions of the Caribbean. In 1660, when the black slave population of the mainland numbered approximately one thousand five hundred souls, Charles II instituted the Company of Royal Adventurers trading to Africa, a state-sponsored joint-stock company with a monopoly over all English trade with the African continent. This organization, reorganized and renamed the Royal African Company in 1672, did not prioritize the mainland as a market for its slaves and did not maintain an agent in Virginia until the late 1680s. Consequently, while some prominent Virginians were able to arrange for consignments of African slaves from the company through their English commercial contacts, the mainland consistently remained undersupplied.[16]

The Royal African Company's position dramatically deteriorated after 1688. An emerging judicial intolerance of monopolies that derived from the royal prerogative targeted the company. In *Nightingale and Others v. Bridges* the plaintiff argued that the Royal African Company's seizure of the cargo of an interloping ship was unlawful because the company's power to enforce its monopoly derived from the prerogative and had been executed through admiralty courts.[17] The company allowed the court's decision to go against it by default and paid damages to the plaintiff. The African Company sent instructions to its colonial agents not to seize or detain interlopers, which reinforced the court's acknowledgment of the potency of the claim against the company in *Nightingale and Others v. Bridges*.[18] Depriving the company of the means to enforce its monopoly appeared to some like an official endorsement of independent slave trading. Interloping slave voyages increased dramatically as a result, despite the onset of the Nine Years' War. The total volume of the English slave trade increased from 1,556 slaves in 1690 to 8,336 in 1692.

With its monopoly undermined in court, the African Company appealed to Parliament for statutory support. It quickly sustained a barrage of interloper attacks. Although mainland American interests did not intervene as early as representatives of the domestic woolen industry and the colonial sugar trade, interest groups representing the Chesapeake colonies came to act at the center of political opposition to the company. Tobacco planters were one of only two colonial petitioning interests with a 100 percent record of opposition to the Royal African Company's monopoly.[19]

The Royal African Company's opponents in Parliament dwelt on the company's failure as a supplier of slaves to the Chesapeake colonies.[20] In the 1690s, the consequences of the company's failure to supply the American mainland with African slave labor became more acute. The Nine Years' War had increased freight rates but had also decreased the supply of indentured labor as the English navy enlarged the scale of its impressments, intensifying Virginia's demand for slave labor. The company persisted, however, in ignoring Virginian demand for slaves. As late as January 1696, the company informed its frustrated agent William Sherwood that it had "no interest in your parts but may do if peace is secured and would, in the meantime like to know of any information regarding demand for slaves in Virginia."[21]

On February, 28, 1696, joint Virginia and Maryland interests first petitioned Parliament against the company under the guise of the "merchants and planters trading to and interested in the plantations of Virginia and Maryland." Their petition appealed to colonial and domestic sentiment by arguing that the said plantations are capable of greater improvements; but want for people to carry on the increase of planting tobacco; and, if they were sufficiently supplied with Negroes, they would produce twice the quantity they now do; which would not only employ more of our shipping, but increase the customs, and render tobacco cheaper, and enable us to furnish the Dutch, and other nations, at cheaper rates than they now make it; whereby, their planting tobacco would be wholly discouraged.

The petition went on to describe the fiscal benefits of an open slave trade, asserting that "one negro will make as much tobacco in a year as must pay 30 or 40£ custom in England." The petition stressed the company's refusal to supply the mainland, insisting that "the African Company have been so far from supplying those plantations, that they have seized all those ships that offered to supply them" and advocated "that the trade for Negroes from Acra to Angola may be left free and open to all the subjects of this Kingdom."[22] These arguments seem to have been compelling, since at the end of the 1696 session the House proposed to sustain the joint-stock company but liberate the slave trade in the areas that the Chesapeake petition stipulated. The session, however, ended without further progress.

It is unclear why the Chesapeake interests intervened in the Africa trade debates later than other colonial lobbies such as the Barbadian and Jamaican sugar interests. It is possible that tobacco interests felt obliged to act by a company proposal in 1698 to open up its southern slave trading areas between Cape Mount and the Cape of Good Hope to independent trade on payment of a 15 percent levy. Chesapeake planters preferred slaves from the northern sections of the company's jurisdiction that the company wished to retain.[23] Tobacco traders quickly pointed out that this disadvantaged the mainland, and MPs dropped the proposal. Some colonial interests also felt uncertain about enlarging the enslaved African population because they feared the potential consequences of a black majority. Both the island and mainland colonies had sizable numbers of African slaves, but the sugar plantations had been better supplied, and by the 1680s and 1690s (and especially during wartime) they sought to manage the ratio of white to black, fearful that a black majority encouraged slave rebellion.[24] In response to this threat, colonial legislatures conceived increasingly brutal punishments for slaves to reassure planters that the black population could be controlled. By the later years of the seventeenth century, a number of severe statutory measures had been adopted in Virginia. A 1669 law, for example, protected masters from felony prosecution for the casual killing of slaves.[25] Colonial interests began to oppose the company's monopoly to improve the supply of African slaves in tandem with the enactment of colonial legislation that had mitigated fears about black majorities.

The timing of the Virginia and Maryland intervention may have been crucial to the achievement of legislation that liberalized the slave trade. The Africa trade discussion that Chesapeake interests initiated in the 1696 session ultimately produced the 1698 Africa Trade Act, which liberated the trade on payment of a 10 percent duty on exports and imports. Another petition from the Chesapeake interest that appeared in the Commons in February 1698 reiterated that the company had undersupplied the mainland colonies with slaves and requested a hearing at the bar of the House of Commons.[26] By May, William Norris, MP for Liverpool and a sympathizer with the Chesapeake tobacco interest, began to chair the Africa trade select committee, and interests oppositional to the company but supportive of its bill petitioned the Lords.[27] When a bill eventually reached the House of Lords, Chesapeake interests were the first to offer a petition, this time as the "Planters of Virginia and Maryland and the merchants trading thereunto" rather than the mercantile-led interest that had petitioned the Commons. Instead of proposing an argument in favor of open trade, it requested that its signatories be heard against the proposed bill in person.[28]

Because this petition to the Lords survives, it is possible to gain an insight into the Virginia planting and merchant interest that opposed the company in the spring of 1698. The petition has eighteen signatories in the following order: Edward Carleton, Edward Chilton, Benjamin Harrison Jr., Fred Jones, Isaac Milner, John Corbin, Henry Hartwell, Benjamin Brain, Thomas Cary, John Munday, Christopher Morgan, Charles Ridgley, John Cary, Thomas Taylor, John Sail, Thomas Corbin, Micajah Perry, and Nathaniel Rous. Eleven of these signatories (Brain, Carleton, both Carys, Thomas Corbin, Milner, Morgan, Munday, Perry, Sail, and Taylor) were tobacco merchants, and with the exception of John Cary (who resided in Bristol) all operated from London. Carleton was a Maryland merchant, while the rest traded predominantly with Virginia. Four of the signatories (John Corbin, Jones, Harrison, and Hartwell) were permanent residents of Virginia, with the latter two members of the colony's Council of State. Edward Chilton was not a permanent resident but lived in Virginia from 1682 to 1694, serving as attorney general of the colony, and on his return to England, policy makers viewed him as an expert on Virginian affairs.[29] So the group, apart from its first signatory, primarily maintained Virginian interests. Five (Carleton, Milner, Munday, Perry, and Rous) also traded in slaves. Only Perry and Thomas Corbin had a business relationship with the Royal African Company, documented by bills of exchange in their name covering payment to the company for contracted slaves. The Chesapeake lobby at this time, then, was first and foremost a Virginian interest combining London tobacco merchants with a handful of influential Virginia expatriates and resident planters.[30]

Four of the petitioners are conspicuous because of their fame in other areas. Thomas Cary became governor of North Carolina, while John Cary authored the famous tract *An Essay on Trade,* in which he advocated an open slave trade. He described the African trade as being "of the most advantage to this Kingdom of any we drive," and went on to argue that "to advise a Government to monopolize, and consequently to lessen this Trade, by confining it to a limited Stock, is the same as to advise the People of Egypt to raise high banks to confine the river Nilus from overflowing, lest it should thereby fertilise their lands."[31] Similarly conspicuous in the list is Micajah Perry, the lynchpin of the British Atlantic tobacco business, prominent financier of the slave trade, and himself a separate trader in 1704 and 1705. Isaac Milner originated from Whitehaven from a nonconformist family. He was also a considerable tobacco merchant with significant influence in the Chesapeake. When he was not shipping slaves himself, many of the Virginia planters purchased slaves with bills on his account.[32]

Although domiciled in Virginia, Henry Hartwell, Benjamin Harrison, and Edward Chilton were, at the time of signing the petition, in London on official business in the imperial capital. They were members of Commissary James Blair's delegation to London to secure the dismissal of Virginia's then governor, Sir Edmund Andros. They were also active in soliciting officials in London to support the proposed College of William and Mary. Benjamin Harrison also sought promotion for himself, securing, on this trip, the position of attorney general of Virginia. Both Chilton and Hartwell coauthored *The Present State of Virginia, and the College* with Blair at around this time. This tract represented a critique of what Blair, Chilton, and Hartwell believed to be an overconcentration of power in the office of royal governor in Virginia. They also sought, in writing this pamphlet, to convince the Board of Trade to encourage the formation of towns and a more mercantile economy in the Old Dominion.[33]

Blair, Chilton, and Hartwell were proponents of reform in Virginia, reform that included the Africanization of the Virginia labor force. To them, the escalation of the slave trade formed a part of a movement to improve the colony. This movement also sought to improve the colony's constitution and its economy. Developing the slave trade was a cause lumped together with progress and a more liberal, decentralized political system and a more diversified and vibrant economy. During a trip to London, Stephen Fouace combined the pursuit of some of James Blair's political designs with the arrangement of slave consignments, assuring Ludwell's son, "I will not fail to do you what service I can in ye business of neg[ro] ships you recommend to me."³⁴ Philip Ludwell Sr. supported Blair's opposition to Governor Francis Nicholson in London and also busied himself with arranging slave consignments for his son's plantation.³⁵ Ludwell was married to the sister of Blair's wife, Sarah, who was herself the sister of Benjamin Harrison Jr. Gawin Corbin, the company's agent at this time remained a stalwart supporter of Governor Nicholson.³⁶ The association between Blair's opponents and the African Company buttresses the connection between political reform and slave trade escalation in Virginia at the turn of the eighteenth century.

Benjamin Harrison Jr. later appeared in person before the Lords' select committee charged with examining the African trade in the summer of 1698. He appeared alongside Peter Paggen, another prominent tobacco merchant in London, Barbadian John Gardner, the leader of the cause for open trade, and Melisha Holder, also a Barbadian sugar merchant.³⁷ Paggen, born in 1651, was a Huguenot immigrant from the Low Countries who began his trading career as a ship captain in the Chesapeake tobacco trade. He soon became one of the most considerable London tobacco merchants of his day. In addition to a vast trade in Chesapeake tobacco, Paggen was a specialist in human cargoes, transporting soldiers during the War of the Spanish Succession, as well as African slaves.³⁸ Isaac Milner, a signer of the Chesapeake interest's 1698 petition to the Commons, had served as Paggen's apprentice in Atlantic trade.³⁹ Harrison, Paggen, Gardner, and Holder succeeded in extracting assurances from the company that independent slave traders would have full access to the company's forts in case they should need to seek shelter. That such a disparate group of Atlantic traders operated together is significant and confirms the importance of Atlantic trade in general as a potent oppositional force to monopoly. The centrality of Chesapeake interests to the antimonopoly campaign also confirms the effect that the 1698 act had in opening up the supply of slaves to mainland America.

In pursuing their cause, the separate traders cultivated and submitted more petitions from a broader constituency and with larger numbers of signatories than the company. The Virginia political interest and the Virginia slave trade had been critical to this effort. The 1698 act produced an explosion in slave-trading activity, with the mainland affected most dramatically because of the numbers of separate traders dispatching slave cargoes to the tobacco colonies. According to Governor Nicholson, in October 1700 the colony had "as many buyers as Negroes, and I think that, if 2000 were imported, there would be substantial buyers for them. They expect several ships from Guiny with Negroes, but I am afraid that no more will come."[40] The best evidence of this trading explosion is the Virginia government's imposition of a duty on slave imports to help finance the construction of the capitol building in Williamsburg.[41]

By 1701, the African Company responded to Chesapeake petitions complaining that the company had refused to supply Virginia and Maryland with slaves. The company ordered the redirection of a Jamaica-bound slaver to Virginia, instructing the vessel's captain that "since your departure wee have considered which may be the best market for the sale of your Negroes, and are of opinion that they will sell much better at Virginia than at Jamaica where wee first intended."[42] In June 1703, the Angola frigate delivered ninety-two Angolan slaves to company agent Henry Fielding on the York River, which marked the beginning of a new spurt of company activity in Virginia. The poor credit of the colony also affected the company. The bills of exchange that Gawin Corbin, the company's other Virginia agent, collected as payment for slaves delivered were, more and more, disputed by merchants in London.[43] Despite the company's burgeoning interest in the Chesapeake, however, it was soundly beaten by the separate traders in the competition to supply the mainland's thirst for enslaved African labor. From 1699 to 1712, English slavers mounted eighty voyages to the American mainland. The African Company managed only seven of these.

Financially crippled by the success of the separate traders' slave trading, by 1707 the company had no choice but to again appeal to Queen Anne to have its monopoly reinstated. The queen passed the company's petition to the reformed Board of Trade and Plantations, which began to umpire the dispute between the company and the separate traders. But the Board of Trade no longer benefited from the access to executive decision making enjoyed by its Restoration predecessor, the Lords of Trade and Plantations. After 1696, the reformed board was instead an information gatherer and a modest governmental attempt to maintain some sense of how the unregulated western British Atlantic economy operated after all attempts to establish American monopoly companies had failed. Because colonists represented the best sources for information about the empire, they enjoyed considerable influence with the board and could engineer the board's consistent opposition to the company.

The first preliminary inquiry that the board made in response to the Royal African Company's petition to the queen in 1707 shows clearly to what extent courting colonial opinion encouraged a predisposition toward the company's opponents. In November 1707, after discussing an act relating to the gauge of tobacco hogsheads, the board's commissioners asked tobacco merchants Micajah Perry and Isaac Milner for their opinion of how the slave trade should be continued. Perry and Milner replied "that the separate traders ... furnished ... above 800 negroes annually, since the passing the late Act, and ... the company had sent none to Virginia and Maryland since, nor seaven years before." They added that "the separate traders ... paid to the company ... more by the ten percent than the ... company have laid ... upon their forts ... [and they] have received all the discouragement imaginable from the company's factors there."[44] Although the board's commissioners scrutinized such testimony, this exchange provides an excellent example of the board's reliance on noncompany opinion. Like many other merchants to Virginia, both Perry and Milner also operated as separate traders.[45] Such men answered the board's call for colonial expertise with opinion grounded both politically and commercially in personal interest.

Who were these independent merchants who began to take an interest in the slave trade to the mainland after the liberalization of 1698? Out of over a thousand named independent slave traders (of which about half can be identified according to their other trading interests), fifty-five independent slave traders specializing in the Chesapeake market can be identified during the term of the 1698 act.[46] These included Virginia residents as well as merchants based in England. A sizable proportion of these traders also took part in anticompany lobbying. Among those who acted politically more than once and whose repeated trading record can be documented, a list of thirty-two elite separate traders emerges. Within the sample, eleven operated predominantly as Chesapeake tobacco merchants, nine were primarily Jamaica sugar merchants, six had ties with Barbados, three operated primarily with the Leeward Islands, and the other with Carolina. They divided, therefore, primarily into Jamaican and Chesapeake circles, representing the two colonies least satisfied by the company's slave-trading operation. Aware of the labor needs of their colonial suppliers, the separate traders served an integrative role in the British Atlantic economy by diversifying into slave trading to increase the size of their sugar or tobacco businesses. Aside from Isaac Milner, Peter Paggen, and Micajah Perry, the Chesapeake separate traders' elite political leadership included Peregrine and John Brown, William Clayton, Robert Cruickshank, John Goodwin, George Nelthorpe, Francis Sitwell, and James Wayte, all English-based tobacco merchants. In the 1690s, sugar merchants formed the core of company opposition. The importance of the tobacco interest to the separate traders' cause during the second phase of parliamentary consideration between 1707 and 1713 confirms the effect that the 1698 act had in opening up the supply of slaves to mainland America.

The separate traders also benefited from the support of several political actors who did not trade in slaves or own plantations. The well-established tobacco lobby offered powerful backing to the cause for an open slave trade. Merchants with interests in the Virginia trade appeared on Commons select committees devoted to the consideration of the future of the African trade during the early stages of parliamentary consideration in the 1690s. Sir Jeffrey Jeffries, a tobacco trading magnate and the Tory MP for Brecon, served in October 1690. James Gould, the Whig MP for Dorchester, also a tobacco trader, served in April 1695. Members of Parliament representing tobacco trading areas—like Gilfrid Lawson, MP for Cumberland, and James Lowther, MP for Carlisle—interested themselves in the tobacco-trading activities of Whitehaven and so supported the open slave trade as a means to develop the tobacco trade. Similarly, Richard Norris and William Clayton, both members for the major tobacco entrepôt of Liverpool, regarded an open trade as a means of enlarging the tobacco trade, and Norris's brother William had chaired the African trade select committee that produced the Africa Trade Act of 1698. Like other Liverpudlians, including Richard Norris, Clayton eventually began to develop slave-trading interests of his own, and several of the politically active separate traders whose trading activity cannot be documented were men who had lobbied on behalf of the tobacco interest in general. But men such as Benjamin Bradley, Godfrey Webster, and several of the signatories to the Chesapeake planters' petition to the House of Lords in 1698 did not diversify from tobacco into slave trading, and the Plymouth tobacco merchants, as we have seen, authored the first Chesapeake petition against the company in 1696.[47] A provincial-colonial network of tobacco traders lobbied against the London-centered Royal African Company. The established tobacco lobby proved a powerful ally to the cause for open slave trading.

The large extent of the Chesapeake traders' involvement in the political campaign to deregulate the slave trade did not reflect the small proportion of the traded slaves who arrived in the Chesapeake prior to 1698. According to the most comprehensive studies of the British slave trade during this period, the mainland received, on average, just 10 percent of the total volume during the term of the 1698 Africa Trade Act.[48] Yet Chesapeake traders regularly made up over a third of those who signed separate trader petitions. Of all the political actions in favor of the separate traders during this period, separate traders with Chesapeake interests accounted for nearly a quarter. This suggests that the Chesapeake separate traders were better organized than their West Indian counterparts, perhaps because of the maturity of the tobacco lobby or the greater strength of its connections with political institutions such as Parliament and the Board of Trade. It may also imply that slave-trade scholars have underestimated the scale of the independent slave trade to the mainland during this period.

When the Board of Trade's first report on the African trade appeared before Parliament, other business pushed it off the agenda. This first pro-separate-trader report showed a particularly strong influence from the tobacco interest after it collated the results of its enquiry:

> The greatest part of the Negroes furnished to Virginia, Maryland, Carolina and New York has been by the Separate Traders, and ... not above two Hundred have been sent to those Parts by the Company since their Establishment. Which not having been contradicted by the Company We must observe upon it that those Plantations so profitably supplyd by the Separate Traders, near one halfe of the Tobacco cou'd not have been produced and brought hither, and how much that would have lessen'd her Majesty's Customs and the Navigation of this Kingdom We need not mention.[49]

Notably, these conclusions underscored the board's report, before the receipt of any testimony from the Chesapeake, suggesting again that tobacco merchants resident in England, including Perry and Milner, exerted considerable influence over the board's deliberations.

The board and Parliament believed, however, that the report lacked the weight of full colonial input. On April 17, 1708, at the request of Parliament, the board embarked on the first inquiry into the transatlantic slave trade to include testimony from all the Atlantic colonies. It asked colonial governors "to confer with some of the principal planters and inhabitants within your government touching that matter, and to let us know how the negro trade was carried on ... [and] in what manner they think the said trade may best be managed for the benefit of the plantations."[50] The board's enquiry placed colonial evidence at the heart of the dispute, to the disappointment of the company, which preferred to focus parliamentary attention on the coast of Africa. It also explicitly privileged the slave trade as a more important aspect of the African trade than the export of English manufactures. In short, the company had to account for its activities to a colonial audience rather than its success as a representative of the British state on the African coast.

The company and separate traders set about influencing the testimony submitted for the board's inquiry. The company dispatched pamphlets to each of its colonial representatives hoping to convince them of the company's position, along with preauthored petitions it hoped planters would sign.[51] Virginian signatories to the company's petitions, however, proved the most difficult to obtain. When the Royal African Company approached Virginian tobacco planters for support, its agent, Gawin Corbin, claimed that planters refused to sign any public petitions, presumably for fear of offending their merchant creditors, many of whom operated as separate traders, including, most notably, Micajah Perry and Isaac Milner, or the powerful anticompany faction in the colony's legislature. Corbin recounted: "Cannot get a Petition to ye Parliament ye people being afraid (through fear or ignorance) to put their hands to any thing that may appear in publick."[52] Such diffidence offers evidence of genuine, though discreetly expressed, anticompany sentiment.

In his official response to the board's inquiry, Virginia's acting governor Edmund Jennings showed how the separate traders "have had much the greater Share" of the slave trade to his colony, despite charging higher prices than the company. Jennings was at pains to report, however, how the open slave trade had produced such an orgy of consumption that "the Inhabitants of this Country in gen'll will not be so fond of purchasing Negros as of late being sensibly convinced of their Error which has in a manner ruined the Credit of the Country." Dissatisfied with this reply, in July 1709 the board's commissioners wrote to Jennings requesting an explanation as to why the separate traders charged higher prices than the company. In his letter of

January 11 of the following year, Jennings answered, "The difference in the price of negroes between the Company and the separate traders was occasioned by the diligence of the latter in sending their ships early, and thereby gaining the advantage, once or twice, of a better market than the Company who came after them."[53] Because many of the separate traders were also tobacco merchants, it is likely they were conversant with the crop's growing season and could therefore arrange to have their shipments arrive at the most advantageous point for their planter correspondents, in contrast to the African company's conspicuous ignorance of such matters. The board reported in favor of the separate traders and added much authority to the separate traders' cause.[54]

The company's prospects looked bleak. In the next parliamentary session, a petition from the combined Chesapeake interests, styling themselves as "merchants and planters, separate traders to Africa, interested in, and trading to, the plantations of Virginia and Maryland," appeared on January, 29, 1709. The petition explained how the 1698 act had profoundly affected the Chesapeake labor force, contending that "since the passing an act for settling the trade to Africa, ... that trade hath been greatly enlarged and improved, to the benefit of the merchant, and satisfaction of the planters, who are now well supplied with Negroes, which before (when the Royal African Company had the trade to themselves) were extremely wanted." The petition also complained about the 10 percent duty ostensibly levied for the maintenance of the company's forts and asked for its repeal, decrying it as an imposition "which is (if rightly applied) much more, than is needful for that purpose." In contrast to the separate traders' solemn 1698 request to the House of Lords that they should have access to the forts, the petition explained that the separate traders "avoid coming near them, to prevent the company's annoying them in their trade."[55]

Other separate-trader pamphleteers singled out the mainland as the arena that best proved the efficacy of a liberalized slave trade. "If we enquire into Virginia, which is so precious a jewel in the British crown," one pamphlet asserted, "we shall find upwards of fifteen thousand Negroes in that colony also; and I defy the African Company to prove, that ever they have imported so many as two thousand into that particular province, since they have been a joint-body." Another remarked that "since the Trade to Africa was by the wisdom of Parliament laid open, the [Chesapeake] plantations in general have flourished and increased." Yet another painted a grim picture of the situation in Virginia before the opening of the slave trade, in which all "the Possessors of many thousand Acres of uncultivated Ground forced to work alone on their own Land bare-foot and bare legg'd." Since "that Province hath been so abundantly supplied with Negroes by Separate Traders," the pamphlet offered by way of contrast, "it now makes yearly 30,000 Hogsheads of Tobacco fit for the Consumption of our Neighbours: To the great increase of Navigation at home, and our vast Benefit in the Balance of Trade abroad."[56] The expansion that the open slave trade effected in the Chesapeake tobacco economies had a further consequence. Tobacco consumption in West Africa began to increase, and more East India goods entered African markets because colonial and East India produce made up 5 and 25 percent of separate trader cargoes respectively in comparison to the company figures of 1 and 4 percent.[57] The separate traders' anticompany crusade appeared, in this sense, like a tobacco adventure to Africa. Their slave-trading supremacy was undeniable.

Virginia planters unanimously criticized the company as an ineffective supplier of slaves prior to its demise. The company, in their eyes, restricted access to labor, the scarcest colonial commodity. The Chesapeake petitions pleaded for an outcome that transpired—a slave trade open to all British subjects. The War of the Spanish Succession and the public humiliation of having its dismal economic and financial record publicized during the second phase of the Africa trade debates in Parliament caused the company's position to atrophy from 1708 onward. The separate traders' more impressive political operation and the size of their collective trade in comparison to that of the company confirmed that the African company was obsolete. Counter-petitioning, such as that by the Virginia and Maryland tobacco merchants, derailed the company's attempts to achieve a statutory endorsement for its charter, and the 1698 act expired in 1712 without a replacement. With the British slave-trade monopoly destroyed, and aided by the onset of peace, the trade began to reach its zenith, and Virginia entered an age in which some planters managed vast armies of African slaves.

The dispute between the Royal African Company and the separate traders sheds new light on the evolution of slavery on the American mainland. It proves how politically active tobacco merchants intervened to solve Virginia's problem of labor supply. Virginian interests worked with other Atlantic trading interests to break the company's monopoly and played an important part in providing leadership for the movement. Alongside Jamaican sugar merchants, they maintained a persistent record of opposition to the Royal African Company. The interventions of the Virginian interests in

Parliament contributed to favorable legislative outcomes, and their petitions proved formative of the content of legislation. American slavery pivoted on an Atlantic moment when, during the latter years of the seventeenth century, British American interests engineered transatlantic political changes to expand their Atlantic economy. American slavery was the product of intentional, political interventions on both sides of the early modern Atlantic.

Notes

1. Stephen Fouace to Philip Ludwell, April 22, 1711, Lee Family Papers, Virginia Historical Society, MSS 1 L51, f. 72.

2. One memorable rendition of this mentality with regard to the empire is Thomas Jefferson's attempt to blame George III for imposing the slave trade on the American colonies in an early draft of the Declaration of Independence. See Julian P. Boyd, ed., *Papers of Thomas Jefferson* (Princeton, N.J., 1950), 1:318.

3. For an overview of the origins debate see Alden T. Vaughan, "The Origins Debate: Slavery and Racism in Seventeenth-Century Virginia," *Virginia Magazine of History and Biography* 97 (1989): 311–54, reprint in Vaughn, *Roots of American Racism: Essays on the Colonial Experience* (Oxford, 1995). See also John Coombs's trenchant analysis in the present volume.

4. For overemphasis on the demand side and focus on local events, see Edmund S. Morgan, *American Slavery, American Freedom: The Ordeal of Colonial Virginia* (New York, 1975).

5. See Russell Menard, "From Servants to Slaves: The Transformation of the Chesapeake Labor System," *Southern Studies* 16, no. 4 (Winter 1977): 363, 389; and David W. Galenson, *White Servitude in Colonial America: An Economic Analysis* (Cambridge, 1981), 152.

6. Winthrop Jordan, *White over Black: American Attitudes toward the Negro* (Chapel Hill, NC, 1968), 44.

7. David Brion Davis, *Slavery and Human Progress* (New York, 1996), 54.

8. The historiography described how slavery created political power, without admitting that slavery was also the result of political decisions. There are some exceptions, but authors rarely accord political decision making a central place in their narratives. Anthony Parent noticed the connection between office holding and slave ownership. See Anthony Parent Jr., *Foul Means: The Formation of a Slave Society in Virginia, 1660–1740* (Chapel Hill, NC, 2003), 2. Edmund Morgan placed the development of slavery within the context of power struggles between overbearing great planters and royal governors. He supposed that Commissary James Blair promoted slavery as part of an appeal to freed servants to raise an interest against the great planters and to divide lower-class whites from blacks, but he does not produce any evidence. See Morgan, *American Slavery, American Freedom*, 354–55. Although primarily interested in slave agency, Ira Berlin pointed out "the slaveholders seizure of power was the critical event in transforming societies with slaves into slave societies." He failed, however, to develop this theme. See Ira Berlin, *Many Thousands Gone: The First Two Centuries of Slavery in North America* (Cambridge, MA, 1998), 2.

9. Galenson, *White Servitude in Colonial America*, 152.

10. These comparisons of separate-trader and company market share are based on annual numbers of voyages rather than numbers of slaves delivered because we can be more precise about the former. They are derived from David Eltis et al., *Voyages: The Transatlantic Slave Trade Database*, available at http://www.slavevoyages.org.

11. For slave volumes, see David Eltis, "The Transatlantic Slave Trade to the British Americas before 1714: Annual Estimates of Volume, Direction, and African Origins," in Robert L. Paquette and Stanley L. Engerman, eds., *The Lesser Antilles in the Age of European Expansion* (Gainesville, FL, 1996), table 10-1 (all total slave-trading volumes are drawn from this article unless stated otherwise).

12. In studying the movement to end the Royal African Company's monopoly of the British slave trade, I hope to respond to the Chesapeake School's obsession with the economic dimensions of social change. I maintain an Atlantic aspect as an antidote to the parochialism of this earlier tradition and place my story within the context of an emerging British empire. Throughout this essay, I equate the entrenchment of mainland American slavery from the 1690s with the escalation of the slave trade.

13. Slaves and gold remained duty free, while redwood incurred a 5 percent duty. See *The Statutes of the Realm* (London, 1820), 7: 393–97. The debates can be followed in *The Journals of the House of Commons* (London, 1803), vols. 11–16. For a more detailed discussion of the "Africa trade" debates in Parliament, see William A. Pettigrew, "Parliament and the Escalation of the Slave Trade, 1690–1714," in Stephen Farrell, Melanie Unwin, and James Walvin, eds., *The British Slave Trade: Abolition, Parliament, and People* (Edinburgh, 2007).

14. I define "modern" in association with any feature of contemporary society that can be traced without significant interruption or mutation to a particular historical turning point.

15. Scholars have noticed before the tendency of the more progressive states to participate most zealously in slave trading. The development of mainland American slavery illustrates how the "slave-free paradox" can be detected in the relationship of slavery to the rise of more inclusive institutions in the mother country after 1688, as well as in the mindset of those individualists who conceived them. David Eltis, *The Rise of African Slavery in the Americas* (New York, 2000), 274. It is only a paradox, of course, with hindsight. But the paradox helps explain the origins of slavery in America. For Morgan's wrinkle on this point, see *American Slavery, American Freedom*, 376. For a more detailed discussion of how political changes aided the escalation of the British transatlantic slave trade, see William A. Pettigrew, "Free to Enslave: Politics and the Escalation of Britain's Transatlantic Slave Trade, 1688–1714," *William and Mary Quarterly*, 3rd ser., 54 (January 2007), 3–38.

16. For details of the mainland's slave population, see US Bureau of the Census, *Historical Statistics of the United States, Colonial Times to 1957* (Washington, DC, 1960), ser. Z, 1–19. For the continued presence of the Dutch after 1650, see "The Rise and Fall of the Virginia-Dutch Connection in the Seventeenth Century," by Victor Enthoven and Wim Klooster in this volume. See also Susan Westbury, "Slaves of Colonial Virginia: Where They Came From," *William and Mary Quarterly*, 3rd ser., 42 (April 1985), 228–37. For the Royal African Company, see K. G. Davies, *The Royal African Company* (London, 1957). For the company's operations in Virginia, see Charles Killinger, "The Royal African Company's Slave Trade to Virginia, 1689–1713" (master's thesis, College of William and Mary, 1969).

17. For the argument of Bartholomew Shower, the *Nightingale*'s prosecuting barrister, see Alexander Renton, ed., *The English Reports* (London, 1900–32), 89: 496–502.

18. See Royal African Company to Henry Carpenter and Thomas Belchamber, March 10, 1691, Records of the Royal African Company, the National Archives, Kew, London, Treasury Series 70 (hereafter T70), vol. 57 (unfoliated).

19. The other was Jamaica.

20. "A Petition of the Merchants and Planters trading to and interested in the Plantations of Virginia and Maryland," February 28, 1696, *Commons Journals*, 11:475.

21. See T70, vol. 57, January 14, 1696 (unfoliated).

22. "Petition of the Merchants and Planters," 11:475. The petition prays for the trade to be "left open" in reference to *Nightingale v. Bridges*. The content of this petition matched that of a petition from the "merchants of plymouth trading to and interested in the plantations of Virginia and Maryland," which suggests that the early incarnation of a Chesapeake interest may have been orchestrated within the Plymouth mercantile community. For the Plymouth tobacco petition, see *Commons Journals*, March 17, 1696 11:517.

23. T70/170, f. 5. See also *Observations on D.T.'s Considerations on the Trade to Africa, Humbly Offered to the Honourable House of Commons, Relating to the Bill Now before Them* (1698), 3.

24. See National Archives, Kew, *Colonial Office Series* (hereafter CO), vol. 28/3, 136.

25. For the creation of a racist slave code in Virginia that legalized white brutality toward slaves, see Kathleen Brown, *Good Wives, Nasty Wenches, and Anxious Patriarchs: Gender, Race, and Power in Colonial Virginia* (Chapel Hill, NC, 1996), 196–206.

26. *Commons Journals*, February 19, 1698, 12:120.

27. These were Chesapeake, Barbadian, and Jamaican interests. See also *Journals of the House of Lords* (London, 1770), May 25, 1698, 16:297, and May 30, 1698, 16:305.

28. See Felix Skene and Edward Taylor, eds., *The Manuscripts of the House of Lords* (London, 1953), ca. June 9, 1698, new ser., 10:1712–14, 3019. See also *Journals of the House of Lords* (London, 1770) May 25, 1698, 16:297. The text of the petition and its signatories are reproduced in Leo Stock, ed., *Proceedings and Debates of the British Parliament Respecting North America* (Washington, DC, 1924), 2:236.

29. See Thad Tate, "Edward Chilton," in Sarah B. Bears, ed., *Dictionary of Virginia Biography* (Richmond, 2006), 3:212–15. I am grateful to Professor Tate for bringing this information and his article to my attention.

30. For evidence of tobacco trading I cite Dr. Perry Gauci's unpublished database of mercantile petitions. I am grateful to Dr. Gauci for granting permission to use this database. For evidence that Chilton, John Corbin, Harrison, Hartwell, and Jones lived in Virginia, see Henry Hartwell, James Blair, and Edward Chilton, *The Present State of Virginia, and the College*, ed. Hunter Dickinson Farish (Williamsburg, VA, 1940), xxxii–xxxv. For Jones see "Public Officers in Virginia, 1702, 1714," *Virginia Magazine of History and Biography* 2 (July 1894): 6; and for Corbin see Richard Davis, ed., *William Fitzhugh and His Chesapeake World, 1676–1701* (Chapel Hill, NC, 1963), 331. For Harrison and Hartwell's councillorships, see "Harrison of James River," *Virginia Magazine of History and Biography* 31 (July 1923), 283; and CO 5/1308, no. 18, respectively. For Thomas Corbin and Perry's arrangement with the Royal African Company, see Killinger, "The Royal African Company's Slave Trade," appendix. For the group's slave-trading interests see T70/1198. For Carleton as a separate trader, see Stock, *Proceedings and Debates*, 2:239.

31. John Cary, *An Essay on the State of England in Relation to Its Trade*, (London, 1695), 74–76.

32. For Thomas Cary as governor of North Carolina, see CO 5/1049, no. 19. See also

John Sheffield to Thomas Starke, August 2, 1699, National Archives E219/446. For Perry, see T70/1198. For Milner, see Nigel Tattersfield, *The Forgotten Trade: Comprising the Log of the Daniel and Henry of 1700* . . . (London, 1991), 332–33; and Killinger, "The Royal African Company's Slave Trade," appendix.

33. See Hartwell, Blair, and Chilton, *The Present State of Virginia, and the College*, xxxii–xxxv and text citations.

34. Stephen Fouace to Philip Ludwell, April 22, 1711, Lee Family Papers, Virginia Historical Society, MSS 1 L51, f. 72.

35. For a memorial against Nicholson whose authors included Ludwell, Blair, Harrison, and another separate trader, Robert Carter, see "Charges against Governor Nicholson," *Virginia Magazine of History and Biography* 3 (April 1896):373–82.

36. For Ludwell's marriage to Blair's sister-in-law, see Morgan, *American Slavery, American Freedom*, 351. For Gawin Corbin's support for Nicholson, see Jack M. Sosin, *English America and Imperial Inconstancy: The Rise of Provincial Autonomy, 1696–1715* (Lincoln, NE, 1985), 66. The persistent connection between Blair's allies for political reform in London and the encouragement of slave trade escalation (as well as the associations between the African Company and Blair's opponents) may provide some much-needed documentary evidence for Edmund Morgan's unsubstantiated but plausible thesis that James Blair sought to increase the size of Virginia's slave population as a means of gathering the support of lower-order whites. The introduction of slavery and the degraded condition it imposed on blacks, so Morgan's thesis runs, improved the relative status of poorer whites, who would feel elevated and therefore supportive of such a scheme's architects. This elevated mass of whites would then provide a plebeian counterweight to the governor's power. See Morgan, *American Slavery, American Freedom*, 344. The proof it offers that Virginia planters intervened directly to escalate the slave trade, however, cannot be disputed.

37. See Skene and Taylor, *Manuscripts of the House of Lords*, ca. June 9, 1698, new ser., 10:1712–14, 3019.

38. For Paggen's involvement in shipping to the colonies, see Gilbert Heathcote to William Blathwayt, May 10, 1701, Blathwayt MSS, vol. 341, Huntington Library, San Marino, CA.

39. Francis Nicholson to Commissioners of Trade and Plantations, August 20, 1698, CO 5/174, no. 52.

40. See Elizabeth Donnan, ed., *Documents Illustrative of the History of the Slave Trade* (Washington, DC, 1930–35), 4:71.

41. *An act for laying an imposition upon servants and slaves imported into this country, towards building the Capitoll* [1699], in Donnan, *Documents of the Slave Trade*, 4:66–67.

42. Royal African Company to Captain Prowde, October 23, 1701, T70/58, f. 18.

43. See Royal African Company to Gawin Corbin, March 11, 1709, T70/58, f. 378.

44. *Journal of the Commissioners for Trade and Plantations* (London, 1920) 1:430.

45. For evidence of Milner and Perry's operation as separate traders, see T70/1198.

46. My prosopographical study of the separate traders represents the only systematic attempt to identify the individuals who opposed the company's monopoly and began independent slave-trading operations. I define "politically active" as someone whose support for a cause within a political context can be documented with a signature or in the minutes of proceedings of an official political institution (in this case Parliament or the Board of Trade; see *Commons Journals* and *Board of Trade Journal*). On these terms, 200 individuals

can be classed as politically active separate traders. For separate trader petitions, see T70/175, f. 100, f. 148, f. 217, and CO 388/11, 388/12, 388/14, and 388/21.

47. For Lawson and Clayton, see *Commons Journals,* April, 30, 1698, 12:247; for Lowther, see T70/175, f. 295. For Norris, see *Commons Journals,* May 13, 1698, 12:268–69. For Clayton as a slave trader, see T70/9 (unfoliated), August 1, 1712. For Bradley, see CO 5/1341, no. 4; for Webster, see CO 5/1315, no. 10. For the Plymouth tobacco petition see *Commons Journals,* March 17, 1696, 11:517.

48. See Eltis, "The Transatlantic Slave Trade to the British Americas."

49. "Some General Observations and Particular Remarks on the Report made by the Lords Commissioners for Trade and Plantations the 3rd February, 1708 Touching the Contents of the Royal African Company's 'Peticion Referred to them by her Majesty,'" T70/175, ff. 87–96.

50. CO 391/20, 108.

51. Royal African Company to Gawin Corbin et al., April 20, 1708, T70/58, ff. 332–35.

52. Gawin Corbin to the Royal African Company, September–October 1709, T70/8, f. 97.

53. Donnan, *Documents of the Slave Trade,* 4:88.

54. For a full transcription of this report, see CO 390/12, 172–282 and CO 389/20, 275–313.

55. See *Commons Journals,* January 1709, 16:29.

56. *A True State of the Present Difference between the Royal African Company and the Separate Traders* (1710); *Some Considerations Humbly Offered to Demonstrate How Prejudicial It Would be to the English Plantations, Revenues of the Crown, the Navigation and General Good of This Kingdom, that the Sole Trade for Negroes Should Be Granted to a Company with a Joynt-Stock Exclusive to All Others* [1698?]; testimony of Benjamin Way, CO 388/15. See also *The African Companies Considerations on the Late Act of Parliament for Settling the Trade to Africa, Answer'd Paragraph by Paragraph* (1709), 1; and *The Case of the Separate Traders to Africa* (1708).

57. See T70/1199.

Conclusion

The Future of Chesapeake Studies

PHILIP D. MORGAN

This impressive collection of essays, coupled with recent conferences commemorating Virginia's quadricentennial in 2007 and the 375th anniversary year of Maryland's founding in 2009, suggest that there is a resurgence of interest in the history of the early Chesapeake.[1] Now is an especially appropriate time for considering the importance of this region in the Atlantic world. What is its role likely to be? What directions are scholars likely to pursue? Where do we go from here?

As befits a historian, I cannot look forward without looking backward. My retrospective musings have me revisiting the introduction to *Colonial Chesapeake Society* that I wrote with Lois Carr and Jean Russo, attempting to summarize the state of Chesapeake history over twenty years ago. So first I offer a reprise, in the form of a three-part schema for thinking about how the Chesapeake has been viewed.

In the good old days—the 1960s and 1970s—the Chesapeake was foil to New England. Using the same techniques pioneered in New England and, before that, early modern England and France, the St. Mary's mafia, as some fondly referred to them—or, more neutrally, the "Chesapeake School" headed by the grande dame Lois Green Carr—explored basic questions about ordinary people's lives. The answers they provided seemed to prove the Chesapeake was everything New England was not: unmarried servants rather than families; dying young rather than living old; the rigors of sotweed cultivation rather than the more relaxed routines of subsistence farming; scattering to the winds rather than settling down together; importing manufactured goods rather than making them; slave labor rather than family labor; looking out for number one rather than everyone. The early Chesapeake, it could be argued, barely qualified as a society at all; rather, it resembled, in Edmund and Marie Morgan's words, "a collection of undisciplined work gangs more than a colony," a Hobbesian nightmare. Ironically, then, the first wave of the "new social history," which sought to understand the Chesapeake experience on its own terms, seemed to confirm New England as normative, the Chesapeake and other regions as deviant.[2]

But during the 1980s and 1990s, as research broadened to other colonies, as some of the starker and more simplistic contrasts between the Chesapeake and New England were moderated, and as New England appeared increasingly exceptional, the Chesapeake gradually moved from outer wings to center stage. Indeed, it began to seem representative of a whole range of British colonial endeavors. If exploitation, materialism, and individualism, for instance, were some of the prominent characteristics of British colonies, then certainly the Chesapeake held its own. Located roughly equidistant from Britain's most northerly and southerly Atlantic colonies, the Chesapeake may be said to represent the middle ground—not in the Richard White sense but in more literal ways. Containing both plantations and farms, an aristocracy and a broad yeomanry, a staple and a mixed agriculture, the Chesapeake was a hybrid, mixing elements from colonies both to the north and south. Indeed, perhaps the Chesapeake, the thinking went, ought to be considered the norm against which to measure all other British American societies. If so, in a sense, the Chesapeake merely resumed the central place that it occupied in the early modern Anglo-American world—the oldest and largest and the most populous, economically valuable, and politically sophisticated region on the mainland. In David Hancock's words, "As went Virginia so went the rest of Anglo-America." In its expansiveness, dynamism, and materialism, the region seemed the prototype for the future United States.[3]

Now, with the Atlantic turn of the last ten to fifteen years, the Chesapeake has retreated again to the margins. Just think of the spate of books that accompanied the quadricentennial celebration of the founding of Jamestown. Yes, some did see the event as the font, the birthplace, the cradle of all good things American, but most described it as, in Karen Kupperman's words, a "shambles of death and despair," "a dismal tale of failure," the "creation story from hell," a nightmare of folly and fecklessness, hunger and starvation, disease and violence. Kupperman credits some trial-and-error efforts, particularly private property in land, a representative assembly, commercial production of a staple crop, to which one might add the transfer of English laws and even more simply the resilience and survivability of the settlement, but subsequent colonizers regarded Virginia as more horror show than inspiration. Precious few lessons seem to have been learned; rather, the moral lay in avoiding Jamestown's grievous mistakes. Jamestown fort and its buildings, we now know, were substantial, and the recovery of more than 1 million artifacts testifies to the Virginia Company's steadfast commitment to making a success of their enterprise, but Jamestown is perhaps most notable as the site of powerful destructive forces—vicious cycles of war, plunder, and the exploitation of natives and later Africans.[4]

Even more telling, when situated in a large context, Jamestown became "an almost trivial event," or as one historian puts it, of "no great significance at the time," "a small part in a great global story," indeed a "small and not always significant part of an Atlantic history."[5] The best accounts of Jamestown ranged far and wide, from Newfoundland to Morocco, from Ireland to Bermuda. In the process, Jamestown shrank in significance. It became one small, risky, and tenuous foray in a global array of English ventures. Many of the key players at early Jamestown—figures such as Sir Thomas Gates; Sir Thomas Dale; John Smith; Captain Christopher Newport; Thomas West, Lord De La Warr; even Pocahontas—were not there long, left Virginia, and never returned (Samuel Argall returned to Virginia as governor in 1617 but lasted only two years). One striking image is that of epic hero and bumptious buffoon John Smith, his genitals more than likely blown off in that gunpowder explosion that forced his departure from the colony, his emasculation accounting, as David S. Shields astutely notes, for his later "compensatory masculine posturing, his preoccupation with the virile body, ... and his repeated and poignant references to 'posterity.'"[6]

Is Smith's likely unmanning a metaphor for our plight today? Has Chesapeake studies lost its vigor, its vibrancy, its potency? Is the death knell of Chesapeake studies being sounded? I detect some definite weariness and lassitude, perhaps even a loss of steam. Yet the waves of new work threaten to engulf anybody trying to keep pace with developments. After all, 43 presenters, 11 discussants, and 9 roundtablers graced the most recent Chesapeake conference.[7] One can hardly claim that the study of this region is moribund. Rather, it is alive, vibrant, definitely dense and thick on the ground—much like the swarms of mosquitoes encountered on a steamy Chesapeake Bay day. So where are we headed? I offer five promising lines of inquiry.

Scale

"One of the deepest tendencies of late-twentieth-century historiography," Bernard Bailyn states, has been "the impulse to expand the range of inquiry, to rescale major events and trends into larger settings, and to seek heightened understanding at a more elevated and generalized plane." Or, as he puts it in his introduction to a recent collection of essays on Atlantic history, "The main stimulus to the proliferation of studies in and references to Atlantic history has been the explanatory power and suggestive implications created by the vision of the Atlantic region as a coherent whole. In that large regional context, otherwise limited, local studies gain heightened meaning at a more general plane of significance."[8]

In a Chesapeake context, one revealing way to reframe matters in a broad way is to explore riverine regional systems. James Rice's study of the fifteen thousand square miles that constitute the Potomac River basin focuses on ecology and Native American life. He asks why, when the whole region offered fertile soil and excellent fishing and hunting, was nearly two-thirds of it uninhabited on the eve of colonization? His answer requires taking a long view and broadening the scale of reference. Seeing the long time horizon means taking note of the Little Ice Age and its impact on shortening growing seasons, which in turn froze out northern Native farmers who moved south. These southward migrations heightened competition for prime village sites and resources. The interior of this region beyond the fall line, an area of roughly ten thousand square miles, became something of a no-man's land, a crossfire zone, a battleground between northern Iroquoian speakers and southern Siouan speakers. The reason, then, that the interior of the Potomac was uninhabited was that it had become a dangerous place, a deadly "shatter zone," to use Robbie Ethridge's term. Naturally, we would certainly like to know more about the Siouan-speaking groups who lived on the upper reaches of the Chesapeake rivers below the Potomac and some of the shadowy groups that arose during colonization—Native groups such as the Doegs. Nevertheless, Rice has advanced our knowledge considerably by enlarging the scale, and by engaging in a polycentric account of all the Native and European actors who both resided in and traveled through his chosen river basin. We could do with more such studies. The Bay, after all, has more than fifty tributary rivers, but since the Susquehanna accounts for nearly half of the total freshwater input and its basin is twice as large as the Potomac's, perhaps it deserves priority, although its study would take one well away from what is conventionally considered part of the Chesapeake region.⁹

What is most refreshing about Rice's approach is that he explores Native American groups from outside the Powhatan confederacy and beyond 1676. Camilla Townsend's essay in this volume suggests that by looking at different perspectives—Spanish as well as English—more can be learned about the early Powhatans. Perhaps that is so, but we seem to be at the point of diminishing returns. Rather, Rice, I submit, suggests the way forward, as does Edward D. Ragan in his essay in this volume, a study of another river valley—the Rappahannock—the northern shore of which was the most densely settled part of Tsenacomoco. Rivers were the true highways of early America. In an Algonquian context, people who lived along a long stretch of river shared more than did those who lived a short distance overland but in different watersheds. Another such study adopting a long time perspective and encompassing non-Powhatans is Martin Gallivan's study of the relations between Powhatans and Monacans in the James River valley.[10]

Atlantic riverine regions also surface in a chapter of a recent book by legal historian Lauren Benton. For her, the political dangers of distant riverine regions were set against their almost mythical promise. European Atlantic geography taught that estuaries would lead to interior riches, trading opportunities, or bodies of freshwater. Yet estuaries themselves offered notoriously difficult conditions for sustained settlement: bad water, poor soil, exposure to severe storms. And once parties traveled beyond the points where deep water could accommodate oceangoing vessels, rivers began to signal not so much opportunity as trouble. They were difficult to navigate safely and to cross. Despite dangers, rivers had a persistent allure. In short, rivers held out much promise but produced confounding results. They were treacherous places, and Benton explores the law of treason in such settings. Her Chesapeake examples include John Smith's entrada up the Chesapeake rivers and Bacon's Rebellion, which she reads as highlighting the geographical distinction between coastal regions and upriver country.[11]

Issues of scale are matters of looking not just outward but also inward. How to disaggregate the region? Is the Chesapeake even a single, coherent unit? Historians of the region have always been well aware that there were significant differences between Maryland and Virginia, between Eastern and Western Shores, between Tidewater and Piedmont, between mountain and interior valley. Surely everyone who has ever studied the region knows that it is a composite of distinct subregions. One way of mapping them owes much to Lorena S. Walsh and her delineation of areas devoted to the production of two types of tobacco—sweet scented and oronoco—and a third area largely devoted to mixed farming. Her tripartite analysis provides one of the most important advances in thinking about subregional differences in the Chesapeake.[12]

But of course there are other ways of doing it. One is to see parts of the Chesapeake as closely allied to its neighbors—another way of looking outward. Thus the northern areas were more akin to lower Pennsylvania and Delaware; indeed in the early republic some Marylanders and Virginians thought of their states as *central* rather than *southern*. The Southside, on the other hand, easily extended into North Carolina, and the Southeast, as Brad Wood is investigating, is certainly connected to the Albemarle region. The Shenandoah valley, as Warren Hofstra points out, is often viewed as a whole world unto itself, a "New Virginia," as it was called, but is certainly connected to an interior world both north and south. The Chesapeake had an extraordinary reach, serving as the seedbed for the antebellum South.[13]

Another way of looking outward has been to search for connections to distant places. There was a time when Ireland was the comparative locale of choice. Those who fought and lived in Ireland learned valuable lessons about how to conquer and colonize, so the argument went, and applied them in the Chesapeake. But to my knowledge few are pursuing those connections now; rather, the opposite tack is in vogue, and it is the lack of linkages and parallels between these two places that is likely to be emphasized. Another outward linkage is to Bermuda, Virginia's true sister colony, these twinned mainland and island ventures harnessing the same expansionist impulses. Fortunately, Mike Jarvis will soon illuminate these enduring links—even as Virginia and Bermuda went their separate ways. Alison Games thinks the Mediterranean connection is the most resonant, but most of those parallels and linkages seem rather tenuous. Others note that Virginia was conceived in the midst of a great contest between Protestant England and Catholic Spain. "The English spent their first fifteen years in Virginia trying to turn their colony into a sort of Protestant Mexico," states Eliga Gould. Lisa Voigt notes that Anglo-America's most famous captive, John Smith, drew on Iberian sources for many of his alleged experiences, perhaps including his tale of rescue by Pocahontas. Much of the colony's immediate and later history, as John Elliott and a number of others have since shown, can be illumined if refracted through a Spanish lens.[14]

Yet another way of conceiving the region is to posit it as the outer edge of the Greater Caribbean. If one thinks of disease patterns and movements, the plantation, and of course slavery, then thinking about the Chesapeake as the northern periphery of a world that stretches all the way to Trinidad and Tobago, the Guianas, and even Bahia is not so far fetched. What might that do? I will offer just one example, drawn from a recent book by J. R. McNeil. In the American Revolution, McNeil argues, the British southern campaigns ultimately led to defeat at Yorktown in October 1781 in part because their forces were much more susceptible to malaria than were the American. Before 1750 some marshy and low-lying parts of England and Germany had hosted vivax malaria, but increasingly English and German youth lacked prior exposure, partly because of wetlands drainage and partly because of an enormous expansion in cattle numbers. Even the few Europeans who did carry resistance to vivax proved vulnerable to falciparum malaria, a routine summer scourge in the Chesapeake, much like the rest of the Greater Caribbean. When in 1780 the British army placed its single largest force in the coastal South, it could no longer recruit men fast enough to offset those it lost. Malaria haunted the core of Cornwallis's army at Yorktown. Cornwallis repeatedly mentioned how much his troops were weakened by sickness; by his account, more than half of his force was too sick to fight. McNeil is not saying mosquitoes and malaria won the American Revolution, but he is saying that they helped make the difference, "snatching victory from the jaws of stalemate," as he puts it.[15]

In short, scale matters. Altering geographical boundaries—whether focusing on a riverine watershed or a settlement system that straddles colonies—raises new questions. The lens employed can be microscopic, exploring subregional differences, or telescopic, contrasting the Chesapeake with other colonial regions or situating it in a much broader—Caribbean or Atlantic—setting; but in all cases, the aim is to reframe and pose new ways of thinking about the subject matter. Context is everything.

Chronology

The introduction to *Colonial Chesapeake Society* noted that a difficulty all colonial historians face in writing the history of a region is how to encompass temporal as well as spatial change, linear and lateral developments. So my second pointer is greater attention to chronology. A subtle and complex narrative must describe the timing of events not just in the heart of a region but also on its continually expanding margins. The progress of settlement demands much more attention than historians have given it. A major task is to determine when differences reflect regional variations in resources as opposed to varying dates of settlement and thus stages of development.[16]

Clearly, progress is being made in dating more precisely the shift to and development of slavery. The stock of the early Atlantic creoles seems to have fallen; their numbers were always miniscule, and what kind of creoles were they, some ask. Linda Heywood and John Thornton have made a heroic, but not wholly convincing, case for the importance of West Central Africa to the formation of slavery in the Chesapeake. Most thoroughly and emphatically, John Coombs shows that Virginia officeholders began buying slaves in the 1640s and 1650s. The most affluent planters had at least ten slaves, and some owned twice that number by then. Investments in slave labor continued in the 1660s, so that he speaks of an emergent black belt, although overall numbers were still small—2,000 by 1670—but they were highly concentrated in the hands of roughly 250 planters who were county commissioners, burgesses, and councilors. What Coombs has shown is that a significant group of Virginians had embraced slavery before Bacon's Rebellion and before the decline in servant immigration. At the same time, he notes, most Virginians derived little benefit from an expanding supply of black laborers. What then seems to have happened is that the distribution of slaves followed the spatial growth of tobacco, with the affluent, sweet-scented tobacco–growing zone between the James and Rappahannock Rivers revealing the highest density of slaves, the marginal staple areas of Southside and Eastern Shore the lowest, and those areas that grew better-quality grades of oronoco leaf somewhere in between. Russell R. Menard is quite right that St. Mary's was a late developer. But what Coombs shows so well, building particularly on Walsh, is that the shift from slave owning to slave society (two ideal types) occurred at different times throughout the Chesapeake region. It would be good to know more about the progress of Native American slavery, which was important in Virginia's southwestern counties in the last third of the seventeenth century.[17]

There are other issues of timing that are receiving new attention. The half century from roughly 1680 to 1729, for example, is attracting much interest, as evidenced by the number of essays at the 2009 Early Chesapeake conference that saw this period as a critical transition. The era has long posed something of a conundrum: stagnation in some respects, dynamism in others. Douglas Bradburn and John C. Coombs have offered a strong critique of Russell Menard's characterization of the period as one of depression. In her magisterial new book on plantation management, Lorena Walsh provides the fullest answers to the puzzle. She notes that the high profits earlier derived from tobacco production diminished to modest, sometimes paltry levels. Most planters, who had exhausted any technological improvements they could make in raising tobacco, faced increasingly hard times. Opportunities for newcomers declined because long-established planters were usually able to set up their children with portions of land, bound laborers, and already-developed farms. Many fewer poor Europeans chose to migrate to the Chesapeake. Since initially only rich planters could afford to buy expensive Africans, the wealthy gained from the shift in labor systems, while ordinary planters suffered.[18]

But there was not stagnation, if by that one means stasis. Rather, there were significant advances—in land speculation and settlement, brick construction, and the rise of the polite house and even the "banqueting" or "party" house, as Cary Carson labels the phenomenon; a few high-gentry families, "alpha-gentlemen," were the fashion leaders and trend setters. Mann Page, as Camille Wells demonstrates, embarked on an extravagant building campaign with his brick mansion at Rosewell; Edward Lloyd II, Amy Speckart notes, was like other native-born members of the Maryland planter-merchant elite, able to take advantage of wide kinship networks (and, in his case, his political leverage as acting governor from 1709 to 1714) to consolidate economic and political power. There were other positive developments for at least some Chesapeake residents: the establishment of new towns; the peaking of a successful livestock-herding system (the "Tobacco Coast" could easily be renamed the "Hog Coast"); new marketing and credit systems as the Chesapeake adjusted to "total war," the term used by Victor Enthoven and Wim Klooster in their essay in this volume. Douglas Bradburn, in a particularly important essay, emphasizes the emergence of an impressive "regulatory regime which constrained, often with violent force, the size, timing, and character of the tobacco market," based on an extension of considerable naval power, and of course there was the rapid development of slavery, for this was a time when Virginia's labor force Africanized, as William Pettigrew notes in his essay in this volume.[19]

Many of these changes are explained by growing inequality among whites, predicated on ever-increasing degradation and exploitation of enslaved blacks. Subregional differences were vital: planters in marginally productive areas abandoned tobacco and turned to diversified agricultural activities, while Virginia planters in the lower Tidewater developed sweet-scented leaf, a new strain of tobacco that for a time commanded high returns in the English market. The fortunes of planters in the more favored areas diverged markedly from those living in less advantaged places. Those at the margins undoubtedly suffered, as Terri Snyder illustrates in her essay in this volume. Overall, planters struggled to maintain or to expand their revenues in the face of stagnant or falling prices for their staple, decreasing availability of good land in long-settled areas, and severe shortages of labor, but the planter and merchant elite—people such as Mann Page and Edward Lloyd II—did remarkably well. The gap between rich and poor became a chasm.[20]

What is at stake here is how best to characterize the developmental process. A simple cyclical model is inadequate. Each wave of settlement cannot be seen as simply replicating earlier stages of development, although important repetitions undoubtedly occurred. Some have posited the model of a helix as more appropriate, because later settlement processes could compress, skip almost entirely, perhaps even elongate elements of earlier stages. A continuous and expanding spiral encourages us to see regional cores and peripheries as constantly interacting. This complex interplay and mutual interpenetration of forces and influences between old and newly settled subregions seems to provide the best way forward for understanding the evolutionary process in the Chesapeake as a whole.[21]

Material Culture

The Chesapeake has always been in the forefront of material culture studies, in part because of the sparsity of conventional documentation, turning its students into "Kremlinologists," to use Cary Carson's description, decoders of elusive clues from the surviving scraps of available evidence. Scholars construct amenity indices, explore postholes in the ground, decipher inscriptions on the landscape, probe teeth and bones for evidence of disease and trauma—in short, make ingenious use of the insignia of past lives. This is therefore my third suggestion of a key future direction of study—a heightened understanding of a rich material culture, drawing on a variety of related disciplines. The approach is represented in this volume by Philip Levy's essay, which uses archaeological information to understand Middle Plantation, a rural neighborhood that ultimately became Williamsburg, but of course no single paper could suggest the almost unlimited possibilities of the material culture approach. Let me just single out some of my own personal favorite findings drawn from recent work.[22]

Jamestown has been a veritable goldmine of information about the lives of the earliest Chesapeake colonists. Their first structures were not wattle and daub, as once thought, but rather "mud and stud," a building tradition derived from Lincolnshire. Apparently, the elite lived in lean-to huts along the palisade walls, and the commoners in communal, mud-and-stud housing, but as early as 1611 Thomas Gates ordered the construction of box-frame row houses—so change came quickly at the fort. It was a vibrant place with much activity devoted to turning a profit. Colonists engaged in glassmaking, pipe making, brickmaking, barrel making, the reworking of armor, and metallurgy. Indeed, they melted copper from English mines in crucibles, indicating that the metal served not only as a trade item but as an ingredient in the search for potential zinc ores, such as calamine stone, needed in England to produce brass. The colonists were not as helpless as often portrayed: they were well equipped with hooks, weights, and seine weights to exploit the rivers and bay, evident in the seventeen different species of fish identified in their food remains. Furthermore, while some of their armor may have been archaic for use on European battlefields, it was useful for guerrilla warfare with Indians. The presence of Indians within the fort, however, is striking; their clay pots, nutting stones, celts, hammerstones, bone needles, tobacco pipes, stone drills, and over a thousand shell beads have been found within the fort. The Indian material culture at Jamestown is much richer than that found at most Native sites—Werowocomoco included. The earliest documented appearance of three different types of beetle in a circa 1611–17 well sample suggests how quickly invasive species colonized the New World. Oyster shells from sealed datable contexts promise to provide benchmarks for measuring the health of the Chesapeake Bay. Furthermore, by correlating these findings with information about drought, it may be possible to read shells chronologically—in the manner of dendrochronology but not in wood. The numerous Catholic artifacts found at Jamestown, it is now conjectured, are not proof of "closet Catholics," but rather of plunder from Spanish and Portuguese ships for use in the Indian trade. One exotic item suggests reading in early Jamestown, not an activity usually associated with the place: a Roman oil lamp presumably illuminated one gentleman's evening hours.[23]

Archaeological fieldwork has allowed museum builders at places such as Colonial Williamsburg and St. Mary's to "raise buildings from the grave." The commitment to inclusiveness is evident in the buildings reconstructed by both institutions: at the former an asylum, a plantation slave quarter, a protoindustrial blacksmith's workshop, a "people's court," the accommodations and work buildings assigned to an urban enslaved labor force, and a hypothetical (but thoroughly researched) small plantation on the edge of town; at the latter a printer's shop and a brick Catholic chapel that literally rises from the ground. Cary Carson provides a tour de force analysis of how people's use of space changed over time from the seventeenth to the eighteenth century in his deconstruction of the changing furnishings of Bacon's Castle in Surry County, Virginia, the oldest surviving building in the Chesapeake region and a wonderful microhistory of Simon Overzee's murder of a slave as seen through an archaeological reconstruction of the crime scene. Vernacular architecture specialists such as Carson can detect status in different kinds of floorboard nails, door trim, paint, and wallpaper and have determined that color coding reinforced seating arrangements at some Anglican churches in Virginia because pews restricted to African American worshippers were sometimes painted black. What can be extracted from the arcana of everyday life by an expert almost defies belief.[24]

Archaeological discoveries have revealed a great deal about how Chesapeake colonists treated their dead. Much has been learned about the use of shrouds and types of coffins. One finding is simply the diversity of coffin types, which may be traced to different English regional origins. Most colonists were not usually buried wearing their clothes, but rather wrapped from head to toe in a shroud, which in turn was usually held in place with ropes tied above the head and below the feet with pins. There were some exceptions—examples of clothed bodies buried in haste, perhaps because of the fear of catching a contagious disease by handling clothes of an infected person. The Chesapeake offers the earliest evidence of embalming in America and the oldest lead coffins.[25]

The wonders of science also can reveal much about human bodies. Did a person, for example, eat primarily corn or European grains, giving a good clue to birthplace? Isotopes of strontium and oxygen, correlated with soil types, can often determine where an individual grew up. Skeletal analysis can provide the most precise estimates we are ever likely to get of a person's height. Archaeologists can reconstruct a person's muscular development and key parts of his or her medical history. Rickets, for example, has been detected among some Chesapeake babies, owing, it has been claimed, to their mothers' swaddling or wrapping them tightly in cloth, thereby preventing their bodies from absorbing sunlight, which, along with poor nutrition, could cause the disease. Demanding work stiffened spines and degenerated joints, head-carrying affected backbones, and all of these symptoms can be detected in the skeletons of African Americans. Evidence of teeth cleaning—the use of a piece of cloth dipped into a gritty paste and scrubbed across the surface—is evident in worn-away enamel. Colonists' teeth show a much higher rate of decay after they began eating a corn-based diet. The heavy consumption of meat (normally thought to be a benefit), alcohol, and tobacco, which was common in the early Chesapeake, actually took a significant toll on colonists.[26]

A very different material culture study—and that does not quite capture its scope—is Shepard Krech's study of birds and Indians. Why, he asks, is the "most persistent visual image of the indigenous people" of the South "that they were feathered"? So the feather can be an object of investigation, or of ethno-ornithology, if one wants to be grandiose. Many Chesapeake Indians wore feathers, bird parts, and even entire birds on their bodies. They fletched arrows with turkey and hawk feathers and made fans of eagle feathers. They wore mantles or blankets made of turkey feathers. They tattooed figures of birds on their bodies. Feathers were important trade items; they also stood for authority and power, as is best indicated by the Powhatan war chief Nemattanew, otherwise known as Jack of the Feathers, who covered himself all over with feathers and fastened swans' wings onto his shoulders. Indians associated feathers with display, aggression, and hostility. Avian imagery pervaded the key elements in the material culture of smoking. The intoxicating power of tobacco presumably conjured up thoughts of flight. Thus John White inscribed his famous representation of an Indian conjuror or medicine man with both arms upraised and a bird with wings spread in his hair above one ear as the flyer. Some birds, most notably the whip-poor-will, represented wandering souls or departed spirits.[27]

Turning from the lightweight feather to archaeological websites is certainly a shift of gears—heavy lifting one might say—but the payoff is that accumulation and standardization of evidence can promote generalizations and comparisons. There are at least two archaeological websites worthy of mention. One, the Comparative Archaeological Study of Colonial Chesapeake Culture, based on eighteen early Chesapeake sites, is the source base for an inventive paper by John C. Coombs, Philip Levy, and David Muraca, which explores variability in how early Marylanders and Virginians pursued their material ambitions. A somewhat more ambitious website is the Digital Archaeological Archive of Comparative Slavery, hosted at Monticello, which fosters intersite comparative archeological research on slavery throughout the Chesapeake, the Carolinas, and the Caribbean. It now contains information from forty-one sites and is beginning to generate important findings. Fraser Neiman, the project director, has likened subfloor pits, an adaptation uniquely Chesapeake, to safe-deposit boxes (lockboxes, as it were). He believes they were clever inventions by enslaved people to increase the security of their food ration in dwellings that housed people in fairly large groups. Over time, as more slaves lived in smaller, family-based groupings over whose membership they had some control, the need for subterranean root cellars declined, and they disappeared from the archaeological record. In two inventive articles, Jillian Galle, the project manager, has shown how African Americans actively participated in the consumer revolution sweeping the late-eighteenth-century Anglo-American world through their acquisition of fashionable buttons and ceramics.[28]

Databases, which might become websites, are also informative. Thus, for example, one ongoing project is to measure the dimensions of Virginia slave housing using a standardized format. The project has found information on more than nine hundred structures and has compiled fully standardized data on more than thirty. Four dwellings date to the period 1789–1816. Another staggering resource derives from Joanna Bowen, faunal expert par excellence, who has analyzed three hundred assemblages from eighty Chesapeake sites, creating one of the largest zooarchaeological databases in the world. During the seventeenth century, she demonstrates, cattle populations flourished and increased in individual size, but by the first half of the eighteenth century, as land degraded, planters introduced the plow, and free-ranging livestock overgrazed the region, cattle size decreased dramatically. Her story is one of ecological and faunal declension.[29]

New technologies are invented all the time. Major advances have occurred in paleoethnobotany, archaeophysics, and dendrochronology. Climate and environmental reconstruction profiles have been especially helpful. New advances will surely reorient perspectives on Chesapeake life- and death-ways in the future. Forensic anthropology in particular promises to provide information about entire groups of people—their mortality patterns, health, general activity, and cultural practices. Genomic studies (DNA sampling and comparisons) of long-established community residents will probably tell us much about Euro-African-Indian intermixing in the future.

Politics and Law

The fourth area that has generated some exceptional work of late—and there is obviously much more in the offing—is the public realm, especially politics and the law. Clearly, these two spheres have not been entirely neglected in the past; one thinks of the work of Jack Greene, Thad Tate, Lois Carr, Warren Billings, Jon Kukla, and Terri Snyder, just to mention a few. The late Emory Evans recently published a book that is a fitting memorial to his lifelong interest in Chesapeake politics and social structure. There is obviously a venerable history of works on the political and legal history of the Chesapeake, but nevertheless the so-called Chesapeake School was most noted for social, economic, and demographic history, and the public sphere tended to be somewhat slighted.[30]

As for law, I have already mentioned the new book by Lauren Benton, which has Chesapeake implications, but there are many other works worth mentioning. Ken MacMillan's recent book on the legal and constitutional foundations of England's emerging American empire focuses a good deal on the Chesapeake. One of his major findings concerns how the English asserted legal title to lands. He demonstrates, contrary to previous claims, that Roman law provided a vital lingua franca in the early modern Atlantic world. An imperial monarchy, equipped with Roman law, was an assertive player, he demonstrates. His sequel to *Sovereignty and Possession* will be a study of what he calls the "Stuart imperial constitution," which will demonstrate how, when, and why the English center, in the form of the monarch and Privy Council, was involved in the peripheries. His broader purpose is to engage with literature that argues for "the end of American independence" around 1675, when in fact he believes the structure of center/periphery relations had been determined much earlier. Many of the essays in the first volume of the *Cambridge History of Law in America* also bear on the Chesapeake. Particularly noteworthy are Anthony Pagden on claims making, Mary Bilder on governance, David Konig on regionalism, and Claire Priest on commerce. One of the contributors to that volume, Holly Brewer, has written an important book on the changing legal status of children, much of which concerns Virginia.[31]

But the most important trend of the recent and forthcoming works is legal pluralism: in other words, in discussions of law and legalities in America, there was a great deal more at play than the reception and inheritance of common-law traditions that dominated much of the legal-historical literature of the twentieth century. This is the subject of a recent short volume and many more projected volumes by William E. Nelson. What the most recent scholarship is emphasizing is that legal cultures consisted of intricate patchworks of disparate legal systems and codes. As just one exemplar, consider Chris Tomlins's recently published magnum opus—

a huge, sprawling work that covers all of British North America—but since it probes the connections between colonizing, work, and civic identity, it has much to say about the Chesapeake. In one arresting section, for instance, he argues that coerced labor was much less central to Chesapeake history than many have claimed. In another, he demonstrates that law was anything but a national singularity; rather, law described both plural discourses and institutions and, within them, a congeries of local particularities. In short, there was not one English legal culture but many. He argues for no generic legal culture of labor unfreedom but rather a stratified version significantly more oppressive than those supposed to be typical of England for some, significantly less oppressive for others. The comparatively greater oppressions of indentured servitude were a condition of the existence of the comparatively greater freedoms of creole artisans and hireling labor.[32]

Just as study of the law is flourishing, so investigation of Chesapeake politics is making something of a comeback. One issue is the intersection of colonizing and English political theory. Some scholars, such as David Armitage and Andrew Fitzmaurice, have explored this issue, but now historians are interested in the language of "commonwealth" and "government" and how it tracks across the Atlantic. Alec Haskell, for instance, is doing notable work on commonwealth building in seventeenth- and early-eighteenth-century Virginia. He takes aim, for instance, at Andrew Fitzmaurice's treatment of commonwealth rhetoric, effectively turning his argument on its head: commonwealth talk was not a humanist ideal opposed to profit making but rather a way of introducing to the realm a commercial conception of colonization. In other pieces and his larger work, he is eager to uncover how contemporaries conceptualized authority and the relationship between the "people" and gentry leaders and how they maneuvered in a world that imagined this relationship in more complex terms than previously recognized. For example, he takes on the issue of deference and defiance, hierarchy and egalitarianism and manages to show how they could coexist. What Virginia politicians recognized, he maintains, was that in the highly uncertain political environment of a developing colony, nobody had a monopoly on legitimacy. All had an incentive, especially in moments of crisis, to ground their actions on a foundation of popular consent.[33]

Peter Thompson explores some of the same territory as Haskell. In seventeenth-century Virginia, householders valued their independence and deferred to good government, but they reserved a right to critique maladministration and resist corruption or immorality. Poor yet loyal householders could offer a moral critique of the pursuit of advancement by antisocial individuals. They did so by invoking the language of commonalty. As used by Virginians, this term referred to the common people of the colony, often figured as a distinct social and political estate oppressed by rapacious grandees. It served as a near synonym for commonwealth, referring to localized polities in which householders were bound together in an organic commonweal. These householders depended on the security of their fundamental rights to liberty and property and on an assortment of privileges and freedoms relating to landholding and locality; within the scope of these rights and privileges, individual ambitions, collective obligations, and obedience to a just and fair government could all coexist.[34]

Maryland politics has been generating important work. Timothy Riordan's microscopic account of Maryland during the war years 1645 and 1646 reveals that the so-called Plundering Time, the rebellion led by Richard Ingle, was no aberration. It was no "isolated incident but fits well into the recurring cycle of revolution and counterrevolution that is characteristic of early Maryland's political climate," which arose from long-festering strains internal to that tiny frontier outpost and "must be interpreted within the context of the English Civil War." Seventeenth-century Maryland politics can seem rather byzantine, but Riordan's exhaustive book and a recent Ph.D. dissertation completed by Antoinette Sutto make these machinations more intelligible. In Lord Baltimore's dispute with the Jesuits, for example, Sutto demonstrates that he was implicitly arguing for the king's role as the ultimate source of law and authority in English dominions. The proprietor of Maryland thus promoted an absolutist theory of law, and there was such a thing as Caroline absolutism in England. She is thus writing the history of the early modern English state and the early colonial world as a single story, which is surely the right way to do it.[35]

Religion

One last area in which there has been something of a renaissance is appropriately enough the spiritual realm. Many scholars have reacted negatively to the depiction of the Chesapeake as heavily secular and materialistic, essentially irreligious, with a dissolute and incompetent clergy, with laypeople lax in observance, and supposedly with many people unchurched. Instead, Chesapeake historians have discovered or rediscovered religion, and there have been many recent studies on the subject, not least Douglas Bradburn's essay in this volume, and, to mention another, the work of David Harris Sacks, both of which reveal the messianic impulses in the thinking of many involved in the early Virginia venture.[36] I do not mean to slight earlier work—and one can go a long way back, to, say, Perry Miller, who wrote an important essay on religion in early Virginia—or in more recent times, Michael Graham on Maryland toleration; Dell Upton on Anglican churches; Joan Gunderson, who in numerous studies has pointed to a vital Anglicanism; Beatriz Hardy on Maryland Catholics; and most recently, Edward Bond, who wrote an important book on Anglicanism in seventeenth-century Virginia; John Nelson, who wrote the companion for the eighteenth century; and John D. Krugler, who has probed the enigmatic relationship between religion and economics among the first three Calvert proprietors. But if one were to single out one person who has provided the most popular account of Chesapeake religion—both established Anglicanism and its most serious evangelical challenger, the countercultural Separate Baptists—then of course it is Rhys Isaac.[37]

Isaac is the key foil for a number of recent historians of Chesapeake religion. Lauren Winner's recent book, *A Cheerful and Comfortable Faith,* takes issue with what she sees as his overly functionalist reading of Anglicanism. In her view, Isaac is not concerned with Anglican religious practice per se but with the ways that Anglican religiosity supported the social order. By contrast, she reveals in compelling fashion that vital religious practices occurred in the household. Yes, the gentry's Anglicanism was a religion at ease with the world; its theology was by and large optimistic and not overly speculative. But liturgical forms of corporate worship, far from being tedious and empty, gave meaning and solace to people. Virginians were not indifferent to religion; they were not, as she puts it, "whited sepulchers just waiting for evangelical revivalists to 'awaken' them to the importance of Christianity." Rather, they wrestled with spiritual matters in their households and made active attempts to use religion to provide comfort, whether that meant reflecting on a wall hanging with a biblical reference, producing religious needlework, organizing meals around the liturgical calendar, or engaging in private and deeply felt mourning practices. Others too are writing in the same vein: a recent Oxford University dissertation explores what it terms the "Anglican Enlightenment"; Jacob Blosser provides an impressive discussion of moral duty and virtue in Anglican thinking in another recent dissertation.[38]

Other parts of Isaac's story have also come under attack. Jewel L. Spangler in her recent book has made a strong case that Baptists were not quite so oppositional as Isaac argued. She persuasively maintains that Baptists' success in Virginia was due in part to their creative ways of upholding and drawing on established communal rituals and norms. Although Baptists "tended to describe themselves as a people apart from the dominant order," Baptist practice "fit with and supported the fundamental social mores of the colony and codes of proper public conduct, as well as reinforcing the hierarchies of gender and race." For example, Baptists' "attempts to restrict the sexual activity of church members" dovetailed with "the code of sexual conduct that civil officials sought to enforce in Virginia." Baptists' concerns about fancy dress engaged Virginians at precisely the moment they were purging excessive luxury from daily life. Baptists, she claims, did not stand in stark opposition to the dominant culture, nor did they represent primarily the marginal. Similarly, Monica Najar argues that early evangelicals created churches that functioned as civil as well as religious entities. As Baptists sought to create a godly religious community, they scrutinized all aspects of their congregants' lives. In addition, Janet Moore Lindman focuses on the body-centered faith of Baptists. Conversion, she says, marked the Baptist body, and disciplining the Baptist body became a principal means of engendering spiritual identity and belief.[39]

Part of the motive for English settlement was sharing the Gospel with so-called Native American "infidels" and, later, alleged African "heathens," but there was always deep ambivalence about this project. Rebecca Goetz in her recent dissertation puts the role of religion front and center in the shaping of race in the early Chesapeake. Holly Brewer is investigating this issue via John Locke's writings. Religious debates were fundamental to race formation. At the same time, protoracial thinking was seriously constrained by the orthodox Christian belief in the monogenesis, or unity, of human origins. All humans descended from a single ancestor. To suggest otherwise was to risk heresy. Biblical sources were a first resort for answering questions such as were Native Americans the descendants of the ten Lost Tribes of Israel? Or were they wandering Tartars from northern Asia? Why were some people black, others tawny, and yet others white? Was the curse of Ham directed at Africans? As Colin Kidd notes, "During the early modern era, theological concerns helped to inhibit—and at the very least to circumscribe—the articulation of racial prejudices and the formulation of identities based upon race."[40]

Much of the religious eclecticism of the Chesapeake could be enriched if people probed even more deeply than they have the boundary of religion and magic. Catholics had available to them crucifixes, beads, popish images, and popish books—a reliance on material objects that proved a vital means by which they expressed their religion. As Elizabeth Roark has shown, Justus Engelhardt Kühn's portraits of eight-year-old Henry Darnall III (a well-known image in colonial American art) and of Henry's six-year-old sister Eleanor were suffused with Catholic iconography. As previously mentioned, at Jamestown, a number of crucifixes, rosary beads, and religious medallions featuring Catholic saints have been uncovered. In Protestantism, prayer books could also be drawn into rituals that historians sometimes categorize as "magical." The use of the prayer book as an object of enchantment should not be surprising. After the Reformation eliminated many so-called superstitious rituals, Protestants often attributed magical power to the holy word. Indeed, doing away with saints' relics, describing the consecrated host in decidedly unmagical terms, and generally purging religious objects imbued with special power left books as the only especially powerful objects to which the laity had access. Bibles placed on heads were thought to help children sleep. Fanning a sick person's face with the pages of a Bible was believed to restore health. Bibles figured in romantic divination. In such areas a considerable folklorization of magic existed in the early Chesapeake, even if there were few witches.[41]

These five are not the only promising directions for Chesapeake studies. Two of the pointers—those of scale and timing—are broad, general concerns; the other three are thematic and focused. It would be easy to add other themes: gender is an obvious candidate;[42] economics another;[43] urbanization a third;[44] literary studies, a real growth area, has much to contribute.[45] The Chesapeake is one of the largest estuaries in the world, but how many are studying it cartographically? Putting the Bay and the Atlantic Ocean into Chesapeake studies, as Jeff Bolster is doing for the Northeast Shelf marine ecosystem, would be invaluable.[46] The study of individuals or families—Ron Hoffman and Sally Mason's continuing work on the Carrolls, Annette Gordon-Reed on the Hemingses, Warren Billings on William Berkeley, Rhys Isaac on Landon Carter, Phillip Hamilton on the Tuckers, Laura Kamoie on the Tayloes, and so on—can be especially illuminating.[47] Charles Royster's *The Fabulous History of the Dismal Swamp Company* is even more timely now than when it was written, since it is such a marvelous dissection of elite pretensions and follies, the cronyism and corruption of the so-called Virginia gentlemen who conjured up the fantastically delusional enterprise of draining and developing a vast "low sunken Morass" along the Virginia–North Carolina border. Other such accounts of speculative schemes would be worth having.[48]

On the whole, the study of the Chesapeake region, then, seems to be thriving. It has always been inventive and eclectic. True, it once tended to be quantitative and demographic, but clearly much recent work is now far more capacious. True, too, it has always allowed a great role for archaeology, vernacular architecture, and material culture studies in general, and this tendency has only deepened of late. The cultural turn has certainly helped—shifting attention to interior, subjective experiences, to values and beliefs. Similarly, the broader Atlantic perspective has been all to the good; the inward-looking quality of much of this region's scholarly literature was once quite striking; attention to details seemed to matter more than far-reaching generalizations. That has now changed. The story of the seventeenth-century Chesapeake awaits a new master narrative. Edmund Morgan's magisterial work has stood for over a generation; it needs updating. The promise of seeing the Chesapeake whole, the sum of its many parts, beckons.[49]

Notes

1. The first conference was held March 4–7, 2004, and resulted in Peter C. Mancall, ed., *The Atlantic World and Virginia, 1550–1624* (Chapel Hill, NC, 2007); the second, The Early Chesapeake: Reflections and Projections, occurred on November 19–21, 2009 (hereafter the Early Chesapeake conference, 2009). The Omohundro Institute of Early American History and Culture, in cooperation with others, sponsored both. John Coombs invited me to deliver the summary plenary address at the latter conference, and, with revision, it has become this essay. I thank John and Doug Bradburn for encouraging me to rework my talk into this conclusion.

2. Introduction to Lois Green Carr, Philip D. Morgan, and Jean B. Russo, eds., *Colonial Chesapeake Society* (Chapel Hill, NC, 1988), 1–46 (some passages are reproduced here from pp. 1–2); Edmund S. Morgan and Marie Morgan, "Our Shaky Beginnings," *New York Review of Books*, April 26, 2007, 21–25, quote on 24. For another account, see Debra Meyers and Melanie Perreault, eds., *Colonial Chesapeake: New Perspectives* (Lanham, MD, 2006), xi–xxiii.

3. Jack P. Greene, *Pursuits of Happiness: The Social Development of Early Modern British Colonies and the Formation of American Culture* (Chapel Hill, NC, 1988), especially 1–54, 81–100, 170–209; David Hancock, *Oceans of Wine: Madeira and the Emergence of American Trade and Taste* (New Haven, CT, 2009), 111.

4. Karen Ordahl Kupperman, *The Jamestown Project* (Cambridge, MA, 2007), 1–3, 5,

8, 11, 253–54, 327. See also James Horn, *A Land as God Made It: Jamestown and the Birth of America* (New York, 2005); Robert Appelbaum and John Wood Sweet, eds., *Envisioning an English Empire: Jamestown and the Making of the North Atlantic World* (Philadelphia, 2005); Camilla Townsend, *Pocahontas and the Powhatan Dilemma* (New York, 2004); Helen C. Rountree, *Pocahontas, Powhatan, Opechancanough: Three Indian Lives Changed by Jamestown* (Charlottesville, VA, 2005); and William M. Kelso, *Jamestown: The Buried Truth* (Charlottesville, VA, 2006). The Atlantic turn has precedents in Chesapeake history, e.g., David Quinn, ed., *Early Maryland in a Wider World* (Detroit, 1982), and, more recently, April Lee Hatfield, *Atlantic Virginia: Intercolonial Relations in the Seventeenth Century* (Philadelphia, 2004).

5. Mancall, *Atlantic World and Virginia*, 2, 24, 25; Kupperman, *Jamestown Project*, 184, 192.

6. David S. Shields, "The Genius of Ancient Britons," in Mancall, *Atlantic World and Virginia*, 489–509, especially 494; J. A. Leo Lemay, *The American Dream of Captain John Smith* (Charlottesville, VA, 1991), 105. For views of Jamestown in large context, see particularly Kupperman, *Jamestown Project*, and Appelbaum and Sweet, *Envisioning an English Empire*; on Indians abroad, see Alden T. Vaughan, *Transatlantic Encounters: American Indians in Britain, 1500–1776* (New York, 2006), especially 42–56, 77–96.

7. See the brochure for the Early Chesapeake conference, 2009, http://oieahc.wm.edu/conferences/chesapeake/index.html.

8. Bernard Bailyn, "How England Became Modern: A Revolutionary View," *New York Review of Books*, November 19, 2009, 44; Bailyn, "Introduction: Reflections on Some Major Themes," in Bernard Bailyn and Patricia L. Denault, eds., *Soundings in Atlantic History: Latent Structures and Intellectual Currents, 1500–1830* (Cambridge, MA, 2009), 2.

9. James D. Rice, *Nature and History in the Potomac Country: From Hunter-Gatherers to the Age of Jefferson* (Baltimore, 2009); Robbie Ethridge, "Creating the Shatter Zone: Indian Slave Traders and the Collapse of the Southeastern Chiefdoms," in Thomas J. Pluckhahn and Robbie Ethridge, eds., *Light on the Path: The Anthropology and History of the Southeastern Indians* (Tuscaloosa, AL, 2006), 207–18; Robbie Etheridge and Sheri M. Shuck-Hall, eds., *Mapping the Mississippian Shatter Zone: The Colonial Indian Slave Trade and Regional Instability in the American South* (Lincoln, NE, 2009); Donald W. Pritchard and Jerry R. Schubel, "Human Influences on the Physical Characteristics of the Chesapeake Bay," in Philip D. Curtin, Grace Brush, and George W. Fisher, eds., *Discovering the Chesapeake: The History of an Ecosystem* (Baltimore, 2001), 60–82.

10. Martin D. Gallivan, *James River Chiefdoms: The Rise of Social Inequality in the Chesapeake* (Lincoln, NE, 2003). See also Edward D. Ragan's essay in this volume; his book MS won the 2009 Francis Jennings First Book Manuscript Prize in Early American Ethnohistory, sponsored by State University of New York Press, and will appear in its new series Ethnohistories of Early America. For other studies that place the Powhatans in larger perspective, see Helen C. Rountree, ed., *Powhatan Foreign Relations, 1500–1722* (Charlottesville, VA, 1993); Robbie Ethridge and Charles Hudson, eds., *Transformation of the Southeastern Indians, 1540–1760* (Jackson, MS, 2002); Dennis B. Blanton and Julia A. King, eds., *Indian and European Contact in Context: The Mid-Atlantic Region* (Gainesville, FL, 2004); Laura J. Galke, "Perspectives on the Use of European Material Culture at Two Mid-to-Late 17th-Century Native American Sites in the Chesapeake," *North American Archaeologist* 25, no. 1 (2004): 91–113; Eric E. Bowne, *The Westo Indians: Slave Traders of the Early Colonial South* (Tuscaloosa, AL, 2005); Gregory A. Waselkov, Peter H. Wood, and

Tom Hatley, eds., *Powhatan's Mantle: Indians in the Colonial Southeast*, rev. and expanded ed. (Lincoln, NE, 2006); Paul Kelton, *Epidemics and Enslavement: Biological Catastrophe in the Native Southeast, 1492–1715* (Lincoln, NE, 2007); and Joseph M. Hall Jr., *Zamumo's Gifts: Indian-European Exchange in the Colonial Southeast* (Philadelphia, 2009). See also the following papers delivered at the Early Chesapeake conference, 2009: Julia King and Dennis Curry, "'Forced to Fall to Making of Bows and Arrows': The Material Conditions of Indian Life in the Chesapeake, 1660–1710"; Maureen Meyers, "Native Trade in a Colonial Sphere: The Westo Indians in the Early Chesapeake"; Stephanie Crumbaugh, "Mergers and Migrations on the Virginia Frontier: Fort Christanna and the Creation of the Saponi Nation, 1670–1740"; and Stephen Feeley, "Pathways and Boundaries: Tuscaroras, Virginia, and Native Networks, 1676–1722."

11. Lauren Benton, *A Search for Sovereignty: Law and Geography in European Empires, 1400–1900* (New York, 2010), 40–103. See also on those two events Helen C. Rountree, Wayne E. Clark, and Kent Mountford, *John Smith's Chesapeake Voyages, 1607–1609* (Charlottesville, VA, 2007); and James D. Rice, "Bacon's Rebellion in Indian Country," paper presented at Washington Area Seminar in Early American History, October 1, 2009.

12. Lorena S. Walsh, "Summing the Parts: Implications for Estimating Chesapeake Output and Income Subregionally," *William and Mary Quarterly*, 3rd ser., 56 (1999): 53–94. For other impressive regional explorations, see Walsh, "The Chesapeake Slave Trade: Regional Patterns, African Origins, and Some Implications," *William and Mary Quarterly*, 3rd ser., 58 (2001): 139–70; and J. Elliott Russo, "The Chesapeake's Invisible People: Labor Resources of Small Planters in Early Eighteenth-Century Maryland and Virginia," paper delivered at the Early Chesapeake conference, 2009.

13. Jack P. Greene, "The Constitution of 1787 and the Question of Southern Distinctiveness," in Robert J. Haws, ed., *The South's Role in the Creation of the Bill of Rights* (Jackson, MS, 1991), 9–31, 147–49; Bradford J. Wood, "The Southward Expansion of the Chesapeake: The Albemarle Settlements, 1660–1730," paper delivered at the Early Chesapeake conference, 2009; Noeleen McIlvenna, *A Very Mutinous People: The Struggle for North Carolina, 1660–1713* (Chapel Hill, NC, 2009) (see also Bradford J. Wood's review in *Reviews in American History* [forthcoming]); Warren R. Hofstra, *The Planting of New Virginia: Settlement and Landscape in the Shenandoah Valley* (Baltimore, 2004); Hofstra, "The Backcountry Counterpoint to the Developing Chesapeake, 1700–1730," paper delivered at the Early Chesapeake conference, 2009; L. Scott Philyaw, *Virginia's Western Visions: Political and Cultural Expansion on an Early American Frontier* (Knoxville, TN, 2004); David Hackett Fischer and James C. Kelly, *Bound Away: Virginia and the Westward Movement* (Charlottesville, VA, 2000).

14. Alison Games, *The Web of Empire: English Cosmopolitans in an Age of Expansion, 1560–1660* (New York, 2008), 117–46, and for Ireland's singularity, 255–87; Andrew Hadfield, "Irish Colonies and the Americas," in Appelbaum and Sweet, *Envisioning an English Empire*, 172–91 (but cf. Kupperman, *Jamestown Project*, 194–209, and Nicholas Canny, *Kingdom and Colony: Ireland in the Atlantic World, 1560–1800* [Baltimore, 1988]); Michael Jarvis, "'In the Eye of All Trade': Maritime Revolution and the Transformation of Bermudian Society, 1612–1800," (Ph.D. diss., College of William and Mary, 1998) (Jarvis is now at work on the seventeenth-century connections between Virginia and Bermuda); Neil Kennedy, "Anglo-Bermudian Society in the English Atlantic World, 1612–1701," (Ph.D. diss., University of Western Ontario, 2002); Eliga H. Gould, "Entangled Histories, En-

tangled Worlds: The English-Speaking Atlantic as a Spanish Periphery," *American Historical Review*, 112 (2007): 764–86, quote on 769; Lisa Voigt, *Writing Captivity in the Early Modern Atlantic: Circulations of Knowledge and Authority in the Iberian and English Imperial Worlds* (Chapel Hill, NC, 2009), 39, 303–19; J. H. Elliott, *Empires of the Atlantic World: Britain and Spain in America, 1492–1830* (New Haven, CT, 2006) and "The Iberian Atlantic and Virginia," in Mancall, *Atlantic World and Virginia*, 541–57.

15. J. R. McNeil, *Mosquito Empires: Ecology, Epidemics, and Revolutions in the Greater Caribbean, 1620–1914* (New York, 2010), 195–234. For other ways of thinking about Virginia as part of the Greater Caribbean, see Philip D. Morgan, "Virginia's Other Prototype: The Caribbean," and Stuart B. Schwartz, "Virginia and the Atlantic World," in Mancall, *Atlantic World and Virginia*, 342–80, 558–70. See also Gregory E. O'Malley, "Beyond the Middle Passage: Slave Migration from the Caribbean to North America, 1619–1807," *William and Mary Quarterly*, 3rd ser., 66 (2009), 125–72.

16. Introduction to Carr, Morgan, and Russo, *Colonial Chesapeake Society*, 33–34. This is as true now as when stated over twenty years ago.

17. Ira Berlin, *Many Thousands Gone: The First Two Centuries of Slavery in North America* (Cambridge, MA, 1998), 29–46; Linda M. Heywood and John K. Thornton, *Central Africans, Atlantic Creoles, and the Foundation of the Americas, 1585–1660* (New York, 2007), especially 242–48; John C. Coombs's essay in this volume and his "Building 'The Machine': The Development of Slavery and Slave Society in Early Colonial Virginia," (Ph. D. diss., College of William and Mary, 2004); Russell R. Menard, "Making Slave Society in Colonial British America: Some Evidence from St. Mary's County, Maryland," paper delivered at the Early Chesapeake conference, 2009. For the distinction between slave owning and slave society, see Philip D. Morgan, "British Encounters with Africans and Afro-Americans, circa 1600–1780," in Bernard Bailyn and Philip D. Morgan, eds., *Strangers in the Realm: Cultural Margins of the First British Empire* (Chapel Hill, NC, 1991), 163. For Indian slavery, see Owen Stanwood, "Captives and Slaves: Indian Labor, Cultural Conversion, and the Plantation Revolution in Virginia," *Virginia Magazine of History and Biography* 114 (2006): 435–63. The seventeenth century poses many conundrums. For an insightful discussion of Mathias de Sousa, often described as the first black Marylander, possibly a Portuguese "mulatto" who also seems to have been capable of passing as white, and the burial of a European with some African-style mortuary features in the 1680s at Patuxent Point, Calvert County, see Julia A. King and Edward E. Chaney, "Passing for Black in Seventeenth-Century Maryland," in Mary C. Beaudry and James Symonds, eds., *Interpreting the Early Modern World through Archaeology* (New York, 2010), as well as David S. Bogen, "Mathias de Sousa: Maryland's First Colonist of African Descent," *Maryland Historical Magazine* 96, no. 1 (Spring 2001): 68–85.

18. Douglas Bradburn and John C. Coombs, "Smoke and Mirrors: Reinterpreting the Society and Economy of the Seventeenth-Century Chesapeake," *Atlantic Studies* 3, no. 2 (October 2006): 131–57; Lorena S. Walsh, *Motives of Honor, Pleasure, and Profit: Plantation Management in the Colonial Chesapeake* (Chapel Hill, NC, 2010), chaps. 3–4.

19. Willie Graham et al., "Adaptation and Innovation: Archaeological and Architectural Perspectives on the Seventeenth-Century Chesapeake," *William and Mary Quarterly* 3rd ser., 64 (2007): 451–522; and the following papers presented at the Early Chesapeake conference, 2009: Cary Carson, "William Berkeley's Green Spring and the Problem of Cultural Readiness"; Camille Wells, "An Embarrassment of Riches: What Rosewell

Meant in Early Virginia"; Amy Speckart, "Fashioning a Role among Maryland's Emerging Native Elite: Edward Lloyd II at the Turn of the Eighteenth Century"; Joanne Bowen, "The Transformation of the Chesapeake"; Paul Musselwhite, "Contesting Cohabitation: Reconsidering the Debate over Towns in the Chesapeake, 1652–1710"; Hank D. Lutton, "'No Towns of Consequence': Contextualizing and Reconsidering Urban Places in the Colonial Chesapeake"; Victor Enthoven, "The Early Chesapeake and the Dutch Connection, 1680–1730"; and Douglas Bradburn, "The Visible Fist: The Chesapeake Tobacco Trade in War and the Purpose of Empire, 1690–1715." On urbanization, see also Silas D. Hurry, *"Once the Metropolis of Maryland": The History and Archaeology of Maryland's First Capital* (St. Mary's City, 2001); Mark P. Leone, *The Archaeology of Liberty in an American Capital: Excavations in Annapolis* (Berkeley, CA, 2005); Christopher E. Hendricks, *The Backcountry Towns of Colonial Virginia* (Knoxville, TN, 2006); and Michael Thomas Lucas, "Negotiating Public Landscapes: History, Archaeology, and the Material Culture of Colonial Chesapeake Towns, 1680 to 1720" (Ph.D. diss., University of Maryland, 2008).

20. Walsh, *Motives of Honor, Pleasure, and Profit*, chaps. 3–4.

21. Introduction to Carr, Morgan, and Russo, *Colonial Chesapeake Society*, 34–36 (again, as true now as when stated over twenty years ago). Walsh's book, as noted, provides a culminating synthesis.

22. Carson, "William Berkeley's Green Spring." In addition to some of the references in n. 19 above, I would also single out three important works: Barbara Wells Sarudy, *Gardens and Gardening in the Chesapeake, 1700–1805* (Baltimore, 1998); Cary Carson et al., "New World, Real World: Improvising English Culture in Seventeenth-Century Virginia," *Journal of Southern History* 74, no. 1 (February 2008): 31–88; and Ann Smart Martin, *Buying into the World of Goods: Early Consumers in Backcountry Virginia* (Baltimore, 2008).

23. I am greatly indebted to Beverly Straube for providing all the information in this paragraph. Her dissertation, "Surprises from the Soil: Unexpected Objects and What They Reveal about Life in England's First Successful Colony" (University of Leicester, forthcoming) is eagerly awaited. For other specifics, see Eric Deetz, "Architecture of Early Virginia: An Analysis of the Origins of Earthfast Tradition" (master's thesis, University of Leicester, 2001); Carter C. Hudgins, "Elizabethan Industries in Jacobean Virginia? An Examination of the Industrial Origins and Metallurgical functions of Scrap Copper at Early Jamestown (c. 1607–1610)" (Ph.D. diss., Royal Holloway College, London, 2005); Hudgins, "Articles of Exchange or Ingredients of New World Metallurgy?" *Early American Studies* 3, no. 1 (2005): 32–64; Daniel Schmidt, "Subsistence Fishing at Jamestown, 1607–1624," *Post-Medieval Archaeology* 40, no. 1 (2006): 80–95; Beverly Straube, "'Unfitt for Any Moderne Service'? Arms and Armour from James Fort," *Post-Medieval Archaeology* 40, no. 1 (2006): 33–61; Hudgins, "A Roman Oil Lamp Illuminates 17th-Century Jamestown," *Ceramics in America* 8 (2008): 78–84; Juliana M. Harding, Roger Mann, and Melissa J. Southworth, "Shell Length-at-Age Relationships in James River, Virginia, Oysters (*Crassostrea Virginica*) Collected Four Centuries Apart," *Journal of Shellfish Research* 27, no. 5 (2008): 1109–15. See also Kelso, *Jamestown*, 51–52, 59–60, 80–89, 102, 104, 106–10, 178–79, 180–89.

24. I am particularly grateful to Cary Carson for sharing with me his illuminating chapter 2 of Edward Chappell, Carl Lounsbury, and Cary Carson, eds., *The Chesapeake House: The Practice of Architectural Investigation by Colonial Williamsburg* (Chapel Hill, NC, forthcoming). See also Garrett Fesler, "From Houses to Homes: An Archaeological Case Study of Household Formation at the Utopia Slave Quarter, ca. 1675 to 1775" (Ph.D.

diss., University of Virginia, 2004); Susan Kern, "The Material World of the Jeffersons at Shadwell," *William and Mary Quarterly*, 3rd ser., 62 (2005): 213–42; Carl R. Lounsbury, *The Courthouses of Early Virginia: An Architectural History* (Charlottesville, VA, 2005); Bernard L. Herman, *Town House: Architecture and Material Life in the Early American City, 1780–1830* (Chapel Hill, NC, 2005).

25. Sally M. Walker, *Written in Bone: Buried Lives of Jamestown and Colonial Maryland* (Minneapolis, 2009), 26. For a more conventional view, see Erik Seeman, *Death in the New World: Cross-Cultural Encounters, 1492–1800* (Philadelphia, 2010), chap. 3; Timothy B. Riordan, *Dig a Grave Both Wide and Deep: An Archaeological Investigation of Mortuary Practices in the 17th-Century Cemetery at St. Mary's City, Maryland*, St. Mary's City Archaeology Series, no. 3 (St. Mary's City, 2000); and Historic St. Mary's City, Project Lead Coffins: Laboratory Analysis, 2007, http://www.stmaryscity.org/Lead%20Coffins/project_lead_coffins.htm. For morbidity, see James D. Alsop, "Royal Naval Morbidity in Early Eighteenth-Century Virginia," in Meyers and Perreault, *Colonial Chesapeake*, 141–77.

26. Walker, *Written in Bone*. The exhibit at the Smithsonian National Museum of Natural History (February 7, 2009–January 6, 2013) in Washington, DC, is breathtaking. For the website, see http://anthropology.si.edu/writteninbone. See also Kenneth Cohen, review of the website Written in Bone: Forensic Files from the 17th Century, in *Journal of American History* 96 (December 2009): 778–81; Douglas H. Ubelaker and Douglas W. Owsley, "Isotopic Evidence for Diet in the Seventeenth-Century Colonial Chesapeake," *American Antiquity* 68, no. 1 (2003): 129–39; R. H. Steckel and J. C. Rose, eds., *The Backbone of History: Health and Nutrition in the Western Hemisphere* (Cambridge, 2002), 208–25; Kelso, *Jamestown*, 125–68; Thao T. Phung, Julia A. King, and Douglas H. Ubelaker, "Alcohol, Tobacco, and Excessive Animal Protein: The Question of an Adequate Diet in the Seventeenth-Century Chesapeake," *Historical Archaeology* 43, no. 2 (2009): 61–82. For the Chesapeake diet, see James E. McWilliams, *A Revolution in Eating: How the Quest for Food Shaped America* (New York, 2005), especially 89–130; and Trudy Eden, *Early American Table: Food and Society in the New World* (DeKalb, IL, 2008).

27. Shepard Krech III, *Spirits of the Air: Birds and American Indians in the South* (Athens, GA, 2009), xi, 63.

28. John C. Coombs, Philip Levy, and David Muraca, "The Death of the Chesapeake? Rethinking Interpretive Scale in the Archaeological Study of Early Virginia and Maryland," paper delivered at the annual meeting of the Society for Historical Archaeology, January 9–14, 2007; A Comparative Archaeological Study of Colonial Chesapeake Culture, http://www.chesapeakearchaeology.org; Digital Archaeological Archive of Comparative Slavery, http://www.daacs.org; Fraser D. Neiman, "The Lost World of Monticello in Evolutionary Perspective," *Journal of Anthropological Research* 64, no. 2 (Summer 2008): 161–93; Patricia M. Samford, *Subfloor Pits and the Archaeology of Slavery in Colonial Virginia* (Tuscaloosa, AL, 2007); Jillian Galle, "Costly Signaling and Gendered Social Strategies among Slaves in the Eighteenth-Century Chesapeake: An Archaeological Perspective," *American Antiquity* 75, no. 1 (January 2010): 19–25; Galle, "Big Island, Small World: The Archaeological Correlates of Male and Female Signaling Strategies in Eighteenth-Century Jamaica and Virginia," in James Delle and Mark Hauser, eds., *The Historical Archaeology of Jamaica* (Tuscaloosa, AL, forthcoming). For another impressive material culture study of slaves, see Garrett R. Fesler, "Living Arrangements among Enslaved Women and Men at an Early-Eighteenth-Century Virginia Quartering Site," in Jillian E. Galle

and Amy L. Young, eds., *Engendering African American Archaeology: A Southern Perspective* (Knoxville, TN, 2004), 177–236.

29. Douglas W. Sanford and Dennis Pogue, "Measuring the Social, Spatial, and Temporal Dimensions of Virginia Slave Housing," (unpublished manuscript, 2009; my thanks to Dennis Pogue for this information); Bowen, "The Transformation of the Chesapeake," paper delivered at the Early Chesapeake conference, 2009; cf. Virginia DeJohn Anderson, *Creatures of Empire: How Domestic Animals Transformed Early America* (New York, 2004), 75–79, 100–105, 107–40. For ecological change, see Henry M. Miller, "Transforming a 'Splendid and Delightsome Land': Colonists and Ecological Change in the Chesapeake, 1607–1820," *Journal of the Washington Academy of Sciences* 76 (September 1986): 173–87; Charles Hardy, "Fish or Foul: A History of the Delaware River Basin through the Perspective of the American Shad, 1682 to the Present," *Pennsylvania History* 66 (1999), 506–34; and, for the most comprehensive look, see the various essays in Curtin, Brush, and Fisher, *Discovering the Chesapeake*.

30. Most of Jack P. Greene's many essays on Virginia can be found in *Imperatives, Behaviors, and Identities: Essays in Early American Cultural History* (Charlottesville, VA, 1992); *Negotiated Authorities: Essays in Colonial, Political, and Constitutional History* (Charlottesville, VA, 1994); and *Understanding the American Revolution: Issues and Actors* (Charlottesville, VA, 1995), 209–46. Warren E. Billings, John E. Selby, and Thad W. Tate, *Colonial Virginia: A History* (White Plains, NY, 1986); Jon Kukla, "Order and Chaos in Early America: Political and Social Stability in Pre-Restoration Virginia," *American Historical Review* 90 (April 1985): 275–98; Kukla, *Political Institutions in Virginia, 1619–1660* (New York, 1989); Woody Holton, *Forced Founders: Indians, Debtors, Slaves, and the Making of the American Revolution in Virginia* (Chapel Hill, NC, 1999); John Ruston Pagan, *Anne Orthwood's Bastard: Sex and Law in Early Virginia* (New York, 2003); Warren M. Billings, *A Little Parliament: The Virginia General Assembly in the Seventeenth Century* (Richmond, 2004); David Thomas Konig, "Virginia and the Imperial State: Law, Enlightenment, and 'the Crooked Cord of Discretion,'" in David Lemmings, ed., *The British and Their Laws in the Eighteenth Century* (Woodbridge, UK, 2005), 206–29; Kevin R. Hardwick, "Narratives of Villainy and Virtue: Governor Francis Nicholson and the Character of the Good Ruler in Early Virginia," *Journal of Southern History* 72 (February 2006): 39–74; Michael A. McDonnell, *The Politics of War: Race, Class, and Conflict in Revolutionary Virginia* (Chapel Hill, NC, 2007); Kevin R. C. Gutzman, *Virginia's American Revolution: From Dominion to Republic, 1776–1840* (Lanham, MD, 2007); Emory G. Evans, *A "Topping People": The Rise and Decline of Virginia's Old Political Elite, 1680–1790* (Charlottesville, VA, 2009).

31. Ken MacMillan, *Sovereignty and Possession in the English New World: The Legal Foundations of Empire, 1576–1640* (New York, 2006); but also see Lauren Benton and Benjamin Straumann, "Acquiring Empire by Law: From Roman Doctrine to Early Modern European Practice," *Law and History Review* 28, no. 1 (February 2010), 3–27; MacMillan, "Crown and Empire: Center and Periphery in the English Atlantic World, 1603–1640" (unpublished manuscript); Michael Grossberg and Christopher Tomlins, eds., *The Cambridge History of Law in America*, vol. 1, *Early America (1580–1815)* (New York, 2008), especially 1–31, 63–103, 144–77, 400–46; Holly Brewer, *By Birth or Consent: Children, Law, and the Anglo-American Revolution in Authority* (Chapel Hill, NC, 2005). For more on children, see Jean B. Russo and J. Elliott Russo, "Responsive Justices: Court Treatment of Orphans and Illegitimate Children in Colonial Maryland," and Holly Brewer, "Appren-

ticeship Policy in Virginia: From Patriarchal to Republican Policies of Social Welfare," in Ruth Wallis Herndon and John E. Murray, eds., *Children Bound to Labor: The Pauper Apprenticeship System in Early America* (Ithaca, NY, 2009), 151–65, 183–97.

32. Christopher L. Tomlins, "Introduction: The Many Legalities of Colonization: A Manifesto of Destiny for Early American Legal History," in Tomlins and Bruce H. Mann, eds., *The Many Legalities of Early America* (Chapel Hill, NC, 2001), 1–23; William E. Nelson, *The Common Law in Colonial America*, vol. 1, *The Chesapeake and New England, 1607–1660* (New York, 2008), 3–48, 101–35; Tomlins, *Freedom Bound: Law, Labor, and Civic Identity in Colonizing English America, 1580–1865* (New York, 2010).

33. David Armitage, *The Ideological Origins of the British Empire* (Cambridge, 2000); Andrew Fitzmaurice, *Humanism and America: An Intellectual History of English Colonisation, 1500–1625* (Cambridge, 2003); Fitzmaurice, "The Commercial Ideology of Colonization in Jacobean England: Robert Johnson, Giovanni Botero and the Pursuit of Greatness," *William and Mary Quarterly*, 3rd ser., 64 (2007): 791–820; Fitzmaurice, "Moral Uncertainty in the Dispossession of Native Americans," in Mancall, *Atlantic World and Virginia*, 383–409; Alec Haskell, "Marchland or Commonwealth? Competing Visions of Polity in the Settlement of the Virginia Colony 1577–1622," paper delivered at the USC-Huntington Early Modern Studies Institute, September 26, 2009; Haskell, "Corrupting the Commonwealth, Jeopardizing Empire: The Founding of Maryland as a Problem (and Opportunity) in Virginia Politics," paper delivered at the Early Chesapeake conference, 2009; Haskell, "Defining the Right Side of Virtue: Crowd Narratives, the Newspaper, and the Lee-Mercer Dispute in Rhetorical Perspective," *Early American Studies* 8 (2010): 120–45; Haskell, *Civility, Rhetoric, and the People's Love: Forging the Bonds of Commonwealth in English Virginia* (Chapel Hill, NC, forthcoming).

34. Peter Thompson, "The Thief, the Householder, and the Commons: Languages of Class in Virginia," *William and Mary Quarterly*, 3rd. ser., 63 (2006): 253–80; Thompson, "William Bullock's 'Strange Adventure': A Plan to Transform Seventeenth-Century Virginia," *William and Mary Quarterly*, 3rd ser., 61 (2004): 107–28.

35. Timothy B. Riordan, *The Plundering Time: Maryland and the English Civil War, 1645–1646* (Baltimore, 2004), especially 5, 14, 330; Antoinette Sutto, "'You Dog ... Give Me Your Hand': Lord Baltimore and the Death of Christopher Rousby," *Maryland Historical Magazine* 102, no. 4 (Winter 2007): 240–57; Sutto, "Lord Baltimore, the Society of Jesus and Caroline Absolutism in Maryland, 1630–1645," *Journal of British Studies* 48 (July 2009): 631–52; Sutto, "The Borders of Absolutism: Restoration Politics, Royal Authority, and the Maryland-Pennsylvania Boundary Conflict, 1681–1685," *Pennsylvania History: A Journal of Mid-Atlantic Studies* 76, no. 3 (Summer 2009): 276–300; Sutto, "Bloodsucking Sectaries, Malicious Papists, and Obedient Protestants: Two Versions of a Revolution in Maryland, 1652–1655," paper delivered at The Early Chesapeake conference, 2009; Sutto, "Built upon Smoke: Politics and Political Culture in Early Maryland," unpublished book manuscript. For other work that sets Chesapeake politics into a larger imperial frame, see Tom Cogswell, "'In the Power of the State': Mr. Anys's Project and the Tobacco Colonies, 1626–1628," *English Historical Review* 123, no. 500 (February 2008): 35–64; and Russell Scott Stoermer, "Constitutional Sense, Revolutionary Sensibility: Political Cultures in the Making and Breaking of British Virginia, 1707–1776" (Ph.D. diss., University of Virginia, 2010).

36. David Harris Sacks, "Discourses of Western Planting: Richard Hakluyt and the Making of the Atlantic World," in Mancall, *Atlantic World and Virginia*, 410–53; David

Boruchoff, "Piety, Patriotism, and Empire: Lessons for England, Spain, and the New World in the Works of Richard Hakluyt," *Renaissance Quarterly* 62, no. 3 (Fall 2009): 809–58; David Harris Sacks, "'To Deduce a Colonie': Richard Hakluyt's Godly Mission in its Contexts, c. 1580–1616," in Daniel Carey and Claire Jowitt, eds., *Richard Hakluyt (c. 1552–1616): Life, Times, Legacy* (London, forthcoming).

37. In chronological order: Perry Miller, "The Religious Impulse in the Founding of Virginia: Religion and Society in the Early Literature," *William and Mary Quarterly*, 3rd ser., 5 (1948): 492–522; Rhys Isaac, *The Transformation of Virginia, 1740–1790* (Chapel Hill, NC, 1982); Michael James Graham, "Lord Baltimore's Pious Enterprise: Toleration and Community in Colonial Maryland, 1634–1724" (Ph.D. diss., University of Michigan, 1983); Dell Upton, *Holy Things and Profane: Anglican Parish Churches in Colonial Virginia* (New Haven, CT, 1987); Joan R. Gunderson, *The Anglican Ministry in Virginia, 1723–1766: A Study of a Social Class* (New York, 1989); Beatriz Betancourt Hardy, "Roman Catholics, Not Papists: Catholic Identity in Maryland, 1689–1776," *Maryland Historical Magazine* 92 (Summer 1997): 139–81; Edward L. Bond, *Damned Souls in a Tobacco Colony: Religion in Seventeenth-Century Virginia* (Macon, GA, 2000); John K. Nelson, *A Blessed Company: Parishes, Parsons, and Parishioners in Anglican Virginia, 1690–1776* (Chapel Hill, NC, 2001); John D. Krugler, *English and Catholic: The Lords Baltimore in the Seventeenth Century* (Baltimore, 2004); Edward L. Bond, *Spreading the Gospel in Colonial Virginia: Preaching, Religion, and Community; With Selected Sermons and Other Primary Documents* (Lanham, MD, 2004); Paul Rasor and Richard E. Bond, eds., *From Jamestown to Jefferson: The Evolution of Religious Freedom in Virginia* (Charlottesville, VA, 2011). For an older but still useful essay, see Darrett B. Rutman, "The Evolution of Religious Life in Early Virginia," *Lex and Scientia: Journal of the American Academy of Law* 14 (1978): 190–214, subsequently reprinted as "Magic, Christianity, and Church in Early Virginia," in Darrett B. Rutman with Anita H. Rutman, *Small Worlds, Large Questions: Explorations in Early American Social History, 1600–1850* (Charlottesville, VA, 1994), 134–57. For the best general survey, see Jon Butler, *Awash in a Sea of Faith: Christianizing the American People* (Cambridge, MA 1990). For a useful overview of this literature, see Brent Tarter, "Reflections on the Church of England in Colonial Virginia," *Virginia Magazine of History and Biography* 112 (2004): 338–71.

38. Lauren Winner, *A Cheerful and Comfortable Faith: Anglican Religious Practice in the Elite Households of Eighteenth-Century Virginia* (New Haven, CT, 2010); Albert Zambone, "Anglican Enlightenment: Intellectual Culture in Virginia, 1690–1750," (Ph.D. diss., Oxford University, 2009); Jacob M. Blosser, "Pursuing Happiness: Cultural Discourse and Popular Religion in Anglican Virginia, 1700–1770" (Ph.D. diss., University of South Carolina, 2006); Blosser, "Irreverent Empire: Anglican Inattention in an Atlantic World," *Church History* 77, no. 3 (September 2008): 596–628; Stuart Schwartz, *All Can Be Saved: Religious Toleration and Salvation in the Iberian Atlantic World* (New Haven, CT, 2008). See also Anne Sorrell Dent, "God and Gentry: Public and Private Religion in Tidewater Virginia, 1607–1800" (Ph.D. diss., University of Kentucky, 2001); and Kevin R. Hardwick, "Anglican Moderation: Religion and the Political Thought of Edmund Randolph," in Daniel L. Dreisbach, Mark David Hall, and Jeffrey H. Morrison, eds., *The Forgotten Founders on Religion and Public Life* (Notre Dame, IN, 2009), 196–219. For a study that praises and builds on Isaac, see Randolph Ferguson Scully, *Religion and the Making of Nat Turner's Virginia: Baptist Community and Conflict, 1740–1840* (Charlottesville, VA, 2008), 19–92.

39. Jewel L. Spangler, *Virginians Reborn: Anglican Monopoly, Evangelical Dissent, and the Rise of the Baptists in the Late Eighteenth Century* (Charlottesville, VA, 2008), 119–66, 184–93; Monica Najar, *Evangelizing the South: A Social History of Church and State in Early America* (New York, 2008); Janet Lindman Moore, *Bodies of Belief: Baptist Community in Early America* (Philadelphia, 2008); Thomas E. Buckley, SJ, "Patrick Henry, Religious Liberty, and the Search for Civic Virtue," in Dreisbach, Hall, and Morrison, *The Forgotten Founders*, 125–44; John A. Ragosta, "Fighting for Freedom: Virginia Dissenters' Struggle for Religious Liberty during the American Revolution," *Virginia Magazine of History and Biography* 116 (2008), 226–61.

40. Rebecca Anne Goetz, "From Potential Christians to Hereditary Heathens: Religion and Race in the Early Chesapeake, 1590–1740" (Ph.D. diss., Harvard University, 2006); Holly Brewer, "'Baptized, Catechized, and Bred Christians': Tracing Slaves, Subjects, Suffrage and Sovereignty through the Religious Debates of the Early British Atlantic," paper delivered at the Early Chesapeake conference, 2009; Colin Kidd, *The Forging of Races: Race and Scripture in the Protestant Atlantic World, 1600–2000* (New York, 2006), especially 54–120, quote on 57. See also Charles F. Irons, *The Origins of Proslavery Christianity: White and Black Evangelicals in Colonial and Antebellum Virginia* (Chapel Hill, NC, 2008).

41. Elizabeth L. Roark, "Keeping the Faith: The Catholic Context and Content of Justus Engelhardt Kühn's Portraits of Eleanor and Henry Darnell III, ca. 1710," paper delivered at the Early Chesapeake conference, 2009; Shona Johnston, "'All the Popes Trinkets': Catholic Artifacts and Religious Practice in the English Atlantic World," paper presented at Georgetown University Early Modern Global History Seminar, November 13, 2009.

42. Apart from Snyder's essay in this volume, some key works include the classic by Lois Carr and Lorena Walsh, "The Planter's Wife: The Experience of White Women in Seventeenth-Century Maryland," *William and Mary Quarterly*, 3rd ser., 34 (1977): 542–71; Kathleen M. Brown, *Good Wives, Nasty Wenches, and Anxious Patriarchs: Gender, Race, and Power in Colonial Virginia* (Chapel Hill, NC, 1996); Mary Beth Norton, *Founding Mothers and Fathers: Gendered Power and the Forming of American Society* (New York, 1997); Linda L. Sturtz, *"Within Her Power": Propertied Women in Colonial Virginia* (New York, 2002); Carole Shammas, *A History of Household Government in America* (Charlottesville, VA, 2002); Terri L. Snyder, *Brabbling Women: Disorderly Speech and the Law in Early Virginia* (Ithaca, NY, 2003); Katherine Kerrison, *Claiming the Pen: Women and Intellectual Life in the Early American South* (Ithaca, NY, 2005); and Sarah Hand Meacham, *Every Home a Distillery: Alcohol, Gender, and Technology in the Colonial Chesapeake* (Baltimore, 2009).

43. For example, see Lois Green Carr, "Emigration and the Standard of Living: The Eighteenth-Century Chesapeake," and Richard S. Dunn, "After Tobacco: The Slave Labour Pattern on a Large Chesapeake Grain-and-Livestock Plantation in the Early Nineteenth Century," in John J. McCusker and Kenneth Morgan, eds., *The Early Modern Atlantic Economy* (Cambridge, 2000), 319–43, 344–63; Jean E. Russo, "'Fifty-Four Days Work of Two Negroes': Enslaved Labor in Colonial Somerset, Maryland," *Agricultural History* 78 (2004): 466–92; Lorena S. Walsh, "Mercantile Strategies, Credit Networks, and Labor Supply in the Colonial Chesapeake in Trans-Atlantic Perspective," in David Eltis, Frank Lewis, and Kenneth Sokoloff, eds., *Slavery in the Development of the Americas* (New York, 2004), 89–119; Eltis, Lewis, and Sokoloff, "The Role of Aristocratic Management Strategies in the Economic Development of the British North American Chesapeake," in Paul Janssens and Bartolomé Yun-Casalilla, eds., *European Aristocracies and Colonial*

Elites: Patrimonial Management Strategies and Economic Development, 15th–18th Centuries (Farnham, UK, 2005), 199–211; Eltis, Lewis, and Sokoloff, "Liverpool's Slave Trade to the Colonial Chesapeake: Slaving on the Periphery," in David Richardson, Suzanne Schwarz, and Anthony J. Tibbles, eds., *Liverpool and Transatlantic Slavery* (Liverpool, 2007), 98–117; Kenneth Cohen, "Well Calculated for the Farmer: Thoroughbreds in the Chesapeake, 1750–1850," *Virginia Magazine of History and Biography* 115, no. 3 (October 2007), 370–411; Justin Roberts, "Sunup to Sundown: Plantation Management Strategies and Slave Work Routines in Barbados, Jamaica and Virginia, c. 1780–1810" (Ph D. diss., Johns Hopkins University, 2008); Alvin Rabushka, *Taxation in Colonial America* (Princeton, NJ, 2008), especially 228–66, 416–36, 519–55, 657–711, 826–63; David Hancock, *Oceans of Wine*, xix, 73, 87, 98, 103, 110–11, 143, 145, 148, 151–55, 163, 179, 210, 275, 288–90, 299–301, 333–34, 358–60, 370, 374, 391.

44. See the works by Musselwhite, Lutton, Hurry, Leone, Hendricks, and Lucas mentioned in n. 19.

45. One subset of literary studies consists of histories of the book; recent works include: Kevin J. Hayes, *The Road to Monticello: The Life and Mind of Thomas Jefferson* (New York, 2008); and Hayes, *The Mind of a Patriot: Patrick Henry and the World of Ideas* (Charlottesville, VA, 2008). Another subset comprises studies of letters: see, for example, Sarah M. S. Pearsall, *Atlantic Families: Lives and Letters in the Later Eighteenth Century* (Oxford, 2008), and Konstantin Dierks, *In My Power: Letter Writing and Communications in Early America* (Philadelphia, 2009), both of which contain a fair amount of Chesapeake material. Edward Kimber, *The History of the Life and Adventures of Mr. Anderson*, ed. Matthew Mason and Nicholas Mason (1754; Peterborough, ON, 2009) is set partly in the Chesapeake, as was of course Defoe's *Colonel Jack* and *Moll Flanders*. It would be easy to multiply the references not just in the literary realm but in the cultural sphere more generally.

46. On maps, see Lisa Blansett, "John Smith Maps Virginia: Knowledge, Rhetoric, and Politics," in Appelbaum and Sweet, *Envisioning an English Empire*, 68–91; Cynthia J. Van Zandt, *Brothers among Nations: The Pursuit of Intercultural Alliances in Early America, 1580–1660* (New York, 2008), 19–64; William P. Cumming, *The Southeast in Early Maps*, rev. by Louis De Vorsey Jr. (Chapel Hill, NC, 1998); Philip D. Burden, *The Mapping of North America: A List of Printed Maps* [to 1700], 2 vols. (Rickmansworth, UK, 1996–2007); Richard W. Stephenson and Marianne M. McKee, eds., *Virginia in Maps: Four Centuries of Settlement, Growth, and Development* (Richmond, 2000); Margaret Beck Pritchard and Henry G. Taliaferro, *Degrees of Latitude: Mapping Colonial America* (Williamsburg, VA, 2002); Edward C. Papenfuse and Joseph M. Coale III, *The Maryland State Archives Atlas of Historical Maps of Maryland, 1608–1908* (Baltimore, 2003); W. Jeffrey Bolster, "Putting the Ocean in Atlantic History: Maritime Communities and Marine Ecology in the Northwest Atlantic, 1500–1800," *American Historical Review* 113 (February 2008): 19–47. For a valuable first effort that focuses as much on the terrestrial as marine component, see Curtin, Brush, and Fisher, *Discovering the Chesapeake*. An impressive microlevel agroecological history is Lynn A. Nelson, *Pharsalia: An Environmental Biography of a Southern Plantation, 1780–1880* (Athens, GA, 2007), which provides an excellent account of Piedmont development in the eighteenth century.

47. Ronald Hoffman in collaboration with Sally D. Mason, *Princes of Ireland, Planters of Maryland: A Carroll Saga, 1500–1782* (Chapel Hill, NC, 2000); Phillip Hamilton, *The Making and Unmaking of a Revolutionary Family: The Tuckers of Virginia, 1752–1830* (Char-

lottesville, VA, 2003); Warren M. Billings, *Sir William Berkeley and the Forging of Colonial Virginia* (Baton Rouge, 2004); J. Kent McGaughy, *Richard Henry Lee of Virginia: A Portrait of an American Revolutionary* (Lanham, MD, 2004); Rhys Isaac, *Landon Carter's Uneasy Kingdom: Revolution and Rebellion on A Virginia Plantation* (New York, 2005); Josephine Little Zuppan, ed., *The Letterbook of John Custis IV of Williamsburg, 1717–1742* (Lanham, MD, 2005); Laura Croghan Kamoie, *Irons in the Fire: The Business History of the Tayloe Family and Virginia's Gentry, 1700–1860* (Charlottesville, VA, 2007); Jon Kukla, *Mr. Jefferson's Women* (New York, 2007); Annette Gordon-Reed, *The Hemingses of Monticello: An American Family* (New York, 2008).

48. Charles Royster, *The Fabulous History of the Dismal Swamp Company: A Story of George Washington's Times* (New York, 1999), 82.

49. As something of an inside joke, this essay leaves till last what is still the best book on the seventeenth-century Chesapeake: Edmund S. Morgan, *American Slavery, American Freedom: The Ordeal of Colonial Virginia* (New York, 1975), although it should be supplemented with James Horn, *Adapting to a New World: English Society in the Seventeenth-Century Chesapeake* (Chapel Hill, NC, 1994).

Contributors

DOUGLAS BRADBURN is associate professor of history at Binghamton University, State University of New York. He has published a number of articles and book chapters on various aspects of early American and British imperial history, including a critique of the economic and social history of the late-seventeenth-century Chesapeake, the role of warfare in British state formation, the causes of the American Revolution, the opposition to the Alien and Sedition Acts, and the problem of citizenship, immigration, and ethnicity in the era of the American Revolution. He has received numerous grants and fellowships including the Gilder Lehrman Research Fellowship from the Robert H. Smith International Center for Jefferson Studies, given to support the completion of his book, *The Citizenship Revolution: Politics and the Creation of the American Union, 1774–1804* (2009). He has recently been recognized with the SUNY Chancellor's Award for Excellence in Teaching (2010).

JOHN C. COOMBS is Associate Professor of History at Hampden-Sydney College. His research focuses on the economy, society, and politics of the early Chesapeake, particularly Virginia. His first book, *The Rise of Virginia Slavery* (forthcoming from the University of Virginia Press), offers a major reassessment of the timing and character of the colony's conversion from servant to slave labor and the role that pivotal transition played in the emergence of a dominant class of gentry planters and the formation of African American society.

VICTOR ENTHOVEN is Associate Professor of History at the Netherlands Defense Academy and the Royal Netherlands Naval College, and he is a Senior Research Fellow at the Free University of Amsterdam, affiliated with the Dutch Atlantic Connections project. He has also worked for the University of Leiden's Institute of European Expansion and the Institute for Dutch History in The Hague. His project on Dutch Atlantic trade and shipping, in conjunction with Johannes M. Postma of Mankato State University, resulted in the edited volume *Riches from Atlantic Commerce: Dutch Transatlantic Trade and Shipping, 1585–1817* (2003), which was named an Outstanding Academic Title in 2004 by *Choice: Reviews for Academic Libraries*. Since 2004, he has regularly participated in Harvard University's International Seminar on the History of the Atlantic World, 1500–1800. He is currently completing a book on Dutch entrepreneurs active in the eighteenth-century Atlantic.

ALEXANDER B. HASKELL is Assistant Professor of History at the University of California Riverside. He received his Ph.D. at The Johns Hopkins University in 2005 and was a National Endowment for the Humanities Postdoctoral Fellow at the Omohundro Institute of Early American History and Culture in 2005–7. He has explored the relationship between rhetoric and political culture in eighteenth-century Virginia in "Defining the Right Side of Virtue: Crowd Narratives, the Newspaper, and the Lee-Mercer Dispute in Rhetorical Perspective," in *Early American Studies*, special issue, "The Atlantic World of Print in the Age of Franklin" (Winter 2010). He is currently completing a book-length study on rhetoric and commonwealth formation in the Virginia colony from the Tudor era forward.

WIM KLOOSTER is Associate Professor of History at Clark University, where he has taught since 2003. He has been a Fulbright Fellow, an Alexander Vietor Memorial Fellow, and an Inter-Americas Mellon Fellow at the John Carter Brown Library; a Charles Warren Fellow at Harvard University; and a Postdoctoral Fellow in Atlantic History at the National University of Ireland, Galway. For the last ten years, he has been coeditor of Brill's Atlantic World book series. Klooster is the author of numerous articles and seven books, including *Revolutions in the Atlantic World: A Comparative History* (2009), *Illicit Riches: Dutch Trade in the Caribbean, 1648–1795* (1998) and *The Dutch in the Americas, 1600–1800* (1997), and coeditor, with Alfred Padula, of *The Atlantic World: Essays on Slavery, Migration, and Imagination* (2005).

PHILIP LEVY is Associate Professor of History at the University of South Florida. He is the author of *Fellow Travelers: Indians and Europeans Contesting the Early American Trail* (2007) as well as numerous articles on colonial Indian relations, historical archaeology, and Virginia history. He has won prizes, fellowships, and awards from the Virginia Historical Society, the Colonial Williamsburg Foundation, the Virginia Foundation for the Humanities, the George Washington Foundation, the National Endowment for the Humanities, and the National Geographic Society. His current work is a study of George Washington's boyhood, the famous cherry tree story, and the Virginia landscapes of Washington's childhood.

PHILIP D. MORGAN is Harry C. Black Professor at The Johns Hopkins University. He is the author and editor of numerous articles and books, including *Slave Counterpoint: Black Culture in the Eighteenth-Century Chesapeake and Lowcountry* (1998), winner of the Bancroft Prize from Columbia University, the Albert J. Beveridge Award from the American Historical Association, the Elliot Rudwick Prize from the Organization of American Historians, Jacques Barzun Prize from the American Philosophical Society, and the Frederick Douglass Award from the Southern Historical Association. His most recent books are (with Jack P. Greene) *Atlantic History: A Critical Appraisal* (2009) and *African American Life in the Georgia Lowcountry: The Atlantic World and the Gullah Geechee* (2010).

WILLIAM A. PETTIGREW is Lecturer in American History at the University of Kent. He is the author of, among other essays, "Free to Enslave: Politics and the Escalation of Britain's Transatlantic Slave Trade, 1688–1714," which appeared in the January 2007 edition of the *William and Mary Quarterly* and has won three international prizes. He has recently completed a study that examines how political changes at the turn of the eighteenth century accelerated Britain's involvement in the transatlantic slave trade, which will shortly be published as a book entitled *Freedom's Debt*. He is now working on a broader study of how political change underpinned economic growth in the British Atlantic world at the threshold of modernity.

EDWARD DUBOIS RAGAN received his Ph.D. from Syracuse University and is currently an exhibit curator and historian at the Valentine Richmond History Center in Richmond, Virginia. He also works in Virginia Indian history with a particular research interest in the settlement and social development of the Rappahannock River valley from its earliest Algonquian residents through the agricultural revolution of the late nineteenth century. His book manuscript, *Where the Water Ebbs and Flows: Place and Self among the Rappahannock People,* won the 2009 Francis Jennings Prize in Early American Ethnohistory and is forthcoming from the State University of New York Press.

TERRI L. SNYDER received her Ph.D. from the University of Iowa and is currently Professor in American Studies at California State University, Fullerton, where she teaches courses on early American studies, women's history, and gender in American culture. Her research focuses on the intersections of gender, law, and violence in the early American South. She is the author of *Brabbling Women: Disorderly Speech and the Law in Early Virginia* (2003). She has also published in the *Journal of American History,* the *William and Mary Quarterly,* and in Christopher L. Tomlins and Bruce H. Mann's *The Many Legalities of Early America* (2001). She is the recipient of several national fellowships, including a National Endowment for the Humanities Faculty Fellowship, and is currently working on a book-length study of the history of suicide in early British North America.

CAMILLA TOWNSEND is Professor of History at Rutgers University. She is the author of *Pocahontas and the Powhatan Dilemma* (2004), *Malintzin's Choices: An Indian Woman in the Conquest of Mexico* (2006), and *Here in This Year: Seventeenth-Century Nahuatl Annals of the Tlaxcala-Puebla Valley* (2010). In 2010 she was named a Guggenheim Fellow and is using the time to pursue a study of indigenous notions of history as found in the earliest colonial records.

LORENA S. WALSH, Historian, Colonial Williamsburg Foundation (retired), is the author (with Lois Green Carr and Russell R. Menard) of *Robert Cole's World: Agriculture and Society in Early Maryland* (1991), awarded a 1993 Maryland Historical Society book prize, and the 1994 Economic History Association Jones Prize; *From Calabar to Carter's Grove: The History of a Virginia Slave Community* (1997); and *Motives of Honor, Pleasure, and Profit: Plantation Management in the Chesapeake, 1607–1763* (2010).

Index

The letter t *following a page number denotes a table;* f *denotes a figure.*

Abbot, Archbishop, 42
Ackersloot, Cornelis, 106
Act of Navigation (1650), 90–91, 96, 99, 102–3, 282
Acts and Monuments, of These Latter and Perilous Days (Foxe), 19
Acts of Trade, 107
Adams, John, 178–80
Advancement of Learning, The (F. Bacon), 25
Advocate, The (Worsley), 46
Africa Trade Act (1698), 285, 287, 290–91
Albion's Seed (Fischer), 4, 11n6
Alexander, William, 48, 56n136
Algonquian Indians: Chief Powhatan and, 57, 76–80, 89n56, 89nn52–53, 207, 210–11; conversion of, 9, 15, 23, 36, 43, 44, 55n121, 209–10, 318; environment for, 208–9, 225, 232n5; exploitation of, 215, 221–22, 235n38, 236n59, 301–2; identity for, 207, 220; Iroquoian raids on, 227–28; lifestyle of, 208–11, 217–18, 228, 232n3; peace with, 226; population of, 210–11, 233n14; research on, 9, 210–12, 233n18; tribute by, 81. *See also* Native Americans
Allen, Theodore, 245, 271n16
Allen, Thomas, 114
Amazon Company, 41

American Revolution, 159, 181, 188
American Slavery, American Freedom (Morgan), 3, 320, 331n49
Ames, Susie M., 243, 255
Anderson, Lancelot, 107
Andrews, William, 247
Andros, Edmund, 286
Anglo-Powhatan wars, 36, 170, 188, 213–17
Anglo-Spanish War, 64
archaeology, in Chesapeake, 186, 192, 309–11
architecture and buildings: artisans for, 199–200, 206n55; rural and urban differences in, 194; in Virginia, 4, 6, 193–95, 197–200, 202n3, 204n32, 206nn54–55, 308, 310
Argall, Samuel, 40–41, 54n108, 69, 302
Arias, Diego Rodrigues, 106, 125n78
Aristotle, 24, 26, 35
Arminianism, as heresy, 42, 44
Armitage, David, 16, 48n6, 315
"Articles of Amite & Commerce," 107
Atlantic Virginia: Intercolonial Relations in the Seventeenth Century (Hatfield), 10, 13n16
authority and power, as negotiated, 6, 165–68, 178, 183n24

338 / Index

Awberry, Henry, 228
Aylmer, John, 18–19

Backer, Jacob, 112–13
Backer, Marten, 97
Bacon, Francis, 25–26, 35, 44–46
Bacon, Nathaniel, Jr., 180, 195
Bacon, Roger, 24, 173
Bacon's Rebellion, 173, 196, 225–26, 228, 245, 249, 255, 258, 271n16, 280, 307
Baffin, William, 44
Bailyn, Bernard, 185–86, 203n22, 203n26, 303
Bale, John, 19, 20, 24–25
Ballard, Thomas, 190
Bates, John, 189
Bean, Richard, 244
behavior, of settlers, 158–60, 182n5
Bell, Philip, 41
Bennett, Edward, 94
Benton, Lauren, 304, 314
Berkeley, William, 90, 100–102, 104, 107–8, 110, 123n65, 180, 225, 248, 319
Berlin, Ira, 240, 245, 255, 257, 259–60, 263, 267, 275nn36–37, 277n53, 295n8
Bermuda Company, 31, 34–36, 38–41, 44, 96, 305
Bernhard, Virginia, 7
Beverley, Robert, 229–30
Bilder, Mary, 314
Billings, Warren, 6, 110, 269n4, 314, 319
Binckes, Jacob, 108–9, 126n90
Bishop, John, 91
blacks: demography of, 7–8, 129, 254–56, 258, 260, 275n42; interracial marriage with, 128–29; as servants rather than slaves, 131, 258, 275n42
Blair, James, 286–87, 298n36
Bland, John, 90, 110
Blenck, Jacob Gerritsen, 99–100
Blosser, Jacob, 317
Board of Trade and Plantations, 288–89
Bolster, Jeff, 319
Bond, Edward, 317
Bonon, Cornelis, 106
Book of Martyrs (Foxe), 15–16, 21, 25, 48n5

Borland, John, 113
Bowen, Joanna, 313
Bradburn, Douglas, vii, 6, 10, 114, 307–8, 316–17
Bradley, Benjamin, 290
Bray, James, 190, 198–99
Breen, T. H., 185–86, 240, 244–45, 255, 258, 263, 267, 269n4, 270n10, 271n16, 275n42
Brewer, Holly, 6, 314, 318
Brief and True Report of the New Found Land of Virginia (Hariot), 73
Briggs, Edward, 24
Briggs, Henry, 44
Brockholls, Anthony, 113
Bromfield, Thomas, 173, 175–78
Brooke, Nicholas, 189
Brooke, 2nd Baron (Robert Greville), 39, 41, 43, 45, 54n112
Brown, John, 106
Brown, Kathleen M., 7, 240
Brown, William, 112
Bruce, Philip Alexander, 243
Bruton Parish Church, 196–97
buildings. *See* architecture and buildings
Burwell, Lewis, 189
Bush, Jonathan A., 9, 269n4
Button, Henry, 29
Byrd, William, II, 131, 203n26, 242, 265

Cabot, Sebastian, 23
Calvert, Charles, 112
Calvinism, 42
Cambridge History of Law in America, 314
cannibalism, in Jamestown, 185
Caron, Noel, 94
Carr, Lois Green, 1, 147, 300, 306, 314
Carson, Cary, 308, 309, 311
Carteill, Christopher, 18
Carter, John, 248, 273n24
Carter, John, II, 249
Carter, Landon, 131, 242, 319
Carteret, Philip, 113, 127n101
Cary, John, 285–86
Cary, Thomas, 285–86
casuistry, 166–67, 172–73, 181
Cecil, Edward, 31

Cecil, Thomas, 30–31
Certaine Errors in Navigation (Wright), 30
Champlain, Samuel, 29
Charles I, 39, 100
Charles II, 109–10, 192, 195, 282
Charlton, Stephen, 104, 260
Cheerful and Comfortable Faith, A (Winner), 317
Chesapeake, region of: chronology of, 306–9; disease in, 60, 217, 229, 311; economic diversity of, 6, 252–53, 274n32; exploitation in, 37, 148, 215, 221–22, 235n38, 236n59, 301–2; literary studies of, 319, 330n45; materialism of, 301, 309–13; mortality rate and trends in, 4, 8; New England's differences from, 300–301; politics and law in, 313–16; religion in, 16, 18, 49n8, 209–10, 316–19; research on, 1–5, 8, 91, 119n9, 300, 302, 312–13, 320, 320n1; subregions of, 250–53, 304–5; treatment of dead in, 311
Chesapeake in the Seventeenth Century, The, 1
Chesapeake School, 5–7, 10, 243, 296n12, 300, 314
Chicheley, Henry, 248, 273n24
Child, Josiah, 113
Chilton, Edward, 286–87
Christianity: Antichrist and Christ for, 16, 19, 24, 26, 32–34, 44; Calvinism as, 42; conversion to, 9, 15, 23, 36, 43, 44, 55n121, 209–10, 318; Huguenots and, 18–19, 27, 29; Jesus' divinity and, 160–63; Middle Plantation parish and, 196–97, 205nn42–44; Roman Catholic Church and, 19, 33, 43–44; slaves and, 261, 277n49
Chronicle (Howe), 34
Cicero, 162
Civil War, 2, 262
Clark, John, 71–72, 87n38, 87n43
Clarke, John, 190
Clavis Apocalyptica (Mede), 36
Clayton, William, 290
Cobb, Robert, 173, 175–78
Cogitata et Visa (F. Bacon), 35
Colclough, George, 246, 248
Coleman, John, 160

College of William and Mary, 191, 196, 286
Colonial Chesapeake Society (Carr, Morgan, Russo), 1, 300, 306
Colonial Williamsburg Foundation, 186, 198, 203n25, 206n51
Comenius, Jan, 44–45
Company of Royal Adventurers, 282. *See also* Royal African Company
Comparative Archaeological Study of Colonial Chesapeake Culture, 312
Condren, Conal, 160–66, 180
conversion, to Christianity, 9, 15, 23, 36, 43, 44, 55n121, 209–10, 318
Coombs, John C., vii, 6, 9, 307–8, 312
Cooper, Elianor, 173, 175
Copland, Patrick, 36
Corbin, Gawin, 229, 287–88, 292
Cornelius, John, 104
Corneliuson, Hugh Cornelius, 104
Cortés, Hernando, 60, 73–74, 89n54
Coughen, Laurence, 106
Council for New England, 31, 39, 41
Council for Virginia Company, 27, 30–31, 36, 93
Countrey Justice (Dalton), 138–39, 155n51
court system, Chesapeake: blacks' testimony in, 138, 142, 144, 154nn45–46; disciplinary violence and, 138, 155n51; doctrine of coverture in, 136, 153n37; on Eastern Shore, 134–35, 138–39, 155n51; for household governance, 128–29, 132–34, 315–16; mastery and, 134, 138–40, 153nn26–27; for women, 128–29, 132–36, 141, 143–45, 147–48, 152n24, 153n26, 156n73, 156n76, 156n78
coverture, doctrine of, 136, 153n37
Covington, Richard, 229
Cowley, William, 113
Cranmer, Thomas, 18–19
Crashaw, William, 30, 32, 34–35
Craven, Wesley Frank, 239–40, 268
creolization, 8, 255–56
Crijnssen, Abraham, 108
Cromwell, Oliver, 16, 26, 39, 46–47, 107
Culpeper, Thomas, 173
Curtin, Philip, 264–65

Custis, John, 195
Custis, Robert, 107

Dale, Thomas, 15–16, 34–35, 37–38, 54n104, 72, 93–94, 302
Dalton, Michael, 138–39, 155n51
Darnall, Eleanor, 319
Darnall, Henry, III, 319
Daule, John, 257
Davis, David Brion, 280
Davis, John, 23, 50n19
Deal, J. Douglas, 240, 255–57, 269n4, 270n10
Decades of the New World, The (Eden), 73
Dee, John, 20–21, 22f, 23, 27, 31, 47
deference: defiance rather than, 158–61, 165, 176–78, 182n5; natural aristocracy and, 178–80, 184n37; for office, 158, 160, 163, 165, 167–68, 176–77, 182n5, 184n37; persona and, 165–68, 172, 174, 176–77, 180–81
De la Warr, 3rd Baron (Thomas West), 30, 31, 34, 67, 82, 302
De officiis (Cicero), 162
De rebus oceanicis et orbe novo decades tres (Martire d'Anghiera), 73, 88n48
Derrickson, Daniel, 104
Devereux, Robert, 2nd Earl of Essex, 18, 26–29, 31, 38
de Vries, David Pietersz, 98–100, 106, 122n47
Digges, Dudley, 29, 31, 36, 38
Digges, Thomas, 31
Digital Archaeological Archive of Comparative Slavery, 312
Discourse and View of Virginia, A (Berkeley), 107–8, 110
"Discourse on Western Planting" (Hakluyt, "the younger"), 20, 23
discrimination, origins debate and, 280
disease, in Chesapeake, 60, 217, 229, 311
Dominicans, in Mexico, 57, 60–62
Doña Marina, 62, 85n13
Dorchester Company, 39
Drake, Francis, 16, 18–20, 23, 47
Dudley, Robert, 18
Dury, John, 44–45
Dutch Sea Beggars, 19

Dutch West India Company, 96, 100, 108–9, 121n31
Dyer, Edward, 21

Eastern Shore: blacks' property rights on, 257–58, 275nn38–39; court of, 134–35, 138–39, 155n51; Dutch traders and, 91–92, 104, 123n67, 124n68; free blacks on, 130, 151n14, 254–55, 257–58, 275nn38–39; indentured servitude on, 130
East India Company, 27, 31, 36, 94
Economic History of British America, 1607–1789 (McCusker, Menard), 4
Eden, Richard, 73
Edict of Nantes, 28
Edmund Custis and Company, 107
Elfrith, Daniel, 41
Elizabeth I, 16–18, 21, 23, 27–28, 34, 37, 93
Elliott, John, 305
Eltis, David, 266
encomienda (Spanish grant), 58, 68, 71
Endicott, John, 43
England: eschatology and, 15, 17, 26, 48n4; expansionism by, viii, 16–17, 20–21, 26, 38, 48n6; House of Trade for, 59, 84n7; mastery in, 147, 157n87; Navigation Acts by, 40, 46, 90–91, 96, 99, 102–3, 109–11, 118, 282; navy of, 21; Netherlands and, 27, 38, 91, 94; political culture in, 281–82, 296nn14–15; privateering by, 91; re-exporting by, 102; regional history of, viii; servants in, 134; ship confiscation by, 100, 102, 106, 112–13, 124n76, 125n88; Spain and, 26–28, 64; trade restrictions by, 40, 46, 90, 96, 99, 101–3, 107–10, 116t
English Civil War, 47, 99, 105–6, 109, 116–17, 174, 194
Enthoven, Victor, 308
Erondelle, Pierre, 29
eschatology: Bacon, F., and, 25, 35, 44–46; Bermuda and, 34–36; colonization and, 17, 32–35, 37, 43–44, 47, 55n118, 56n134; England and, 15, 17, 26, 48n4; expansionism and, 16; history and, 24–26, 32–33; humanism and, 23–24; knowledge and, 24–26; Native American conversion for,

9, 15, 23, 36, 43, 44, 55n121, 209–10, 318; nature and, 25; as Protestant and apocalyptic, 15; Raleigh and, 26; Reformation and, 19; Spain and England regarding, 26; Virginia Company and, 43; Worsley and, 45–46
Essay on Trade, An (Cary, J.), 286
Essex, 2nd Earl of (Robert Devereux), 18, 26–29, 31, 38
Ethridge, Robbie, 303
Evans, Emory, 314
Evertsen, Cornelis, 108–9, 126n90
expansionism, by England, viii, 16–17, 20–21, 26, 38, 48n6
exploitation: of Algonquian Indians, 215, 221–22, 235n38, 236n59, 301–2; in Chesapeake, 37, 148, 215, 221–22, 235n38, 236n59, 301–2; in Jamestown, 37, 301–2; through mastery, 148, 301

Fabulous History of the Dismal Swamp Company, The (Royster), 319–20
Fauntleroy, Moore, 216–17, 219, 221, 235nn40–41
Feria, Pedro de, 61–62, 85nn10–11
Fernández de Ecija, Francisco, 69–70, 77, 82
Ferrar, Nicholas, 24, 36
Fielding, Henry, 288
First Anglo-Dutch War, 99, 102, 108
Fischer, David Hackett, 4, 11n6
Fitzhugh, William, 195, 252
Fitzmaurice, Andrew, 16, 48n6, 315
Fouace, Stephen, 279, 287
Foul Means (Patent), 245–46
Fox, David, 195, 248
Foxe, John, 15–16, 19, 21, 24–25, 32, 48n5
France, 17–18, 31, 63
Frederick of the Palatinate, 29
Freeman, Bridges, 104
French Company, 31
Frith, John, 33
Frobisher, Martin, 18, 23

Galenson, David, 244–45, 250, 266, 271n15, 272n20, 280–81

Galle, Jilliam, 313
Gallivan, Martin, 304
Games, Alison, 305
Gardner, John, 287
Gates, Thomas, 34–35, 93–94, 212, 302, 310
Gauden, John, 45
General and Rare Memorials Pertayning to the Perfect Arte of Navigation (Dee), 20–21, 22f
George III, 295n2
Gilbert, Adrian, 23
Gilbert, Humphrey, 23
Gill, Stephen, 104
Glover, Richard, 103–4, 123n65
Godfrey, William, 265
Goetz, Rebecca, 318
Goffman, Erving, 165–66
Gordon-Reed, Annette, 319
Gorges, Ferdinando, 41
Gould, Eliga, 305
Gould, James, 290
governance, household: courts for, 128–29, 132–34, 315–16; mastery in, 130–33, 135, 152n24
Graham, Michael, 317
Great Britain. *See* England
Greene, Jack P., 4, 178, 185–86, 314
Greville, Robert. *See* Brooke, 2nd Baron
Grey, Jane, 18
Grinsted, William, 261
Guasco, Michael J., 9
Guinea Company, 39, 40
Gunderson, Joan, 7, 317

Hack, Georg, 105
Hakluyt, Richard, "the elder," 21–22, 25–26, 29–30, 50n29, 73
Hakluyt, Richard, "the younger," 16, 20, 23, 24–25
Hall, Francis, 175
Hamilton, Patrick, 33–34
Hamilton, Phillip, 319
Hamor, Ralph, 34–36, 169–70, 173
Hancock, David, 301
Hapsburgs, of Spain, 17, 19, 93
Harcourt, Robert, 29

Hardin, David Scott, 5
Hardy, Beatriz, 317
Hariot, Thomas, 20, 23, 27, 44, 73
Harrison, Benjamin, 286
Harrison, Benjamin, Jr., 287
Hart, Samuel, 91
Hartlib, Samuel, 44–45
Hartwell, Henry, 286–87
Harvey, John, 99, 173, 188, 192–93
Hashaw, Tim, 9
Haskell, Alec, 315
Hatfield, April Lee, 9–10, 13n16, 269n4, 275n42
Hatton, Christopher, 21
Hawkins, John, 19
Henrico, settlement at, 36, 38, 253
Henry of Navarre, 27
Henry Stuart, Prince of Wales, 26, 28–31, 37–38, 42, 52n52
Henry VIII, 28
Herbert, Andrew, 105
Herrman, Augustine, 105
Hewes, Mary, 143–44
Heywood, Linda M., 9, 240, 256, 258, 269n4, 275n36, 307
Higginson, Robert, 190
Hill, Thomas, 189
History and Present State of Virginia (Beverley), 229–30
History of the World (Raleigh), 26
Hoffman, Ron, 319
Hofstra, Warren, 305
Holder, Melisha, 287
Holland. *See* Netherlands
Holt, Robert, 104
Hooker, Richard, 43
Horn, James, 6
Horse Path, 191, 196, 200, 203n25
House of Trade, 59, 84n7
Howard, Francis, 113–14
Howe, Edmund, 34
"How her Majesty may Annoy the King of Spain" (H. Gilbert), 23
Hudson, Henry, 29, 31
Huguenots, 18–19, 27, 29
humanism, 16, 23–24, 50n25

Image of Both Churches, The (Bale), 19
indenture, for servants, 4, 128–30, 137, 149n1, 245, 247, 247t, 272n21
Ingle, Richard, 316
Innes, Stephen, 255, 258, 275n42
Iroquois Indians, 227–28
Isaac, Rhys, 317–19

Jacobson, Peter, 104
James Fort. *See* Jamestown
James I, 28, 37, 41, 42, 65, 93, 96, 193, 212
James II, 281
Jamestown: adventurers in, 16, 17; archaeology in, 192; architecture for, 198, 310; cannibalism in, 185; charter for, 30, 67, 93; Chief Powhatan and, 77–80; culture of, 4, 310; development of, vii, 16–17, 309–10; Dutch trade with, 6, 90; eschatological vision for, 17, 32–35, 37; exploitation of, 37, 301–2; fire in, 200; General Assembly at, 214; General Court at, 168, 173–74; hardship in, vii, 6, 32, 34, 68, 72, 78, 185–86, 301–2; men in, 7; militarism in, 82, 171, 302; Native Americans and, 71, 77–83, 90, 310; Native Americans' labor in, vii, 36, 58, 60, 67, 73–75, 86n27, 88n45, 88n48; Pocahontas and, 36, 72; privateering from, 65–67; Protestantism in, 28, 32; religious warfare in, vii, 15–17, 28, 32–37, 49nn7–8; Roman Catholicism and, 33; settlement of, vii–viii, 2, 10, 13n6, 15, 57, 64–65, 76, 82–83, 300, 301; significance of, 301–2; slavery in, vii, 4, 41, 47, 95; Spain and, 64–72, 86n19; trade with, vii, 6, 37, 46, 73, 77–78, 80–82, 89n57, 90; women in, 7, 174
James VI, 27
Jansen, Abraham, 104
Jansz, Abraham, 112
Jarratt, Devereux, 158, 160–67, 178, 180
Jarvis, Mike, 305
Jasperson, John, 91
Jefferson, Thomas, 178–81, 295n2
Jeffreys, Herbert, 226
Jeffries, Jeffrey, 290
Jennings, Edmund, 263–64, 292–93

Jennings, John, 265
Jesuit order, 18–19, 31, 63
Jewel, John, 18–19
Johnson, Anthony, 255–56
Johnson, John, 104, 124n68
Johnson, Robert, 33, 34
Jordan, Arthur, 257
Jordan, Winthrop, 280
Jourdain, Silvestre, 35
Julich-Cleves succession, 29

Kamoie, Laura, 319
Kant, 181
Kemp, Richard, 99, 189–94
Kendall, William, 112, 260
Kennon, Richard, 265
Key, Elizabeth, 260–62
Key, Thomas, 260–61
Key to the Millennium, The. See *Clavis Apocalyptica*
Kidd, Colin, 318
Kindt, Franck Cornelisz, 97, 99
Klein, Herbert, 264–65
Klooster, Wim, 308
Knightly, Richard, 43, 45
Konig, David, 314
Krech, Shepart, 312
Krugler, John D., 317
Kühn, Justus Engelhardt, 319
Kukla, John, 186
Kulikoff, Allan, 4, 8, 264–65
Kupperman, Karen, 301

Lachard, Govert, 91
Lambeth articles (1595), 41
Lane, Thomas, 265
Laud, William, 42
Law, Society, and Politics in Early Maryland, 1
Lawson, Gilfrid, 290
Leaguers, of France, 19
Lebsock, Suzanne E., 7
Leicester, Earl of (Robert Sidney), 21, 26–27, 29, 31, 93
Leigh, William, 229
Levy, Philip, 309, 312

Lindman, Janet Moore, 318
Lloyd, Cornelius, 247
Lloyd, Edward, II, 308, 309
London Company, 96
López de Gómara, Francisco, 73
Lost Flocke Triumphant, The (Richard Rich), 34
Low Countries. *See* Netherlands
Lowther, James, 290
Ludlow, George, 104
Ludwell, Philip, Sr., 190, 193–95, 200–201, 279, 287
Ludwell, Philip, Jr., 279, 287
Ludwell, Thomas, 190, 192, 193–95, 200–201, 258
Lugir, John, 106
Lundsford, Thomas, 190–91
Lymbry, Francis, 70–72

MacMillan, Ken, 314
Main, Gloria, 244–45, 272n20
Major, Edward, 104
manumission, of slaves, 254–56, 259–60
Many Thousands Gone (Berlin), 255, 275n37
Map of Virginia, A (Smith, John), ii
Marable, George, 197
marriage, interracial, 129
Martin, John, 170
Martin, William, 105
Martire d'Anghiera, Pietro, 73, 88n48
Mary, Queen of Scots, 18, 19
Maryland: Dutch trade with, 91–92, 104, 111, 123n67, 124n68; Plundering Time in, 316; religious wars in, 47; Virginia's similarity to, 4, 10. *See also* Eastern Shore
Mason, Sally, 319
Massachusetts Bay Company, 38–39
mastery: court system for, 134, 138–40, 153nn26–27; in England, 147, 157n87; in household governance, 130–33, 135, 152n24; by intimidation, 138–40, 154n48, 155n61; over servants, 131–32, 140, 147–48; over slaves, 147, 157n88; resistance to, 139, 143; through sexual exploitation, 148, 301
Mathews, Samuel, 107, 247

344 / Index

Maurice of Nassau, 29, 31, 100
McCartney, Martha, 9
McColley, Robert, 9, 242, 271n15
McCusker, John J., 4
McNeil, J. R., 306
Mede, Joseph, 36
men: in Jamestown, 7; Rappahannock lifestyle for, 208, 232n3
Menard, Russell R., 4, 7, 91–92, 111, 242, 244–45, 250, 270n10, 272n20, 280, 307–8
Menédez de Avilés, Pedro, 59–63
Menefie, George, 190
Mercator, Girardus, 20
Merchant Adventurers, 95
Mexico, 18–19, 57–58, 60–63, 68, 71, 73–74, 85n9, 89n54
Michael, John, 112, 113
Michielsz, Jan, 104, 124n68
Middle Plantation: archaeology for, 309; architecture for, 197–98; Horse Path for, 191, 196, 200, 203n25; land holdings at, 189, 203n20, 206n51; palisade at, 171, 187–90, 192f, 200; parish for, 196–97, 205nn42–44; settlement of, 190–91, 192f, 196. *See also* Williamsburg
Milbourne, Jacob, 113
Mildmay, Henry, 45
militarism: in Jamestown, 82, 171, 302; at Middle Plantation, 171, 187–90, 192f, 200; against Native Americans, 213–15, 234n29; Puritanism and, 27, 51n45
Miller, Perry, 317
Milner, Isaac, 286–87, 289–90, 292
Molina, Diego, 70–72, 87n43
Monson, William, 69, 71, 87n32
Montagu, Richard, 42
Monticello, viii–ix, 312
Moore, John, 175
More, Thomas, 28
Morgan, Edmund, 1, 3, 95, 242, 244–45, 255, 262, 270n10, 271n16, 295n8, 298n36, 300, 301, 306, 320, 331n49
Morgan, Marie, 301
Morgan, Phillip, 266, 300
Mormon Church, 3

Morris, James, 198
mortality, Chesapeake rate and trends in, 4, 8
Muraca, David, 312
Muscovy Company, 31
"Myne Own Ground" (Breen, Innes), 255, 275n42

Najar, Monica, 318
Namontack, 80
Napier, John, 24
National Endowment for the Humanities, 2
National Science Foundation, 2
Native Americans: in Caribbean, 73, 88n46; census of, 223; conversion of, 9, 15, 23, 36, 43, 44, 55n121, 209–10, 318; disease among, 60, 217, 229, 311; documentation on, 9; Hariot's study of, 23; holy war against, 36; interaction with, 9; Jamestown and, 71, 77–83, 90, 310; killing of, 16; labor by, vii, 36, 58, 60, 67, 73–75, 86n27, 88n45, 88n48; material culture of, 312; militarism against, 213–15, 234n29; research on, 9, 210–12, 233n18; as servants and slaves, 129, 220, 253, 274n31; of Spanish America, 75, 88n50; survival strategies by, 9, 225–26; trade with, vii, 6, 37, 46
natural aristocracy, 178–80, 184n37
Navigation Act (1651), 40, 46, 96, 102, 282
Navigation Act (1660), 109–11, 118
Necotowance, 214–15
Neiman, Fraser, 313
Nelson, John, 317
Nelson, William E., 314
Netherlands: agents and factors for, 97–98, 106; confiscation of ships of, 100, 102, 106, 112–13, 124n76, 125n88; England's alliance with, 27, 38, 91, 94; New Netherland and, 96, 104–5, 107; revolt in, 18; slave trade by, 113, 282; States General for, 91, 93–94; tobacco cultivation in, 92–93, 118t; tobacco for, 6, 28, 51n45, 90–92, 95–96; trade by, for Virginia, 90, 96–97, 102–3, 105–6, 113, 121n37

New England: Chesapeake's differences from, 300–301; church and state in, 179; colonization in, 16; Council for, 31, 39, 41; eschatology and, 17, 47, 56n134
New England Company, 31, 39, 41, 43
"New Life of Virginia, The" (R. Johnson), 34
New Netherland, 96, 104–5, 107
Newport, Christopher, 34, 65, 79–80, 212, 302
Nicholson, Francis, 287
Nightingale and Others v. Bridges, 283, 297n22
Nine Years' War, 265, 283
Nobles, Greg, 159–60, 165–66, 178, 182n3, 182n5
Nork, Elizabeth, 145
Norris, Richard, 290
Norris, William, 285, 290
North, Robert, 41
North Carolina, 23
Northwest Passage, 18, 23, 44, 63–64
Northwest Passage Company, 27, 31

Of Consuming Interests, 6
office: abuse of, 162, 164–65, 167, 170–74; casuistry and, 166–67, 172–73, 181; conduct in, 164, 176–77; continuity of, 165; deference and defiance towards, 158, 160, 163, 165, 167–68, 176–77, 182n5, 184n37; duties of, 166–67, 177; expectations for, 169; interrelationship of, 162–64, 166–67; language of, 160–61, 172, 178; parody of, 181; persona and, 165–68, 172, 174, 176–77, 180–81; status and authority for, 6, 165–68, 178, 183n24
Okeham, John, 248
Old Dominion. *See* Virginia
Omohundro Institute Conference, 1
Opechancanough, 36, 79, 83, 170, 188, 213–17
"Order and Chaos in Early Virginia" (Kukla), 186
Order of the Garter, 29
origins debate: racial discrimination and, 280; research on, 6, 239–44, 268n2, 269n4, 270nn5–6, 271n11, 277n49, 280; on slavery, 6, 239–48, 268, 268n2, 269n4, 280; supply and demand for, 245–46, 279–81
Overzee, Simon, 100, 311

Pagan, John, 99, 111
Pagden, Anthony, 314
Page, Francis, 190, 197–200, 205n50
Page, John, 189, 190, 195–97, 200
Page, Mann, 308, 309
Paggen, Peter, 287, 290
Paggen, William, 265
Pal, Jan Jacobsen, 100
Palatinate, 29, 38
Paquiquineo, 57–64, 68, 75–77, 84n2, 84nn4–5, 84nn7–8, 85n16, 89n53
Parent, Anthony, 240
Parsons, Robert, 27, 33
Patent, Anthony, 245–46
patents, for land, 189–90, 198, 203n20, 216–17, 221, 226, 229, 247
Peale, Francis, 189
Pearce, James, 265
Pedro, John, 257, 275n41
Penman, Thomas, 189
Percy, George, 34, 89n55
Percy, Henry, 20, 23, 26, 29, 50n22
Perez, Marcos Antonio, 70–71
Perry, James R., 3
Perry, Micajah, 265, 286, 289–90, 292
Peter, Hugh, 42
Petit, Daniel, 113
Pett, Phineus, 29
Pettigrew, William, 263, 308
Philip II, 18, 20, 58
Philip III, 57, 64–72, 77, 83, 87n29
Pigot, Francis, 260
Pincus, Steven, 46
"Plaine Description of the Barmudas" (Jourdain), 35
Plaine Discovery of the Whole Revelation of St. John (Napier), 24
Plantation Duty Act (1673), 111
Plant-Cutting Riots, 173, 196
Plato, 162
Pleasants, John, 265
Plundering Time, 316

Plymouth Company, 39, 41. *See also* Virginia Company
Pocahontas, 36, 40, 69, 72, 80, 302, 305
politics: deference and defiance in, 158, 160, 163, 165, 167–68, 176–77, 182n5, 184n37; instability in, 172–73, 176, 183n28; language of, 160, 182n5; religion and, 18, 49n8; as sexual, vii; slave trade and, 281–82, 285, 287–91, 293–95, 295n8, 296nn12–13, 297n27
Ponet, John, 18–19
Popeley, Richard, 189
Poppen, Paul, 98
Powell, Joan, 128–30, 132–36, 143–48, 149n1, 151n9, 152n24, 156n73, 156n78
Powell, John, 40
power. *See* authority and power
Powhatan, Chief, 57, 76–80, 89n56, 89nn52–53, 207, 210–11
Powhatans. *See* Native Americans; Powhatan, Chief
Poynter, Johannah, 173, 175–76
Poynter, Thomas, 174–76
Present State of Virginia, and the College, The (Blair, Chilton, Hartwell), 286
Preston, John, 42
Priest, Claire, 314
Principal Voyages (Hakluyt, "the elder"), 26
Principle Navigations (Hakluyt, "the elder"), 25
privateering, 28, 40, 65–67, 91, 254, 256, 282
"Proffits humbly presented to this kingdome" (Worsley), 45
Protestantism, 9, 15–18, 23, 26–30, 32, 36–37, 43–44, 47, 55nn120–21. *See also* Christianity
Providence Island Company, 39, 41, 43–44, 46
Providence Plantations, 40
provisioning, of servants, 133–34, 140, 153n26, 155n58
Purchas, Samuel, 16, 37, 43, 47, 53n100, 73
Puritanism, 18, 26–27, 51n45
Pursuits of Happiness (Greene), 4
Pym, John, 43, 44, 45

Ragan, Edward D., 9, 304
Raleigh, Walter, 18, 23, 24, 26–29, 31, 50n28
Rappahannock Indians: Articles of Peace with, 227; independence of, 216, 219, 222–23, 225–26, 230–31, 237n69; interdependence of, 227, 230–32, 238n84; land of, 215–16, 226–27, 237n72, 237n81; lifestyle for, 208, 232n3; recognition of, 231, 238n100; resettlement of, 223–26, 228, 230, 237n69, 237n73, 237n78; treaties with, 214–20, 235n40; tribute by, 214, 231. *See also* Algonquian Indians; Native Americans
Rappahannock River Valley, 218f
Reade, George, 189
Reformation, 15–19, 27, 48n5, 319
Republic (Plato), 162
research: chaos-to-order for, 185–87, 202n3; on Chesapeake, 1–5, 8, 91, 119n9, 300, 302, 312–13, 320, 320n1; databases for, 312–13; DNA studies for, 313; on Native Americans, 9, 210–12, 233n18; on origins debate, 6, 239–44, 268n2, 269n4, 270nn5–6, 271n11, 277n49, 280; records for, 2, 7, 9, 186–87, 223, 255, 257, 275n41, 275nn38–39, 276n43, 276nn46–47
Restoration, 194–95
"Revelation of the Antichrist" (Hamilton, Patrick), 33–34
Rhode Island, 40
Rice, James D., 9, 303–4
Rich, Charles, 38
Rich, Nathaniel, 34, 38, 40, 42, 44–45
Rich, Richard, 28
Rich, Robert. *See* Warwick, 2nd Earl of
Rich Neck Plantation, 191–96, 200, 204n32
Ridley, Nicholas, 18–19
Riordan, Timothy, 316
Roark, Elizabeth, 319
Robert H. Smith International Center for Jefferson Studies, viii–ix, 10n2
Robins, Obedience, 104
Roe, Thomas, 29
Rolfe, John, 36, 72, 95, 120n26
Roman Catholic Church, 19, 33, 43–44. *See also* Christianity

Rountree, Helen, 9, 238n84
Royal African Company, 250–51, 263–64, 281–83, 285–86, 288–95, 296n12, 297n19, 297n29. *See also* slave trade
Royster, Charles, 319–20
Rufus II, 20
Rump, the, 46–47
Russo, Jean, 300, 306
Rutman, Anita H., 3, 5, 8, 240, 243, 269n4, 270n10
Rutman, Darrett B., 3, 5, 8, 243, 269n4, 270n10

Sacks, David Harris, 25, 50n29, 317
Saines, John, 189
Sandys, Edwin, 18–19, 36, 41, 95, 120n26
Sandys, George, 36
Sarmiento de Acuña, Diego, 72, 88n44
Savage, Thomas, 128–29, 131–32, 134, 137, 140–42, 147, 151n10, 151n18
Say and Sele, Lord, 39, 43, 45
Scarborough, Edmond, 112
Scott, James C., 166
Scott, Thomas, 26, 31, 38–39, 43
Second Anglo-Dutch War, 108, 112, 125n88
servants: abuse of women as, 133–35, 139, 152n24, 155n56; in England, 134; as indentured, 4, 128–30, 137, 149n1, 245, 247, 247t, 272n21; mastery of, 131–32, 140, 147–48; migration of, 203n26; Native Americans as, 129, 220, 253, 274n31; provisioning of, 133–34, 140, 153n26, 155n58; resistance by, 143; slaves versus, 131, 258, 275n42; as witnesses, 143–44
Seymour, John, 265
Sherwood, William, 283
Shields, David S., 302
Sibsey, John, 247
Sidney, Philip, 18, 21, 26, 29
Sidney, Robert, Earl of Leicester, 21, 26–27, 29, 31, 93
slavery: on Bermuda, 40–41; institutionalization of, 129, 258–59, 262–63; in Jamestown, vii, 4, 41, 47, 95; legal status of, 241, 254, 256, 257, 261, 269n4; origins debate about, 6, 239–48, 268, 268n2, 269n4, 280;

supply and demand for, 245–46, 279–81; transition to, 243–45, 247t, 247–50, 249t, 253–54, 256, 262, 272n18, 273n25
slaves: auction for, 279, 282; blacks as servants rather than, 131, 258, 275n42; census of, 265–67, 278n60, 278n62; as charter rather than plantation generation, 256, 275n36; Christianity and, 261, 277n49; codes for, 129; creolization of, 8, 255–56; cultural adjustment by, 256, 263–64, 267, 277n53; freedom petition by, 260–62, 277nn49–50; free trade in, 281, 283–84, 296n10, 296n12, 297n22; General Assembly laws for, 258, 262–63; geographic distribution of, 242, 252–53, 268; headrights for, 248, 253, 273n22, 273n26; manumission of, 254–56, 259–60; mastery over, 147, 157n88; Native Americans as, 253, 274n31; ownership of, 248–49, 249t, 251t, 257, 273n27, 275nn38–39; privateering and, 254, 256, 282; property rights deeds for, 257, 259, 275nn38–39, 276n44; punishment for, 284–85; quarters for, 195, 313; rebellion by, 284; servants rather than, 131, 258, 275n42; sex ratio of, 258, 276n43; treatment of, 147, 157n88, 311
slave trade: Africa Trade Act for, 263, 285, 287, 290–91; Board of Trade and, 291–92; Board of Trade and Plantations and, 288–89; deregulation of, 291, 293–94; Dutch in, 113, 282; duty on, 293; intercolonial commerce for, 280–82; politics and, 281–82, 285, 287–91, 293–95, 295n8, 296nn12–13, 297n27; privateering for, 254, 256, 282; records for, 7, 255, 257, 275n41, 275nn38–39, 276n43, 276nn46–47; Royal African Company and, 250–51, 263–64, 281–83, 285–86, 288–95, 296n12, 297n19, 297n29; separate traders in, 281–82, 287–94, 296n10, 298n46; sources for, 264–67; supply and demand for, 245–46, 279–81; tobacco and, 242, 256, 290–91, 293, 308
Smith, Henry: abuse by, 133, 135, 139, 145–46, 155n56, 156n73; in court, 133–36, 152n24, 155n61; estate of, 128–29, 131, 149n1, 151n9, 151n18; homicide charges

Smith, Henry (*continued*)
    against, 135, 148, 153n30, 157n90; mastery by, 131–32, 140, 147–48; political office for, 148; provisioning by, 140, 155n58; resistance to, 145–46
Smith, Joanna Matrum, 135–36, 144–45, 148, 153nn31–32
Smith, John, ii, 75–77, 79, 81–82, 88n50, 210–11, 217, 232, 235n42, 302, 305
Smith, Nicolas, 91
Smith, Robert, 192
Smith, Thomas, 29, 31, 33
"Smoke and Mirrors: Reinterpreting the Society and Economy of the Seventeenth-Century Chesapeake" (Bradburn, Coombs), vii
Snyder, Terri L., 7, 309, 314
Somers Islands Company. *See* Bermuda Company
Sovereignty and Possession (MacMillan), 314
Spain: in Americas, 19–20, 33, 58; as Antichrist, 26; Armada of, 27, 64; in Asia, 64; England and, 26–28, 64; Hapsburgs of, 17, 19, 93; imperialism by, 18–20; Jamestown and, 64–72, 86n19; Native American abductions by, 57–60, 84n2, 84n4; Native Americans' labor and, 58, 60, 67, 73, 86n27; Portuguese corruption by, 20; Reformation and, 17; Virginia colony and, 57, 65–72, 84n1, 86n19
Spangler, Jewel L., 317–18
Spanish Match, 26, 38, 41, 64, 86n18
Spanish Netherlands, 91, 124n76
Speckart, Amy, 308
Sprieteman, Thomas, 112, 127n99
St. John, Oliver, 46
Stam, Arent Cornelisz, 104–5
Stam, Dirck Cornelisz, 99, 104–5
Staple Act (1663), 110–11, 118
Stone, Thomas, 100
Stoughton, John, 42–43
Strachey, William, 35, 39, 74–75, 88n48
Straughan, Adam, 175
Sturtz, Linda L., 7
Sutto, Antoinette, 316
Synod of Dort (1619), 41–42

Tate, Thad, 314
Taylor, Philip, 247
Thierry, Jacques, 91
Thierry, James, 91
Third Anglo-Dutch War, 108–9
Thomas, Robert, 244
Thompson, George, 100
Thompson, Maurice, 39, 45
Thompson, Peter, 315–16
Thorndale, William, 9
Thornton, John K., 9, 240, 256, 258, 269n4, 275n36, 307
Thorpe, George, 36, 212–13, 234n21
Thorpe, Ortho, 190
Throckmorton, John, 94
"Titles to Foreign Lands" (Dee), 23
tobacco: agents and factors for, 97–98, 106; convoy system for, 114–15, 118; cultivation of, in Netherlands, 92–93, 118t; Dutch trade for, 90, 95–96; English imports and exports of, 96, 116t; London Company import of, 96; for Netherlands, 6, 28, 51n45, 90–92, 95–96; prices for, 115, 117t; profits from, 308–9; Royal African Company and, 290–291; slave trade and, 242, 256, 290–91, 293, 308; soil for, 5; Somers Islands Company import of, 96; trade restrictions on, 40, 46, 90, 96, 99, 101–3, 107–10, 116t; types of, 114–15, 127n113; of Virginia Company, 169; Virginia's economy and, 4, 5, 28, 90, 169; for West India Company, 96
Tobacco Revolution, 255–56
Tocqueville, Alexis de, 159
Tomlin, Chris, 314–15
Topp, Aries, 104, 124n68
Townsend, Camilla, 9, 10, 304
trade: Acts of Trade for, 107; Africa Trade Act for, 285, 287, 290–91; agents and factors for, 97–98, 106, 265; "Articles of Amite & Commerce" for, 107; bills of exchange for, 106–7, 125n82; Board of Trade and Plantations for, 288–89; convoy system for, 114–15, 118; disguised ships for, 111–12; between Dutch and Chesapeake, 6, 28, 51n45, 90–92, 96–

97, 101, 104, 111, 123n67, 124n68; duty on, 109–13; as free for slaves, 281, 283–84, 296n10, 296n12, 297n22; House of Trade for, 59, 84n7; with Jamestown, vii, 6, 37, 46, 73, 77–78, 80–82, 89n57, 90; with Maryland, 91–92, 104, 111, 123n67, 124n68; with Native Americans, vii, 6, 37, 46; with Netherlands, 113, 282; restrictions on, 40, 46, 90, 96, 99, 101–3, 107–10, 116t; with Virginia, 90, 96–97, 102–3, 105–6, 113, 121n37. *See also* slave trade

Trans-Atlantic Slave Trade Database, 8

Treaty of London, 64

Treaty of Westphalia (1648), 47

Tsenacomoco, tribes of, 57. *See also* Powhatan, Chief; *specific tribes*

Tucker, William, 100, 319

Turner, Frederick Jackson, 159

Twelve Years' Truce, 96

Tyler, Henry, 189, 190

Tyler, William, 169–73, 176–77

Upton, Dell, 317

Utie, John, 169–70

Uttamatomakin, 83

Valerious Termininus (F. Bacon), 25

Vane, Henry, 39

Vaughan, Alden T., 9, 239, 241–42, 245, 263, 268n2, 270n6

Vaughan, Richard, 260

Velasco, Alonso de, 68–69, 71–72, 87n43

Velasco, Luis de. *See* Paquiquineo

Velázquez, Antonio, 58–59

Verbrugge, John, 105, 124n71

Vergil, Polydore, 24

Vermande, François, 100

Vethuysen, Ysbrant, 100

Virginia: Act of Navigation (1650) for, 90–91, 96, 99, 102–3, 282; Acts of Trade and, 107; Algonquian population of, 210–11, 233n14; architecture in, 4, 6, 193–95, 197–200, 202n3, 204n32, 206nn54–55, 308, 310; "Articles of Amite & Commerce" for, 107; Bermuda's links to, 305; Council for Virginia Company and, 27, 30–31, 36, 93; Council of State for, 246; counties of, xii; Dutch attacks on, 108–9; Dutch in, 99–100, 104–5, 122n49; Dutch smugglers in, 111; Dutch trade with, 90, 96–97, 102–3, 105–6, 113, 121n37; English Civil War and, 105–6; founding of, 300; free trade in, 101–2, 104–5; General Assembly of, 107, 120n26, 188, 207, 217, 219; General Court of, 168–69, 173–74, 260–62; Indian policy by, 207–8, 220; instability in, 173, 176, 183n28; Maryland's similarity to, 4, 10; Navigation Act (1651) for, 40, 46, 96, 102, 282; Navigation Act (1660) for, 109–11, 118; settlement of, 94; sex ratios in, 129; slavery in, vii, 4, 41, 47, 95; Spain and, 57, 65–72, 84n1, 86n19; spelling of Dutch names in, 95, 120n23; tobacco and economy of, 4, 5, 28, 90, 169; voyages to, 26, 28–30, 37; West India Company and, 96

Virginia Assembly, 90, 102

Virginia Company, 18–19, 24, 29–31, 37–41, 93; charter of, 170; dissolution of, 37, 39, 53n98; eschatologic mission of, 43; goals of, 212–13; Indians and, 220, 236n51; as Plymouth Company, 39, 41; promotion by, of Virginia, 67, 69, 226; tobacco of, 169

Virginia Council, 29

Virginia Magazine, 242

Virginia State Library, 3

Voigt, Lisa, 305

Vox Populi (Scott), 26

Wageman, Henrick, 104

Walker, Peter, 258

Walsh, Lorena S., 5–6, 147, 250, 266, 274n32, 305, 308

Walsingham, Francis, 18, 23

Warwick, 2nd Earl of (Robert Rich), 18, 24, 28, 34, 36, 38–42, 44–46, 54n106, 55n121

Watkins, Ryse, 171

Webb, Elizabeth, 146, 156n82

Webb, Giles, 91

Webb, Jane: children of, 137, 141–43, 145–46, 148, 153n39, 154n40, 155n66, 157n85; contract between Savage and, 129, 136–38, 141–42, 153n35, 154n44; court system for, 132–33, 136, 141, 145, 148, 156n76; doctrine of coverture for, 136, 153n37; as indentured, 128–29, 137; marriage of, 128–29; resistance by, 144–45; status of, 128, 141, 149n2, 151n10; witnesses for, 144. *See also* Savage, Thomas
Webb, Nanny, 146
Webster, Charles, 44
Webster, Godfrey, 290
Weeks, Robert, 198
Wells, Camille, 308
West, Thomas, 31, 302
Westbury, Susan, 265
Wetherell, Charles, 8
Whitaker, Alexander, 32–33
Whitaker, Edward, 189
Whitaker, William, 32
White, John, 43, 312
whites: inequality among, 308; opportunity for, 6, 298n36
William and Mary Quarterly, 242
Williamsburg, Virginia: archaeology in, 186, 198–99, 203n25, 206n51; Colonial Williamsburg Foundation for, 186, 198, 203n25, 206n51; Department of Historical Research for, 3; land holdings at, 189, 203n20; Nassau Street structure in, 198–99; palisade at, 187–90; platting of, 187–90; as Virginia capital, 186

Williamson, Robert, 260
Winner, Lauren, 317
Winthrop, John, Jr., 39, 42–43
women: abuse of, as servants, 133–35, 139, 152n24, 155n56; agency by, 132, 152n22; alliances by, 145–47; court system for, 128–29, 132–36, 141, 143–45, 147–48, 152n24, 153n26, 156n73, 156n76, 156n78; entitlements of, 131; as free blacks, 129, 150n8; in Jamestown, 7, 174; legal strategies for, 131; Rappahannock lifestyle for, 208, 232n3; resistance by, in home, 132, 143–44; unwed pregnancy in, 129, 137, 143, 148, 153n39, 156n71; upward mobility of, 129
Wood, Brad, 305
Woods, Elizabeth, 173–77
Woods, John, 174–76
Wormeley, Ralph, 104, 242
Wormeley, Ralph, II, 249–50
Worsley, Benjamin, 45–47
Wren Building. *See* College of William and Mary
Wright, Edward, 30, 44
Wyatt, Francis, 170, 171, 188, 190
Wyatt, George, 189

Yeardley, Argoll, 103
Yeardley, George, 41
York House Conference, 42

Zuckerman, Michael, 159, 178, 182n3
Zúñiga, Pedro de, 64–68, 86n19

EARLY AMERICAN HISTORIES

A series of studies on early modern North America and the Caribbean from 1500 to 1815, EARLY AMERICAN HISTORIES promises innovative research and analysis of foundational questions central to the work of scholars and teachers of American, British, and Atlantic history—books that bring the early American world into focus.

Douglas Bradburn and John C. Coombs, editors
   Early Modern Virginia: Reconsidering the Old Dominion

www.ingramcontent.com/pod-product-compliance
Lightning Source LLC
Chambersburg PA
CBHW021149230426
43667CB00006B/310